SEA OF GRASS

SEA OF

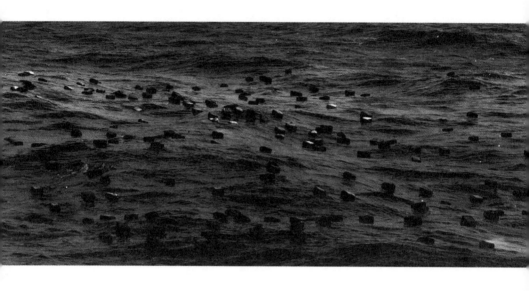

Charles M. Fuss, Jr.

GRASS

The Maritime Drug War
1970–1990

Naval Institute Press / Annapolis, Maryland

Library of Congress Cataloging-in-Publication Data
Fuss, Charles M., 1930–
   Sea of grass : the maritime drug war, 1970–1990 / Charles M. Fuss, Jr.
     p.   cm.
   Includes bibliographical references and index.
   ISBN 1-55750-276-5 (alk. paper)
   1. Narcotics, Control of—United States. 2. Drug traffic—United States.
3. Marijuana—Government policy—United States. 4. Seizure of
vessels and cargoes. I. Title.
HV5825.F87 1996
363.4'5'0973—dc20   96-16534

Printed in the United States of America on acid-free paper ∞

03 02 01 00 99 98 97 96   9 8 7 6 5 4 3 2

First printing

Frontispiece: Marijuana bales and an oil slick mark the passing
of a grass boat. *(Official U.S. Coast Guard photograph)*

Aboard the USCGC *Courageous* over the Puerto Rican Trench, Atlantic Ocean, February 1977:

Lookout: Sir, I think she's about to go under. There she goes! Look at that!

Officer of the Deck: Quartermaster, note the time and our position. Log this—M/V *Calabres* sank, boarding party clear.

Lookout: Right over the bow—some of those bales are popping up. There's more—by God, there's hundreds of them things. It's a regular Sea of Grass.

ADAPTED FROM HANK MESSICK, *OF GRASS AND SNOW*

Contents

List of Illustrations ix

Foreword xi

Preface xv

Acknowledgments xix

Prologue The First One Hundred Years 1

1 It Begins, 1970–1973 7

2 Crosscurrents, 1974–1976 29

3 The Flood, 1977–1978 43

4 High Water, 1979–1981 63

5 Battle Lines, 1982–1983 91

6 The Offensive: Part One, 1984 123

7 The Offensive: Part Two, 1985 149

8 The Ebb, 1986 171

9 Back-strapped, 1987 199

10 Silence and Eddies, 1988 229

11 A Victory at Sea, 1989 253

Epilogue 279

Notes 287

Bibliography 309

Index 315

Illustrations

FIGURES
1. Approximate U.S. Coast Guard marijuana seizures,
   1973 to 1993   xiv
2. Drawing of a hidden marijuana compartment aboard
   the *Querube II*   117

MAPS
1. Early marijuana routes to Florida   23
2. Typical marijuana routes to the eastern United States   99
3. Typical marijuana routes to the western United States   197

PHOTOGRAPHS
A marijuana field in a Latin American country   10
Suspect lobster boat anchored in Bahamian waters   12
A Gulf shrimper typical of those that carried much of
   the Caribbean pot   18
The *Don Emilio* being brought to the U.S. Coast Guard
   base at Miami Beach   37
A marijuana mothership at sea   45
The USCGC *Vigorous* intercepts a mothership off New Jersey   59
Paper found aboard a marijuana mothership showing
   emergency, day-frequency, and alphanumerical codes   73

Grass boats loading on the Guajira Peninsula of Colombia   77
Florida Marine Patrol's Lt. Mike Minski with the *Orion*   81
The USCGC *Dauntless,* premier drug buster   85
The USS *Mississippi,* the first navy ship to seize a drug boat   97
Suspect go-fast boat anchored by Ragged Island in the Bahamas   105
A Coast Guard petty officer searches the double bottoms of
    a freighter.   115
The USCGC *Lipan*   119
Sanctuary officer Bennie Davis at Point Willie   128
The icebreaker *Northwind,* flagship of Operation Wagon Wheel   131
An oil rig tender used as a marijuana mothership   135
The burning and sinking mothership *Pacific Star*   147
A U.S. Customs Blue Thunder interceptor hunts go-fast coke
    runners off Miami.   153
Fast lobster boats along Route 26   157
The *Argana II*   159
MAP vessel with sea-based aerostat   167
Crewmen aboard the patrol hydrofoil USS *Taurus*   179
"Guajira Dog" found aboard the *D'Milu's One*   187
Concealed compartments aboard the *South C. Express*   189
The USS *McCloy*   194
Vice President George Bush at a meeting of the National Drug
    Interdiction Operations Oversight Group   203
The shrimper used in Harold King's last run   209
The crew of the *Lady Hamilton III* being processed   214
The rig tender *Triton Express*   217
A Canadian smuggler identified by the master and chief
    engineer of the freighter *Carmiel*   221
The *Grace Caroline* being intercepted by the USCGC *Attu*   239
The smuggler tug *Intrepid Venture* tows a barge with tons
    of hash and pot on board.   245
USCGC *Boutwell* fires on the *Encounter Bay.*   249
Fred Schellenberg with the *Turtola*   259
Cocaine from the seized coastal freighter *Barlovento*   263
The sailboat *Savage Shrimp,* caught with 347 pounds of pot   267
A navy P-3 Orion rigs the suspect freighter *Sea Chariot* in
    the eastern Pacific.   281
The "Gray Terrors" of Hydrofoil Squadron Two   285

Foreword

The 206-year history of the U.S. Coast Guard is replete with long interludes of exciting and controversial operations in support of national policy objectives. In my time, there have been "market time" coastal interdiction patrols in Vietnam; enforcement of the two-hundred-mile economic zone; the Cuban exodus of 1982, which was preceded by the Cay Sal patrols of the 1960s; and Haitian interdiction operations that later assumed the politically correct sobriquet "Illegal Migrant Interdiction Patrols." Because this service is so small, in a relative sense, as compared to the Department of Defense as a whole, any commitment becomes almost total. This contradicts the multi-mission dynamic upon which we base our budget. At times, this contradiction is felt most acutely within the Coast Guard itself. Certainly no operation had a greater effect upon the Coast Guard than the "War on Drugs."

During this so-called war, programs were severely truncated so that, as one commandant put it, we could "grow from within." Charlie Fuss, in his extremely well-documented *Sea of Grass*, describes this period of history in which uncertain public policies conflicted with agency vision. Unintended rivalries developed. Extraordinary steps were taken to coordinate the war on drugs without exercising control. The National Narcotics Border Interdiction System, under the vice president, was one such mechanism for coordinating the interdiction efforts of the U.S. Coast Guard, the U.S. Customs Service, the Department of Defense, and the intelligence community.

Charlie Fuss stepped into this arena, a one-of-a-kind individual whose good nature, gift for analysis, and ability to work with people and agencies gave him an opportunity to develop the perspective necessary to describe these events in such a way as to be entertaining, informative, and unbiased. He has written this book much as the legendary Ernie Pyle described World War II—from the perspective of the frontline "grunt."

I first met Charlie in 1980, when, at the behest of Vice Adm. Robert Price, the commander, Atlantic Area, the Offshore Law Enforcement Branch organized a "User's Conference." Our purpose was to determine a "best way" to allocate resources to enforce fisheries laws incorporated in the Fisheries Conservation and Management Act of 1976 and to improve our opportunities to interdict the flood of marijuana coming up from Colombia. Charlie was there to represent his organization, the National Marine Fisheries Service. Six years later, I remet him in my capacity as chief, Operations Division, Seventh Coast Guard District. I was surprised to step into his office at our base in St. Petersburg, Florida, and find him so thoroughly expert in the conduct of this war on drugs.

Sea of Grass is a "fun read." It owes its appeal to at least three things. First, as one caught up in the Coast Guard's law enforcement mission from 1970 to my retirement, I thought I knew most of what there was to know about our successes and failures. This book is full of surprises and lessons. Charlie's interviews with the drug war's villains, the smugglers themselves, are particularly edifying. Second, the internecine character of our law enforcement efforts is not ignored. "Body count" or "bale count" was a fact of life, and cooperation often hinged on who got the credit. In many cases, it was easy for the Coast Guard. We arrived with prisoners literally in tow behind gleaming white ships and boats. We were floating "photo opportunities." Last, Charlie describes an effort that evolved from complete naïveté to one of passionate creativity and determination to defeat the smuggler, an effort which consumed more than one-quarter of the Coast Guard's budget in an era as confused about its social goals and objectives as any in our history. Charlie describes another Prohibition era with all the ambiguities and frustrations of the 1920s.

Alexander Hamilton established the Coast Guard's ancestor, the Revenue Marine, to deter smuggling, which had become an American tradition. The commodity changes from decade to decade, but the "industry" prevails. As you trace the Coast Guard's evolution, this mission has been a constant thread. It is ironic that with each new challenge, the Coast Guard searches to pick up that thread and weave it back into its multi-mission tapestry.

It was my pleasure and privilege to serve with the men and women mentioned within these pages. I know that as they read this book, they will be pleased, proud, and occasionally chagrined by its contents. Charlie could not tell it all, of course. Many tales remain untold. For example, the coordinating and controlling attempts of the Office of National Drug Control Policy—the "drug czar"—or the entry of the Secretary of Defense and the Joint Chiefs of Staff into the war on drugs; the individual efforts of men and women to lead their agencies toward greater cooperation and success.

Nevertheless, *Sea of Grass* is a success story, concluding with Adm. Paul A. Yost's assessment that the combined law enforcement effort of twenty years defeated marijuana smuggling. A drug problem persists, and public debate continues as to how best to curb its effect. This book is a history of one such effort. As with any history, once read, the reader will be better able to enter this debate and contribute to a coherent, beneficial public policy. President Harry Truman wrote, "Men make history, not the other way around. In periods when there is no leadership, society stands still. Progress occurs when courageous, skillful leaders seize the opportunity to change things for the better." Charlie Fuss's assertion that there must be a barrier to this vice finds reinforcement among those whose exploits are told in these pages.

Rear Adm. W. T. Leland, U.S. Coast Guard (Ret.)
Chief, Office of Law Enforcement and Defense
Operations, 1989–1991

Preface

This story needs to be told to honor the thousands of American men and women who serve at sea, in the air, in far-off places, and along our coasts in the longest war in our country's history. It is about the rise and fall of maritime marijuana smuggling by boats and motherships; an account of the drug war at sea must also include some discussion of cocaine, although coke is mainly smuggled by aircraft. The narrative is set against the political and bureaucratic battleground of the period. Sea interdiction forces eventually cut the primary marijuana supply lines between the Caribbean basin and U.S. Atlantic and Gulf waters, and later between Southeast Asia and the Pacific coast. Their accomplishment is a true success story in the seemingly endless drug war.

War on drugs was publicly declared by President Richard Nixon in the summer of 1969, fifty-five years after the Harrison Act of 1914 provided for federal narcotics control.[1] Nixon's declaration coincided with the beginning of the drug war at sea. Land border seizures and a drought in the traditional growing areas of Mexico caused the "marijuana famine of 1969."[2] Colombian and Jamaican grass growers responded with relish. Sea shipments of marijuana to the United States began in earnest in the early 1970s and grew in volume and sophistication until the late 1980s. Most marijuana imported after the mid 1970s was delivered by sea. By 1990, marijuana flow to the United States had been reduced to a trickle.

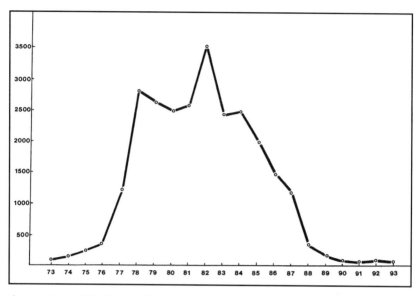

Approximate U.S. Coast Guard marijuana seizures, 1973 to 1993 (thousands of pounds)

(From U.S. Coast Guard records and other sources)

I entered the drug war in the closing months of 1983 as the National Oceanic and Atmospheric Administration (NOAA) representative to Vice President George Bush's National Narcotics Border Interdiction System (NNBIS). As a senior special agent with NOAA's National Marine Fisheries Service (NMFS), my first job for NNBIS was to create a guide for identifying drug-carrying fishing boats. They represented about a third of all smuggling vessels. I also developed methods for postseizure inspections and for debriefing cooperating defendants to collect intelligence on routes and procedures. Many imprisoned smugglers described their tactics. On the basis of this experience, I was chosen to prepare the maritime smuggling scenarios for the 1988 Drug Interdiction Games at the Naval War College.

As my agency's only representative to the national counternarcotics effort, I supported all the NNBIS centers and participated in briefings for the vice president. In 1989 I was detailed to the Office of National Drug Control Policy (ONDCP) as a maritime smuggling expert. I served as a consultant to emerging Department of Defense and intelligence community counternarcotics programs until my retirement from federal service in August 1990.

My experience in counternarcotics work gave me a unique opportunity to observe operations, from the front lines to the highest levels of government. I also had the advantage of spending time with the opposition in prison interviews. Major drug-smuggling defendants described their activities with much candor and detail. Many are now in the Federal Witness Protection Program and cannot be cited in this work. In some cases names have been changed to protect individuals from reprisals, possibly deadly ones.

Classified and sensitive drug interdiction intelligence and operational reports influenced my understanding of and opinions about the drug war. They cannot be identified as sources or used in this work. Notwithstanding these limitations, I have tried to make this brief history factual, with the best documentation I can provide. Familiar case histories are used as examples of smuggling methods and interdiction tactics. There are thousands of others, but I am constrained by space and by knowledge of the events. When classified intelligence was used to make seizures, reference is made to "special intelligence" without source notations.

This account touches briefly on undedicated smuggling vessels: the otherwise legitimate cargo and passenger vessels, yachts, and fishing boats used to transport concealed narcotics. Usually the owners and operators of such vessels do not know about the smuggling venture, but they can be held liable if contraband is found on board. Maritime container smuggling is a serious problem today.

Air smuggling is discussed only when it impacts on vessel smuggling; the discussion is therefore restricted to aircraft drops at sea to boats or to airstrip deliveries in the Bahamas for transshipment to vessels.

This work concentrates on vessels whose only purpose is to deliver narcotics to the United States. Usually the master has, or is alleged to have, full knowledge of the illegal enterprise. In many cases bogus cargoes are used or real fishing is conducted as a cover for the illicit trade. The detection and apprehension of dedicated smuggling vessels is the pure application of maritime interdiction and the story of the drug war at sea. It involves the collection and use of intelligence, the detection of suspects, the deployment of patrol vessels and surveillance aircraft, the search and seizure of boats, and the arrest of transport vessel crews and off-load personnel. It is a sailor's war, fought mostly from small patrol craft, frequently in rough seas and inclement weather, and against wily and audacious adversaries. They who go down to the sea to do this work deserve our everlasting gratitude. They have received little.

In the beginning, a few seagoing Drug Enforcement Administration (DEA) agents were the main line of resistance. Since 1973 the U.S. Coast Guard has been the primary player in the war at sea, followed closely by marine, air, investigative, and intelligence components of the U.S. Customs Service. The Posse Comitatus Act (18 U.S.C., 1385) was amended in 1981 to allow military support of civil law enforcement. Since then the U.S. Navy and other military services have supplied maritime reconnaissance aircraft. In recent years the navy has also provided ships as platforms for Coast Guard law enforcement detachments.[3]

The Drug Enforcement Administration plays a critical role in supporting interdiction by collecting intelligence on drug movements, conducting investigations after seizures, and having case agents assist the offices of the U.S. attorney in prosecutions. DEA also sponsors the El Paso Intelligence Center, a multiagency effort and the main repository for all drug-trafficking information. When the military was authorized to support the counternarcotics mission, certain elements of our foreign intelligence community became active in drug interdiction. Their efforts have produced exemplary results, especially in the maritime arena.

In 1982 the Federal Bureau of Investigation (FBI) got concurrent jurisdiction with DEA to investigate drug-related crimes. Even agents of the National Marine Fisheries Service and rangers of the National Park Service have played a lonely part in apprehending smuggler vessels. No discussion of the drug war would be complete without acknowledging the daily contributions from state and local enforcement agencies.

To all of the above, this book is dedicated.

Acknowledgments

I am indebted to many for their contributions to this account. Some cannot be identified, for their own protection. To those who have been assigned fictitious names, I ask their forbearance. As for those mentioned in the text and source notes, their assistance should be obvious. Numerous drug smugglers, willing and unwilling, assisted me.

Special thanks go to Fred Schellenberg of the Central Intelligence Agency and to Rear Adm. W. Ted Leland, USCG (Ret.), who waded through the entire manuscript, making gifts of their comments and suggestions. Special Agent J. Thomas Maher, U.S. Customs, on his own time and at his own expense, converted rough sketches to professional art. This help was invaluable. I am also indebted to Rear Adm. Richard A. Appelbaum, USCG, for publication advice and to Rear Adm. John E. Shkor, USCG, for guidance in the use of certain references.

Comdr. William Baker of the Coast Guard Institute helped locate active and retired personnel, provided anecdotes, reviewed the chapters that covered Route 26, and helped in many other ways. Comdr. George Heim, USN (Ret.), late of ONDCP, gave me valuable counsel on my assessment of the rise and fall of NNBIS. Comdr. Andy Anderson, USCG (Ret.), reviewed a sample chapter and gave early encouragement. Lt. Comdr. Daniel Laliberte supplied seizure statistics from Coast Guard Headquarters and helped with the location of other data. Lt. Comdr. James Howe, public affairs officer, Seventh

Coast Guard District, helped me resolve conflicting records of some major marijuana seizures. Boatswain's Mate First Class Edward Rubertas, USCG, located some senior enlisted people and gave details of the *Turtola* case.

Richard Keating, retired Customs Service assistant district director, reviewed the early chapters and gave me otherwise unavailable reference sources. Special Agents Daniel Dunn and David Weatherly of Customs reviewed later chapters and gave valuable input. Special Agent Tom Maher, a former Customs air interdiction officer, provided insight into air support operations and aircraft descriptions. Customs National Marine Support Unit chief James Connelly gave me leads on early boat cases and recent changes in Customs boat operations. Customs marine enforcement officer Kenneth Hysell brought me up to date on boat operations in South Florida.

Investigator James Decker of the Collier County state's attorney's office reviewed the later chapters and supplied excellent background on the operative Popeye. Special Agents Stanley Jacobsen, FBI (Ret.), Ronald Dearmin, NMFS, and Samuel Murad, DEA, supplied details on certain investigations/operations that considerably improved the narrative. John Willing and Fran Dyer, Internal Revenue Service/Organized Crime Drug Enforcement Task Force special agents, set me straight on a number of Pacific cases covered in the final chapters. Fisheries Service scientist Rolf Juhl clarified many Mexican and Caribbean fishing issues and provided useful statistics. Dick German, neighbor and computer wizard, saved the day more than once by making the machine well.

Photographs were located by the following: Dr. Robert Browning and Scot Price, USCG Office of the Historian; Richard Toppings, chief journalist, Navy Office of Information; Lt. Comdr. M. E. Woodring, Seventh Coast Guard District; Mr. Ted Hoge, Coast Guard Pacific Area; Joe Fariello, U.S. Customs, Miami; and Fisheries Service agent Mac Fuss, Marathon, Florida.

The staff at the U.S. Naval Institute Press graciously agreed to review a lengthy first draft and convinced me to trim the manuscript down to publication weight. Content editor Mary Yates gave invaluable technical assistance and saved me from embarrassing errors.

To all of the above, I am grateful. Most of all, I am indebted to Carol Ann, my wife of thirty-six years. Without her steadfast devotion and skill this project would have foundered. She has deciphered reams of unintelligible script, typed thousands of pages, and edited everything. Carol is my best critic and my lifetime friend. She has my everlasting love.

In the course of this endeavor I have received an abundance of comments, corrections, and suggestions. Most of these have been incorporated into the manuscript. I am, however, solely responsible for the content and views herein.

SEA OF GRASS

Prologue

The First
One Hundred Years

Drugs have been delivered to our shores in merchant ship cargoes and in the baggage of individuals since the end of the nineteenth century. The first known culprits were Chinese immigrants who brought opium into San Francisco circa 1870. The habits from China were acquired by American-born Chinese in the opium dens of the Gold Coast.[1]

In the early part of this century Beirut was the source of Middle Eastern heroin shipped to the ghettos of New York and other large cities in the Northeast. By the 1920s, organized crime families in New York had developed a substantial heroin distribution business. On 1 July 1930 the Bureau of Narcotics was created within the Treasury Department to fight the growing menace. It targeted the eastern Mafia networks.[2]

The Coast Guard's first organized brush with drug smuggling dates back to the mid-1930s. Opium smuggling was increasing on the Pacific coast. Crewmen on freighters inbound from the Orient were dropping watertight containers overboard, to be retrieved by fishing vessels, pleasure craft, and possibly seaplanes. Coast Guard patrol boats tried to catch the opium smugglers, who responded by making the drops further offshore. When the 327-foot Hamilton-class cutters came into service in 1936, a solution to surveilling offshore areas seemed to be at hand. Reconnaissance seaplanes (J2F Ducks and SOC-4 Seagulls) were embarked on the cutters and lowered over the side for launch-

1

ing. There is no record of opium smugglers being apprehended by the cutter-seaplane combination, but later the idea came to fruition.[3]

During World War II, traffic in heroin from the Middle East and opium from the Far East slowed. Supply did not meet demand. Chinese entrepreneurs from San Francisco went down to Sinaloa, Mexico, and experimented with poppy cultivation. Along came black-tar Mexican heroin.[4] This event, totally overshadowed by a world at war, was the precursor of future supply-demand imbalances that changed the sources, routes, and methods of smuggling narcotics into our country.

After World War II, Marseilles replaced Beirut as the primary conduit of Middle Eastern heroin. The French Connection was born. Corsican gangs supplied Mafia families with heroin to feed the ghetto addicts. Most of it was shipped from France to New York in merchant vessel cargoes. A preferred method was to conceal the dope in French-made automobiles.[5]

On the other side of the world, Chiang Kai-shek was losing his war with the communists. In 1949 some twelve thousand of Chiang's old Kuomintang army gave up and fled across the border into Burma. With no battles to fight, they turned to poppy cultivation and opium production on a grand scale. Remnants of this army migrated into Laos and Thailand. This Golden Triangle became the world's premier producer of opium.[6]

In the early years of drug smuggling there was little need for seagoing enforcement. From the time the problem was first recognized in this country until the 1960s, drug trafficking usually meant opiate distribution to ethnic groups and minorities. Users received scant public sympathy. Around the turn of the century there was serious morphine and cocaine abuse associated with wonder-drug anesthetic dependencies, but this abuse did not affect large segments of the population. Mexican marijuana, brought across the land border, showed up in the mid-1930s but was confined to the barrios of our southwestern states.[7]

Maritime smuggling during this period (1870s–1960s) was limited by three factors: (1) the addict population was small, (2) the drugs of choice were high-potency/low-volume types, and (3) the existing demand could be supplied by legitimate vessels of opportunity and couriers. Dedicated smuggling ships were unnecessary. Counternarcotics enforcement was conducted at land borders, in our ports, and in large cities.

An event occurred beyond our shores at the close of the 1950s that would facilitate the spread of domestic narcotics in the years ahead. In January 1959 Fidel Castro led his victorious ragtag army into Havana. The liberation of Cuba was at hand, and most of the resident underworld made straight for Miami. These proponents of pure capitalism recognized the real philosophy of the Castro regime long before most of the pundits in the United States. They established themselves on the ground floor of a drug industry that exploded in the 1960s. Home-grown entrepreneurs would do the heavy work, but the Cubans had the advantage of being able to converse with the importers to the south.[8] The stage was set for South Florida to respond to the shift in narcotics supply and demand that occurred almost exactly a decade later.

The drug culture spread to middle America in the 1960s. The social upheaval dominating much of American life was exemplified by youth rebellion and the widespread use of marijuana. Grass was characterized as a soft drug, and smoking it was termed recreational rather than abusive. This ambivalence, soft versus hard, allowed drugs to become pervasive. Marijuana, however, was illegal in most states and had been outlawed by the Federal Marijuana Tax Act of 1937. Possession was prohibited by the Boggs Act of 1951.[9]

Mexico sent 80–90 percent of the marijuana imported into the United States. Cuban expatriates dominated transportation from the borders to northern metropolitan areas. Acapulco Gold was getting to be a household term in America. The Pot Revolution was upon us. We experienced the greatest national disregard for the law since Prohibition.[10]

A harbinger of the role that boat smuggling would play in satisfying America's appetite for grass occurred at Dinner Key, Miami, in March 1961. Undercover agents purchased 4 ounces of marijuana from Gerald Seidler, his wife Mary Beth, and Thomas O. Masters aboard the 38-foot yacht *Blow Me Down*. Four other people were arrested in Hialeah and Oldsmar, Florida. The defendants were Anglos, and their average age was twenty-four. News accounts claimed "Florida Dope Ring Crippled" and named the marijuana source as Nassau, Bahamas.[11] It probably originated in Jamaica.

The *Blow Me Down* case was a minor incident, considering the flood of grass rising across the land border from Mexico. It did, however, identify aspects of early maritime drug trafficking: (1) the involvement of young Americans stimulated by the youth and pot revolution of the 1960s, (2) the use of small pleasure and fishing craft for imports, and (3) the importance of Florida and the Bahamas as the initial route of seaborne marijuana to the United States. By the end of the 1960s, pot smuggling from Ensenada, Mexico, to southern California by yachts and high-speed launches had been reported, but there are few specifics and little information on arrests.[12]

The commitment of American troops in Vietnam indirectly gave a boost to the drug culture at home. On 14 November 1965, gallant regulars of the U.S. Seventh Cavalry entered the Ia Drang Valley in the central highlands of Vietnam. They engaged and defeated the Thirty-third North Vietnamese People's Army Regiment. American forces drove General Vo Nguyen Giap's troops into Cambodia. Our victory convinced the U.S. high command that we could win a conventional war in Vietnam. Casualty rates mounted, covered in great detail by the popular press. The antiwar movement was off and running, with more young people embracing the drug culture as a means of escape.[13]

Estimates of marijuana use vary, but a reputable study conducted in San Francisco in 1967–68 showed that 50 percent of the men and 33 percent of the women between the ages of eighteen and twenty-four had used grass one or more times.[14] No one was really concerned, but seizure rates give some indication of use. In 1966, 5 tons were seized; in 1967, 13 tons; then in 1968 the rate jumped to 35 tons.[15]

In 1968 President Lyndon Johnson created the Bureau of Narcotics and Dangerous Drugs from the Federal Bureau of Narcotics and the Bureau of Drug Abuse Control. John Ingersoll was the first director.[16] He was an early proponent of education as the only real solution to drug abuse—an idea that took twenty years to germinate. Education as a solution received short shrift then because no one could figure out how to teach the 1960s generation anything.[17]

Opinions about drug use were changing, and the age of users dropped rapidly to the elementary-school level. A 1969 *Newsweek* article stated that the National Student Association was no longer trying to educate students about drugs but together with the American Civil Liberties Union was challenging the constitutionality of drug laws.[18]

Apologies for pot use were given credibility by authors calling for the repeal or rewriting of pot laws. Antoni Gollan, of *National Review,* stated his case eloquently: "When government sees fit to protect the private citizen from his own activity, the paradox transcends jurisprudence into a not always lucid moral dilemma." Gollan asked, "How can we justify the imprisonment of people who have done things of which one may disapprove, but which have not disturbed others or harmed themselves?"[19] Such was the moral thinking of the time, which led to one of the greatest tragedies in our country's history.

The attitudes and philosophies of the 1960s, including rationalizing drug use as an escape from the televised bloodbath in Southeast Asia, set in motion a demand for narcotics that the existing market could not hope to meet. One author estimated that 300 tons of illegal narcotics entered the United States in 1969, with a probable increase in traffic of more than 500 percent in just three years.[20] That year the nation's underground experienced the worst marijuana famine since the pot epidemic began. Although 70,000 pounds were seized at the border, a drought in the growing areas of Mexico and a sharp increase in use were apparently the real causes of the famine.[21]

President Richard Nixon closed the Mexican border for twenty-one days in 1969 because of the deluge of Acapulco Gold. Operation Intercept began on 21 September and had some impact on the supply of marijuana to the United States.[22] By the end of the decade the U.S. drug trade was estimated at $5 billion per year.[23] Things were bad enough, but the floodgates were about to open.

1

It Begins
1970–1973

Aboard a shrimper loaded with 8 tons of grass, somewhere in the Yucatán Channel:

Captain: I hear a goddamn airplane.
First Man: Where? I don't see nothin'.
Captain: Kick her ahead hard and make a wake.
First Man: O.K., Cap, but you're a paranoid SOB.
Captain: There goes the red-tipped bastard, headed for Catoche. What did I tell you!
First Man: Well, he ain't payin' no attention to us.
Captain: Of course he ain't. We pointin' south. They're only looking for northbound boats.
First Man: We may be pointin' right, but it's gonna take us weeks to get through this miserable ditch goin' backward.
Captain: O.K., Roach, he's gone. Slow 'er down to idle but keep her headed 180. We got almost 4 knots of current here setting us to the north. We makin' about 3 knots over the ground—slow but safe!

FROM A PRISON INTERVIEW WITH AN OLD-TIME SMUGGLER

Near the end of 1970, five men and a woman were arrested in Long Beach, California, for floating 900 pounds of marijuana up the coast from Mexico in a lowly salvage barge.[1] Maritime drug smuggling had come into its own. A voracious demand for marijuana in our permissive society was outstripping the traditional Mexican supply. Intensified enforcement along our land border was an impetus for developing marine routes. It was no surprise that the first serious grass boaters appeared on the Pacific coast; Tijuana, Mexico, just south of San Diego, was the pot capital of the world.[2]

The salvage barge case was eclipsed in May 1971 when a 57-foot fishing vessel, the *Mercy Wiggins,* was seized in San Francisco with 5 tons of pot. Eleven people were convicted in this landmark maritime case. The *Mercy Wiggins* and the 36-foot yacht *Andiamo,* which was used as a floating communications center, departed Newport Beach on 28 March allegedly bound for San Diego to make wildlife documentaries for a fictitious company. The case was broken by a wiretap on the home of the venture's transportation manager, who received coded status reports from the vessels via the marine radio-telephone system. On 29 April the two boats were sighted by a patrol aircraft 14 miles west of the Mexican Todos Santos Islands. They were making way to the north. Intermittent aircraft surveillance was established. When the *Andiamo* entered San Francisco Bay on 3 May, the *Wiggins* was 20 miles off Half Moon Bay. U.S. Customs nabbed the *Andiamo* and put agents aboard the Coast Guard patrol boat *Point Barrow* (WPB-82348) to intercept the *Wiggins.* When Customs agents with guns drawn boarded the vessel, Captain James Lee Olson said, "Please, gentlemen, you don't need guns. We are professional smugglers, not gangsters."[3]

The next year a seizure occurred in Europe that is worth noting. In March 1972, off the Riviera coast, French Customs agents had to fire shots across the bow of the shrimp boat *Caprice des Temps* to stop the vessel. Marcel Boucan, owner and master, threw papers overboard just before he was boarded, and threw himself overboard while the *Temps* was being taken into Marseilles. He was recaptured the next morning, wet and exhausted. Monsieur Boucan apparently had a strong desire to distance himself from his shrimp boat. Agents had been watching the *Temps* for some time because of Boucan's past association with cigarette smugglers. He had refitted the boat for transatlantic crossings.

An initial search revealed nothing. Authorities were hard pressed to hold the boat or the night-swimming owner, except for failing to stop when ordered. The next day the intrepid agents noticed that the boat's concrete ballast seemed oddly placed. "*Voilà! Quelque chose est drôle.*" Out came pickaxes and wrecking bars for an attack on the cement. The assault paid off. Buried in the concrete was a space that contained 934 pounds of pure heroin in plastic bags, the largest single heroin seizure anywhere.[4] The incident foretold a smuggling method that would become commonplace in the next decade: the use of ingenious hidden compartments to transport narcotics. The *Caprice des Temps* case is one of the few documented incidents of a vessel especially dedicated to the transportation of heroin.

When Mexico failed to supply the domestic marijuana market, Jamaica and Colombia responded with relish. The Blue Mountains of Jamaica and the Sierra Nevada and Perija Mountains of Colombia had near-perfect conditions for the cultivation of pot. There was a host of desperately poor farmers to work the fields. There was also a long tradition of smuggling in the Caribbean islands and Latin America. The bubble traders of the Antilles had smuggled liquor and other items for ages.[5] On the Spanish-speaking mainland of South America, the cult of the *contrabandista* was etched in the psyche of the people.[6]

Jamaican pot farmers put up a good fight for the maritime grass market. The island was English-speaking and 400 nautical miles closer than Colombia to the United States. U.S. dollars were hard to come by, because the tourist trade was declining and the government was leaning toward socialism. The American dollars offered by drug smugglers stimulated more than the illegal agricultural industry. Many otherwise legitimate businesspeople in Kingston were happy to change the smugglers' money for them. Farmers could then be paid in the local but fluctuating currency, and businesses got greenbacks to buy needed products and services in the States. All concerned were content with the arrangement.[7]

Colombia had a much larger area to cultivate as well as an existing smuggling apparatus. Moreover, the political situation was in chaos. *La Violencia* between conservatives and liberals gave marijuana growers a free hand.[8] Colombian producers saw the vast profits being made by Mexican growers. They could offer a superior product known as Colombian Gold, soon to become the "smoke of connoisseurs."[9] Colombia eventually took the lead in pot production.

A marijuana field in a Latin American country *(Author's collection)*

In the beginning, marijuana smuggling was done by a large number of entrepreneurs using small boats. They were usually U.S.–registered fishing vessels, sailboats, and cabin cruisers, manned by young American crews. Purchases from growers were financed by little groups of investors and arranged by trips to Jamaica and Colombia. The entire transportation and distribution phase of the venture was handled by Americans.

A kingpin grass smuggler gave insight into the early days. Ambrose Weldon (a fictitious name for a real person now in the Federal Witness Protection Program) was originally a commercial fisherman. Weldon claims he was intimidated by the marijuana growers during his first trips to Colombia. He had a real problem with the language. A cure for this impediment was easy: he formed a loose business arrangement with a tough Cuban expatriate who made the procurement trips.[10]

By an accident of geography, Florida was closer than any other state to the developing Caribbean marijuana sources. It soon became the center of the infant maritime smuggling industry. With over 8,400 miles of shoreline riddled with secluded inlets and rivers and a vast network of residential canals, Florida provided innumerable off-load sites. The state also had a large Cuban underworld population, courtesy of Fidel, to link Colombian growers with home-grown American smugglers.

The coast from Miami to Palm Beach was an ideal off-load area. The nearby Bahamas gave cover and concealment. The islands extended southeast from Grand Bahama for 470 miles to Great Inagua, only 50 miles from the Windward Passage between Cuba and Hispaniola. East through the Windward and up by the Bahamas was the most direct and protected route from Jamaica and Colombia for early smugglers in their frail craft.

Lobster boats and large cabin cruisers could make the run from South Florida to Jamaica in only forty-eight hours. Some smaller boats found it necessary to carry 55-gallon drums of fuel, usually lashed to objects on deck. The drums were one of the first indicators of suspicion used to identify smugglers by the few patrols roaming the Bahamas and the Caribbean. Our offshore presence in the early 1970s was more devoted to fishing conflicts and Cuban counterrevolutionary problems than to drug enforcement. A lobster war was raging in the Bahamas, and Cubans were leaving Fidel's paradise in all manner of flotation devices.[11] The threat of narcotics traffic through the Bahamas was recognized, but violent incidents in the fishing conflicts demanded immediate attention.

Some drug cases did occur despite the thrust of other missions. The first Coast Guard–controlled drug seizure took place on 8 March 1973 about 12 miles west of North Cat Cay, Bahamas, in the Florida Straits. The USCGC *Dauntless* (WMEC-624) seized the *Big L,* a 38-foot sports fisherman. Roy Warren, owner of the motor vessel *Adventurer III* moored in Miami, was approached by Michael Parks about picking up a load of marijuana in Jamaica. Warren told the story to the Bureau of Narcotics and Dangerous Drugs (BNDD), soon to become the Drug Enforcement Administration (DEA). Agents encouraged Warren to accept the offer and helped to outfit his boat for the trip. Two undercover agents served as crew.

On 5 March, Warren called the drug agents from Grand Cayman, a fuel stop on the way to Jamaica. Plans had changed. Warren would pick up the grass in Jamaica, but he would rendezvous with the *Big L*

Suspect lobster boat with fuel drums on deck anchored in Bahamian waters, early 1970s *(Official U.S. Coast Guard photograph)*

near Riding Rocks in the Bahamas. Parks would be there to transfer the load to the *Big L*. Warren did not know where the grass would come ashore. The drug agents went to the Coast Guard for help.

The *Dauntless* was ordered to stand by at the Miami Beach Coast Guard base. A BNDD aircraft would watch the *Adventurer III* and the *Big L*. On the morning of 8 March the *Dauntless* got under way. With position reports from the BNDD aircraft, the cutter established radar contact but stayed beyond visual range of the vessels. After sunset the *Dauntless* doused her lights and closed the range. At 1930 a radio call from Warren verified that the marijuana had been transferred to the *Big L*. A few minutes later he reported that the drug boat had broken down and he would have to take her in tow.

The *Dauntless* charged in at flank speed with her 3-inch deck gun manned and ready. At 600 yards the Coast Guardsmen illuminated the boats with a searchlight. There was no resistance. A boarding party was put aboard the *Big L* at 2028. They found over a ton of marijuana. Four crewmen were arrested. Michael Parks was later found hiding aboard the *Adventurer III*. The five were convicted for conspiring to import marijuana into the United States. It was just the beginning.[12]

Often the Coast Guard discovered dopers while assisting disabled or sinking boats. Such was the case on 14 June 1973, when the 95-foot patrol boat *Cape Shoalwater* (WPB-95324) encountered the go-fast boat *Mr. Lucky* 15 miles east of Fort Lauderdale. The speedboat's two-man crew had met a freighter near Cat Cay in the Bahamas. After taking on 4,500 pounds of compacted pot, the boat ran out of fuel and was disabled in high seas. The next morning the sports fisherman *Golden Lamb* came upon the *Mr. Lucky*. There was an unsuccessful attempt to tow the disabled boat. The unsuspecting skipper called the Coast Guard despite pleas by the dopers that they did not need help. When the *Cape Shoalwater* arrived, Lt. (jg) Dave Henrickson, the cutter's CO, found the *Mr. Lucky* occupied by two men in bathing suits. The boat was slowly taking on water. They hesitantly accepted a tow to Fort Lauderdale. Henrickson had no idea he was offering assistance to a grass boat.

Safely home, Lieutenant Henrickson sent a petty officer to make an inspection of the boat for his search-and-rescue (SAR) report, and the Coast Guardsman discovered what they had fished from the Florida Straits. Henrickson had never arrested anyone, but he managed to take the two dopers into legal custody. There were no handcuffs aboard the *Cape Shoalwater*. The young officer improvised and had his charges locked in the small cutter's office. Henrickson told the gunner's mate to draw a weapon from the armory and to post himself as sentry in front of the locked office. He left to phone Ted Weed, the appropriately named BNDD resident agent. When Henrickson returned, he noticed that the sentry had no ammunition clip in his weapon. The gun was not loaded! The indignant gunner's mate informed his CO of the policy of separating weapons from ammunition except in authorized cases. To their chagrin, they suddenly realized that the ammo was in the ship's office with the prisoners! The lifesavers were learning a new profession. Henrickson hurried ashore to purchase handcuffs with petty cash.

The *Mr. Lucky*'s name was also appropriate. At the time, it was necessary to prove that smugglers caught on the high seas intended to land their contraband on U.S. shores (i.e., there had to be conspiracy to import). A clever defense attorney argued that Henrickson was the one guilty of importing the marijuana by literally dragging his clients and their boat into a U.S. port when they had no intention of coming home with the grass. Surprisingly, some of the jury believed that two American citizens on a Florida-registered 28-foot boat packed with grass did not intend to import contraband. The trial ended with a hung jury. Assistant U.S. Attorney Pat Sullivan reindicted the two and convicted them at the second trial. Sullivan commended Lieutenant Henrickson, Chief Engineman D. E. Green, and Gunner's Mate James Ellis for their valuable assistance and professional testimony at trial.

Unfortunately, after the trial a juror commented to the defense attorney that he had been coerced by other jurors to agree to a guilty finding. Charges against the two smugglers were dismissed. The government did not indict a third time.[13]

On 17 September 1973, as the cutter *Courageous* (WMEC-622) was patrolling the Bahamas in the vicinity of Cay Sal Bank between Florida and Cuba, a lookout sighted a boat heading for Anguilla Cay. Comdr. A. R. Larzelere, CO of the *Courageous*, decided to investigate. The contact was the U.S.–registered lobster boat *Gilma I*. The boat had no traps or other fishing gear. She did, however, have some 55-gallon drums on deck and other cargo covered with a tarp. When ordered to stop for boarding, the two men on the *Gilma* looked the other way and continued toward Anguilla Cay, about 11 miles away. Larzelere maneuvered the *Courageous* alongside the lobster boat and tried to block her obvious run to Bahamian waters. The *Gilma* slowed, seeming to acknowledge the cutter's orders. Suddenly she backed down hard, ducked close under the cutter's stern, and made good her escape into shoal water. As Commander Larzelere tried to get permission to enter Bahamian waters, the *Gilma*'s crew were seen throwing drums and packages over the side. When permission was finally granted, Coast Guardsmen recovered about 4 tons of pot. Bale markings and newspaper packaging showed that the marijuana was from Jamaica. The *Gilma*, however, was out of sight.

The next morning a Customs aircraft located the elusive lobster boat. The *Courageous* was ordered to shadow the *Gilma* from international waters. The U.S. government exchanged messages with the newly independent Bahamas to see who would go after the smugglers. Customs kept discreet air surveillance until relieved by DEA. The *Gilma* was seen landing packages on North Anguilla Cay. The boat then got under way and headed north along the barren islands. The

Coast Guard sent a helicopter from Miami with DEA and Customs agents aboard. Late in the day permission was granted for the helo to land on the island. The agents and the helo crew recovered twelve more bales of grass.

As night approached, the DEA aircraft went home and the *Courageous* tracked the *Gilma* by radar. The two vessels proceeded slowly north, on opposite sides of the island chain. There was a break in the chain with a mile-wide strip of international waters between Damas Cays and Dog Rocks. Commander Larzelere threaded the 210-foot blacked-out cutter through the rocky islands and over the poorly charted bank. The *Courageous* was now on the same side of the island as the lobster boat and 3 miles astern. They crept north outside the Bahamian territorial sea, hoping the *Gilma* would remain oblivious to the big white cutter. Radar picked up other boats anchored in the *Gilma*'s path. Was it a rendezvous? As Commander Larzelere pondered this development, the target went dead in the water. The *Gilma* was anchored near the others.

About midnight the 82-foot patrol boat *Point Barnes* (WPB-82371) arrived on the scene to assist. The *Courageous* moved to cover the north end of the chain; the *Point Barnes* was ordered to the south end. They waited for dawn. About 0800 one of the boats got under way and headed north toward the cutter. Had this boat taken on contraband from the *Gilma* during the night, or was she a decoy to draw off the cutter while the smuggler made a run for it? The cutter's CO moved to intercept the unknown lobster boat. It was the *Odin*. A boarding ascertained that the *Odin* was a legitimate fisherman.

While the boarding was going on, the cutter's people were amazed to see what appeared to be the *Gilma* coming straight toward them. A Customs aircraft verified that the *Gilma* was indeed on a course directly toward the *Courageous*. When the *Gilma* crossed the 3-mile limit, the cutter signaled her to come alongside. The lobster boat came up to the *Courageous* as though it were their first meeting. The *Gilma*'s two-man Cuban-American crew were arrested and brought aboard the cutter. They were docile until they saw the mound of marijuana on the cutter's fantail. The men complained loudly that the Coast Guard had no authority to board them in international waters. They were separated for questioning by two federal agents who had arrived by helo. Both decided to cooperate, and their mysterious behavior was explained.

The *Gilma*'s crew had no idea that they had been seen dumping the pot overboard or that an aircraft had spotted them off-loading. They had bought lobsters and a few traps from the other boats to give the appearance of legitimate fishing. When they came out to the cutter, they had intended to apologize for not stopping two days earlier, using the excuse that engine problems had made it impossible for them to stop. The men told the agents the rest of the story. They had been hired in a Miami bar for $30,000 and had gone to Jamaica with a representative of the buyer. The pot had been purchased for about $100,000. The third man had supposedly been lost over the side in rough weather while transiting the Windward Passage. The plan had called for delivery to small boats off North Florida. Case closed.[14]

In a few days the *Courageous* was at sea again, headed back to Cay Sal Bank. A helo came from Miami to help locate American lobster boats fishing in Bahamian waters, and to deliver Special Agent Jorge Picon of the National Marine Fisheries Service to assist Commander Larzelere. The agent was bilingual and was a valuable asset in warning Cuban-American fishermen of the hazards of violating Bahamian fishing laws.

On 25 September 1973 Picon was returning to the cutter in the helicopter when he spotted the cabin cruiser *Moby Dick* with spare fuel drums on deck proceeding toward Anguilla Cay. Commander Larzelere must have experienced déjà vu. The chase was on again, but this time there would be no under-the-counter dodges. When the *Moby Dick* was overtaken and boarded 15 miles east of Anguilla, approximately 2,000 pounds of marijuana were found in a forward cabin. The boat was seized, and the crew of four Anglo Americans, including one female, were arrested.[15]

The *Courageous* had scored on two drug boats within a week in the same part of the ocean. Were these isolated events? No one knew for sure, but the Coast Guard was not going to cry wolf. At this point the service was just entering the drug war. It was not a planned evolution.

Capt. A. B. How, USCG, predicted the Coast Guard's future in an article for the *Proceedings* of the U.S. Naval Institute. The article was published in May 1974, but it must have been written at the end of 1973. In the section "Enforcing the Laws," Captain How discussed fisheries enforcement, fishing gear conflicts, and oil pollution problems. He stated, "The area that may well see the most expansion in Coast Guard service in the future is that of law enforcement."[16]

Captain How did not even mention drug interdiction. Perhaps many senior people in the Coast Guard tuned out drug interdiction because of lingering memories of Prohibition. The service had suffered the worst public abuse in its distinguished history during the Rum War of the 1920s. There was also a fear of being heavily invested in a single mission, especially with the lack of national consensus.

Debates raged within the Coast Guard over the pros and cons of a policy to arm boarding parties. Many senior officers who had come into the service after World War II were focused on the lifesaving mission and did not favor exchanging their white-hat image for that of a maritime police agency.[17] The historical roots of the organization, however, were in the enforcement of revenue laws. Despite its reluctance, the Coast Guard was forced into the drug war in 1973 and soon became a major player.

When the U.S. Navy closed its operating base in Key West in the early 1970s, the local economy was devastated. The growing demand for marijuana offered salvation to the independent-thinking population of our southernmost city, so strategically located on the developing grass routes from the Caribbean. The hundreds of miles of mangrove shoreline and countless isolated islands in the lower Keys were perfect off-load sites for the bulky pot bales known as "square grouper."

Only 158 miles via the Overseas Highway to the Miami market center—there was good reason for the Conch Kingdom to become a major marijuana port of entry. Corruption was more or less a way of life in Key West. There was little respect for the law and a tradition of smuggling everything from booze to aliens. The only thing needed was a fleet of smuggling vessels and trained seamen to do the job. Key West had an abundance of both.[18]

During the winter months more than three hundred shrimp boats operated out of Key West on the Tortugas shrimp grounds. Many were year-round residents. There were also over one hundred spiny-lobster boats home-ported in Key West. Some were very fast rigs with open-deck carrying capacity. The shrimpers, however, had below-deck capacities to carry 10 tons of pot or more concealed from casual observers. They also had the range for nonstop trips to Colombia with no telltale fuel drums on deck. It was common for American shrimpers to transit to and from the lucrative shrimp grounds off Central and South America. Back on the shrimping grounds north of Tortugas,

A Gulf shrimper typical of those that carried much of the Caribbean pot
(*Official NOAA photograph*)

they could blend in with legitimate vessels and wait for the best time
to come in for an off-load. Considering the huge profits available, it
was no surprise that so many Key West fishermen entered the drug
trade. The carrying capacity alone of renegade shrimp boats was a
meaningful factor in the steady rise in volume of marijuana imports.
In time they would account for over 60 percent of the fishing vessels
seized for drug smuggling.[19]

An early-1970s shrimp boat marijuana trip to Colombia was
described by Ambrose Weldon in a later prison interview. He and his
crew made the voyage in a 67-foot DESCO-built wood trawler, a
pilothouse-forward square-stern Gulf shrimper—a good sea boat with
lots of freeboard, but she would roll your guts out in a beam sea.
There were no sophisticated communications and chart codes then.
They made a legitimate fishing trip to the Tortugas grounds and
unloaded at one of the processing facilities on Stock Island, just east
of Key West. Fuel and supplies were taken on as though they were

preparing for another routine fishing trip. A Key West native who coordinated the smuggling venture with some people in Miami gave Weldon instructions just before departure. They were to proceed straight to Santa Marta and anchor off the town where contact would be made by a Colombian supplier. A direct route was set through the Yucatán Channel off Cape San Antonio, Cuba, with a warning to stay well clear of Cuban waters.

On a dark night the boat slipped out of Stock Island and set course for the Yucatán. The LORAN (long-range navigation) electronic navigation system was not reliable in the Caribbean. It depended on inaccurate signals reflected from the ionosphere. To make sure they stayed on track, Grand Cayman and Pedro Bank southwest of Jamaica were chosen as way points. The captain and the two crewmen had never been to Colombia; they were apprehensive. The crew took a terrible beating from northeast trade winds in the open Caribbean. The wind took them broad on the port beam and caused the empty shrimper to roll her sides under. Even the flopper-stoppers, torpedo-shaped devices suspended from outriggers on both sides, did little to reduce the roll. Because of sea conditions, speed was reduced to an average of 7 knots. It took a week to cover 1,150 nautical miles. Weldon made a night landfall on a dark coast that he hoped was Colombia. There were no lights visible, and the neophyte smugglers had a helpless feeling.

Correctly figuring that the boat had been set to the west by the trades, they crept east along the coast, which veered north. Finally, in the predawn hours, the welcome glow of Morro Grande Light appeared. The crew motored slowly—and, they hoped, unnoticed— into Bahia Santa Marta and anchored on the outer edge of the shelf, as far away from town as possible. Inland stretched the snow-capped mysterious Sierra Nevada de Santa Marta mountains. As the day wore on they waited and sweated and waited some more. The men feared a boarding by the Colombian Navy or other officialdom. By sunset they wanted to forget the whole thing and head for home. Darkness brought a small measure of security. A night watch was set, and the would-be smugglers waited for dawn.

Perseverance paid off. After midnight a small boat with two Colombians came alongside. One man spoke broken English. He said he was their contact and directed Weldon to a fuel dock. They topped off with No. 2 diesel at first light. Then the Colombian guided them to a loading site south of town where a small river emptied into the bay. Just after sunrise a number of bongos (canoelike craft) showed up loaded to the gunnels with bales of grass. In short order, dark-skinned Colombian Indians loaded the shrimper with about 8 tons of pot.

Off they sailed toward home with the boat riding much better from the weight of the cargo. The now buoyant smugglers felt that the only danger still ahead was the passage north through the Yucatán Channel. Weldon had been warned that occasional Coast Guard aircraft patrols covered the Yucatán and might take note of northbound vessels. Our captain was a clever mariner as well as a good fisherman. He had read *Sailing Directions*, published by the Naval Oceanographic Office. The publication told him that a current up to 4 knots set north through the Yucatán from the Caribbean Sea to the Gulf of Mexico. If the seas were relatively calm, why not let the current take you backward through the channel while appearing to head south? That was what he did, then and in the future. Any airplanes approaching out of the sun would see a boat heading south. All you had to do was advance the throttle to make a good wake, and you were convincing. In really good weather you could even run the engine astern through the Gap, as the channel was known.

So they came to pass stern-first through the Yucatán. Arriving undetected off Smith Shoal Light, northwest of Key West, Weldon notified the grass owners. A representative of the organization soon showed up in a fast boat with off-load instructions. The next night they went in as close as possible to the Snipe Keys and transferred the cargo to small boats. No sweat (other than the wait at Santa Marta), no strain (only the wallowing trip south). The captain was paid $60,000 and each crewmen $30,000 for two weeks' work. Not bad money for fishermen, but considering that the load was worth about $6.4 million wholesale, their share was not exorbitant. They were hooked on the dope trade.[20]

The shrimp captain's story was interesting, and accurate to the best of his memory. His worry, however, about Coast Guard aircraft in the early to mid-1970s was mostly unfounded. Grumman HU-16 Albatross flying boats, affectionately known as Goats, did fly over the southern Gulf and the Yucatán in those days, but most flights were search-and-rescue missions. Some were IRT (infrared radiation thermometer) flights, taking surface temperatures of the Gulf on a monthly basis. Sightings of fishing boats were also recorded (but not which way they were going), and schools of fish, sea turtles, and whales. Drug boats were not even a consideration. Many flights were fishery enforcement patrols.[21] Surely some Coast Guard aircraft were tasked with assisting Customs or DEA in the interdiction of smugglers in the early 1970s, but it was not routine.

Oceangoing sailboats, those white-winged beauties so common in tropical seas, were in on the grass float from the very beginning. Sailboat pot smugglers, as a rule, are more laid back and less greedy than their power-boat counterparts. With a few notable exceptions in the Pacific, sailing vessels have a limited carrying capacity, and their usual grass load amounts to only a few hundred pounds. According to one, "You didn't make millions bringing home the 'herb,' but it paid the mortgage notes, bought the groceries, and provided unlimited rounds of Margaritas at beach bars all over the Caribbean."[22] You could even bring wives or girlfriends along. The women were great cover for making the boat and its people look like fun-loving cruisers. This was especially true when the girls lounged on deck in the nude. Girls and spinnakers—what better bluff for a casual drug run to Montego Bay?

In those days Jamaica was a favorite source of marijuana for sailboaters. You did not have to be part of a smuggling organization or bother with off-load crews. No sophisticated radio communications were necessary. Stop at a few other places, such as Grand Cayman or any of the Bahamas, and get your passport punched to show that you were a cruising tourist. All you had to do was anchor in some convenient cove and let it be known at the closest bar that you might be interested in purchasing some "Ganja." The Man would show up, and a transaction would be completed without fanfare. It was a good idea, however, to clear Jamaican waters quickly after the cargo was on board and secured in whatever space was available.[23]

The Jamaica Defense Force Coast Guard was established in February 1966, from the old Jamaica Sea Squadron. Three modern patrol craft built in Louisiana were added to the fleet the next year. The force was under the command of Capt. J. E. Farnol, DSC, Royal Navy (Ret.). They made their first drug seizure in 1972.[24]

Once clear of the island, with the Blue Mountains fading astern, a sailor need not fear interception on the way home. If he went by way of the Caymans and the Yucatán, all he had to do was give Cuba a wide berth. He would probably elect a route through the Windward

Passage, then northwest on an easy beam reach with the trade winds over his starboard side. He could make a stop at any number of Bahama islands without hassle. The Bahamian Defense Force patrols stayed close to Nassau and operated only during daylight. There was only one British navy guardship covering all of the Commonwealth islands.

Entering the Florida Straits from either direction, the sailboat smuggler mingled with hundreds of other boats in the sailing community. If he was cautious, his boat would be tied up at some intermediate marina and left to age with the pot on board. After a time, depending on the nerve of the owner and minus the appearance of any law enforcement, the boat would be unloaded. Sailboat smugglers were hard to catch, then as now. All aspects of the delivery were handled by very few people. Not much chance of leaks to shoreside cops in those tight little groups, and there was little risk of getting intercepted at sea.[25]

The Gold Coast and the Keys were not the only Florida terminuses for embryonic pot conveyors. Commercial fishermen in Cortez, a picturesque village on the Gulf coast, felt the call of the square grouper. Ben Green, in his chronicle of Cortez, noted that "by 1970, Bubba Capo, who had fished with my grandpa for many years, started building big storage compartments on his fishing boat, saying he wanted to go after deep-water mackerel and needed the extra space."[26] No one knows for sure when Bubba and his crew got involved with grass. But by 1973 the whole world knew who they were.

Gulf coast smugglers were prone to transit the Yucatán Channel to Jamaica and Colombia. The route was about the same distance as the Windward Passage, but there were advantages. Traffic through the Yucatán seldom encountered Coast Guard surface patrols. Most available 210-foot cruising cutters were deployed in the Bahamas to deal with pirates and poachers. The Gap was unguarded. A look at the chart will show that more open sea had to be traveled on the western route. Nonetheless, a shrimper was perfectly capable of making that transit with fuel to spare. The smuggling shrimper could mingle with his own over much of the route to grass country. Not only did he have good cover, he could carry more pot than his East Coast competitors. "Go west, young man," must have been the watchword.

Beliefs that the Sunshine State's drug trade was concentrated in South Florida were shattered on 5 March 1973. Officers on the North

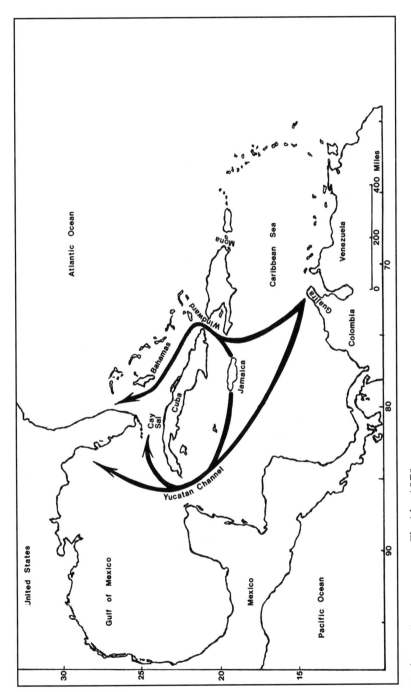

Early marijuana routes to Florida, 1970s

Florida Gulf coast discovered over 9 tons of marijuana on a grounded barge near the isolated fishing village of Steinhatchee. It was the largest pot bust anywhere.[27]

The Steinhatchee haul dwarfed other seizures in South Florida and almost doubled the 5-ton record of the *Mercy Wiggins* in California. Writing on the bales showed they were from Jamaica. By volume and location, the Steinhatchee find revealed a major and unknown grass route up from the Caribbean into the Gulf of Mexico. Was this the handiwork of some sinister and foreign drug organization violating the tranquil marshes of the Gulf coast's Big Bend?

The grounded barge and its big grass load were found at the mouth of Rocky Creek, 4 miles south of Steinhatchee. Credit for the discovery went to Harold O'Neal, an inquisitive citizen who appeared at the Dixie County sheriff's office with a sack he had found near the barge containing plant debris. The sheriff's office identified the sack's contents as marijuana, and O'Neal guided deputies to the scene. One look at the barge and the massive load of grass prompted the locals to call in the Florida Department of Law Enforcement.[28] Surveillance was established at the site, both on the barge and on an isolated island where some of the pot had already been stashed. Down the dirt road came three individuals in a car. At the last minute they saw the officers and tried to flee. A short chase ensued, ending in the capture of James G. Maslanka (twenty-four), Michael J. Knight (twenty-three), and Walter R. Ercius (twenty-two), all of St. Pete Beach, Florida.[29]

Not long after the first three arrests, four men in a boat came up to the island stash site where the law was waiting. At the wheel was none other than "Bubba" (Floyd Farrel) Capo, forty, of Cortez, who had built the big storage compartment on his boat in 1970 to go after "those deep-water mackerel." Bubba had moved up to Horseshoe Beach in Dixie County and opened his own fish house. With Floyd were David Strongosky (twenty-three), Barry W. Korn (twenty-three), and Steven G. Lamb (twenty), also of St. Petersburg. They were all charged with felony possession of marijuana under state laws. On 7 March, U.S. Customs brought federal charges against the men, now known as the Steinhatchee Seven. Under federal laws, they were charged with conspiracy to import marijuana, importation, conspiracy to possess for resale, and possession for resale.[30] This was not some evil foreign conspiracy; it was the work of a bunch of local youngsters and a salty commercial fisherman.

The government prevailed at trial against the famous Houston attorney Percy Foreman, who defended the now infamous Steinhatchee Seven. The seven were found guilty of all charges on 9 October 1973. Some of the prosecution's best physical evidence was burlap fibers taken from the clothes of the defendants that matched burlap fibers from the marijuana bales.[31]

Later that month six of the seven were sentenced to twenty-year prison terms. Only Walter Ercius, whose father was the former mayor of St. Pete Beach, got a lighter sentence of ten years. The judge felt that Ercius had not been involved in the caper to the same extent as the others.[32] None of the men served anything close to the sentences allotted. They were not criminals in the general view; marijuana was really not so bad, and the jails were crowded.

The Gold Coast's reputation for drug smuggling was sullied by the Gulf coast smugglers. It was hit even harder in a few months. In the meantime, marijuana continued to arrive on a regular schedule in small pleasure craft and fishing vessels. It came mostly from stash locations in the Bahamas and usually did not exceed several tons per delivery. The use of stash houses or sheds in the Bahamas let U.S. smugglers maintain control of their loads at safe locations and slip their products piecemeal to Florida.[33]

A bad omen occurred in the southern Gulf on 7 November 1973, though it was hardly noticed at the time. The 40-foot yacht *Pompero*, crewed by two Americans and two Jamaicans, was seized off the west tip of Everglades National Park with 3,000 pounds of grass.[34] It was a minor seizure, but the location boded ill for the future.

The 70 miles of Everglades coastline from Cape Sable to Naples was an ideal marijuana off-load zone. With vast coastal marshes, inaccessible rivers and bays to the south, and the Ten Thousand Islands to the north, the Everglades is a formidable area to police. Marjory Stoneman Douglas in her excellent book about the Everglades called it a River of Grass.[35] Her 1947 description was prophetic. It was one of the final holdouts of multi-ton marijuana smuggling.

Maritime smuggling's early phase peaked at the end of 1973. On Christmas Eve a drug task force composed of federal, state, and local lawmen closed in on a smuggling ring in the Florida Panhandle. Approximately 25 tons of pot were seized, and eleven people were arrested. Headlines again proclaimed the "nation's largest marijuana bust." The primary stash house was a barn in Alachua County that housed about 14 tons of grass. Additionally, 7 tons were seized in a truck in Alabama and just over 4 tons in Leon County, Florida. A fishing boat directly connected to the grass in the barn was seized. The barn was located by a confidential informant carrying a transponder who was tracked by aircraft. The marijuana was from Colombia. Follow-up investigations resulted in the seizure of two shrimp trawlers, one at Apalachicola and the other at Pensacola.[36]

Florida had set two world records that year in pot seizures. Consideration was given to forming a special state grand jury to investigate the obvious menace of the exploding drug industry.[37] When it came, the statewide grand jury would change things, but not in the way most people hoped.

On the national level, President Richard Nixon created the Drug Enforcement Administration in March 1973, under the Department of Justice. DEA was built around the Bureau of Narcotics and Dangerous Drugs, with the involuntary transfer of many agents from the Bureau of Customs. The purpose of the reorganization was to put all federal drug investigators in one house. It was a noble enterprise, despite vocal complaints from a lot of old-time Customs people who got drafted. Anglo agents who had worked narcotics in Florida, in California, and along the Mexican border were less than enthusiastic about joining their Latin-flavored counterparts in BNDD. They all expected to end up working heroin cases in New York. In fact, there was a heroin shortage in the country, possibly related to the arrest of the infamous Frank Matthews, New York's heroin king. The emphasis of drug enforcement was shifting to marijuana and cocaine.[38]

Despite the advantages of having all federal drug investigators under DEA, a new aspect of enforcement known as drug interdiction was rapidly emerging. Interdiction involves the interception of drugs approaching our borders by patrol efforts, either by cold hits or on the basis of intelligence. It targets the transportation platforms rather than the smugglers. The goal is to remove drugs from the pipeline where they are most highly concentrated. Intelligence for interdiction could come from the investigative side, but it was not willingly surrendered. The agents wanted to make arrests on their turf; they were rated on the basis of arrests and seizures. The patrol force consisted of Coast Guard people (with little investigative capabilities) and Customs Patrol officers (who could not conduct investigations on their own).

Reorganization Plan Number Two, which established DEA, also prohibited agents who remained in Customs from conducting drug investigations. This was intended to eliminate competition and duplication of effort. Customs Patrol and the Coast Guard had to turn their seizures over to DEA. Investigation and interdiction were thus effectively separated by agency boundaries, always a barrier to information flow. This happened at a time when there was a great need for the primary parts of drug enforcement to be talking on the same circuit. Somehow the best-laid plans of government to improve operations seem to be overtaken by events. It was a full decade before an attempt was made to straighten out this mess and improve interagency communications with a coordinating organization. Congress abolished that organization in just six years, mostly because of political considerations. Politics and bureaucratic infighting are a large part of the drug war.

Maritime drug smuggling in the early 1970s had unique characteristics that separate this phase from later periods. The end of 1973 is a good point to end this account of the first round of the drug war at sea. As we have seen, the start of maritime smuggling was prompted by a demand for marijuana in America that could not be met by the land supply from Mexico. The availability of pot in Jamaica and Colombia necessitated vessel transportation. The sheer bulk of the product required a sealift capability. Boat smugglers were mostly young American adventurers and some not-so-young fishermen with boats and the knowledge to deliver the goods.

Commercial fishing is, in the best of times, a hard and uncertain business. The temptation to equal or surpass a year's wages with one or two square-grouper expeditions was more than many could resist. The fishing industry was an ideal cover for drug smuggling. It involved the comings and goings of a large number of vessels at odd hours, and the landings of catches at out-of-the-way places. Shrimp boats had the capacity to carry multi-ton loads of grass. Over four thousand offshore shrimpers operated out of southeastern ports.[39] They routinely fished at night (shrimp burrow into the bottom in daylight to escape predators), they had extensive ranges, and many migrated to newly explored fishing grounds in the Caribbean. They made it possible to stockpile large quantities of marijuana on the Florida Gulf coast.

Vessels used for smuggling on the other side of Florida were more cosmopolitan, including yachts, sports fishing vessels, and lobster boats. Smugglers on the East Coast had the advantage of being able to use the nearby Bahamas as a way point and a secure storage area for their product. They could use a variety of small boats for final delivery to the United States. In California both pleasure and fishing craft were used to bring marijuana from Mexico, but nowhere near the volume being imported from the Caribbean.

In the early 1970s there was a shortage of long-range enforcement vessels and a preoccupation with other missions. Only four 210-foot medium-endurance cutters were home-ported in the Seventh Coast Guard District. Those were heavily involved in peacekeeping missions in the Bahamas and saving people fleeing from Cuba. The Bureau of Customs (soon to be designated the U.S. Customs Service) had only a minuscule marine capability. Most of its counternarcotics efforts were concentrated on our land border with Mexico. The Bureau of Narcotics and Dangerous Drugs was still focused on heroin traffic in the Northeast, with just a stirring of interest in the marijuana trade. For our fledgling boat smugglers, the road to the market was wide open.

By the end of 1973 the Coast Guard had seized only six grass boats with a little over 20,000 pounds of pot.[40] Most enforcement victories against boat smugglers were accomplished through traditional shore-based investigative techniques using surveillance, informants, record checks, wiretaps, and bugs. They were few in number, but the investigations that produced results were definitely eye openers. Multi-ton grass seizures in California and in Florida revealed the extent of maritime drug smuggling.

Round one at sea went to the smugglers by default. We were unprepared, in both resources and attitude, to engage the enemy. More to the point, we hardly knew who they were.

2

Crosscurrents
1974–1976

It's the old, old road and the old, old quest
  Of the cut-throat sons of Cain,
South by West and a quarter West,
  And hey for the Spanish Main.

JOHN MANSFIELD, "THE BUCCANEER"

Important foreign and domestic changes occurred in maritime drug smuggling in the middle of the 1970s. Some were planned, and some were not. Drug delivery procedures were established that lasted for fifteen years. The triennium of 1974–76 was a pivotal time.

The most nefarious development was the advent of marijuana motherships. Mothershipping contraband to our shores was not a new concept. Captain William S. McCoy, a former yacht builder from Jacksonville, Florida, established Prohibition's "Rum Row" off New York in 1921. McCoy used his British-registered auxiliary schooner *Tomoka* to deliver illegal liquor just outside the U.S. 3-mile territorial limit. There were abundant small, fast boats along the coast to complete the operation under cover of darkness. McCoy was immune from U.S. enforcement as long as he stayed outside the limit. The *Tomoka* was immune from U.S. enforcement on the high seas because of her foreign registry. The booze motherships flourished. They were the Coast Guard's primary target in the Rum War at sea.[1]

Former Royal Navy officer Harold Derber is credited with introducing the marijuana mothership in 1974. Somewhere along his track from Old Albion to South Florida the dapper Englishman studied the tactics of Rum Row's founder, William "The Real" McCoy. If Derber was not the first to use this highly efficient method to transport the bulky contraband, he certainly set the pace.

Derber appeared on the Florida scene in the late 1960s as a modern-day Scarlet Pimpernel. He devised a plan to rescue people who wanted to escape Cuba and actually brought out a dozen or so paid-in-advance refugees. It was the other thousand whose relatives paid the $50 advance with no result that got Derber into trouble with the authorities. Derber was deported, but he soon managed to return to the United States for "business purposes."

Our wily Briton needed a good man on the beach to implement his marijuana mothership concept and achieve his goal of controlling the whole delivery process. He selected John D. Steele, the former mayor of Hallandale, Florida, and twice an unsuccessful candidate for the U.S. Congress. Besides his political activities, Steele had prospected for diamonds in Venezuela and gold in Honduras. All he got from these adventures was a fungus infection from bat droppings in caves.

The Derber-Steele association came to light in September 1974. Monroe County sheriff's deputies stopped a suspicious truck crossing the Overseas Highway from the Florida Keys. In it they found Harold Derber, John Steele, and 3,000 pounds of marijuana. Charges were dismissed because of a technicality. There was no proof that the grass was from a mothership, but the event marked the start of the Derber-Steele mothership operation.[2] The modus operandi for transporting large volumes of marijuana to the United States was irrevocably changed.

A capacity increase in maritime marijuana transportation was needed. Colombian Gold was becoming more popular every day. Colombian growers saw huge profits in the Mexican marijuana boom of the 1960s and early 1970s. Their product sold for $400–600 a pound wholesale. That was almost double the cost of Mexican commercial-grade grass, but the Colombian product was more potent and more attractive, with fewer stems and seeds. Colombians soon surpassed their Mexican rivals in both volume and quality of marijuana produced. Some was delivered to the United States by cargo and light aircraft, but most of it came by ships and boats. Round-trip small-boat deliveries declined drastically in a few years, but they never disappeared.

Colombian grass production and maritime transportation to American markets received a boost in 1975, when the government of Mexico gave in to U.S. pressure and agreed to an aerial drug crop eradication program using the herbicide 2,4-D. Our government's primary goal was to persuade the Mexicans to spray the poppy fields of the Sinaloa-Durango-Chihuahua highlands to reduce opium production. The Mexican aerial eradication eventually spread to marijuana, with devastating results for pot growers. This program in Mexico shaped the future of the U.S. marijuana supply into the 1980s.[3]

The source and transportation of marijuana were not the only changes; people changes were also in the wind. A Florida statewide grand jury impaneled in February 1974 to combat the drug menace was one instrument of change. It grew out of the 1973 multi-ton Christmas Eve seizure in the Florida Panhandle. Investigators fingered Raymond Grady Stansel, Jr., a forty-three-year-old Tarpon Springs fisherman, as the kingpin of Florida's largest smuggling organization. When Stansel was arrested in June 1974, his briefcase contained cash receipts for a new Mercedes-Benz to be picked up in Germany, blank visas signed by Nicaraguan president Anastasio Somoza, and bank cards for accounts in several foreign countries. Stansel was released on $500,000 bond and quickly left the country, promising to return for trial. Information was developed alleging that Stansel had been smuggling marijuana from Jamaica and Colombia since the late 1960s. He owned or had interest in six or more companies, four in the Caribbean countries and two in the United States. Stansel also owned at least six oceangoing boats, either personally or through his corporations. The Stansel organization used fish trucks to transport pot around the country. Prosecutors were so intent on convicting Stansel, the master smuggler, that most of his prospective co-defendants were given immunity from prosecution in exchange for testifying against him.[4]

It all fell apart on 6 January 1975, when Stansel was scheduled to go on trial in Daytona Beach, Florida. His attorney appeared, but Stansel did not. The attorney announced that his client was missing and presumed dead. Stansel was said to have drowned on 31 December 1974 while scuba diving with his girlfriend, Janet Wood, off Roatán, Honduras. Ms. Wood disappeared ten days after Stansel was reported missing. Stansel left a wife and four children in Tarpon Springs. Law enforcement authorities felt certain that he had faked his death. Stansel sightings in various parts of the world continue; the most recent was in 1987. He is a legend and a folk hero in the drug culture.[5]

With Stansel gone and the other known members of the organization immune from prosecution, the state apparently had little to show for the yearlong grand jury investigation. In fact, the statewide grand jury and an increase in federal enforcement did have an impact on the drug smugglers. Those given immunity in the Stansel investigation and their associates knew they were being watched. Consequently, many independent domestic smugglers were forced out of business along with the small boats they used. The organized criminal elements in Colombia, in concert with American marijuana distributors, moved into the void with the mothership fleet. Henceforth, foreigners would handle most seaborne transportation up to the American contiguous zone. The Colombians expanded their participation from production and packaging into transportation and distribution.

The use of foreign and stateless boats and ships became common. As the size of vessels increased, the coastal freighter became the profile smuggler. There were legal challenges to jurisdiction over stateless and foreign vessels, but the great majority of cases were upheld in the courts. Seizures increased with the number of participants in the marijuana trade. By the end of 1974, the number of Coast Guard drug interdictions had doubled over the previous year; Coast Guardsmen had independently seized eleven vessels and cooperated in the seizure of four others. Some countries resisted U.S. efforts to enforce our laws on their ships.[6] It would take time to work out diplomatic procedures.

The authority to take enforcement action against a foreign vessel was the "statement of no objection" (SNO) procedure. Under the 1958 Geneva Convention, one nation's naval or coast guard unit must receive permission from another nation's government to board the latter's vessels on the high seas. To obtain an SNO, a U.S. Coast Guard cutter commander petitions the appropriate Coast Guard district or area command for permission to board what appears to be a foreign vessel to enforce U.S. laws. The suspect in fact may be stateless. In the message requesting an SNO, the unit commander articulates his suspicion that the sighting is a possible drug smuggler. If the operational commander agrees, the SNO request is endorsed and sent priority to the commandant of the Coast Guard in Washington. This message is received in Flag Plot, headquarters operation center. If the commandant or his designee approves the request, concurrence is immediately sought from the Justice Department and other agencies for prosecution standards. The State Department is responsible for petitioning the flag state for permission to board and seize if drugs are found during the search. It is a cumbersome procedure, but SNOs are usually received within a few hours. When the master of the suspect vessel gives permission to board, no SNO is necessary. If contraband is found after a consensual boarding, an SNO is necessary to seize. The SNO procedure, developed in the 1960s for foreign fishery enforcement boardings off the U.S. coast, is still in use.

Foreign and stateless mothership crews soon learned that U.S. laws held the ship's master to higher standards of responsibility than the crewmen. In other words, it was the captain who got prosecuted if they were caught. He was presumed, under general maritime usage, to know what was aboard his vessel. Smugglers responded with the "recently departed master" syndrome. When the Coast Guard or Customs boarded a foreign or stateless pot boat and asked for the captain, the people on board would say that he had "recently departed" in a small boat, or something to that effect. The suspect might be miles at sea with no land or other vessels in sight, but it was not incumbent upon the crew to prove that the master was not on board. Authorities had to prove that he *was* on board, which was extremely difficult if the crew stuck to their story.

Foreign politics was also instrumental in drug-smuggling changes. The government of the Bahama Islands decided to get rid of the Cuban-American lobster fishermen who had plagued them since 1970. On 9 July 1975 the Bahamians enacted a law declaring the spiny lobster a creature of their continental shelf. All foreign lobster boats were prohibited from fishing on the Bahama Banks.[7]

About 260 Florida-based lobstermen, many recently arrived from Cuba, were forced out of the Bahamas. When the Cubans tried to fish in the Florida Keys, they were roughed up by the locals and their traps were burned. Most of these people could barely speak English. Their options for an alternative livelihood were severely limited. Some were veterans of the Bay of Pigs invasion, and some had since been employed by the Central Intelligence Agency (CIA) for raids along the Cuban coast. Now came an opportunity many could not resist. The Colombians were producing marijuana at a record rate. U.S. demands for pot were spiraling. Cuban lobster fishermen had the boats, albeit in shabby condition, and they were desperate for work. They were naturals for the grass trade.[8]

By the mid-1970s U.S. Customs was cranking up its marine program to target drug smugglers. Customs Patrol officers (CPOs) could work narcotics cases up to the seizures. They were not affected by the reorganization order of 1973 prohibiting Customs agents from investigating drug cases. CPOs, however, depended on DEA or local agencies to follow through with investigations and prosecutions after seizures. The patrol had only a handful of small confiscated boats. Cooperation with the Coast Guard was not good. The Coast Guard was still wrestling internally with the concept of once again becoming a maritime police organization. The CPOs worked the beaches and ports. They covered merchant ship smugglings dockside, as had their predecessors, the Customs port investigators. Now the patrol officers realized that there was a role for them to play in going after marijuana mothership off-load crews. These seizures were mostly small boats in inshore waters. The CPOs did a creditable job despite their "dry feet." In 1975, Customs captured 129 vessels with approximately 500,000 pounds of grass.[9] In a few years, the statistics would skyrocket.

Late in 1975 a group of Colombian marijuana producers reportedly met with Cuban ambassador Fernando Ravelo-Renedo in Bogotá to discuss plans for the free passage of drug ships through Cuban waters. The deal allegedly involved payments of up to $800,000 per boatload. Cuba would provide refueling and repair facilities and the use of its ports and flag. Cuba would also assign gunboats as escorts. A *U.S. News and World Report* article claimed that Cuba made $10 million a month on the deal and purchased weapons and supplies to support Sandinistas in Nicaragua and marxist insurgents in El Salvador and Guatemala.[10]

There was enough evidence against Ambassador Ravelo for a Miami federal grand jury to indict him in 1982, along with a member of the Cuban Communist Party Central Committee and two other Cuban officials. The extent of Ravelo's involvement in drug transits through Cuba, and of Fidel Castro's knowledge of the deal, may never be known. Some cooperating drug defendants claimed that the money was "put in the drawer for Fidel."[11]

Ravelo was not arrested with Gen. Arnaldo Ochoa Sanchez and thirteen other Cuban officers in Castro's drug purge of June 1989. Cuba confirmed the involvement of military and Interior Ministry officials with Colombian and American drug traffickers. The official explanation by Cuba blamed a U.S. embargo on trade with Cuba and CIA corruption for the downfall of their officials. The embargo forced Cuba to set up a special unit within the Ministry of the Interior to smuggle critically needed American goods to Cuba. It was easy and lucrative for officials involved in this venture to facilitate the movement of drugs the other way. They claimed that all it took was some corrupt U.S. government agents to put things in motion.[12]

Regardless of who was involved in the deal, drugs were being shipped through Cuban waters as early as the mid-1970s. At that time most of the contraband through Cuba was marijuana. It was common knowledge in Key West that large fishing vessels, such as shrimpers, could move with impunity through the territorial waters of Cuba for a fee of $50,000.[13]

The door was open for the drug boats to come from Jamaica and Colombia with pot for the U.S. market. Protected passage was available through Bahamian and Cuban waters to jump-off points less than 100 miles from our coasts. Street intelligence obtained by local, state, and federal agencies indicated that the elusive motherships were out there somewhere. But a major seizure was needed to document the existence of these phantom ships.

Harold Derber had set up a forward command post in Colombia. In February 1976 Derber reportedly dispatched seven ships loaded with marijuana for Florida and points north. Derber's partner and off-load boss John Steele was overwhelmed with the volume of grass. Steele frantically negotiated with associates for assistance in unloading along the Florida Straits. The mothership *Gina IV* made a partial off-load near Orange Cay in the Bahamas, then allegedly went to New England waters to dispose of the rest. The distribution system in South Florida was overloaded by the amount of pot arriving, but it was no longer a problem for Derber. On 22 March 1976 he was shot and killed on a Miami street. His murder appeared to be an execution.[14]

Now came Larry Spivey, a young Atlanta businessman and confidential informant for the Georgia Bureau of Investigation (GBI) and some federal agencies. Spivey had successfully worked an air smuggling case for the GBI and a gun case for the Treasury's Bureau of Alcohol, Tobacco and Firearms. In February 1976 he was in Fort Lauderdale, Florida, on loan to the local state's attorney's office when he met defense attorney Charles Gould. The lawyer believed that Spivey was a big-time drug dealer who was paying the fees for a client of his. After some preliminary word sparring, Gould offered Spivey a chance to buy tons of marijuana from a freighter known as the *Don Emilio*.

Drug enforcement agencies in the Southeast knew there was a mothership off the coast, but they did not have her name. A shrimp boat with 18 tons of grass seized at Southern's Bluff, Georgia, and the sailboat *Odessa* seized after unloading 3 tons of pot at Savannah in the summer of 1975 were thought to have been supplied by a phantom freighter. The people arrested either did not know the name of the freighter or were afraid to give it up. Gould assured Spivey that his group could supply any amount of grass on a regular basis. He said that the *Don Emilio* made a run every three weeks. Spivey reported this conversation to the Customs Intelligence Section in Miami.

Customs identified a Panamanian vessel named *Don Emilio*. Moises Torrijos, brother of Panamanian president Omar Torrijos, was a stockholder of the company that owned the ship. A description of the freighter was distributed to U.S. surface and air patrols. If the vessel was found, she could be boarded under the Hovering Vessel Act (19 U.S.C. 1401), an old Prohibition statute giving the Coast Guard authority to board foreign ships outside our territorial waters if there was cause to believe they were violating our laws.[15]

The *Don Emilio* with her record 160-ton pot cargo being brought to the U.S. Coast Guard base at Miami Beach, October 1976

(U.S. Naval Institute photograph)

It took eight months to corner the *Don Emilio*. On 13 October 1976 the U.S. Coast Guard cutter *Sherman* (WHEC-720) found the 325-foot coastal freighter 100 miles east of Acklins Island, Bahamas. It was not necessary to use the Hovering Vessel Act; permission was obtained from the Panamanian government to board and search the ship. On board were 160 tons of marijuana.[16] This was the largest seizure in history, a record that has never been surpassed. A mothership on the grand scale had been documented.

Motherships would eventually sail up the Atlantic coast to New England and the Maritime Provinces of Canada. The first seizure of record there was the *Struggle* in the Gulf of Maine. There is scant information about the 1975 event 37 miles east-southeast of Rockland. To accommodate the 40,000 pounds of marijuana that were seized, the *Struggle* would have had to be a small coastal freighter or a large fishing vessel. A second unnamed vessel was seized in the Gulf of Maine during 1975. In early 1976 the *Nutri I* was seized in the same area.[17]

In March 1976 the Coast Guard found the Panamanian *Kaki* off Beaufort, North Carolina, with marijuana residue. Then came the *Lucy* and *Valborg* near the mouth of the Chesapeake Bay on 2 December 1976, with 5,880 pounds of pot.[18] These modest seizures were scattered in time and location, but they proved that some grass off-loads were moving to the north. There is speculation that the far-ranging *Don Emilio* may have supplied some of these vessels.

In 1976 Donald Steinberg, a twenty-six-year-old Vietnam veteran from the Chicago area, met Lynn Mizer in Fort Lauderdale at Mizer's Star Jag garage. Steinberg was a low-level marijuana dealer with natural business acumen. Mizer was a mechanic with a 40-foot cabin cruiser named *Starship*. They decided to import marijuana from Colombia. Mizer's brother-in-law put them in contact with Samuel Alarcon, a Colombian pot broker. A load of 10,000 pounds was purchased on credit for delivery by mothership to the Bahamas. Steinberg and Mizer were not proficient sailors. They hired Pete Wagnor, a friend of Steinberg's, to captain the boat and bring the pot to Fort Lauderdale. Wagnor was a Vietnam veteran with considerable combat experience. The *Starship* made the pickup but encountered heavy weather on the return trip. She took on so much water that Wagnor barely made it into a Fort Lauderdale canal before the boat sank in shallow water. Wagnor escaped by swimming to shore. The *Starship* and the grass were seized by Customs on 31 December 1976. No one was arrested.

After this less than auspicious beginning, the trio formed a major marijuana-smuggling organization. Mizer handled the Colombian contacts, and Wagnor supervised boat operations. Steinberg was the brains with the business ability. They soon had a fleet of more than thirty yachts and high-performance speedboats for off-load work along Fort Lauderdale's canals. They bought and rented waterfront homes called water houses. The grass was moved by truck and camper to "stash houses" further inland. Steinberg's organization was a model for pot movers. It was run like a modern business—no long hair, jeans, or wild T-shirts, nothing to attract the attention of law enforcement.[19]

The "Black Tuna Gang," working from a houseboat moored along fashionable Collins Avenue in Miami Beach, was another example of youthful vigor applied to the pot industry. Robert Meinster and Robert Platshorn, known as Robby and Bobby in the trade, were operating a fleet of ships and planes importing grass from Colombia. Mark Phillips, vice president of a yacht brokerage firm, was their maritime specialist. They used stash houses in wealthy neighborhoods and even rented a restaurant as a pot warehouse. South Florida Auto Auction was used as a money laundry. The organization had at least fifty members; most were sophisticated and educated young men in their mid-thirties. Gold chains with tuna medallions were worn by the group as a sign of recognition and status. Drug agents estimated that the Black Tunas brought in $300 million worth of drugs between 1974 and their demise in 1977 after a raid in Wilmington, North Carolina. DEA's Robert Feldkamp admitted that the Tunas were the best-organized drug ring the agency had encountered to date. At one point they were believed responsible for 8 percent of the nation's drug-smuggling total. They would be surpassed, but Robby and Bobby were pacesetters.[20]

Out West, nothing much had happened since the *Mercy Wiggins* in 1971. No significant seizures were recorded for four years. In 1975 there were only two seizures: a pleasure craft in San Diego was apprehended with 1,200 pounds of pot, and the fishing vessel *Silverware* was seized in Puget Sound with 8,000 pounds. Seizures in 1976 included the fishing vessel *Red Baron* near the Channel Islands in January (10,000 pounds), the F/V *National* in February in Bodega Bay, California (10,000 pounds), the pleasure craft *Siboney* in Santa Barbara (6,000 pounds), and the F/V *Nana II* in Astoria in November (10,000 pounds). This was a fourfold increase over 1975 in grass volume.[21] Pacific seizures continued to fluctuate widely over the years. Few vessels were seized, but some had very large loads.

The Gulf of Mexico seemed to have been abandoned by serious grass smugglers in the middle 1970s. Seizures were nil, but things were cooking. A future import center was developing in the Everglades City–Chokoloskee area of the River of Grass. Everglades City's Willard Wooten was identified as a pot smuggler. Wooten would change sides ten years later. Known by the code name Popeye, he would play a singular role in severing the primary Caribbean marijuana sea route to the United States through the Yucatán Channel.[22]

U.S. Customs in Tampa, Florida, made an unusual dockside seizure in June 1976. Cocaine was not a hot maritime item in those days, but

crewmen from the 329-foot banana boat *Ea* had been caught making
a number of small deliveries. The Liberian refrigerated vessel made
regular runs between Tampa and Turbo, Colombia. Customs routinely surveilled the vessel when she was in port. At about 0200 on 15
June, Customs Patrol officers observed packages being passed from
an *Ea* porthole to a man on the dock. Approximately 230 pounds of
cocaine were seized, a record at the time, and several crew members
were arrested. The *Ea* was seized on 19 June, and a complaint for forfeiture was filed by the U.S. attorney with the district court of the
Middle District of Florida. The vessel's owners responded with a peti-
tion for release, noting that the *Ea* was a common carrier and therefore immune from seizure and forfeiture. The government held that
the vessel was a "private carrier" transporting bananas for a single
company. By definition, they said, a common carrier is one who
openly professes to carry for hire the goods of all persons who may
choose to employ him. A civil trial was held, and the government prevailed. District Judge Ben Krentzman found that whatever the vessel's
carrier status, the ship's master had sufficient knowledge of the smuggling operation to justify seizure and forfeiture. The *Ea* was sold to
the highest bidder for $2,225,000. She was the first and last com-
mercial vessel to be seized and forfeited for smuggling drugs.[23]

A seemingly unimportant event occurred in the southern Gulf on
29 November 1976. The Coast Guard boarded the U.S.–registered
Teal for a random safety inspection. The 86-foot motor vessel was an
offshore oil rig service and supply boat known as a rig tender. Documents on board showed that she was owned by Platform Service,
Inc., of New Orleans. She had been purchased by Platform for transfer to a foreign flag. There was no contraband aboard the *Teal,* but
she was well equipped with electronics and fully stocked and fueled
for a long voyage. The master was known to law enforcement. He
would later be recognized as the head of a major Florida drug organization.[24] The *Teal* was probably the first oil rig tender to be used for
smuggling grass. Vessels of this type were ideally suited for the purpose.

A related and deadly aspect of maritime drug smuggling was publicly acknowledged in the summer of 1974: boat theft and boat piracy
were named serious threats to the boating public by the Coast Guard
and the Subcommittee on Coast Guard and Navigation of the U.S.
House of Representatives. Congressman John M. Murphy (D., New
York), chairman of the subcommittee, found that no single federal

agency was responsible for piracy investigations. The Coast Guard said it was responsible for searches when a vessel was first reported missing, but not for long-term investigations. The Federal Bureau of Investigation (FBI) kept records of stolen boats but did not have the resources or expertise to investigate cases.

Murphy's group found that there had been 611 reports of missing pleasure craft in areas adjacent to the United States or in the Caribbean between 1970 and 1974. Thirty or more of these cases had the earmarks of hijacking.[25] Had the buccaneers returned? Many felt that these events had been boat hijackings, and that the root cause was drug smuggling; after all, smugglers need a variety of boat types for their operations. Nevertheless, it is easy to steal a boat despite the hull identification numbering system established by the Federal Safe Boating Act of 1971. Why hijack a boat and possibly kill someone when it is so easy to steal one?

By 1976 the U.S. Coast Guard had finally come to terms with its image crisis. Adm. Owen W. Siler, commandant, stated in a published article, "I see the Coast Guard as a law enforcement agency; in this context we are all operational with a central fundamental purpose." The commandant addressed profound changes at an unprecedented rate. He mentioned fisheries law enforcement and drug interdiction as recently acquired, burgeoning aspects of the Coast Guard's traditional law enforcement roles.[26] Admiral Siler's comments signaled a new policy, but changes were slow. The Coast Guard was at least ready to address its role in the drug war at sea.

Maritime drug-smuggling patterns changed quickly in the mid-1970s. Independent American entrepreneurs surrendered the trade to multinational groups with volume capabilities. Domestic marijuana demand outdistanced the supply, creating a huge illicit market. Mexico was still an important source country, but the U.S.–sponsored aerial spray program had created consumer doubt about the safety of the Mexican product. The Florida statewide grand jury caused changes in the players by opening the field to more daring criminals. Boat piracy by smugglers had been publicized. Cuba had opened its door for safe passage of drug boats. The emergence of the marijuana mothership, however, was by far the most important event of the period.

3

The Flood
1977–1978

All the fountains of the great abyss burst forth, and the
floodgates of the sky were opened.

GENESIS 7:11

By the late 1970s there was a great deluge of marijuana flowing into the United States. Prophets forecast the doom of society. Many of our youth welcomed the expansion of the drug culture and viewed pot as an instrument of enlightenment and joy. They scoffed at their elders for making a distinction between marijuana and liquor. The older generation was either indifferent to or aggravated by the rise in youthful lawlessness. Regardless of our views at the time, society is still paying a huge price for the ravages of the drug culture.

As 1977 dawned, the motherships were at sea. Harold Derber was in his grave, but the Derber-Steele flagship, the 180-foot coastal freighter *Night Train*, was steaming north from the Guajira Peninsula of Colombia. She had replaced the legendary *Don Emilio*. The rusty coastal freighters coming from the Caribbean were the profile marijuana transports that received special attention from the few ocean-going Coast Guard cutters stationed in Florida. The Seventh District cutter *Dauntless* (WMEC-624), captained by Comdr. J. C. Uithol, had made the first solo Coast Guard pot seizure. The *Night Train* (now *Labrador*) and the *Dauntless* had a rendezvous.[1]

DEA agents in Miami, posing as a prospective off-load crew, learned the arrival time and coordinates for a huge pot delivery by an unnamed mothership. Veteran undercover agents Kevin Foley and John McCutcheon chartered the sports fishing vessel *Catchalot II* for the job. They also made arrangements with the Coast Guard for backup. On the night of 27 January 1977, McCutcheon, three other agents, and the vessel's captain set out for a position east of Great Abaco Island in the Bahamas. The *Dauntless* trailed at a safe distance.

The *Catchalot II* made contact with the freighter on 31 January. Agent McCutcheon persuaded smuggler captain Nino Rinsi Cadena to let them come alongside in daylight. They delivered needed supplies and took some bales to measure holes cut in the deck for quick transfer. McCutcheon read the name *Labrador*. Visible under the name were the raised letters of the former name, *Night Train*. The agents contacted the Coast Guard on a special radio frequency. There was rejoicing in Coast Guard and DEA headquarters.

As planned, the *Catchalot II* moved 5 miles away to wait for darkness. The agents had to keep the *Night Train* in place until the *Dauntless* arrived. McCutcheon had enough contraband to make the seizure. After dark the freighter captain made repeated radio calls to the

A marijuana mothership at sea *(NNBIS slide series, source unknown)*

off-loader in Spanish. Finally the exasperated smuggler shouted in ragged English, "Bastards! What damn you doing?"

Just then the cutter arrived at full speed with searchlights trained on the freighter. The *Night Train*'s captain ignored radio and light signals to stop and tried to ram the *Dauntless*. Shots were fired across the renegade's bow. Gun flashes prompted a passing British tanker to radio the cutter to determine who was under attack. The *Night Train* finally stopped after Commander Uithol had his 3-inch deck gun trained on the maverick's pilothouse. Thirteen Colombians were arrested and 52 tons of marijuana seized. The smuggler ship had finally been brought to bay.[2]

While the *Night Train* saga unfolded between the Florida Gold Coast and the Bahamas, a $1.1-million 75-foot luxury yacht went missing in the Gulf of Mexico. The *Pirate's Lady* vanished on 26 January 1977, en route from Apalachicola to Clearwater, Florida. Multi-millionaire businessman Charles D. Slater of New Orleans, the yacht's owner, was waiting in Clearwater. He planned to make a fishing trip to the Bahamas. Captain Tony Latuso, a veteran skipper, and college student David Diecidue were aboard when the yacht disappeared.

That day law enforcement officers in North Florida found 3,000 pounds of marijuana abandoned on the Intracoastal Waterway near Sandy Creek, the stream that flows into East Bay by Panama City. The site of the abandoned grass load was about 36 miles as the crow flies northwest of Apalachicola. Sandy Creek would soon be headline news.

The search for the *Pirate's Lady* got started the next day. The south-sector search was interrupted almost immediately. In an apparently unrelated incident, the shrimp trawler *Gunsmoke* was sighted sinking off Egmont Key at the mouth of Tampa Bay. Coast Guardsmen searched the area as an oil slick spread. They found eleven bales of marijuana but no people. Were the *Gunsmoke*, the abandoned pot at Sandy Creek, and the disappearance of the *Pirate's Lady* somehow connected? Eventually most of the pieces of this grisly puzzle fell into place, but a mystery would remain.[3]

Testimony at subsequent drug and murder trials told most of the story. On 23 January 1977 the *Gunsmoke,* with tons of grass, put in to East Bay via the Intracoastal Waterway. The plan was to off-load to small boats, which would deliver the load somewhere along Sandy Creek. That afternoon at a bar on U.S. 98 (the main east-west highway), two men and two teenaged sisters got together for a good time. Sheila and Sandy McAdams drove to the bar with Douglas Hood in a blue camper-pickup. They met George Sims, an ex-convict.

The foursome set out for Sandy Creek, where Sims frequently fished. Later that night the two couples accidentally came face to face with the *Gunsmoke*'s off-load crew. Sims was shot and killed on the spot. The two girls and Hood were tied up and taken away in a van with Sims's body. About half of the *Gunsmoke*'s cargo was ashore. After the shooting, the crew panicked and fled, leaving part of the load and an off-load boat at the scene. The *Gunsmoke* got under way and made for the Gulf and a watery grave.

In August 1978 two divers found the weighted bodies of the McAdams sisters, Sims, and Hood in a sinkhole in Taylor County, 150 miles east of Panama City. Hood and Sheila had been gagged and shot in the back of the head. Sims had been shot in the chest. Investigators could not determine how Sandy had been killed. It was time to look for the *Gunsmoke*. The *Pirate's Lady* was long since forgotten.

In November the wreck of the *Gunsmoke* was located by survey vessels of the National Oceanic and Atmospheric Administration (NOAA) in the Gulf off St. Petersburg. Florida Marine Patrol and

NOAA divers identified the vessel. David Capo, son of the infamous "Bubba" of Steinhatchee fame, Walter Steinhorst, David Goodwin, and seven others were indicted by a federal grand jury for conspiracy to smuggle marijuana with the shrimper. Two pled guilty before trial. Capo and three others were convicted. Four were acquitted, including Steinhorst and Goodwin. Steinhorst, Goodwin, Capo, and two others were indicted by a state grand jury for the Sandy Creek–Taylor County sinkhole murders. Steinhorst and Goodwin were convicted of first-degree murder.[4]

State and local law enforcement officials along Florida's west coast speculated for years that the disappearance of the *Pirate's Lady* was somehow connected to the *Gunsmoke*'s smuggling operation. It was not until May 1992 that commercial divers working out of Carrabelle, 31 miles east of Apalachicola, found the remains of the *Pirate's Lady* in 90 feet of water. The owner, Charles Slater, does not believe that the big yacht's disappearance was accidental, because she had an array of sophisticated safety equipment on board and an experienced captain. Slater identified the boat from videotapes taken by divers. According to Florida Marine Patrol investigators and Slater, the yacht was broken into many pieces. There was no trace of Captain Tony Latuso or his young crewman.[5] Remains are not likely to be found in a littered wreck after fifteen years on the bottom.

The Sandy Creek massacre demonstrated that drug smuggling, even the simple pot variety, could be a deadly game. People were accustomed to intense warfare among smugglers along the Mexican border and the Gold Coast of South Florida, but they were shocked when innocent bystanders in a sleepy community in northwestern Florida became victims of smugglers.

The loss of the *Pirate's Lady* is typical of the missing-boat cases suspected of being drug-related. There is no evidence that the yacht was hijacked or in any way related to the *Gunsmoke* case. She simply disappeared when a smuggling operation was going down in the vicinity. Slater's theory to the contrary, the boat may have been the victim of an internal explosion. A recent Florida Marine Patrol investigation, based on recovered wreckage of the vessel, concluded that the *Pirate's Lady* had suffered an engine room fire and a sudden loss of electrical power.[6] Then again, the people who scuttled the *Gunsmoke* got off somehow. No admission from these participants is likely, considering the deaths of the yacht's master and crewman. The mystery is still on the books.

Speculation about drug smugglers pirating boats continued to crop up. Coast Guard and other law enforcement officials questioned claims for good reasons. There would certainly be friends and family of the people aboard pirated vessels who would report them missing and provide descriptions of the boats. The Coast Guard and other enforcement agencies would receive "overdue" reports and establish lookouts for missing vessels for a reasonable length of time. With adequate information from survivors, searches would be conducted. Officials reasoned that drug smugglers would hardly want to use a "hot" vessel when they could purchase one with their huge resources. The only flaw in the theory is the limited reasoning capabilities of smugglers like the Sandy Creek gang.

Three weeks after the *Night Train*'s capture, the Coast Guard located another suspect off the east coast of Florida. The USCGC *Courageous* (WMEC-662) found the 125-foot coastal freighter *Calabres*. When the cutter showed up, the freighter started moving south. The vessel fit the profile of a marijuana mothership. Had she already offloaded? The *Calabres* story was leaked to the media. Tracking the mystery ship became a nightly television drama for Florida viewers. As the *Courageous* and her prey progressed toward the Caribbean, the Seventh District ordered the old buoy tender *Sagebrush* (WLB-399) out of San Juan to assist. After steaming for ten hours, the *Sagebrush* met with the *Courageous*. By that time the cutter was close aboard the freighter, illuminating the suspect with searchlights.

After the tender arrived on the scene, the *Calabres* stopped. Smoke rose above her pilothouse. The crew began jumping overboard. When the Coast Guardsmen fished them out, they claimed that the captain had left the ship somewhere off Florida. The *Courageous* and *Sagebrush* lay alongside the freighter to fight the fire. They put a lot of water into the ship. They also put pumps aboard to get the water out. As soon as the fire was controlled, a boarding party made a quick inspection. The ship proved to be full of marijuana. The holds, engine room, and passageways were stuffed with bales of pot. Suddenly the fire reflashed. More water was poured in until the boarding party was ordered away from the burning hulk. The *Calabres* sank by the stern. First the bubbles rose, then the bales; a few, then hundreds surfaced. It was a Sea of Grass. Boat crews cut open as many bales as possible to make them sink. The cargo of the *Calabres* was estimated at 120 tons.[7]

José Martinez (a fictitious name for a real individual) typifies the corrupting influence of the dope flood. He was born in a small fishing village on the southwest coast of Cuba and grew up during the Batista reign. Trained as a fisherman by his father, young Martinez received little formal education. When the revolution came to Cuba, Martinez was too busy trying to make a meager living to take any interest in politics. In the early 1960s he was conscripted into the Cuban Revolutionary Army. Our young fisherman decided he was not a communist.

After release from active service, Martinez and his brother made an irrevocable decision: they took a village boat and made a perilous crossing of the Yucatán Channel to Mexico. The intrepid refugees abandoned the boat on the rocky limestone coast near Puerto Juarez and left the sparkling turquoise sea behind. They eventually got to the United States and down to Miami. The Cuban community counseled them to seek refugee parole status from the U.S. government.

Martinez worked hard at a series of jobs and saved his money. In the late 1960s he was finally able to buy a small fishing boat. He avoided conflicts with local fishermen by making the dangerous trip across the Florida Straits in an open boat to fish for lobster and bottom fish on the Bahama Banks. He continued to work and save and found a bride in Little Havana. Key West appealed to the young couple. They moved there in the 1970s, and Martinez bought a larger boat. He fished on Cay Sal Bank. The small islands around the bank and the bank itself are Bahamian territory. It was seldom patrolled and was becoming a place for marijuana mothership off-loads.

In the spring of 1977, near a place called Elbow Cay, Martinez was tempted beyond his ability to resist. His lobster and fish traps had been set all night. Now it was early morning, and the fisherman was preparing for another dawn-to-dark workday. He preferred working alone, though hauling traps up from 4–6 fathoms was back-breaking labor. Martinez was pulling the anchor from the sandy bottom when he saw the first one, a brown burlap bale that appeared from nowhere in the tranquil turquoise water. Then he saw others. They stretched away to the east across the bank like a file of troops marching straight and mute right to his boat. What should he do? Martinez knew he was looking at bales of pot. He told himself he would be a good citizen to his adopted country; he would retrieve the contraband and deliver it to the authorities. Martinez brought the square grouper aboard. It was just as hard as hauling traps. He manhandled more than fifty bales into his boat. There were more, but he could not take them. The reeking, sodden stuff was stowed in every available space. The boat's bilge was ankle-deep in brown pot water. Martinez started the run to Key West.

On the way home he met a friend and fellow fisherman coming out to the bank. Martinez could hardly hide his cargo, so he revealed his plan to take the marijuana to the Coast Guard station in Key West. The man suggested an alternative: Stick with his story if he was stopped by the Coast Guard or Customs. If not, call this number and ask for Dermi, who would pay him well for the grass. Martinez got to his moorings at Stock Island without even seeing an enforcement unit. He sold the grass to Dermi for more money than he could ever make from fish and lobsters. Martinez was hooked. He bought a bigger boat and went to work off-loading pot for a man Dermi recommended. He became one of the biggest marijuana off-load masters in South Florida, with a fleet of boats. The barefoot fisherman from Cuba via the wilds of Mexico was now a kingpin in grass smuggling.[8] We will hear more of him in a later chapter.

About the same time José Martinez was getting started in the marijuana off-load business on the Atlantic side of the Keys, Ambrose Weldon was organizing his operation in the lower Gulf. Weldon, the ex–commercial fisherman who hated his early trips to Colombia, had found his niche. No more dealing with people he could not understand. Let somebody else back boats through the Yucatán Channel to confuse the Airedales. The motherships were coming, and they needed to be unloaded. Weldon had the organizational ability to do the job. He also had a lifetime of experience navigating the myriad shallows and mangrove islands of the Everglades, that vast River of Grass.

Weldon was able to concentrate on the off-load phase of marijuana traffic because of an alliance with a former Cuban freedom fighter in the Keys. This stalwart dealt with the Colombian suppliers and was greatly feared in the South Florida smuggling community because of his paramilitary background. He stood up to the Colombians, and of course he spoke their language. The man arranged for and scheduled mothership transports. Weldon took care of off-loads and ground transportation to stash locations.

Weldon used fishing vessels exclusively for his operation. He found fishermen who were about to default on boat mortgage payments and evaluated them as prospective participants. If the individual appeared to be sympathetic to smugglers, Weldon made an offer that could not be refused. Recruits were given radios and placed on call for off-loads. The Cuban notified Weldon when a mothership was headed north. It was a matter of weight and distance to Weldon. He would select an off-load position and figure how many boats were needed. The off-load craft, usually shrimpers, lobster/stone-crab trap boats, or fast mackerel net boats, would be mixed. By using vessels of varying capacity and speed, Weldon avoided overwhelming the bale handlers at the final landing site.

A coordinated meeting between the mothership and the off-load boats was essential. Weldon selected an appropriate nautical chart. Random letters were assigned to latitude and longitude lines in advance. As a security measure, the actual off-load positions were not given to the pickup boats until the last minute. They were directed to the rendezvous by radio. For example, the letter B could be used to identify 26° north and the letter M for 86° west. A broadcast of "Bravo 15, Mike 20" on a prearranged frequency told the pickup boats that the off-load would take place at 26°15' north and 86°20' west. Sites were constantly varied to avoid patterns and confuse law enforcement.

Shoreside off-load crews were also recruited in advance for last-minute call-up. They manned the skiffs or reported to the beach site as laborers. Off-loads of multi-ton marijuana shipments were labor-intensive. Weldon's organization and other similar groups along the Gulf coast facilitated the flow of huge marijuana cargoes into the Gulf through the Yucatán Channel. Because of its location, Everglades City was a hub for off-load operations. It is the only town located in the Everglades. Many economically stressed fishermen in this small and isolated village reached an unbelievable standard of living from the grass trade.[9]

Maritime marijuana trading was directly linked to the Mexican aerial eradication program sponsored by the United States. That program assured the supremacy of Colombian marijuana. U.S. government officials tried to prevent the diversion of Mexican spray efforts from poppy fields to marijuana plantations, because opium was still our primary drug concern. The Mexicans, however, said they had an internal pot abuse problem. Despite our objections, they began using their American-built helicopters to spray grass fields. The herbicide 2,4-D worked well on poppies but not so well on hardy pot plants, and so Mexicans substituted the deadly plant poison paraquat. It readily killed marijuana plants. Paraquat could also kill people. In 1977, when the big grass freighters were coming into use, reports started trickling in that poisoned pot from Mexico was being sold to Americans. Official inquiries were authorized by the Carter administration. When word reached the press, American consumers sounded the death knell for Mexican grass. Why risk paraquat poisoning when Colombian Gold was arriving by the tons in old and rusty motherships? It cost a little more than Mexican commercial, but it was better for your health.[10]

Colombian grass was reaching U.S. shores in massive quantities. Donald Steinberg's organization, The Company, was doing a booming business in beautiful Fort Lauderdale. Steinberg delivered his grass loads to expensive "water houses." Wholesalers who flocked to the Gold Coast for Steinberg's bonanza often bought marijuana by the houseful. Not by bales or truckloads—by addresses! When a wholesaler purchased an address from Steinberg, he expected to receive approximately 10,000 pounds of Colombian pot. Grass merchants didn't quibble over a few hundred pounds.[11]

By 1977, marijuana was arriving in such volume along the Gold Coast of South Florida that land transportation north had become a serious problem for traffickers. A few motherships had been sent up the Atlantic coast for off-loads adjacent to New England in 1975–76. Seizure statistics for 1977, however, show that a lot of grass was delivered to the Northeast. Between May and October three off-load boats were seized along the Maine coast, and the Honduran mothership *Juliana I* was seized off Cape Ann in the Gulf of Maine. The combined marijuana cargo of the vessels was approximately 95,000 pounds.[12] A conservative estimate of pot delivered to New England was close to a million pounds. The flood tide had moved up the Atlantic seaboard.

Not all northbound motherships were destined for the Gulf of Maine; there was also a grass market in the mid-Atlantic states. On 20 November 1977 the 378-foot high-endurance cutter *Gallatin* (WHEC-721), Capt. Alan Breed, USCG, commanding, was on a fishery patrol off the Atlantic Bight. A priority message from the Atlantic Area Command (ComLantArea) interrupted routine boardings of foreign trawlers. ComLantArea, the senior Coast Guard command on the East Coast, had operational control of the big cutters. The *Gallatin* was ordered south to a position off Cape Fear, North Carolina, at her best speed. An enforcement agency had just received information from an informant that a grass off-load was about to take place.

The mothership was code-named Martha. The *Gallatin* cranked up to 28 knots and put a groove in the Gulf Stream heading south. The cutter's 165 crewmen were anxious to catch a doper. Two National Marine Fisheries Service agents on board were resigned to a break in counting squid. Periodically the cutter radioed "Martha" on a specified frequency, identifying herself as Fishhawk, a code name for one of the pickup boats. At midnight Captain Breed ordered his engineer to light off the Pratt-Whitney gas turbines to max their speed against the Stream. Breed did not know if "Martha" was a U.S. or a foreign vessel. His approach to the target depended on her flag. If she was foreign, he needed grounds to obtain an SNO from the flag country.

The next morning "Martha" suddenly called "Red Fox." The *Gallatin*'s people had no clue who Red Fox was. They mumbled something on the radio about poor reception and hoped for the best. Breed ordered flank speed toward the suspect. A U.S. Customs aircraft sighted the target and gave the cutter her position. Lookouts had her in sight. She had a rusty gray hull with a white pilothouse aft, and was about 100 feet long. They could make out her name: *Sea Crust,* NASSUA—had to be Nassau spelled wrong. The *Gallatin* slowed to make her approach look like a casual close-aboard passing. The *Sea Crust* increased speed on a course away from the cutter. "Martha" was running.

The *Gallatin* went to battle stations. The 20 mm guns and .50-caliber machine guns were manned and ready. Crewmen donned their tin hats. The armed boarding party was closed up by the duty motorboat. The *Sea Crust* refused to answer radio calls. Breed ordered the international flag signal "identify yourself" broken out from the yardarm. In return, the *Sea Crust* ran up the Bahamas flag. The quartermaster of the watch logged it; they would need this for an SNO. Finally someone aboard the *Sea Crust* radioed the cutter. He told Breed he was bound from Trinidad to Baltimore. Captain Breed was satisfied. "Martha" had just admitted that she was bound for the United States. That statement was admissible evidence of conspiracy to import contraband. Breed sent his message to ComLantArea requesting an SNO. He had reason to believe that the target was violating the law. She had refused to stop and had admitted that she was heading for the United States.

The *Sea Crust* changed course frequently and then headed southeast, away from the U.S. coast. The Coast Guardsmen settled down for a long and slow stern chase. They followed the target all night. A sharp lookout was maintained in case "Martha" started dumping things overboard. The next morning, 22 November, dawned on a moderate sea, a fine day in the Gulf Stream. Then it came: the Bahamian government gave permission for the Coast Guard to board the *Sea Crust* to search her cargo spaces. Back to the guns! Even the 5-inch deck gun was manned and trained on the target.

The *Sea Crust*'s master refused to be intimidated. He responded to Breed's order to stop and be boarded with "No. I have not violated no law. I am on the high seas. You cannot come aboard my vessel." When Breed explained that he had permission from the Bahamian government, the spunky captain of the little freighter suggested that the *Gallatin* could follow him to the nearest British port. Breed continued his demands. He finally brought the *Gallatin* close aboard the rusty fugitive to demonstrate that he meant business. Then the unexpected happened: the *Sea Crust* suddenly came hard left, directly toward the cutter's high, white side. She was going to ram the menacing cutter. Breed shouted the order for emergency flank ahead. The *Gallatin* barely cleared the bow of the freighter. Alan Breed would take only so much from the suspect smuggler. When they were settled on a new course abeam of the *Sea Crust,* he released his 20 mm battery. They fired a short burst well ahead of the *Sea Crust*. Nothing happened. Another burst of fire. Smoking splashes went up as shells impacted the water ahead of the freighter. Finally the *Sea Crust*'s master called the cutter: "Captain, if you want me to stop, I'll stop." As the sun set, the *Sea Crust* came to a stop. The rest is anticlimax. The *Gallatin*'s boarding party found 6 tons of marijuana. Most of the grass had already been unloaded. The hold was almost empty. At 1900 on 22 November the *Sea Crust* was seized 230 miles off the North Carolina coast. Eight people were arrested, including Nollie Alexander, the gutsy little Bahamian master of the mothership "Martha." He was later convicted of conspiracy to smuggle marijuana. His load of grass was just a tiny fraction of the million-plus pounds the Coast Guard seized that year. The Coast Guard had indeed gone to war.[13]

Down on the main line of resistance off Florida, seizures rose in 1977. December was a banner month. Ten vessels were seized in the

Florida-Bahamas area. Coast Guardsmen took down the Venezuelan-registered mothership *Isla de Aruba* just north of San Salvador and the *Ecopesca IV* near Orange Cay. They also picked off the *Miss Connie* of Panama. The three foreigners contained over 50 tons of Colombian grass. Others were U.S. yachts and fishing boats used for off-loads. Most were seized at docks along Florida's east coast. They accounted for another 28 tons of pot.[14]

Not all the action was on the Atlantic side of Florida. On 28 December 1977 the 82-foot patrol boat *Point Thatcher* (WPB-82314) intercepted the 110-foot coastal freighter *Marania* at the mouth of Tampa Bay with 30 tons. The Coast Guard took part in capturing fifty-two dope-carrying vessels in calendar year 1977.[15]

A few seizures were made along the Pacific coast. The only significant one was the motor vessel *Cigale* at Bandon, Oregon, on New Year's Day 1978. Recall was sounded aboard the old Coast Guard tug *Modoc* (WMEC-194), lying snug at her berth in Coos Bay, Oregon. Like sailors worldwide, most of the crew were off at their various haunts having a tot to celebrate the arrival of another year. Lt. Comdr. Pete Busick, the *Modoc*'s CO, and Ens. Bill Baker, the first lieutenant and morale officer, were roasting nuts over a hibachi. They had to send out the duty section to bodily retrieve part of the ship's company. District told Busick to investigate a report by the Coos County sheriff's office of a drug boat hovering off Bandon, only 18 miles to the south. In due course Captain Busick got under way with a fairly sober crew. They were accompanied by a 52-foot motor lifeboat with a maximum speed of 9 knots. The Coast Guardsmen could not believe there was a drug boat in their backyard. This was 1978. It was the Pacific, and the Northwest at that. Drug boats happened on the East Coast.

The *Modoc* arrived at the scene of the crime early on New Year's Day. They found the 80-foot yacht-turned-freighter *Cigale* blatantly landing pot on the beach with two surplus World War II amphibious trucks (DUKWs). Sheriff's deputies and federal agents were in position near a farm where the marijuana was being stored in a new barn. The DUKWs drove across the beach and right up to the barn to unload. When the smugglers realized they were surrounded, wild shots were fired from dug-in defense positions around the beachhead. A just-arrived Coast Guard helo ducked for cover. It was all over in a few seconds. The men raised their hands and waited for the cuffs. One person, however, broke and ran for the woods. The next day an off-duty deputy gave a ride to a grubby hitchhiker near the farm. Later the strange traveler was tentatively identified as Brian Peter Daniels, whom we will hear from later.

The final pot count was about 16,000 pounds, believed to be of Colombian origin. It was the largest load of grass seized so far in the North Pacific. If the smugglers had not fenced off a salmon stream with chain link topped with barbed wire, the off-load site might have gone undetected. You do not fence salmon streams in the Northwest without the Wildlife people or the sheriff's office investigating.[16]

Smugglers focused on the Gulf coast in 1978. On 14 April the 82-foot patrol boat *Point Swift* (WPB-82312) apprehended the 75-foot Panamanian-registered motor vessel *Albazul* 90 miles southwest of Tampa Bay with 10,000 pounds. Thirteen Colombians were arrested. Intelligence about the vessel was developed by drug agents when they searched a waterfront house in Fort Myers the day before and found 2,700 pounds of pot. On 23 May U.S. Customs intercepted the 65-foot stripped-down trawler yacht *Running Bear* in Southwest Pass at the mouth of Tampa Bay with 20 tons of Colombian marijuana. Five Americans and one Cuban were arrested. The next month there was another 20-ton seizure. The USCGC *Point Swift* was out again. The little cutter intercepted the 70-foot U.S. motor vessel *James Island* out of Key West and a 35-foot cabin cruiser from Miami 20 miles west of Johns Pass. A Florida Marine Patrol helicopter assisted in the two-boat seizure. By the end of June 1978, Coast Guard and Customs officers in the Tampa–St. Petersburg area had seized 551,119 pounds of marijuana, compared with 274,102 pounds in all of 1977. Dick Keating of Customs Patrol in Tampa estimated that 20–25 percent of the grass headed for the bay area was being intercepted.[17]

Smugglers felt enforcement pressure along the Florida-Bahamas interface in 1978. Some of the less reckless grass runners moved a little further north. Drug agents in Charleston suspected that the 48-foot steel-hulled charter vessel *Helen L II* out of New York was a drug boat. They asked the local Coast Guard station for help. On 8 January the suspect got under way, shadowed by a patrol boat. The Coast Guard lost the target in bad weather off South Carolina's coast. Two days later the *Helen L II* showed up at Stem Creek, near Charleston. She was boarded and searched. Agents found marijuana residue and a chart with pencil markings at Hutchinson Island. The island was raided on 11 January. Agents found 19,000 pounds of pot and evidence that the *Helen* had met a mothership offshore. She was seized, and numerous people were arrested.[18] This was one of the first documented off-loads in South Carolina.

A fortuitous event occurred in April. The Florida Marine Patrol found a 25-foot cabin cruiser with four Cuban parolees adrift in the Atlantic off Port Salerno. They were out of gas. Sheets of paper with Spanish writing found on board turned out to be an off-load plan with positions, radio frequencies, and codes. DEA agents borrowed a 40-foot boat and hurried to meet the 100-foot coastal freighter *Moctezuma* in Bahamian waters. Pretending to be a pickup boat and using codes obtained from the Cubans, the agents took twenty bales of pot from the mothership. The 95-foot Coast Guard patrol boat *Cape Shoalwater* (WPB-95324) moved in and seized the freighter under the Hovering Vessel Act. When she was brought to Palm Beach, 57 tons of grass were found on the mothership.[19]

Seizures continued in the Bahamas at a fair rate during the first half of 1978 but declined after that summer. Perhaps delivery of the Colombian spring harvest was complete. Some said that the motherships had become invisible. More likely the reduction in intercepts occurred because Colombia withdrew permission for U.S. enforcement aircraft to fly over pot loading areas along the Guajira Peninsula. Before that, unmarked planes had surveilled loading places and photographed ships and boats taking on marijuana. The government of Colombia decided that this was an infringement of its sovereignty.[20] Use of the aircraft and results of their intelligence prompted rumors that the United States was using satellites to track grass boats.

On 22 July 1978 the *Washington Post* reported that U.S. Navy Ocean Surveillance Satellite data had been used to assist DEA and the Coast Guard in the seizure of forty drug ships with over a million pounds of marijuana. The paper said the effort ran from December 1977 until April 1978. It was called Operation Stopgap.[21] The navy was helping the Coast Guard and DEA in 1978. It is unlikely, however, that U.S. satellite assets were being used then to track drug ships. The Posse Comitatus Act of 1878 prohibiting the military from enforcing civil laws was still strictly applied. It was not amended by Congress until 1981, when the armed forces were allowed to support civilian law enforcement but still forbidden to take part in seizures and arrests. The *Post* article may have resulted from information intentionally leaked to the press to take the heat off certain Colombian officials who had tacitly allowed our civilian enforcement aircraft to invade Colombian airspace. However the rumors and press articles originated, they put a temporary damper on mothership operators, who believed that their ships were being tracked by satellites. It was good use of disinformation.

A factor that certainly influenced drug boat seizures in 1978 and 1979 was Fidel Castro's Operation Cuban Reunification, announced on 6 September 1978. Castro released 2,728 ex-prisoners and 4,421 relatives of prisoners. Releases began on 21 October and continued until 1980. Other "escapees" joined the undesirables in fleeing Cuba. The Mariel boatlift tied up Coast Guard resources.[22] Forced to monitor the exodus from the Cuban port of Mariel, these units were diverted from intercepting motherships coming north from the Caribbean.

Although satellite rumors helped to slow things down, there was still a huge grass flow from the Caribbean to the United States in 1978. Most seizures occurred along our southeastern sea frontier, despite the Coast Guard's distraction with the Cuban boatlift. The Seventh Coast Guard District, including its Greater Antilles Section in the Caribbean, reported 102 vessels seized with 2.8 million pounds of marijuana.[23] If the seizure rate was at the estimated 10–20 percent, between 14 million and 28 million pounds of maritime pot got through to the Atlantic and Gulf coasts alone.

Seizures in the second half of 1978 indicated a trend toward grass deliveries north of Florida's Gold Coast. The *Helen L II*'s off-load at Hutchinson Island was not an isolated event. On 29 July 1978 the 80-foot fishing vessel *Mister Sidney* was seized at Saint Simons Island, Georgia, with 41,459 pounds of pot. Fourteen people were arrested in this case. Evidence indicated the widespread distribution of marijuana along our entire eastern seaboard. Two months later, on 6 October 1978, the 100-foot coastal freighter *Bocas* was nabbed by the Coast Guard 20 miles east of Brunswick, Georgia, with 8,840 pounds of grass remaining in the hold. The *Bocas* had already off-loaded 30,376 pounds to two contact vessels. The total of 39,216 pounds was a sizable delivery to the Georgia coast.

These two big seizures in Georgia may have caused off-load movement even further north. On 18 December a joint enforcement effort by DEA, Customs, the Coast Guard, and local authorities ended with

The USCGC *Vigorous* (WMEC-627) intercepts a mothership off New Jersey. *(Official U.S. Coast Guard photograph)*

the seizure of the 70-foot fishing vessel *Chris Covey* in New Hanover County, North Carolina, with about 30,000 pounds of marijuana. The common thread in these seizures was a connection to Florida-based smuggling groups.[24] This was further evidence that enforcement pressures were being felt by grass importers along the Gold Coast.

There was a definite surge in off-load activity off the Northeast in 1978. Twenty-four vessels of all types were seized that year, compared with six in 1977. Groups of large seizures cycled between the Gulf of Maine and the Long Island, New York, area. In April and May the U.S. vessels *Onalay* and *Southern Belle* were intercepted near the coast of Maine with 55,000 pounds. Then in October and November the *Scott Bader, Darlene C,* and *Terry's Dream* were seized in the vicinity of Long Island with 111,000 pounds. Back again to the Gulf of Maine. In December the Panamanian *Tusker* and a British vessel with no recorded name were taken with approximately 90,000 pounds. About 318,000 pounds of maritime marijuana were intercepted off the Northeast that year.[25] Assuming a 10 percent seizure rate, if that much was taken, almost 3 million pounds must have been successfully delivered to the North Atlantic coast in 1978. The Sea of Grass had truly reached our northern shores.

In 1978 the National Narcotics Intelligence Consumers Committee (NNICC) was established to coordinate collection and analysis of foreign and domestic drug intelligence. The deputy assistant administrator for intelligence of DEA chaired the committee. Membership included representatives of the Coast Guard, Customs, the FBI, the Department of Defense, the Internal Revenue Service, the Immigration and Naturalization Service, the State Department (International Narcotics Matters), the Treasury, the National Institute on Drug Abuse, and the White House Drug Abuse Policy Office. Representatives of the Central Intelligence Agency and the National Security Agency attended NNICC meetings as observers. The NNICC initiated the annual Narcotics Intelligence Estimate, which contains an estimate of the quantity and sources of drugs consumed in the United States. It also addresses the amount and distribution of drug money.[26] NNICC is a forum for agencies to exchange strategic drug intelligence. It is not, however, a system for supplying tactical intelligence to operating agencies, and it does not help in locating smuggler vessels and aircraft.

Before leaving 1978, two important events should be noted that impacted marijuana smuggling. Carlos Lehder, the notorious cocaine air transporter for the Medellin cartel, occupied Norman's Cay in the Bahamas. With his island air base, Lehder revolutionized cocaine smuggling methods. He transformed the industry from one that transacted business in kilo units to a mammoth growth industry that dealt in tons of white powder. Robert Vesco, an equally notorious U.S. fugitive residing in the Bahamas, allegedly helped Lehder negotiate necessary payoffs to high-level Bahamian officials.[27] The fantastic success of the coke business from 1978 on, and the explosive use of cocaine in America, eventually attracted some kingpin maritime grass smugglers to the much more lucrative cocaine air traffic.

A second event revealed the sophistication of the opposition. On 6 April 1978, Miami police, investigating a suspected cocaine operation run by Ricardo Morales, raided a house in north Dade. They found drugs, but the real payoff was written on paper beside a radio scanner. Two legal-sized sheets listed radio frequencies used by DEA, the FBI, the Coast Guard, and the Secret Service. These frequencies were so secure that even the Federal Communications Commission did not have a complete list. The programed radio scanner was tuned to monitor ten frequencies assigned to DEA. Law enforcement officials were shocked. Plans were implemented to protect enforcement frequencies, but it would take a long time to repair the damage.[28] The enemy was regarded in a new light. It would be years before we could estimate their order of battle.

Total maritime marijuana seizure statistics for 1977–78 compared with 1975 give some idea of the tremendous increase in grass smuggling. They also indicate an increase in U.S. interdiction efforts. In 1975 a little over 200,000 pounds were seized by all forces from a handful of vessels. As the motherships started rolling north, seizures soared to over a million pounds in 1977, with a catch of fifty-two boats and ships. Then came the great flood of 1978, with grass seizures reaching almost 3 million pounds and 115 intercepted vessels.[29]

Colombia replaced Mexico as the primary source of grass to an ever-expanding U.S. market. The Mexican paraquat scare helped the transition. Sophisticated transport and off-load organizations developed from Florida to California to handle landings. People from all walks of life were corrupted by the grass bonanza and its astronomical profits. Violence followed, ashore and afloat. Motherships tried to ram Coast Guard cutters. Cutter crews began to treat grass boats as dangerous adversaries. The flood of grass spread north along the Atlantic and also touched our Pacific shores. Cocaine had just begun to undermine the marijuana industry, but the grass trade was still very much alive. The Sea of Grass had reached high tide.

4

High Water
1979–1981

There lies the trail to Sunnydale,
  Amid the lure of laughter.
Oh how can we unhappy be,
  Beneath its leafy rafter!
Each perfect hour is like a flower,
  Each day is like a posy.
How can you say the skies are grey?
  You're wrong, my friend, they're rosy.

ROBERT SERVICE, "TO SUNNYDALE"

After the flood there was a period of stability in the flow of maritime marijuana to the United States. Coast Guard seizures declined for a while, probably because of the Cuban boatlift. There were indications that the northeastern supply also faltered for a few months. Marijuana smuggling remained well above anything we had seen before the great flood of 1978. This was indeed a high time for pot boats and their customers.

In 1979 there was either an increase in the number of pot smokers in the metropolitan Northeast or a decrease in the amount of grass that got past our slim defenses. A December *New York Times* article reported that dealers and police had noted a marijuana shortage caused by storms in Colombia, federal agents in Florida, and Soviet troops in Cuba. The article quoted Michael Chase of the drug-culture rag *High Times,* who declared 1979 the worst year for pot suppliers in recent times. Chase blamed the weather in Colombia. He credited rumors of navy ships stopping everything moving near Cuba. Chase admitted he did not know if the U.S. military's response to the Soviet brigade in Cuba had anything to do with the pot shortage but speculated that many smugglers were afraid to move through the Caribbean. The article said domestic marijuana production had increased to 15 percent of the total supply.[1]

If the smugglers were concerned with military activity in the Caribbean, it was understandable but not well founded. On 1 October 1979 President Jimmy Carter announced that we would respond to the presence of a Soviet combat brigade in Cuba with increased surveillance and the establishment of a Caribbean joint task force. Sixteen days after his press release, eighteen hundred leathernecks of the Thirty-eighth Marine Amphibious Unit landed at Guantánamo, Cuba. The landing was a demonstration of naval power after the Soviets' refusal to withdraw their combat troops.[2]

The news was enough to give grass shippers second thoughts. Military interest in their activities, however, was nil to none. Just as with the previous year's rumors of satellite tracking, there was little likelihood of direct military involvement in drug interdiction. Posse Comitatus was still in full force.

The way north for the motherships was more open now than it had been for the past two years. The Mariel boatlift was under way in 1979. According to the Cuban refugee program in Miami, 374 boat arrivals were recorded that year, compared with 19 in 1978.[3] Coast

Guard cutters came south to help the beleaguered Seventh District deal with the motley collection of small boats transporting Mariel people. There were many cutters at sea between Cuba and Florida, but they had little time to look for drug boats.

At the same time, the interdiction forces were improving their performance. The USCGC *Steadfast* (WMEC-623) was on patrol east of Little Bahama Bank when she encountered a rusty 65-foot fishing vessel, the *Don Alvaro*. When the Dominican Republic denied the vessel's claim to its flag, the *Don Alvaro* was declared stateless and was boarded. The boarding party found 35 tons of pot. The crew were arrested and transferred to the *Steadfast*. A Coast Guard prize crew got under way for Miami in the captured boat. While the *Steadfast* was off checking a radar contact, a light aircraft dropped a message to the grass boat. It gave the time and place of the off-load. The Coasties decided to follow through with the plan.

The *Don Alvaro*, with her crew of Coast Guard smugglers, proceeded to the appointed place off Great Abaco. They carefully stayed in international waters. Along came the 50-foot U.S. cabin cruiser *Quester* looking for a load of grass. The Coast Guardsmen obliged by tossing a few bales to the pickup boat. Then they arrested the two-man crew and seized the yacht.[4] On-scene innovation thus produced two seizures with little additional effort.

DEA noted the departure of the 157-foot Panamanian coastal freighter *Karen Danica* from Cristobal, Canal Zone, on 24 March 1979. Several of her crewmen had narcotics records. The suspicious freighter declared for Curaçao, Netherlands Antilles. The drug agents were not convinced. She was placed on the lookout list that went out each month from the El Paso Intelligence Center (EPIC) to Coast Guard, Customs, and DEA field units. A DEA investigation in Miami identified a pending mothership off-load in or near the Bahamas. The USCGC *Active* (WMEC-618) intercepted the *Karen Danica* near the Bahamas on 29 May. With an SNO from Panama, the freighter was boarded and searched. She contained 50,000 pounds of Colombian pot.[5]

There was definitely traffic into the Gulf of Mexico. Harold King (a fictitious name for an individual in the Federal Witness Protection Program) made his first grass run with a Gulf shrimper in early 1979. King is a happy-go-lucky, robust fisherman from Fort Myers, Florida. His maiden pot voyage was all the way from Colombia, via the

Yucatán, to Mobile Bay. King had to anchor off Bon Secour, where he intended to deliver the load, because of heavy fog that night. No sooner was the hook down than a Coast Guard utility boat showed up with a crew of three very young Coasties. As they slowly approached, King had to physically restrain his two crewmen from jumping overboard and swimming for what they hoped was shore.

With the crew in hand, King was ready to deal with the Coast Guardsmen. They stopped a few feet from the shrimper and asked if they could tie up alongside until the fog cleared. King welcomed the youngsters, then dashed to the galley and put on a big pot of coffee. He stayed on deck for an hour, topping off their coffee mugs and talking about anything and everything. King could not believe that the Coasties did not smell the pot; perhaps it was the strong coffee. The utility boat crew left happy.

King was now able to off-load the 15,000 pounds of grass to his friends waiting out in the fog. The lesson he learned was that when caught with your pants at half-mast, be friendly, talk fast, and always have plenty of strong coffee on board.[6]

Before leaving southern waters, we should note a seizure near the south end of Cay Sal Bank. The 95-foot Coast Guard patrol boat *Cape Current* (WPB-95307) intercepted the U.S. cabin cruiser *David* on the Fourth of July. She was found to be loaded with 3,000 pounds of pot, probably from Jamaica. The *Cape Current*'s CO arrested the yacht's crew and seized the boat. Lt. Susan I. Moritz, USCG, the only commissioned officer and the only female in the *Cape Current*'s fourteen-person complement, became the first Coast Guard woman to take down a drug boat.[7]

In the Northeast the first big seizure of 1979 occurred on 17 March off Sandy Hook, New Jersey. The 82-foot patrol boat *Point Francis* (WPB-82356) seized the 189-foot Liberian freighter *Olaug* with 40,000 pounds of grass. Happy St. Patrick's Day! Two days later the *Point Franklin* (WPB-82350) took out the *Kristen Jane,* a 70-foot U.S. fishing vessel with another 40,000 pounds, near the entrance to Delaware Bay. After March, seizures were minor. The total volume of grass seized in the Northeast was about 80,000 pounds, compared with over 318,000 pounds in 1978.[8] If seizures are indicative of traffic, they confirmed the northeastern pot shortage that year.

Though seizures were slow on the Atlantic coast in 1979, it was a good year for grass hauls on the Pacific side. The total volume of marijuana and hashish seized, or believed destroyed by scuttled vessels, was over 350,000 pounds. That volume would not be surpassed for ten years. Vessel seizures did not increase.[9] Two vessels accounted for most of the total.

Up first was the 142-foot ex–salvage vessel *Samarkanda* off a remote beach at Vancouver Island, British Columbia. On the foggy morning of 22 May 1979 a combined Royal Canadian Mounted Police (RCMP) and Canadian Forces strike force descended on a heavily forested cove on the coast of Vancouver. The Mounties surprised a bedraggled multinational gang of smugglers with a cache of 67,000 pounds of Colombian pot. They looked more like survivors than drug runners. Just off the beach, the *Samarkanda* lay at anchor with a broken engine. In all, twenty-three people were arrested, including the Colombian captain and seven Americans.

The trial was a remarkable case of innovative defense. Lawyers put forth a "defense of necessity." They insisted that the *Samarkanda* had been making for Alaska when her engine began to fail. Her crew had no choice but to seek shelter in the Vancouver cove. The trial judge instructed the jury that a defense of necessity had never succeeded in Canada and could only be used in a case of peril to life and limb. To everyone's surprise, the jury rejected the Crown's theory of blatant smuggling and acquitted all the "survivors."[10]

What could have been the grand-slam maritime pot seizure for the West Coast came next. On 1 August a Coast Guard aircraft sighted the 320-foot Panamanian freighter *Gladstone* 300 miles southwest of San Francisco, dead in the water. The ship was surrounded by four fishing vessels. Aircrewmen saw people transferring bales from the freighter to the boats. When the boats were loaded, the crews evidently saw the aircraft circling at a distance and took off at maximum speed in four different directions. The Coast Guard Pacific Area Command dispatched the *Midget* (WHEC-726), a high-endurance cutter. District commands sent three 82-foot patrol boats to look for the off-load boats. Air surveillance was maintained over the *Gladstone*. About four hours after the off-load, a Coast Guard aircraft reported that the ship was down by the stern, suggesting that the engine room was being flooded. No distress signal was broadcast, but the freighter's crew abandoned ship in a lifeboat.

The next day the *Midget* rescued the eleven-man crew 20 miles from the ship's original position. The freighter was nowhere in sight.

The master was a Chilean; the others were Latin except for one American who was identified as a "stowaway." No bales were recovered. One suspect off-load boat was intercepted about 100 miles from the freighter's last known position. She was clean.[11]

The *Gladstone* case prompted a senior DEA official to speculate that marijuana mothership operations were moving to the West Coast. It was more than speculation. Intelligence indicated that the *Gladstone* was delivering 240,000 pounds of Colombian marijuana to the Pacific shores of the United States.[12] The *Gladstone*'s load would have been surpassed only by the *Don Emilio*'s cargo of 320,000 pounds seized east of the Bahamas in 1976. It would certainly have been the largest grass seizure on the West Coast.

The Coast Guard seized approximately 2.6 million pounds of marijuana in 1979, associated with 110 vessels. This was a decline from the 115 vessels and nearly 3 million pounds of pot taken in 1978.[13] The best explanations for the 1979 pause are related to the Cuban boatlift. Expanded Coast Guard operations off Cuba and Florida deterred some mothership operators. Also, the focus of the Coast Guard effort on the boat exodus reduced the chance of drug boat interceptions.

Meanwhile, demand for cocaine was increasing rapidly. It could be shipped by air and was much easier to handle than marijuana. The 1980s are known as the decade of cocaine for good reason. DEA estimated that between 40 and 48 metric tons were imported in 1980, an increase of more than 40 percent over the previous year. Cocaine availability and abuse were expanding at a phenomenal rate.[14]

Coca is grown primarily in Bolivia and Peru and is refined into cocaine hydrochloride in Colombia. Plants have a life span of about thirty years. The leaves can be harvested three to six times a year, and the plant can be grown in soil unsuitable for other crops. Coca prices in the producing countries accelerated in 1980 to twenty times their previous level, reflecting the growing demand in the United States.[15]

Miami was the central conduit for coke. Crime was getting out of control. Colombian trafficking organizations were establishing distribution systems. Machine-gun shootouts were common. Into this chaos came approximately 120,000 "Marielitos," arriving in South Florida in the spring and summer of 1980 via the boatlift. About five thousand were Cuban criminals who continued to practice their trades in and around Miami. Citizens were desperate.[16]

How did this violence affect the usually placid grass boaters? It brought national attention to the drug trade. People who were tolerant or ambivalent in their attitude toward drugs were much less complacent when confronted with violent crime. A grass-roots movement against narcotics use and trafficking was emerging. Politicians at all levels of government reacted vigorously to constituent pressures for antinarcotics programs, especially law enforcement. Narcotics became one of the most important political issues of the 1980s. Marijuana smugglers, as a rule, were not "Cocaine Cowboys," but they would soon be lumped with their cocaine relatives in the government's crusade against narcotics. Grass boaters were more vulnerable to detection because of their bulky cargoes and labor-intensive off-load procedures.

Cocaine had undoubtedly been included in maritime grass shipments in the past. There were reports by Coast Guard cutters of marijuana ships deep-sixing small packages before being boarded. It was a common opinion in the law enforcement community that smugglers felt more liable for cocaine than pot. When interception was inevitable, they dumped the coke first. Many American grass smugglers wanted nothing to do with cocaine. They had no moral qualms about importing tons of pot but expressed revulsion at the idea of carrying a few kilos of coke, a dangerous drug! Some old-timers claimed that they would not allow cocaine on their boats, even for recreational use. Others admitted that when their marijuana ventures were about to fail, they tried cocaine smuggling but felt guilty.[17]

Some multi-ton Colombian grass shipments normally delivered to South Florida were diverted to the northern Gulf of Mexico in 1980. It became known as the Bayou Bypass. Smugglers were worried about the increased Coast Guard presence around South Florida because of the Cuban boatlift. They were also worried about getting shot. The USCGC *Point Francis* (WPB-82356) put fifty-five machine-gun rounds into the drug boat *Thomas E* as she fled toward the Bahamas on 10 October 1980. They were the first disabling shots fired at sea.

The Louisiana coast was a good alternative. Unmanned offshore oil rigs were ideal rendezvous points. Coastal marshes with miles of little-known oil rig canals and natural bayous were ideal water highways for moving bulk marijuana. Great numbers of the fast, low-profile Lafitte skiffs of the inshore fishing fleet were available. There were also underutilized crew boats for unloading operations. These boats attracted little attention cruising among the myriad offshore rigs and through the inland waterways.

In October 1980 a 100-foot barge moored along the Louisiana Intracoastal Waterway west of New Orleans with 80 tons of grass was discovered by Customs officers and local police. The barge was equipped with conveyor belts for fast loading and unloading. It was a floating grass warehouse for mothership cargoes, and a near-record seizure. Customs figures for December show more than 250 tons of pot seized in the bayou areas since October, three times the amount seized during the three previous years.

The area was hot. It was also the setting for the second shots fired by the Coast Guard in the drug war. The 82-foot patrol boat *Point Spencer* (WPB-82349) was given permission to use disabling fire to stop the U.S.–registered supply boat *Polaris* on 20 November 1980. The *Point Spencer* used forty rounds of .50-caliber machine-gun fire to stop the escaping drug boat. Seventy tons of pot were seized and sixteen people arrested.[18]

Before the year ended, the *Point Spencer* scored another bust in the Mississippi River Gulf outlet east of New Orleans. The patrol boat came upon the 100-foot Norwegian coastal freighter *Tysfjord* on 11 December. The little freighter was aground on a mud bank. An inspection of the vessel was the natural thing to do. The eleven people on board were not ordinary Scandinavian seamen. It did not take the boarding party long to find the 40-plus tons of grass in the cargo hold.[19] The Bayou Bypass was sufficiently documented.

The first major seizure of the new decade in the Northeast occurred off Long Island on 23 March. The USCGC *Cape Strait* (WPB-95308) sighted the Venezuelan motor vessel *José Gregorio* off Montauk Point. The cutter's crew became suspicious because of the battered appearance of the loitering vessel. The Coast Guard received an SNO from Venezuela, but rough seas prevented the 95-footer from boarding. The *José Gregorio* moved offshore in the gathering darkness. The Coast Guardsmen followed, wallowing through mounting seas. They observed about two dozen bales being tossed over the side of the rusty suspect but could not recover them. The next morning the *Cape Strait* was relieved by the 210-foot medium-endurance cutter *Vigorous* (WMEC-627). Finally, with moderating weather, the *Vigorous* was able to put a boarding party on the Venezuelan 38 miles south-southeast of Montauk Point. Approximately 15 tons of marijuana, minus whatever had been fed to the fish, were found in the hold. Two Americans and seven Colombians were arrested.[20] Some of the grass bound for the deprived New York area was thus removed from the pipeline.

As 1980 progressed there was an apparent move to the north for Atlantic mothership operations. The Coast Guard and the RCMP snagged the Honduran motor vessel *Patricia* with 37,400 pounds of grass about 70 miles southeast of Cape Sable, Nova Scotia, on 30 May. The load was probably destined for off-load in the Gulf of Maine. It was a common ploy for foreign motherships to declare for Halifax and then double back to the gulf for off-load. The British motor vessel *Persistence,* with 16,000 pounds of pot, was intercepted and seized by Coast Guard and Customs officers on 12 August about 50 miles northeast of Cape Cod as she entered the gulf. On 23 September the USCGC *Tamaroa* (WMEC-166) stopped the 204-foot Panamanian coastal freighter *Roon Diep* east of Georges Bank. The freighter yielded 20 tons of marijuana. Four Americans and three British subjects were arrested. Next came the largest northeastern seizure for the year. The Coast Guard, DEA, and the Maine State Police apprehended the Canadian motor vessel *Jubilee* on 20 October 1980, just off Penobscot Bay, Maine, with 34 tons of marijuana.[21]

Motherships targeted the mid-Atlantic area in December. On 15 December the U.S. fishing vessel *Terry and Joe* was seized by the Coast Guard 55 miles south of Cape Lookout, North Carolina, with 40,000 pounds of pot. Six days later the Panamanian motor vessel *Silvano* was taken off Newport News, Virginia, with another 40,000 pounds. Then on the twenty-ninth the U.S. *Don Frank* was intercepted off the mouth of Chesapeake Bay with 14,000 pounds of pot.[22] The pattern of alternating delivery points because of enforcement pressure was common in the northern Atlantic area as in other places.

Pacific marijuana seizures declined in 1980. The maritime take plummeted to 71,402 pounds from a record high of 350,351 pounds in 1979. Vessel seizures, however, remained about the same. There were only three seizures in the multi-ton range. The largest of the year occurred in September. Customs, the Coast Guard, and DEA cooperated in the apprehension of two large pleasure craft, the *Valkyure* and *Potomac,* in San Francisco Bay. A total of 40,000 pounds of marijuana was seized.[23]

The case involving the latter vessels is interesting. The 165-foot *Potomac,* originally the Coast Guard cutter *Electra,* had at one time been the official yacht of President Franklin D. Roosevelt. She was used for crucial strategy sessions during World War II. Such luminaries as Winston Churchill and King George VI met with Roosevelt aboard the *Potomac* in her heyday. In the wee hours of the morning of 11 September, federal agents, state officers, and Coast Guardsmen found the *Potomac* and the 100-foot *Valkyure* moored at Pier 26 in San Francisco. Enforcement teams swarmed aboard the vessels after a bullhorn announcement of their intention to board. Six Colombians were arrested aboard the *Valkyure*. Fourteen Americans were also arrested at the scene. No pot was found aboard the *Potomac,* but she was seized for supporting the *Valkyure*'s 20-ton delivery. A confidential informant identified a tractor-trailer truck that was traced to the pier and found partially loaded with pot. The smuggling organization was operating as the bogus Crippled Children's Society of America.[24] This group set a record for the degradation of American principles.

The Coast Guard seized about 2.5 million pounds of maritime grass in 1980. Approximately 1.5 million pounds were taken in the Caribbean and along the southeastern U.S. coast. In all, 134 vessels were seized, 101 of them in the Southeast.[25]

Two events occurred in September 1980 that helped maritime drug interdiction. First, the Biaggi Act (21 U.S.C. 955a) was passed by Congress. This new law expanded U.S. jurisdiction over U.S. and stateless vessels carrying drugs. It was no longer necessary to prove intent to import contraband into the United States; the boarding officers' pro forma "Where bound?" was not critical. The mere possession of narcotics with intent to distribute was sufficient grounds to seize vessels and arrest crews. Second, the Cuban boatlift ended in September. Coast Guard resources were again free to track drug boats.

By the 1980s, maritime marijuana smuggling had evolved into a highly efficient business. Organizations operated according to a specialized division of labor. They involved people of different nationalities, backgrounds, and expertise. The possibility of inadvertent information leaks by off-loaders and disclosure by informants was a major concern.

Final off-load coordinates were passed at the last minute to delivery vessels by radio alphanumerical or simple pad codes. Alphanumerical codes were a random selection of letters that represented numbers from 0 to 9. A pad code could be any set of ten letters such as the phrase "Can you help?" where the first letter, C, stands for 0, the

Emergencias

1- **Silverado** = Estoy a la deriva.
2- **Bronco** = Me falta combustible.
3- **Samuray** = Me falta agua y comida.
4- **Renegado** = Me persigue un guardacosta.
5- **Toyota** = Un avion me sobrevuela.

Para cuando este llegando al sitio.

1- Me caso con: Ana = Lunes.
2- " " " : Patricia = Martes.
3- " " " : Silvia = Miercoles.
4- " " " : Jessica = Jueves.
5- " " " : Josefina: Viernes.
6- " " " : Maria = Sabado.
7- " " " : Rosa = Domingo.

HORA Siecle Pinoniner

Caballero R.T.

POLLITO.

20 mts	40 mts	2 mts.
14.460.	7.400.	31.25.
14.325.	7.460	
14.500.	7.465	
14.375.	7.480	
14.400.	7.468	
14.446.	7.85	
14.480.	7410	

B	H	I	T	K	M	P	O	A	E
1	2	3	4	5	6	7	8	9	0

Paper found aboard a marijuana mothership showing emergency, day-frequency, and alphanumerical codes
(Author's collection)

second letter, *A*, stands for 1, and so on to the last letter, *P*, for 9. Obviously the phrase could not contain repeated letters. The old method of using navigational charts marked with random letters designating degrees of latitude and longitude was still used.

Other measures were taken by maritime smugglers to preserve operational security—OPSEC, in military parlance. Aircraft flew surveillance around delivery vessels and overflew Coast Guard stations to note the absence of cutters. If a cutter was away from her moorings, she was somewhere at sea and a threat to the smugglers. Two-meter line-of-sight hand-held radios were used to coordinate final off-loads as a communications security measure. They were so indicative of smuggling that crews often dropped them over the side before being boarded. Shore watchers in small boats at vantage points along the beach and at roads leading to landing sites also used the ubiquitous radios to report approaching enforcement units.

The chase boat was the best security for smugglers at sea. A chase boat was a very high speed "cigarette" or "formula"-type boat equipped with sophisticated radio, electronic navigation, and radar equipment. They were capable of speeds up to 60 knots. A few hours before the pending off-load, the alerted chase boat operator would be given coordinates, frequencies, and codes. He would proceed to the off-load area and conduct a visual and radar search for enforcement vessels or aircraft. If the coast was clear, he would advise the control station. Chase boats stayed about half a mile away while delivery vessels transferred contraband to pickup boats. A roving lookout for enforcement units was maintained while the smugglers frantically transferred the marijuana bales. In the unlikely event that a Coast Guard cutter or a Customs boat appeared on the scene, the chase boat would dash in and take off the smugglers. The boats' presence was also a great boost to the smugglers' morale; many would not do off-loads without one.

One experienced smuggler captain, who successfully delivered numerous multi-ton loads of grass to the Gulf coast between 1976 and 1987, had his own special demands for a chase boat. Harold King, whom we have met before, captained shrimp boats from Colombia or picked up grass loads from motherships offshore. About 2 miles from the final off-load point, King would slow down to a few knots and engage the shrimper's automatic pilot. He would call the chase boat on his 2-meter radio to take him and his crew off the pot-loaded shrimper. They would follow the unmanned boat a few hundred yards astern until they got to the approximate position. If no suspicious vessels or aircraft were seen, they would quickly reboard, make for the exact coordinates, and radio for the pickup boats.

Another common OPSEC measure was to change the name of the vessel, sometimes en route. Motherships loitering in Colombian or Panamanian ports frequently changed their names after loading a cargo of grass and heading north. By now they were aware of DEA planes and spies recording names and descriptions of possible motherships. Quick-change name boards were common. In some cases motherships were even repainted down to the waterline during transit. It was also a good idea to paint the waterline high so that the vessel would seem empty. Name changes were also frequent among pickup boats. Possession of a lookout list, purchased for thousands of dollars from a corrupt law enforcement person, was not a sure bet; your boat's name could have been added in the last few days. Smart smugglers would therefore pick the name of a legitimate boat of similar type and size. If the Coast Guard or other enforcement agencies checked the bogus name, it would come back as a valid registration.[26]

Smuggling ventures are financed by a principal. This may be an individual or a group. It may consist of otherwise legitimate investors who put up money for a quick return and remain isolated from the venture. Front money for expenses comes from the principal. All kinds of people have invested in drug ventures for astronomical returns, vastly better than certificates of deposit or mutual funds. Some are ostensibly pillars of the community. Few have been prosecuted. The dirty work is done by the midlevel managers or middlemen.

The middleman is the operations chief of the smuggling venture. He makes things happen. He also serves as a shield for the principal, who usually has no contact with other members of the smuggling organization. The principal is thus protected from detailed knowledge of the operation. He is immune from prosecution unless a link can be found between him and the middleman. A midlevel manager has a host of duties. He must contact a supplier in a source country and negotiate payment for the load. He has to find and purchase or lease a primary transport vessel or mothership, get a captain and crew, and select a route. Then the middleman selects the off-load site, establishes communication procedures and schedules, procures off-load boats and land transportation vehicles, and implements security measures.

He is also responsible for land distribution to stash houses and protection of the facilities. In addition to his other duties, the middleman pays crews and supplies bribes to corrupt officials.

Colombian marijuana crops were harvested in the spring (April and May) and fall (October and November); the spring crop was usually half the volume of the fall harvest (or smaller). Marijuana was grown in the mountains. Harvested leaves were dried in the growing areas, then sorted, most of the stems being removed manually. Sorted leaves were baled with trash compactors into 25- to 100-pound bales, then wrapped with plastic or burlap or both. Wrapped bales were transported by mule carts or trucks to loading points or warehouses on the coast. Although harvesting took place only twice a year, baled grass was generally available year-round.

Motherships were usually loaded along the Colombian Guajira Peninsula. Until this time, small freighters ran right up to the beach. The scene was reminiscent of World War II amphibious operations. Trucks shuttled between grass warehouses and the beach. Bales were loaded across floating platforms or directly up ramps to vessels. After 1980, when smugglers became aware of our intelligence capability to photograph vessels at the beach, they started loading at night a few miles offshore. This process required a fleet of large 40-foot "bongo" boats to lighter the pot cargoes out to transport vessels. After loading, the transports usually shaped a course north from the Caribbean through the Windward (between Cuba and Haiti) or Mona (between the Dominican Republic and Puerto Rico) Passage or through the Yucatán Channel (between Cuba and the Yucatán Peninsula of Mexico).

The few marijuana motherships plying the Pacific sailed north from Colombia or east across the vast ocean from Southeast Asia. Allegedly, some Colombian-loaded ships embarked grass cargoes in Buenaventura on the Pacific coast. That city, however, was a long way from the primary marijuana growing region in the Sierra Nevada de Santa Marta—530 miles away over the mighty Cordillera Central. Pacific motherships loading in Colombia probably did so on the Guajira and then transited the Panama Canal. Southeast Asian pot usually came from Thailand. Motherships loaded at ports in the Gulf of Thailand. It was a long and tedious voyage to off-load points, usually a few hundred miles off the West Coast. The customary route out of the South China Sea was through the Luzon Strait (between Taiwan and the

Grass boats loading on the Guajira Peninsula of Colombia in a scene reminiscent of World War II amphibious operations
(NNBIS slide series, source unknown)

Philippines), then via the great-circle track across the Pacific. A few Asian motherships took their cargoes to French Polynesia for transshipment to large U.S. sailing vessels. The logistics problem associated with Pacific transport of bulk marijuana cargoes was momentous.

Ordinarily mothership masters and crewmen were foreign nationals. The masters and engineers were often licensed mariners with considerable sea experience. Although many were from South and Central America, it was not uncommon for captains to come from Europe and the Orient. Crewmen were generally from Colombia, Panama, Venezuela, and Honduras. A few motherships were manned entirely by Orientals, mainly Koreans. Most off-load crews were U.S. nationals or resident aliens who had regular and legitimate jobs. Pickup boat operators were fishermen or marine industry people with experience and the critical local knowledge needed to deliver bulky loads to coastal waters, bays, inlets, rivers, and canals at night without lights. Humpers, or bale handlers, came from all walks of life.

Many were young fishermen, and some were related to experienced off-load operators.

Air reconnaissance was critical to maritime smugglers. Planes located law enforcement units, served as communication relay stations, and transported personnel and spare parts for vessels. In a routine operation, an aircraft flew to a temporary base in the Caribbean, the Bahamas, or Mexico a few days before the mothership or primary transport vessel was to depart from the source country. A standard ploy was for airmen to pose as tourists or visiting businessmen. They scouted the planned route and tried to locate Coast Guard or naval vessels in the area. If sightings were made, they were reported by radio to a control station during flight or by telephone after landing; routes were then changed or departures delayed. Once under way, daily flights went over and ahead of the transport, searching for interdiction forces. Direct radio contact was avoided unless the aircraft determined that an interception was likely. In some operations, surveillance was restricted to perceived danger areas such as narrow passes or locations of recent Coast Guard patrols. Frequently, air reconnaissance was conducted in the general off-load area just prior to or sometimes during the event. Some captains reported that surveillance aircraft gave them a warning before they were boarded. The warnings were transmitted by 2-meter radio to reduce the chance of interception. Codes for the direction and distance of enforcement sightings were commonly used. A simple example would be "Red 23," meaning a Coast Guard cutter is north of you at 23 miles.

Other security measures and ploys were used by more sophisticated smuggling organizations. Decoy vessels, behaving like smugglers and sometimes transmitting meaningless radio codes, drew enforcement resources from the track of transport vessels and off-load areas. False distress calls were common. Decoys occasionally went to the extreme of taking on water to fake a sinking condition, necessitating the delivery of pumps by the Coast Guard.

Dipole directional antennas were used by many boats and mobile shore stations to reduce the chances of transmission intercept. One cooperating smuggler told boarding officers to look for small holes drilled in the top of pilothouses or living spaces, implying temporary use of the antennas. He claimed that smugglers would not leave the dipoles mounted because they thought the antennas suggested smuggling activity. The source also explained how they modified radios to "get between the bands": they took the limit off the dial and extended the capability to higher or lower frequencies between normal bands.

When a mothership was 100–500 miles offshore, she was directed to the off-load position by a control station using prearranged frequencies and codes. Commonly, motherships transferred the grass to fishing vessels or large yachts well offshore. Pickup boats went to isolated docks or waterfront homes or to secondary off-load positions close to shore. If a secondary option was used, pickup boats transferred cargoes to small inshore fishing boats or fast small boats, depending on final delivery location and the vessel population of the area. For example, if the cargo was bound for the Florida Gold Coast, pickup boats were yachts, open fishermen, or racing-type boats. They went directly to homes or marinas on the many canals and waterways. If final delivery was to the Everglades, a secondary transfer was made to shallow-draft mullet boats or gill-netters.

Off-loads required many people, depending on the size of the load. To reduce the chance of identification by local enforcement officers, organizations frequently assembled crews in motels some distance from the off-load site. The crew moved to the site in separate vehicles a few hours before the pickup boats arrived. Unloading took place as quickly as possible. The bales of pot were sent by truck, van, or motor home to distant stash houses. Portions of the load not already consigned were sold directly to wholesalers for distribution throughout the country.

Profits were huge. In 1980, commercial-grade Colombian marijuana could be purchased for $35 a pound, mostly on credit, then sold wholesale in the southeastern United States for $400 a pound. This gross profit margin of 91 percent gave the principal a markup of over ten times the initial investment. Put another way, a modest 20,000-pound load costing $700,000 in Colombia and selling for $8 million in the United States made a gross profit of $7.3 million.

There were expenses, but they were small compared with the profits. A load of this size cost about $1 million to import. The primary transport vessel and crew cost around $300,000. Say a 72-foot steel-hulled shrimp trawler was used for the long voyage from Colombia to the U.S. Gulf coast. The captain received $125,000 and the three crewmen got $50,000 each. The remaining $25,000 went for fuel and boat expenses, including updating the electronics equipment. A support aircraft staged out of Grand Cayman, Mexico, and Fort Myers

(Florida) flew six sorties to get the boat safely through the Yucatán Channel for the off-load near Naples, Florida. Add another $250,000 for the aircraft, pilot, and observer-radioman. The high-speed chase boat with an experienced operator required $100,000 for forty-eight hours of intense effort. Ten bale humpers in the off-load crew each got $20,000, for a total of $200,000. Four bale handlers drove trucks to a distant stash house for a bonus of $5,000 each, which added a paltry $20,000 to the bill. Use of the final shoreside off-load site cost the operation another $75,000. The remaining $55,000 went for on-call coast watchers, highway lookouts, and miscellaneous expenses.[27]

Our prime-mover middleman could take up to $1 million for his share and expenses, including any necessary bribes. The principals still came away from the venture with a net profit of $5.3 million. If an individual put up $50,000 for purchase of the load, he could have a return of over $300,000 in approximately forty-five days. The fantastic rate of return was more than many otherwise legitimate investors could resist. It was a travesty that the multitude of investors in "harmless marijuana" escaped prosecution; they helped to build the drug culture that has paralyzed this nation for so many years.

Despite the growing sophistication of maritime drug smuggling, the slim cutter force and its allies did well in 1981. Seizures rose to about 2.6 million pounds of marijuana, a bit higher than the previous year. The total number of vessels seized by the Coast Guard was 146. There was a vast increase in cocaine air smuggling, but only 40 pounds of maritime coke were seized by the cutters in 1981.[28]

The great majority of marijuana, and now cocaine, entered the United States through Florida. According to intelligence estimates in 1981, Florida was targeted for 68 percent of all maritime drug smuggling and 47 percent of all air smuggling. It was a matter of distance. Florida was closest to the primary sources. Colombia provided about 79 percent of the marijuana imported into the States and up to 75 percent of the cocaine. With Jamaica's contribution of 10 percent, nearly 90 percent of the pot consumed in the United States was produced closest to Florida.[29]

The inshore patrol off Florida was mighty slim in 1981. Even the Fisheries Service ran afoul of pot smugglers. Special Agent Ron Dearmin, a Marine Corps Vietnam veteran, was a good choice for the ordeal that occurred on the night of 25 February off the lower west coast of Florida. His two associates were no less qualified for the task.

Florida Marine Patrol's Lt. Mike Minski with the *Orion*, which he commanded in 1981 *(Photograph by NMFS agent Logan Gregory)*

Dearmin was charged with enforcing compliance with a line of separation to reduce conflicts between shrimp and stone-crab boats. The arbitrary line ran roughly from Fort Myers to Key West. Shrimpers had to fish west of the line. Crabbers could fish both sides but were encouraged to stay east. Under a cooperative agreement between the National Marine Fisheries Service (NMFS) and the Florida Marine Patrol (FMP), the FMP provided federally deputized officers and boats. The mainstay of the line patrol was the FMP 50-foot boat *Orion*, commanded by Sgt. Mike Minski and home-ported in Key West.

Dearmin and Minski were aboard the *Orion* accompanied by FMP officer Andy Brown. They anchored about 3 miles southwest of Naples and monitored vessel activity with radar. Around 1900, two targets crossed the line from west to east, possibly shrimp boats entering enemy territory. The *Orion* got under way to investigate. It was completely dark.

As they approached the first target, Sergeant Minski energized the searchlight. It was not a shrimper. The 48-foot gillnet boat *Miss Jill II* was deck-loaded with bales stacked as high as the pilothouse. They ran for a while, but the heavily loaded net boat could not stay ahead of the 25-knot *Orion*. While the chase was on, Sergeant Minski called for backup—from anybody! He was told that no enforcement unit could get there in less than four hours. Shortly thereafter the *Miss Jill II* stopped, and her crew of four surrendered. There were almost 15,000 pounds of pot on the boat. Officer Brown went aboard the captured boat as a one-man prize crew with the vessel's master. Minski and Dearmin locked the three prisoners below and took off to search for the second target. There were other boats in the area; after terrorizing two lovers on a sailboat by boiling up to them blacked out and then blinding them with a searchlight, they found what they suspected was the other target. She was also loaded with bales. The 45-foot crab boat *McRich* refused to stop. The chase was on again.

About 9 miles from the first capture, Minski and Dearmin grew concerned about Officer Brown. He was back there alone with a prisoner and 7.5 tons of pot. Who knew what other characters might be lurking in the pitch-black Gulf? Minski yelled to Dearmin over the screaming noise of the engines to take the shotgun and fire a round over the fleeing grass boat. Dearmin was actually running the line mission, but Minski was captain of the *Orion*. Like a good marine, Dearmin took the Remington off the rack and struggled onto the pitching, wind-swept deck. When he raised the weapon and chambered a round, Dearmin had two thoughts: the NMFS firearms policy that prohibited warning shots, and the plight of Andy Brown. As he started to squeeze the trigger, the *McRich* slowed. With a sigh of relief Dearmin began to safe the weapon. Just then the smuggler took off again. Dearmin fired a round over the *McRich*'s pilothouse. The flame from the muzzle of a shotgun on a dark night is a fearful sight; the *McRich* went dead in the water. Minski brought the *Orion* alongside and hailed the people to come on deck with their hands up. There were five: four locals and a Colombian. The boat had about 11,000 pounds of marijuana on deck.

Agent Dearmin herded the new arrivals up to the *Orion*'s foredeck with the shotgun. He ordered them to lie facedown, hands behind their backs. Dearmin did not tell them he was out of handcuffs. Sergeant Minski somehow managed to get a line on the *McRich*. It took them about an hour to tow this boat back to the first. With great relief, they found Officer Brown still in charge. The Fisheries agent and the two FMP officers now held two captive boats, nine prisoners, and almost 26,000 pounds of marijuana. Still no reinforcements. They tried to tow the boats with the *Orion,* but it was hopeless. Officer Brown went back to the *Miss Jill II* with the vessel's captain. They would tow the *McRich* to Key West, 90 miles to the south. Minski decided to run the arrested men into Key West as fast as he could. Brown was left behind again, with two boats full of pot and only a partially paroled smuggler for help. At 0200 the *Orion* met an FMP go-fast boat coming out of Key West to assist. They sent the two officers north to locate Brown. Luckily they found him at about 0400 and helped him bring the boats in. It was a close thing.[30] The episode stressed the desperate need for more Coast Guard resources in the southeastern Gulf.

An interesting fact of law arose pretrial in the federal district court. Florida Marine Patrol officers had authority to arrest drug smugglers within Florida territorial waters. Minski and Brown were deputized to enforce federal fisheries laws on the high seas within the jurisdiction of the National Marine Fisheries Service. NMFS, however, had no authority to arrest drug smugglers. Despite raging motions from defense lawyers to dismiss for lack of jurisdiction, the trial judge ruled that the FMP officers and Agent Dearmin had made valid citizen's arrests within the maritime jurisdiction of the United States. The defendants who went to trial were convicted. Agent Dearmin received a letter of commendation from the Florida attorney general. He was also ordered by the NMFS Washington office to show cause why he should not be charged with a firearms violation. Dearmin's boss threatened to go to the newspapers with both documents. The firearms matter was dismissed, but the event was not forgotten. A little over a year later, Congress amended the Fishery Conservation and Management Act to give NMFS agents and their deputized state officers authority to arrest for violations of any federal law committed in their presence.

The undermanned Seventh Coast Guard District was responsible for the primary drug defense line around Florida. The district was responsible for the Florida peninsula, Georgia, South Carolina, Puerto Rico, and the U.S. Virgin Islands. The Coast Guardsmen did well with what they had. It is not surprising that the Seventh District accounted for about 1.6 million pounds of the marijuana and 126 of the vessels seized in 1981.[31] By spring of 1981 the cutter *Dauntless* (WMEC-624) had forty green marijuana leaves painted on her stack; each little leaf represented a grass seizure. Since her debut in 1973 the *Dauntless* had become the premier drug buster of the Coast Guard fleet. Comdr. Michael Murtagh was skipper, ably assisted by Lt. Comdr. Andy Anderson, the executive officer, and Lt. Larry Yarborough, the operations officer. They had developed special skills in identifying drug boats.

In April the *Dauntless* was on patrol in the Yucatán Channel. What looked like a U.S. shrimper was sighted inside the 12-mile territorial sea. The cutter kept the shrimper in sight as the vessels moved north. Finally the Seventh District got permission from Mexico for Commander Murtagh to take a closer look. At 3,000 yards the shrimper ran up a U.S. flag; that simplified the authority-to-board issue. Soon the bridge crew could read *Blue Seas,* Hilton Head, S.C., on the transom of the fishing vessel. She was not on the lookout list. There was nothing suspicious so far. It was neither illegal nor unusual for American shrimpers to transit through Mexican waters.

Murtagh and his officers studied their prospective prey with binoculars. The shrimp nets were a mess. Gear on the trawl deck was tangled. She had not been fishing lately. Murtagh ordered the covers off the two .50-caliber machine guns. He also directed Lieutenant Yarborough to make radio contact with the *Blue Seas.* There was no reply to repeated calls, including some in Spanish. Radio aerials were clearly visible on the shrimper. No one was on deck. The pilothouse doors were closed. By now the cutter was close alongside the plodding shrimper. Commander Murtagh could see that the waterline had been painted high to make the vessel look empty. This was a good indication that the boat was hauling grass.

Suddenly the pilothouse door facing the cutter was thrown open. A bare-chested man in jeans appeared, followed by three others. They acted as if they had just crawled out of their bunks, with much rubbing of eyes and stretching. They were obviously building an excuse for their failure to answer the radio calls. Yarborough called them again on the radio. In response to his query about their last port of call, an individual replied, "Aruba." This was a bad answer. Aruba was a frequent stop for drug boats heading to the United States. When asked where they were bound, the voice said, "U.S.," but another voice was heard in the background saying, "Shut up! Mexico!" This was enough for Murtagh. He ordered the *Blue Seas* to stop immediately.

The USCGC *Dauntless* (WMEC-624), premier drug buster
(U.S. Naval Institute photograph)

Andy Anderson, XO of the *Dauntless*, went with the boarding party. The cutter's battery of heavy machine guns were trained on the shrimper for effect. It did not take long for Anderson and his crew to find what they fully expected to find: about 20 tons of Colombian pot crammed into the fish hold. The *Dauntless* chalked up her forty-first drug seizure.[32]

Unfortunately, the majority of motherships and smaller transport vessels made it through the thin white line of cutters. The *Break Sea* apparently made the delivery but not the round trip. Early on 6 June 1981 a Coast Guard aircraft spotted the 351-foot coastal freighter loitering near Bimini in the Florida Straits. The aircraft commander decided that the rusty freighter looked suspicious. A patrol boat chased the freighter to the southwest until the 210-foot *Steadfast* (WMEC-623) arrived. The *Break Sea* was obviously headed for the Yucatán Channel.

Repeated radio calls to the fleeing rustbucket produced no response. Queries to countries and references of registration failed to identify the vessel's nationality. She flew no flag. By the second day of the chase, which had now covered 350 nautical miles, a decision was made to declare the suspect stateless. The *Steadfast* was authorized to use disabling gunfire to stop the ship. Machine-gun bursts over the bow got no result. Now the order was passed to the gun crews: "Battery released for disabling fire!" The gunner laid a stream of .50-caliber fire into the ship's hull.

The *Break Sea*'s engine was rung down, and she glided to a stop, almost in the Yucatán Channel. A heavily armed boarding party climbed aboard. Only a few pounds of marijuana residue were found in the holds. The foreign master and twenty-five crewmen were arrested. The ship was seized and escorted to Miami.[33]

When the *Break Sea* arrived in Miami, shoreside intelligence indicated that part of the marijuana cargo was still aboard. It was also discovered that the vessel's real name was *Snowflake* and she was registered in Panama. A thorough search by Coast Guard and Customs officers found 350 pounds of marijuana tucked away in different parts of the ship. It was not enough for the U.S. attorney, who declined to prosecute. The crew was deported. The ship went to Customs for storage until forfeiture proceedings were complete. She was laid up for two years, then sold at auction. When the new owner was preparing the vessel for sale, he made a remarkable find: almost 3 tons of marijuana in the fuel tanks.[34]

This vital piece of intelligence concerning use of concealed compartments to hide large quantities of marijuana was denied to the operating forces for two full years. Heroin was known to be hidden in concealed spaces; remember Marcel Boucan and the French shrimp boat *Caprice des Temps* in 1972. But not marijuana! In 1981, pot smugglers depended on avoiding detection. The few who got caught were just a write-off, a cost of doing business. The people who put together the *Break Sea* (a.k.a. *Snowflake*) load were reading the tea leaves. Concealed compartments for huge grass loads were just a few years ahead.

The marijuana residue adrift in her holds and the size of the ship indicated that the *Break Sea* had successfully delivered a multi-ton load of grass somewhere along the U.S. coast. This platform had been removed from the grass pipeline, but a multitude of other ships lay in reserve at ports in South and Central America. The old and rusty ships with their throw-away Third World crews were a small expense in the lucrative pot trade of the early 1980s. The chance of interception was too small to be a serious consideration for international pot smugglers.

Things were changing in the Caribbean, making drug enforcement a little easier. On 13 November 1981 the United States and the United Kingdom entered into an agreement whereby the U.S. Coast Guard could board British vessels without an SNO if there was reason to believe that drugs were on board. If drugs were found, the United Kingdom would not object to seizure. The agreement was limited to the Gulf of Mexico, the Caribbean Sea, and adjacent parts of the Atlantic Ocean.[35] Other drug agreements with Caribbean basin countries followed, but none was as liberal as the 1981 U.K. agreement. Some said it was too bad so few British-flag vessels transported grass through the Caribbean.

In Florida and other areas, progress was made in identifying the people on this end who initiated and organized smuggling operations. The big news came with the federal indictment of 155 U.S. citizens in Florida, Georgia, and Louisiana on 12 March 1981. Operation Grouper, named after the synonym for marijuana bales (square grouper), was a long-term undercover investigation by drug agents. As many as fourteen different but connected smuggling organizations were taken down at one time. Some estimates claimed that the combined group was responsible for 30–40 percent of the marijuana coming into the United States from Colombia. Seizures included 1.5 million pounds of grass, $1 million in cash, thirty vessels, and two aircraft. Operation Grouper was the largest pot smuggler roundup so far.[36]

There were fewer seizures along the upper Atlantic seaboard in 1981. Seizures peaked in the third quarter (July, August, and September), as they consistently did each year; the reasons for this trend were unknown, but intelligence analysts suspected that it was related to the spring marijuana harvest in Colombia and decent weather in the North Atlantic during late summer and early fall. There were no 40,000- to 60,000-pound seizures in 1981 as in previous years.[37]

The most unusual case in northern waters began on 18 July, 60 miles southeast of Nantucket Island. A suspicious 70-foot Honduran fishing vessel was sighted by the 95-foot cutter *Cape Fairweather* (WPB-95314). The cutter hailed the *Coral I* and asked permission to board. Surprisingly, the captain agreed. The *Fairweather*'s boarding party soon found that the *Coral I* was loaded with pot. "So what?" said the pot boat captain. He refused to follow the cutter into U.S. waters. He ordered the Coasties off his boat and made to the southeast. The *Cape Fairweather* followed, waiting for an SNO to reboard and seize the vessel. Just after midnight the *Coral I*'s crew set the marijuana cargo afire. They also tried to scuttle the boat. Still no SNO from Honduras. By now the pot boat was almost 120 miles east-southeast of Montauk Point, Long Island. As the grass blazed and the *Coral I* settled lower in the water, the Coast Guardsmen reacted in their lifesaving role. They reboarded the vessel, extinguished the fire, and stopped the flooding. The *Cape Fairweather* towed the now derelict vessel to the Coast Guard station at Montauk Point. The twelve foreigners aboard the *Coral I* were thus rescued. So were 22,000 pounds of Colombian grass.[38]

The oceans occasionally give up their secrets in mysterious ways. On 24 October 1981 several 130-pound bales of hashish, made from the resinous secretions of the marijuana plant, washed up on a beach in Ocean County, New Jersey. About the same time, the tug *Sunfish* reported floating bales off New York Harbor. Customs sent a small boat to retrieve the bales and mark the spot. These floating bales were also found to be hash. It was believed that the mysterious bales came from a sunken ship or boat. The Coast Guard dispatched the buoy tender *Red Beech* (WLM-686) with a diving team. After two days of searching, the tender found a small freighter on the bottom 12 miles off Sea Bright, New Jersey, in 100 feet of water. The unidentified vessel had extensive damage. There was no recent record of any vessel in distress in the area of the wreck. Divers recovered over thirty bales. Authorities estimated the total hash cargo to be about 10,000 pounds.[39]

How long the ship had been down was anybody's guess, but the bales were in good shape, indicating recent arrival. It was not the first time, and certainly not the last, that floaters would lead drug sleuths to a source. Floating bales were usually the result of drug boats jettisoning their contraband cargo after being spooked by enforcement units. In this case the contraband carrier met with more than a close encounter with some unknown avenger.

In the usual Pacific rhythm, seizures rose again on the West Coast but did not equal the peak of 1979. Eleven vessels with 254,700 pounds of pot were seized in 1981. Three of those vessels accounted for 75 percent of the marijuana seized. Two were intercepted in July. The pleasure craft *Tiki* was caught by Coast Guard and Customs officials near Bellingham, Washington, with intelligence from DEA and the RCMP. The *Tiki* was trying to off-load 60,000 pounds of Colombian pot. The 150-foot Honduran motor vessel *Islander* was seized by the Coast Guard 165 miles west of Eureka, California, with 74,000 pounds of pot, the largest catch of the year. In September the motor vessel *Polaris* was boarded 100 miles southwest of San Francisco. She had about 60,000 pounds of pot, but the vessel sank from scuttling before she could be brought in.[40]

An air-smuggling event at the end of 1981 was momentous. The intensified interdiction effort over South Florida forced some air smugglers to take different routes. One was across the Gulf of Mexico to central Florida. An inbound aircraft on this track came in too high and too fast. Bells rang in the Air Defense Command, and two F-16 fighters responded. They chased the suspect back and forth over the Tampa Bay area for two hours, breaking the sound barrier. While this was going on, the smuggler co-pilot was frantically throwing duffle bags of coke out the door. Some landed in Tampa Bay and the nearby Gulf. Fishermen found coke bags the next day and turned them in.[41]

Max Mermelstein, responsible to the infamous Colombian drug lord Jorge Ochoa for safe delivery of the load, was frantic; he knew how the Medellin gang handled failures. Max decided to bluff it out. He called Ochoa to report the fiasco. Max opened with "We learned an important lesson today—coke floats!"[42] Properly wrapped coke did indeed float. It was not long before cocaine pilots were making regular drops over water. That would open a whole new maritime drug problem.

In December 1981 Congress decided to give the military greater leeway in helping civilian enforcement stem the flow of drugs. They amended Posse Comitatus with a new Chapter 18 of Title 10, United States Code, governing military assistance to law enforcement. The legislation reaffirmed the traditional prohibition against direct military participation in law enforcement by arrest, searches, and seizures. It gave specific authority for indirect assistance, including sharing of intelligence collected during military operations, use of military equipment and facilities, and training of civilian law enforcement personnel. This assistance could not adversely affect military preparedness.

The new law was implemented by Department of Defense Directive 5525.5, "DoD Cooperation with Civilian Law Enforcement Officials."[43]

What did the amendment to Posse Comitatus do for the drug war at sea? It gave the navy a clear role in providing combat ships as platforms for Coast Guard tactical law enforcement teams (TACLETs). It also allowed the routine use of navy aircraft, regular and reserve, in detecting drug boats. The amendment authorized use of the air force's aerostat balloon at Cudjoe Key with its over-the-horizon radar to detect and track smugglers approaching Florida. One of the best things to come out of the military's highly publicized entry into the drug war was confusion to the enemy. Maritime drug smugglers would henceforth look at navy ships and aircraft as a threat to their welfare.

By the end of 1981 Miami was under siege by drug traffickers. They were murdering each other with machine guns on city streets in broad daylight. FBI statistics showed that Dade County was number one on the nation's crime list. A survey by the group Miami Citizens Against Crime revealed that 38.9 percent of Miami residents would leave South Florida if given the opportunity. Almost two million Americans in South Florida lived in fear. They went to the White House for help.[44]

Seizures at sea declined. The Cuban boatlift's dilution of Coast Guard interdiction efforts was the probable cause. A concentration of navy and Coast Guard ships in the vicinity of Cuba because of Soviet troops and the boatlift made some grass boaters avoid South Florida; they moved to the Gulf and the upper Atlantic. All of this may have contributed to an increase in maritime grass deliveries to the Pacific coast, but Atlantic-Gulf marijuana imports remained at a much higher level than before the flood. Smuggling was now an organized and well-run business. Coast Guard interdiction forces were unable to intercept smugglers in substantial numbers. Drug trafficking was not yet a national concern. According to many longtime grass smugglers, this was the apex of their careers.

5

Battle Lines
1982–1983

We're rejecting the helpless attitude that drug use is so rampant
that we're defenseless to do anything about it. We're taking
down the surrender flag that has flown over so many drug
efforts; we're running up the battle flag.

PRESIDENT RONALD REAGAN, 24 JUNE 1982

T
he year 1982 marked a watershed in the drug war. People in South Florida in particular, and in the nation as a whole, finally decided that enough was enough. The lobbying by Miami Citizens Against Crime got President Reagan's attention. On 28 January 1982 he created the South Florida Task Force (SFTF) under the direction of Vice President George Bush. Never before had the White House taken a hand in a specific law enforcement effort.

Within weeks, hundreds of federal law enforcement agents and officers were detailed to South Florida. More Coast Guard cutters were sent south to bolster the Seventh District. Three old navy salvage tugs were de-mothballed and commissioned in the Coast Guard fleet. Three new experimental surface-effect ships were also procured for duty out of Key West. To meet the expected demand for increased prosecutions, additional assistant U.S. attorneys and federal judges were assigned to the Southern District of Florida.[1]

The SFTF did not command the antidrug forces. It was established to coordinate the activities of all agencies involved. A coordination center was installed in the Miami federal building with two primary functions: interdiction operations and intelligence. It was staffed by the Customs Service, the Coast Guard, and the military. DEA and the FBI took part to a limited extent. Charles F. Rinkevich was the on-scene task force coordinator.[2] Rinkevich's title gave him clout in dealing with the interagency rivalries plaguing drug interdiction and enforcement efforts. Appearances by the vice president at SFTF functions reinforced Rinkevich's position. He was recognized and respected as the White House's man in the trenches. The battle lines were drawn.

The SFTF was not without detractors. Democratic senator Dennis DeConcini of Arizona charged that the task force was merely displacing the drug problem to other parts of the country. Others on Capitol Hill complained that the task force's funding was a budgetary shell game. No new funds had been appropriated; money was simply transferred from other programs. Opponents were not limited to politicians. DEA administrator Francis Mullen felt that the task force might solve a political problem in Florida but would cause DEA to neglect important drug investigations in other places. The plan called for DEA to handle follow-up investigations after seizures of drug vessels and aircraft. DEA officials felt that their agents would be more productive penetrating drug rings at a higher level and making conspiracy cases against kingpins. Mullen did not agree with the drug interdiction plans of retired navy admiral Daniel Murphy, Vice President Bush's chief of staff. Viewing the program from a military prospective, Murphy was instrumental in persuading the Pentagon to provide resources and intelligence. If we could detect Soviet submarines, why not drug smugglers? Murphy's concept of using military technology to track potential smuggler boats and aircraft irked some traditional lawmen like Mullen. He asserted that identifying potential targets without specific information was a waste of time. Friction between Murphy and Mullen caused DEA's support for the SFTF to be less than enthusiastic.[3]

The General Accounting Office (GAO) found that more than 60 percent of interdiction cases were not followed up by investigations. To rectify this situation, the attorney general granted limited authorization to designated Customs special agents to investigate cases under DEA direction, but only in the SFTF area of operations. The GAO report saw the fragmentation of federal efforts as a longstanding problem in drug enforcement.[4]

The El Paso Intelligence Center was a DEA asset that played an important role in the task force concept from the very beginning. EPIC is a multiagency effort managed by DEA with representatives from Customs, the Coast Guard, and other federal enforcement agencies. Each state has a designated police agency that serves as a clearinghouse for other state, county, and local agency queries to EPIC. The center's charter directs EPIC to provide overall intelligence on drug movements by land, sea, and air throughout the world as they relate to the United States; to provide time-sensitive information on drug movements; and to support other programs of interest to EPIC's participating agencies.

At the time, EPIC was organized into two components: the Watch Section and the Analysis Section. The Watch published lookouts on suspect smuggling conveyances. When a suspect was sighted, the Watch notified the agency that posted the lookout and other interested agencies. The Analysis Section developed tactical intelligence reports on drug movements such as criminal organizations, smuggling routes, concealment techniques, and other pertinent information. In 1982 EPIC handled an average of seventeen thousand intelligence transactions monthly.[5] With improved data-processing and physical facilities, EPIC functions in much the same way today.

The amendments to Posse Comitatus gave routine military help to drug enforcement through the mechanisms established by the SFTF.

Helping in the war against drugs was a new role and mission for the armed forces.[6] It was appreciated by the civilian enforcement agencies, but there were serious concerns. Many enforcement officials believed that participation by the Department of Defense (DoD) might be unmanageable. DoD had seemingly unlimited resources. Many senior lawmen feared that a very heavy tail could end up wagging the dog.

DoD personnel assigned to the task force coordination center in Miami included the first full-time representative of the national foreign intelligence community (NFIC). This man was an expert in the collection and analysis of communications intelligence. He played a major role in putting together a system that would greatly help the interdiction of both maritime and air smugglers. Security dictated the exclusion of any publicity about the program. Many otherwise knowledgeable law enforcement officials would later question the contributions of the NFIC to the drug interdiction effort. Most were unaware that the communications intelligence program existed. They did not have a need to know. That kind of operational security was new and irksome to civilian enforcers. Even those who knew something about the program responded with "Don't tell me anything that I can't use in court." From their point of view, it was a valid argument. The challenge was to isolate potential government witnesses from sources of classified information used to detect smugglers.

Despite political posturing, continuing interagency battles, and civilian fears about a military takeover, the SFTF was an unprecedented success in multiagency coordination and cooperation. People with a common goal were working together across agency lines. The SFTF was not a panacea, but it was better than anything produced so far in the drug war. Almost everyone agreed—including Democratic congressman Glenn English of Oklahoma, who chaired the 1983 congressional hearings on the administration's drug interdiction effort— that the direct involvement and leadership of the vice president was the key to its success.[7]

The national focus on drug enforcement in South Florida and the Caribbean made governors and senior police officials in other parts of the country nervous. It was common knowledge that maritime drug smugglers were targeting other coastal areas to avoid the enforcement buildup in the Sunshine State. In July 1982 the Southern Governors' Conference convened in Hilton Head, South Carolina. The governors agreed that international drug trafficking was an issue of major regional concern. Their concerns spread to other states and attracted the attention of Congress and the administration.[8] The political heat was turned up for more drug warriors nationwide.

President Reagan responded to the escalating narcotics threat on 14 October 1982 by establishing thirteen Organized Crime Drug Enforcement Task Forces (OCDETFs) under the attorney general. These OCDETFs were in key locations throughout the United States and had orders to target major organizations that financed and distributed drugs. Task forces worked independent of but in close cooperation with the offices of the U.S. attorney in their respective areas. They were staffed with Justice Department attorneys; DEA, Customs, and FBI agents; state and local officers; and representatives of other agencies.[9] They differed from the SFTF, which emphasized the interdiction of drugs approaching the United States. The OCDETFs focused on kingpins by using standard investigative techniques. Some OCDETFs set impressive indictment records over the next few years. They had little direct involvement with the drug war at sea, except for some Pacific seizures, but they helped to dismantle big maritime smuggling organizations.

For the sea war the most important part of the 1982 enforcement buildup in South Florida was the assignment of extra medium-endurance cutters. There were now nine of these workhorses home-ported in the Seventh Coast Guard District. Even though three of the newcomers were very slow World War II–vintage tugs from the navy mothball fleet, they had long legs. The district was also supported by one or two 378-foot high-endurance cutters deployed south by the Atlantic Area Command. By the end of the year the Coast Guard had commissioned two very fast 110-foot surface-effect cutters (SESs) and assigned them to Key West. Another came the next year. They were the first single-mission vessels designated for the drug war. Long-range navy patrol aircraft also supplemented the Seventh District's nine fixed-wing aircraft and fifteen helicopters used for surveillance.

The Coast Guard maintained a more or less continuous presence in the Caribbean choke points where most of the marijuana came north in the ragtag fleet of motherships. Smuggler vessels went through the passes, giving cutters a better chance of interception. The Seventh District's seizures peaked in 1982, at 145 vessels containing almost 2.4 million pounds of marijuana. Rear Adm. D. C. Thompson, the Seventh District commander, credited the impressive record with increased presence in the choke points and enforcement coordination through the South Florida Task Force. He cautioned that intelligence showed some smugglers breaking out of the Caribbean further to the east and circling around behind the Bahamas. Admiral Thompson predicted that these routes would lead to the Middle Atlantic States and New England.[10]

In May 1982 a navy and Coast Guard operations order spelled out how the navy would help the Coast Guard. Part of the order covered the deployment of Coast Guard tactical law enforcement teams, or TACLETs, aboard the gray ships. On 4 June 1982 a navy ship helped the Coast Guard in a drug seizure for the first time. The guided-missile destroyer USS *Farragut* (DDG-37) took charge of two vessels seized by a Coast Guard cutter in the Caribbean. The *Farragut* towed the U.S.–registered *Miss Cecile* with 30,000 pounds of pot and escorted the stateless *Rio Panuco* with over 100,000 pounds to San Juan, Puerto Rico. The minesweeper USS *Fidelity* (MSO-443) relieved another cutter of the U.S. vessel *Yvette* with 13,000 pounds of grass and delivered her to Key West.[11]

The navy did more than tow and escort; it also provided muscle. On 8 September 1982 two 95-foot Coast Guard cutters began chasing the 125-foot suspect freighter *Mont Baron* off the Georgia coast. Intelligence said the vessel was armed and the crew might resist boarding. Two days into the chase, it became obvious that the *Mont Baron* was not going to stop. One cutter was almost out of fuel. A call went out to the navy for help. The guided-missile frigate USS *Clifton E. Sprague* (FFG-16) responded on a flank bell. The *Sprague* refueled the 95-footer and joined the chase. The navy then dispatched two A-7 attack aircraft, which made below-mast-level passes on the suspect. The people on the *Mont Baron* finally decided the odds were against them and surrendered. The Coast Guard boarding team found marijuana residue in the suspect's hold. The residue and the prolonged refusal to stop were reason to seize the ship and arrest the eleven people on board. The message to the smugglers in the navy's show of force was to beware of gray ships prowling the drug routes.[12] It was good propaganda but more fiction than fact; only a few navy ships were out with Coast Guard TACLETs.

By far the greatest demonstration of U.S. sea power in the drug war occurred in November 1982. A Coast Guard TACLET was deployed aboard the supercarrier USS *Nimitz* (CVN-68) exercising in the

The USS *Mississippi* (CGN-40), the first navy ship to seize a drug boat
(Official U.S. Navy photograph by PH3 Jim Swanstrom)

western Caribbean. On the morning of 20 November an E-2C Hawk-eye early-warning aircraft from the *Nimitz* spotted the oceangoing tug *Recife* 70 miles off the Colombian coast. The aircraft crew photographed the tug, which flew the flag of Honduras. The TACLET officer, Lt. Patrick L. Shuck, USCG, was suspicious. With permission from the battle group commander, Shuck and his seven-man team were transferred by helicopter from the *Nimitz* to the nuclear-powered missile cruiser USS *Mississippi* (CGN-40) to run down the suspect. Responding to a radio query, someone on the tug said they were on a rescue mission. The persistent Coast Guard officer was not convinced. He requested more information on the tug through the Coast Guard SNO process. Honduran officials denied that the *Recife* was theirs. The tug became a stateless vessel, subject to Coast Guard boarding. With all her weapons, the formidable *Mississippi* dwarfed the little tug. The *Recife* hove to at the first order. Within minutes the TACLET was aboard, doing a standard sweep procedure. The *Recife* was seized with 50,650 pounds of Colombian marijuana. Her master and ten crewmen were arrested. Score one for the *Nimitz* battle group![13]

The *Recife* case was a legal test for the Posse Comitatus Act amendment. The drug tug's crew went to trial in January 1983 in the U.S. district court at San Juan, Puerto Rico. Counsel for the defendants submitted a motion to dismiss for violation of Posse Comitatus. The defendants contended that it was unlawful for a navy ship to serve as a conveyance for a Coast Guard boarding team. The court rejected the motion and upheld the government's position that it was in full compliance with the amended Posse Comitatus. The jury returned guilty verdicts against the *Recife*'s crew. The Department of Defense, navy, and Coast Guard had a sound legal precedent to continue using navy assets in the drug war at sea.[14]

In the air, navy P-3 Orions from reserve Patrol Wing Atlantic were working with the Coast Guard and Customs to identify and track maritime smugglers. Orions were usually deployed to Puerto Rico for drug interdiction operations. P-3 patrols in November 1982 identified 217 vessels; 35 were classified as suspicious vessels by the SFTF's operation center. Intercepts by law enforcement units accounted for the seizure of 21 tons of marijuana.[15] The southern ocean was no longer the sole province of the smuggler.

The navy was out in force to support the drug interdiction effort, but its main job was training for war. Its institutional heritage and the caveats in the Posse Comitatus amendment did not allow it to do otherwise. The mainstay of the maritime drug battle line was still the white cutters with the red stripes. The cuttermen knew that for every drug boat they took, nine more got through. But they were good sailors. They had their orders, and they would persevere.

Detractors to the contrary, the South Florida Task Force had an impact on drug smuggling. It caused major shifts in traffic routes to other areas. By October 1982 over 100 tons of marijuana had been confiscated in six major seizures in the New England area; only 9 tons had been seized during 1981. In the New York sector, 363 tons of grass were seized in the same time frame, compared with 70 tons in all of 1981. Northern seizures confirmed that motherships were still getting out of the Caribbean and into the Atlantic for the run north.[16] No one doubted that the smugglers would do whatever they could to outflank the SFTF defense perimeter.

In the summer of 1982 a secondary patrol line north of Bermuda would have been productive. The motherships breaking out of the Caribbean through the eastern passes were coming north well offshore.

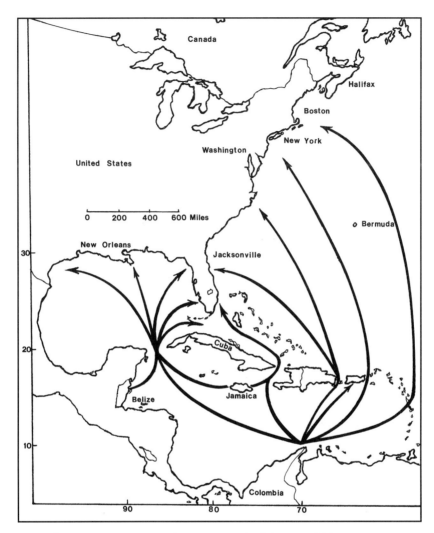

Typical marijuana routes to the eastern United States, 1980s

Intelligence was improving, and there were a few cutters controlled by the Coast Guard Atlantic Area Command to work in blue water. The first significant hit was the Netherlands Antilles freighter *Moby Dick*, intercepted 325 miles northwest of Bermuda on 3 June with about 100,000 pounds of grass by the USCGC *Cherokee* (WMEC-165), an ex-navy tug. Two weeks later the Venezuelan motor vessel *Ricardo* with 38,000 pounds of pot was captured 290 miles north-northwest of the British island.

That summer there was a record Atlantic seizure. The Danish trawler *Trio Senior* (a.k.a. *Grimurkamban*) was taken with almost 120,000 pounds of marijuana. The high-endurance cutter *Bibb* (WHEC-31), one of the old breed, discreetly tracked the 116-foot suspect about 400 miles due north of Bermuda. Clearance to board the big trawler was granted on 17 July approximately 58 miles west of Nantucket Island, where she was seized. Only four days later the 55-foot U.S. fishing vessel *Shanti* was detected in roughly the same position where *Trio Senior* had been first sighted. The *Shanti*'s crew dumped at least 136 bales before they were stopped and searched. The Coast Guard boarding party found 7,400 pounds of pot still on board. Five days after *Shanti*, on 26 July, the U.S.–registered *Surprise* was nabbed 200 miles north-northeast of Bermuda with 45,000 pounds of pot. In just two months five vessels had been intercepted passing Bermuda with over 300,000 pounds of marijuana.[17]

The motherships could stay in deep water, but the pickup boats had to make a run for the beach. Inshore seizures showed where major grass loads were headed. North Carolina and the Chesapeake were important destinations for offshore marijuana shipments throughout 1982. The New York City area was a prime target for deep-sea motherships, and Massachusetts received its fair share of maritime pot to supply the big Boston market.[18]

Motherships normally off-loaded to local fishing vessels and yachts well offshore. The case of the 71-foot Florida snapper-grouper boat *Tiki X* is illustrative. Police in the town of Fairhaven, acting on an informant's tip, followed a tractor-trailer to Mullen's Wharf on 6 November. They watched over 30 tons of marijuana being unloaded from the *Tiki X* into the huge truck. They went for the truck. The Coast Guard was called to take down the boat as she left the wharf. Twenty-six people were arrested. The investigation was a case for Bristol County's Drug Task Force. Soon after the *Tiki X,* the motor vessel *Dominable* was apprehended just off Rockland, Maine, with 60,500 pounds of grass. By the end of the year over 420,000 pounds of marijuana had been seized in or near New England, almost ten times the amount taken in all of 1981. The U.S. attorney for Maine, Richard Cohen, explained that the drastic rise in pot seizures was a result of smuggler dislocation because of the South Florida Task Force. While Cohen was making his news release, President Reagan was in Miami presenting a Presidential Unit Citation to the cutter *Dauntless* for a two-year drug seizure record. The cutter had made 126 arrests and seized 459,000 pounds of grass. The *Dauntless* accounted for almost as much marijuana as the total seized around New England for the same period.[19]

The day after the *Tiki X* seizure, the ancient 1936-commissioned cutter *Duane* (WHEC-33) intercepted the 240-foot Panamanian freighter *Biscayne Freeze* with 63,980 pounds of marijuana about 270 miles north-northwest of Bermuda. After receiving an SNO to board the vessel, the *Duane* had to fire .50-caliber rounds across the freighter's bow to bring her to a stop. Twenty-two Colombians were arrested. Investigators believed that the *Tiki X* had picked up her 60,000 pounds of grass from the *Biscayne Freeze* during the first days of November.[20] If their assumption was correct, the freighter had been carrying almost 124,000 pounds of Colombian grass, a record for the North Atlantic. If the transfer occurred near the seizure position of the *Biscayne Freeze,* the *Tiki X* had to run about 360 miles to deliver her cargo to Fairhaven, perhaps a record off-load trip of over 700 miles. Whether or not the fishing boat met the freighter, the seizure of the *Biscayne Freeze* north of Bermuda showed that motherships were still transiting well offshore in late 1982.

Two facts are evident from maritime seizure statistics for the northeastern United States in 1982. First, seizures peaked that year, with a total of thirty-four vessels carrying 727,735 pounds of marijuana. The amount was more than double that seized in the two previous peak years of 1978 (318,475 pounds) and 1980 (310,780 pounds). Northeastern maritime pot seizures in 1983 (546,471 pounds) would not be far behind, but the 1982 record would not be exceeded.

The second noteworthy fact from the 1982 statistics concerns the number of vessels seized far offshore. Eleven of the thirty-four vessels seized were in the offshore category, including some seized more than 25 miles from the coast. That's eleven in a single year; between 1975 and 1981, by contrast, there had been a total of only fourteen seizures in the offshore category. Five of the eleven offshore seizures were in blue water north of Bermuda.[21] There can be no question about the marijuana motherships flanking the South Florida Task Force patrol line, probably through the eastern passes from the Caribbean, and transiting north by Bermuda. From the huge increase in grass seizures in the Northeast during 1982 by a small patrol force, it is clear that the SFTF effort was displacing maritime smugglers in a material way.

This was not the case in the Pacific. Maritime marijuana seizures on the U.S. Pacific side dropped to a mere 14,373 pounds in 1982, the lowest since 1975. Two vessels were seized dockside in January: the fishing vessel *Sunburst* in Huntington Harbor with 5,495 pounds of pot, and the pleasure craft *Fourwinds* at Marina Del Rey with 5,668 pounds. The only other seizure of note that year was the sailing vessel *Orca,* intercepted in June in the North Pacific almost 1,000 miles south of the Aleutian Islands and over 3,000 miles from the U.S. mainland.[22] The interception was a cold hit; there was no prior intelligence on the vessel. It accounted for only 3,210 pounds of pot, from a Southeast Asian source, and is worth mentioning only because of subsequent events.

The *Orca* was sighted by the high-endurance cutter *Boutwell* (WHEC-719) on 20 June 1982 on a routine Alaska fisheries patrol. The boarding and seizure were uneventful. Three people on the 39-foot sloop were arrested and transferred to the cutter. The *Boutwell* took the sloop in tow and headed for Kodiak. While en route, strange things began to happen to the cutter's main propulsion machinery; something was causing the reduction gears to overheat. The ship was stopped so that the engineers could take things apart to find the cause. As the *Boutwell* drifted, a young crewmen tried to slide down the towline to board the *Orca.* He was washed off the line and drowned before a boat could reach him. The engineers then discovered that sand or metal filings had been deliberately poured into the gears. The *Boutwell* had been sabotaged! An investigation revealed that three of the cutter's crew, including the man who drowned, had disabled the ship and planned to steal the pot-laden sailboat and make their way to the coast.[23] This harebrained plan with little chance of success cost one perpetrator his life. The incident further highlights the corrupting influence of narcotics on our society, even in the ranks of the dedicated interdiction forces.

The year 1982 marked the apex in maritime marijuana seizures. Coast Guardsmen seized 3.5 million pounds of grass, a record that has not been equaled. They also seized 173 vessels and arrested over a thousand people.[24] Perhaps more marijuana was at sea in 1982 than in any previous year. Maritime forces were improving interdiction strategies and tactics. More ships and aircraft were in the right places. The seagoing drug warriors were getting better at identifying suspect vessels. Some credit for the record year goes to the coordination efforts of the South Florida Task Force. The SFTF also promoted improved intelligence on drug vessel movements and interdiction support by the military. Almost 70 percent of the maritime marijuana seized was within the SFTF area.

In 1982 the volume of grass taken at sea was overwhelming evidence that marijuana destined for the United States was primarily being delivered by vessels from Colombia and Jamaica. The National Narcotics Intelligence Consumers Committee estimated that 13,215 metric tons (29,139,075 pounds) of marijuana were available for consumption here in 1982. The NNICC estimated that Colombia was the source of 67 percent of the imports, Jamaica 19 percent, and Mexico only 6 percent.[25] The amount of marijuana seized in 1982 was 4,469,542 pounds. Sea interdictions accounted for 93 percent, land interdictions for 1 percent, and air interdictions for 6 percent.[26] Marijuana seized by the interdiction effort was only 15 percent of the estimated total available for consumption. Of special importance, however, was the role that sea forces played in disrupting the marijuana flood.

Cocaine was not a serious maritime threat in 1982, but the explosion of imports that had begun in 1980 went unabated. It was coming by air through South Florida in ever-increasing amounts. DEA knew that Colombia's Medellin traffickers had formed a cartel led by Jorge Ochoa, Pablo Escobar, and Carlos Lehder. These miscreants planned to mass-market the drug in the United States. Their goal was to handle all aspects of the trade, from production in Colombia to distribution here. They had a good incentive: in 1982, cocaine sold wholesale for $47,000–60,000 per kilo.[27]

"Coke Floats" Max Mermelstein, the Medellin transporter based in Miami, was testing his theory in Long Island, Bahamas. After one of his planes was forced to shower Tampa Bay with coke parcels, he became convinced that air drops to boats were a plausible alternative method of delivery. Max selected a 26-foot Duskie open fisherman, customized with long-range gas tanks and compartments big enough for 200 kilos, for the initial trials. He used 200-horsepower Evinrude outboards but put 140 hp covers on the engines to make them look smaller. The boats were equipped with used fishing gear, ice, bait, and fish bought in the Bahamas. They were also fitted with required safety equipment. No "Miami Vice" Cigarettes, Magnums, or Scarabs for Max; they attracted attention.[28]

Max and his crew used flour wrapped in plastic and packed in duffle bags for the first trials. They calculated that the bags would hit the water at 75–80 miles per hour when dumped from a height of 125 to 150 feet. The first test was a failure. The bags leaked, and the phony coke was soaked. They added two more layers of plastic and wrapped the packages with heavy-duty filament tape. It worked; they were ready. The first real coke delivery from Colombia arrived on schedule. Down came the bags where the Duskies waited. The boat crews watched in horror as a white powder slick formed on the surface of the turquoise water. Ten of the twenty-six packages had ruptured on impact. It cost the cartel over $2 million. Max had to do some explaining to Ochoa again. It turned out that the people in Colombia had not wrapped the packages properly.[29]

They finally got it right. The drops were made so that the Duskies could make the run to Florida on Sunday afternoons. They looked like weekend fishermen returning from the Bahamas. Fishing tournaments were also used as cover for the runs. Mermelstein's air-to-boat delivery system was just out of the shakedown stage when the SFTF got cranked up. His crew set up a radio monitoring station in a penthouse overlooking Haulover Cut to Miami. They used scanners to listen to enforcement activity and maintained lookouts with telescopes and night-vision glasses. Spotter planes tracked boat runs to Florida. The Maule Lake Marina on Biscayne Bay was used for landings. Boats were trailered to a warehouse where the coke was unloaded.

Max lasted until 1985. When he was arrested, he flipped and became a government witness. In 1987 he was sentenced to time served and placed on lifetime special parole. Max wrote a book about his smuggling career published in 1990.[30]

Cocaine air drops to small boats in the Bahamas became routine. They were a difficult interdiction problem. The planes landed empty, usually in the Bahamas, if they landed at all on the north end of the run. Drop zones were shifted at the last minute from one side of an island or reef line to another, frustrating surface patrol vessels. Pickup boats were extremely fast, were highly maneuverable, and could run on-the-plane in a few feet of water. They could also outrun anything in the surface patrol force. Even with good intelligence, interception

Suspect go-fast boat anchored by Ragged Island in the Bahamas—the new threat *(Official U.S. Coast Guard photograph)*

of air drop pickup boats was problematical at best. The most efficient chase vehicle for air drops was the helicopter or light aircraft, which usually had to come from Miami and be on station at the right time. If the smuggler boats detected the surveillance aircraft, they could dash in to one of the Bahama cays and wait things out or stash the load. It is not surprising that maritime cocaine seldom appeared in the interdiction statistics of the early 1980s.

Cocaine aircraft also began overflying Cuba to reach drop zones in the Bahamas around this time. The planes flew less than 30 miles to reach some drop areas after clearing Cuba.[31] The first quasi-official charge by the United States against Cuba for complicity in drug smuggling came on 5 November 1982. A federal grand jury in Miami indicted four Cuban officials and ten Cuban Americans. The indicted included Cuban Vice Adm. Aldo Santamaria Cuadrado; Rene Rodriguez Cruz, a member of the Central Committee of the Communist Party; Fernando Ravelo Renedo, former ambassador to Colombia; and Gonzalo Bassols, former counselor at the Bogotá embassy. Also

indicted was Jaime Guillot Lara, the known international drug traf-
ficker from Colombia accused of smuggling arms from Cuba to left-
ist guerillas in his country. Admiral Santamaria Cuadrado and Rene
Rodriguez Cruz were close associates of President Fidel Castro. The
Cuban Interests Section in Washington said, "Lies, all lies."[32] However, evidence of Cuban officials directly involved in smuggling drugs
through the island would build over the years.

A shaft of light pierced the storm clouds over the Bahamas in April
1982: OPBAT was born, with little fanfare. It was initiated by a contingent of the SFTF, with DEA as the primary agency. The U.S. Army
provided two helicopters. OPBAT stood for Operation Bahamas and
Turks/Caicos, a joint U.S.–Bahamas drug interdiction project. Helos
ferried Bahamian police detachments to the islands identified as air
and boat transshipment sites. Some said that Prime Minister Lyndon
Pindling agreed to the project to counter charges against him and
other Bahamian officials of accepting bribes from traffickers. OPBAT
was credited with the seizure of over 49 tons of marijuana, twenty-
one vessels, nineteen aircraft, and $89,000 in drug assets during its
first year, as well as the arrest of seventy-five people. It was a good
start. In 1983 the U.S. Air Force assumed responsibility for supporting the project with two UH-1N helicopters. The agreement with the
Bahamas and the United Kingdom for the Turks and Caicos Islands
also gave U.S. interdiction forces the right to fly in the islands' air
space and patrol their contiguous waters.[33]

By the end of 1982, federal efforts had reduced crime in Miami to
an acceptable level.[34] The same could not be said for the little isolated
town of Everglades City, 78 miles to the west across the River of Grass.
Two years earlier the secretary of the interior had told that community
to prepare for a ban on commercial fishing in and around Everglades
National Park. Much of their fishing was done in the waters affected,
so he suggested they find some other source of income. They did:
smuggling marijuana.[35]

DEA and the Florida Department of Law Enforcement (FDLE)
focused on Everglades City. With the help of a few Collier County
investigators, feds and state agents had painstakingly gathered evidence on the Everglades off-loaders for a number of years. It was difficult work. There is only one road leading to the town from the
Tamiami Trail through the Glades. State Highway 29 crosses a canal
bridge as it enters the community. To the right after the bridge, a small

convenience store with an outside pay phone was a favorite place to post a lookout, who identified any incoming out-of-town vehicles. The investigators persevered. Operation Everglades hit the community like a storm on 7 July 1983. Twenty-eight grass smugglers were arrested on the first sweep. The investigation went into the next year with thirty more arrests.[36] Off-load organizer Ambrose Weldon went down in the second phase. He appealed and was free on bond until 1987. During that time Weldon organized about sixteen off-loads with seven successful deliveries. Operation Everglades caused only a temporary disruption of grass deliveries.

Congressman Glenn English completed his hearings on the administration's drug interdiction efforts in July 1983. The hearings were held in Miami, New Orleans, El Paso, and San Diego. English and his subcommittee spoke with almost everyone in the drug interdiction program. They published a 589-page report, *Review of the Administration's Drug Interdiction Efforts*. The subcommittee found fault with the air interdiction program but offered no specifics for improving sea interdiction. They did provide a milestone summary of where we were in 1982. Near the end of the hearings Congressman Ronald D. Coleman (D., Texas) made prophetic statements. In San Diego on 9 July Coleman predicted:

> I am more than ever convinced that the adaptability of the smuggler that the chairman referred to is evidenced. I am convinced that the southwestern United States and the 2,000 mile stretch of border of land from Brownsville, Texas to San Diego, California will become an even greater trafficking area than we have ever known before and I think part of that is because of the efforts of the Coast Guard in the Gulf, along with the South Florida Task Force that will necessarily force drug smuggling to new and varied routes.[37]

The southwestern border would become the primary target for cocaine air smugglers in a very few years. Ships can't go that way.

The task force, major increases in federal enforcement in South Florida, and record grass seizures in 1982 caused some smugglers to take alternative routes to the United States. It was enough to make political forces in other parts of the country hammer the White House for added protection. The demands of politicians, supported by media exposés of new drug threats in the Gulf, the Middle Atlantic, and the

Northeast, caused a dilemma for the Reagan administration. The Southeast was still the primary target for drug smugglers. The president was attempting to reduce government spending in all areas except defense. How could a law-and-order president, who had just run up the battle flag over the drug interdiction effort, ignore pleas for help?

The answer was to expand the South Florida Task Force concept along all our borders. There was general consensus in political circles and in most of the law enforcement community that the SFTF had improved agency coordination. Funding and personnel came from participating agencies. Expanding the SFTF to the rest of the nation would be a drain on the personnel assets of line enforcement agencies, but soldiers, sailors, airmen, and marines could help man SFTF-type centers.

On 23 March 1983 the president announced the formation of the National Narcotics Border Interdiction System (NNBIS) to interdict narcotics. A White House press release defined the general organization and functions of NNBIS. It would be headed by the vice president, who would chair an executive board including the secretaries of state, treasury, defense, and transportation, the attorney general, the counselor to the president, the director of central intelligence, and the director of the White House Drug Abuse Policy Office. In setting down the mission of NNBIS, the key word was *coordination*. NNBIS would coordinate, not direct, the work of those federal agencies with responsibilities and capabilities for the interdiction of narcotics. The announcement said, "NNBIS will complement but not replicate the duties of the regional Drug Enforcement Task Forces (OCDETFs) operated by the Department of Justice." The function of interdiction, primarily a Coast Guard and Customs mission (later to include the Border Patrol) with DoD and intelligence community help, was separated from the investigative function. That was mainly the mission of DEA and the OCDETFs with input from the FBI.

The vice president would oversee drug interdiction; the attorney general would supervise drug investigations. The only real change was the expanded role of the VP. He would, however, have no oversight for drug investigations or drug use reduction. The announcement specified that "NNBIS will monitor suspected smuggling activity originating outside national borders and destined for the United States, and will coordinate agencies' seizures of contraband and arrest of persons involved in illegal drug importation." In closing, the White House release said, "The coordinating board for NNBIS will be headed by Adm. Daniel J. Murphy, chief of staff to the vice president, who has chaired the working group of the South Florida Drug Task Force." The board would consist of senior officials of the departments represented on the executive board and their subordinate agencies.[38] The SFTF thus became the nucleus of the NNBIS Southeast Region and a pattern for other regions. The system became operational that summer.

Capt. Nick Schowengerdt, USCG, was the first staff director of NNBIS in the Office of the Vice President (OVP). Captain Schowengerdt reported directly to Admiral Murphy and often briefed the vice president on NNBIS matters. He was assisted by a minuscule staff consisting of Customs air officer Jim Howell; Customs inspector Kevin Cummings; Comdr. Jack Bookhultz, U.S. Navy; Lt. Col. Joe Zadareky, U.S. Air Force; a representative of the Central Intelligence Agency reporting to the intelligence community; and Lt. Comdr. Terry Hart, USCG. They were housed in the Old Executive Office Building next to the White House. The staff director had a private office on the fourth floor. The others were all crammed into an atticlike room in the rear of the monolithic granite building. In December a Fisheries Service agent was assigned to provide expertise on fishing vessel operations and identification. Admiral Murphy let him work from a Coast Guard station in Florida. There was no room in the attic.

Each staff member was responsible for coordination with one NNBIS region and had collateral duties for liaison with one or more of the enforcement agencies, the intelligence agencies, and the military services. The military members did not wear uniforms or use military titles. The junior people at NNBIS headquarters had clout with the operating agencies because they were White House staff, titled assistants to the vice president's chief of staff. They were responsible for obtaining commitments of cooperation and personnel from the enforcement agencies and monitoring the activities of the NNBIS regions. They also got commitments and resources from the military services in supporting the drug interdiction mission. This small group accomplished amazing feats in moving the multitude of government entities toward a unified interdiction system in a very short time. Morale was never a problem at OVP/NNBIS.

Eventually the staff moved into a decent suite of offices, and representatives from the State Department, DEA, the Immigration and Naturalization Service, and the army were assigned. Capt. Howard

Gehring relieved Schowengerdt in 1985, about the time Admiral Murphy was replaced by Craig Fuller, the VP's new chief of staff. Fuller did not have the background or the inclination to coordinate day-to-day functions of NNBIS; the job fell squarely on the shoulders of the junior Coast Guard captain. Gehring had to interface with the vice president, various cabinet members, agency heads, and a host of flag and general officers. A testimony to his effectiveness was the vice president's personal request to the commandant of the Coast Guard to keep Gehring at NNBIS past his rotation date. Capt. John Shkor relieved Gehring in the fall of 1988. He had the unenviable task of decommissioning NNBIS the next year and taking the remains to the new Office of National Drug Control Policy.[39]

The NNBIS regions were ready to go in June 1983. Miami was already in place as the SFTF. The Miami center would coordinate interdiction operations for NNBIS Southeast, covering the lower Atlantic coast from Florida to North Carolina and most of the Florida Gulf coast. The rest of the Atlantic coast north was the province of NNBIS Northeast, with a center in New York. Gulf coast areas west of Cape San Blas, Florida, were covered by NNBIS New Orleans. The Pacific Region, headquartered in Long Beach, was responsible for the whole Pacific coast; later a western Pacific district was established in Honolulu, becoming the Western Pacific Region. The Northern Border Region, headquartered in Chicago, covered the Canadian border. The Mexican land border was the responsibility of the Southwest Border Region, headquartered in El Paso, Texas; this center was later relocated to Houston. Within each region the vice president designated a senior Customs official or a Coast Guard flag officer as his representative and regional coordinator. Day-to-day command of the NNBIS centers was the responsibility of the regional staff director. He was either from the Coast Guard (usually a commander) or Customs (usually a GS-14-level agent). All centers were supposed to operate like the model SFTF with an Operations Information Center (OIC) and an Intelligence Information Center (IIC). Only New York, New Orleans, and Long Beach had enough people or the need to realize this goal. Most NNBIS people came from the Coast Guard, Customs, and the military, but many federal agencies were represented. All NNBIS centers had representatives from state and local enforcement agencies.[40]

The regional centers evaluated and collated intelligence from participating agencies, EPIC, and in some cases internal sources. They identified smuggler targets and tagged those with the best potential for seizure. A tagged target, vessel or aircraft, was tracked in OIC. Once it had been tagged, the OIC watch officer tried to find an interdiction resource in the target's path. He then recommended that the target be intercepted. It was up to the agency owning the resource to make the decision to intercept, board, search, seize, and arrest. This regional approach to the coordination of interdiction efforts had merit. The centers were places where people worked together unencumbered by agency turf prerogatives.

There was a lot of brass associated with NNBIS, from the vice president down to the admiral/commissioner regional coordinators, and only about 150 troops. The VP could not spend much time with the program, but he regularly attended quarterly regional coordinators'/staff directors' meetings and the National Drug Interdiction Operations Oversight Group meetings. He also visited the NNBIS regions. Vice President Bush's major contribution was promoting morale in the ranks and allowing his name to be used to further program goals.

Regional coordinators and deputies were also busy people with responsibilities in their regular assignments. They were charged by the vice president to encourage cooperation among the agencies. NNBIS was really run by the staff directors, but they had the delegated clout to get things done.

NNBIS was by no means perfect. It was a political football touted by the administration on the one hand and deprecated by the Democratic Congress on the other. Many old-time drug warriors called it a system for producing press releases. The Murphy-Mullen conflict grew in intensity, reaching embarrassing proportions. They fought over who would take credit for what, contacts with foreign governments, definitions of intelligence, and how to operate an interdiction program.[41] The sad result of the hostility between these dedicated and capable men was a lack of enthusiasm on the part of DEA in support of the coordinated drug interdiction effort.

A lack of timely intelligence from individual agents also detracted from the NNBIS mission. DEA street agents, working within the United States with cooperating local and state officers, were conducting innumerable drug-trafficking investigations. Intelligence from these investigations concerning the importation of drugs went into DEA files. However, only the information on pending drug imports that agents passed to EPIC had a chance of reaching the interdiction forces. Agents and officers traditionally hold on to their information, especially information received from confidential informants, so that they can make the bust on their own ground; it is part of the human condition, something related to rewards and promotions. DEA felt that it was better to use hard-earned intelligence to pursue kingpin drug traffickers and not waste it on interdicting "mules." Their views had merit. NNBIS, however, was trying to coordinate a massive program without DEA's intelligence, which was locked in case files. Volumes of index data were contained in DEA's Narcotics and Dangerous Drugs Information System (NADDIS) listing individual names, vessel names, and the like. A NADDIS check told where to go for specific case information. NNBIS centers could access NADDIS through EPIC, but they had to know what they were looking for. NADDIS was of limited value unless NNBIS had a specific name.

The problem was not limited to DEA files. Customs also had drug movement data in its case files. It had an index similar to DEA's contained in the Treasury Enforcement Communications System (TECS), which was readily available to the centers. You still needed a name to get something out of TECS. Customs officers and agents, however, were more apt to feed time-sensitive information directly to the NNBIS centers. After all, Customs was a major player in the interdiction program.

Getting time-sensitive information from case files into the interdiction system has never been satisfactorily achieved, although progress has been made. Computer resources at all levels of the federal system have been upgraded to speed up the transmission, collation, and integration of information from sources at EPIC and other intelligence centers. The basic problems still remain, however. How much information are investigators willing to give to national databases? How strictly do agencies enforce the requirement to share information with others? After all, agencies and their investigators need arrest and seizure statistics to justify appropriations; that's how the system works.

There were kinks in the system, but interdiction was coming of age. By 1983, marijuana smugglers had been forced to alter their methods and routes. Motherships were diverted into the deep Atlantic for runs north with off-loads far at sea. Payoffs were allegedly being made in Mexico for passage through the Mexican territorial sea by Cape Catoche on the Yucatán Peninsula; the Gap between Mexico and Cuba was getting too hot.

Smugglers bought sophisticated radio scanners to scan enforcement frequencies. Even when the interdiction forces used secure scrambler equipment, the opposition could hear the "noise" (i.e., microphone keys depressed to transmit) and log the number of transmissions. When enforcement transmissions increased, it was wise to call off a delivery or go somewhere else. Boat smugglers had become much more conscious of the need to maintain radio silence. They used microphone clicks and whistles to show they were monitoring certain frequencies. Listeners were put in bars near Coast Guard stations to pick up loose talk about cutter movements and special operations. Bags of cement were used to shield pot loads from suspected infrared detection. Some smugglers believed that U.S. infrared sensors could detect heat produced by pot cargoes inside a boat or ship. They were correct as far as the technology was concerned, but off on the degree of its sensitivity. Look-alike boats were used to confuse patrols. To avoid setting patterns, off-loads were never made in the same place. False ship's papers, forged personal identification documents, and bogus logbooks appeared. Dropping a few grass bales in coastal waters or on the beach told smugglers if enforcement resources were nearby. From concealed places they could identify adversaries. Even false distress calls were used to divert sea and air forces from off-load positions.[42]

Smugglers typically respond to enforcement initiatives with countermoves; maritime marijuana smugglers did so in 1983. Before, they piled multi-ton cargoes into anything that would float and sent it north from the Caribbean or east from the Gulf of Thailand. Then came the U.S. perimeter defense. Smugglers could no longer depend on unimpeded voyages, even if they detoured. The obvious countermeasure was to hide the contraband. Because of the volume, this would require ingenuity. No one ever accused dope smugglers of being short of that attribute.

Hidden compartments had been found in the past, but they were isolated events, especially in the grass trade. Then came the 1983 crop; it was a bumper yield. Over seventy vessels with hidden compartments were seized that year. Nearly 40 percent of all vessels intercepted by the Coast Guard and Customs had concealed contraband. The expensive construction of hidden compartments, even on rustbuckets, was a good indication that interdiction efforts were hurting smugglers.[43] Intelligence pointed to a number of ship- and boatyards in Colombia and Panama specializing in the installation of concealed compartments. Inaccessible voids were built into engine spaces, cargo and fish holds, fuel and water tanks, and double bottoms to accommodate drugs. A new Third World industry arose almost overnight to support smuggler needs.

A Coast Guard directive proclaimed that widespread use of hidden compartments presented the greatest challenge in the maritime drug interdiction effort. Boarding officers were told that perseverance and ingenuity were keys to detecting concealed spaces. They were directed to measure the vessels carefully, inside and out, to locate inaccessible voids. Indicators of suspicion were fresh paint, fresh welds, new gaskets, worn studs, padeyes in the overhead for lifting with no obvious hatches below, and attempts to mask the smell of marijuana with Lysol, diesel fuel, or pine oil. Crews were advised to tap bulkheads and decks for hollow sounds and to sound fuel and water tanks. Because of the complexity of thorough space-accountability searches, commanding officers were reminded to use the old 1935 Hovering Vessel Act whenever possible to bring vessels into port for better examination.[44]

Finding hidden compartments was no small task. The 75-foot swordfish longliner *Xiphias* was boarded in April 1983 by a Coast Guard law enforcement detachment (LEDET) from the hydrofoil USS *Aries* (PHM-5) near Cay Sal Bank. (The term LEDET was now used in place of TACLET.) Enough marijuana residue was found for them to seize the boat and take it to Islamorada in the Florida Keys. A dockside search was exhaustive but negative. The *Xiphias* was placed in temporary storage at a local marina. A few days later the marina operator noticed a person aboard the vessel late at night. He called the Islamorada Customs office. An agent responded and found someone trying to remove the large 30-kilowatt generator from its mountings in the engine room. The man's explanation left much to be desired, but it gave Customs agents a clue. They removed the generator and found access through a false bottom under the machine to a huge concealed compartment containing 27,500 pounds of baled grass.[45] How the audacious smugglers planned to remove a multi-ton load from a vessel in custody remains a mystery.

Other hidden-compartment cases followed in rapid succession, but November was a singular month. Cutter crews were learning fast. On 3 November the USCGC *Dallas* (WHEC-716) met the 150-foot British coastal freighter *Narwal* butting through the Windward Passage. She was boarded under the U.S.–U.K. agreement. The master was most

A Coast Guard petty officer searches the double bottoms of a freighter—the dirty work of the unsung heroes. *(Author's collection)*

cooperative, which made the boarding officer suspicious. An apparent void was found just aft of the forward peak tank. A sounding seemed normal, but when water was pumped from the tube, the level dropped 6 feet with only a gallon removed. The *Narwal's* gracious captain gave permission to drill. A borescope was used to look inside the tank and void, where many bales could be seen. In all, 29,900 pounds of grass were removed.

Seven hundred miles west, on 15 November, the old ex-navy tug *Ute* (WMEC-76) wheezed up to another tug pointed north toward the Yucatán Channel. The master of the 70-foot Panamanian *Querube II* gave permission for the *Ute's* people to come aboard. Much measuring was done, but the boarding party could not account for about 180 cubic feet in the forward part of the vessel. There was a scarred manhole cover on the foredeck. A nearby sounding tube smelled of diesel fuel. When pumped, the fuel level dropped 4.5 feet after only a half gallon had been removed. Another pumping job was necessary. At the boarding officer's request, the captain grudgingly gave permission to remove the cover. They saw a tank that appeared full of fuel. At this point the *Querube II*'s master grew surly. He ordered the *Ute*'s men off his boat. It did not take them long to get an SNO from Panama to reboard. A false fuel tank with a cone-shaped top over a 9-foot cylinder was found under the manhole cover. The real tank held 22,550 pounds of Colombian commercial-grade grass.[46]

Not all dopers hid their cargoes; they were more prone to run. Some ran hard in the face of overwhelming odds. The first navy ship to fire her guns in the drug war was the guided-missile destroyer USS *Kidd* (DDG-993). Cruising east of the Bahamas in the open Atlantic with a Coast Guard LEDET, the gray warship sighted a shabby motor vessel making to the north on 15 July 1983. The LEDET officer requested the captain of the destroyer to close with the target. Soon the 72-foot M/V *Ranger,* flying the Honduran flag, was close aboard. The *Ranger*'s master returned the hail, saying he was heading north in ballast. The vessel was riding low in the water. The LEDET officer-in-charge requested permission to make a courtesy boarding. The *Ranger* refused and kept running north. An SNO request was initiated for permission to board. In a few hours Honduran officials denied that the vessel was theirs. The *Ranger* was declared stateless. The *Kidd* closed again and ordered the *Ranger* to stop for boarding. Again, the master refused. What audacity! The little boat was dwarfed by the big destroyer bristling with space-age weapons. Now the process of obtaining permission to use force began, in this case involving the commander-in-chief, Atlantic Fleet.

A navy ship had never been asked to use deadly force in the drug war; it took deliberations at high levels. Finally the *Kidd* was given permission to use .50-caliber machine-gun fire. The *Ranger* was hailed again. The master was told to get his crew up on the bow before he was shot in the tail. The *Ranger*'s defiant captain told the *Kidd* he would do with his people as he saw fit. It took only eighteen rounds fired into the stern of the *Ranger* to bring her to a stop. The LEDET found 57,265 pounds of marijuana stuffed into the hold. The *Ranger* was seized and her unruly nine-man crew arrested. The Coast Guard buoy tender *Sagebrush* (WLB-399) towed the prize to San Juan.[47]

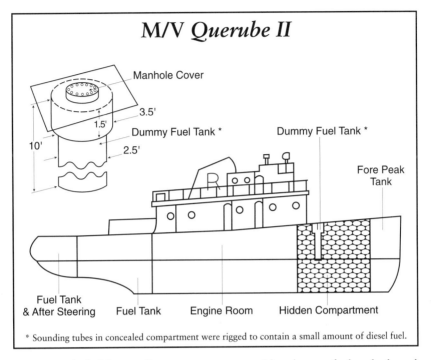

M/V *Querube II*

Manhole Cover

3.5'

1.5'

10'   2.5'

Dummy Fuel Tank *   Dummy Fuel Tank *

Fore Peak Tank

Fuel Tank & After Steering   Fuel Tank   Engine Room   Hidden Compartment

* Sounding tubes in concealed compartment were rigged to contain a small amount of diesel fuel.

Drawing of a hidden marijuana compartment with a dummy fuel tank aboard the *Querube II* (*Reproduced with permission of the U.S. Coast Guard*)

Then there were those who just got off and left the spoils to the victor. On 25 March a Coast Guard inshore patrol boat approached two fishing vessels in Florida Bay a few miles north of Islamorada. The Coasties beheld frantic activity ahead. All hands from the two vessels leapt aboard a go-fast boat and sped away to the north. There was no chance of catching the fleeing "fishermen." The abandoned boats were the 65-foot shrimp trawler *Cayman* and the 45-foot lobster boat *Zoila,* containing about 20,000 pounds of grass. The two F/Vs had probably received their loads from a mothership somewhere north of the Dry Tortugas. This was a good example of the expeditious use of the chase boat preferred by Gulf smugglers as a form of insurance. A few days later, officers found an abandoned Scarab go-fast in Everglades National Park.[48]

There were some record seizures by individual cutters in late 1983 in southern seas. The 378-foot *Dallas* (WHEC-716), down from Governors Island, New York, to work the Caribbean choke points, took out six vessels with 102,685 pounds of grass between 25 October and 16 December. Fifty-one smugglers were arrested in this outstanding single deployment. The cutter's victims included the *Saint Nicholas, Wammer Jammer, Narwal, Miss Debbie, Nistanova,* and *W&V.* She didn't have to fire a shot.[49]

On the heels of the success of the *Dallas* came the even more spectacular achievement of the ex-navy tug *Lipan* (WMEC-85). The old-timer got four vessels with twenty-five people and 80,000 pounds of pot in twenty-four hours. It all started on 30 December in the Caribbean approaches to the Windward Passage. In rapid succession the *Lipan* intercepted an 82-foot Panamanian-registered motor vessel and a 60-foot U.S. shrimper. While escorting her prizes to the naval base at Guantánamo Bay, Cuba, she intercepted a stateless vessel with a marijuana cargo and added another smuggler to her train. By this time the cutter was getting short of people to man the captured vessels. Just shy of her destination, the *Lipan,* with her flotilla of grass boats, ran down another recruit. It took messcooks and firemen to board this one, a U.S. lobster boat out of Florida.[50] The *Lipan*'s eventful twenty-four hours' catch was an all-time record for one cutter. The white cutters and the gray ships were doing a good job in the major Caribbean choke points.

The primary Caribbean passes to the north were now fairly well patrolled, but a lot of pot still leaked into the Atlantic through the eastern passes. Although only 9 percent of vessels seized were in the upper Atlantic, 26 percent of maritime marijuana seized in 1983 came from that area. These figures show a preponderance of motherships intercepted to the north, carrying very large cargoes of grass.[51] Typical of the large pot carriers going north was the Honduran freighter *Civonney,* intercepted by the vintage cutter *Duane* (WHEC-33) 215 miles southeast of Atlantic City on 16 March 1983. The *Civonney*'s crew set her on fire and abandoned ship in a lifeboat as the cutter approached. The *Duane*'s crew fought the fire but finally had to abandon the freighter when she began to sink. The freighter supposedly carried 120,000 pounds of Colombian grass. If she did, it was a near record for the Northeast. The old *Duane* had missed another chance for fame. A total of twenty-eight maritime seizures were made in the

The USCGC *Lipan* (WMEC-85). The old navy salvage tug set a twenty-four-hour seizure record in 1983. *(U.S. Naval Institute photograph)*

Northeast in 1983. The seizures produced 546,471 pounds of mari-juana, 20,000 pounds of hashish, and 350 pounds of cocaine.[52]

Maritime seizures along the Pacific coast in 1983 were mostly dockside or in harbors. In total, 158,483 pounds of pot were seized in the Pacific region from eight vessels. Cocaine was showing up in Los Angeles and San Francisco in small shipments aboard merchant ships. Over 1,000 pounds were seized in six cases. All involved attempted imports by individual crew members.[53]

Cocaine from Colombia, traditionally imported by private and commercial aircraft, began to arrive aboard merchant ships in 1983 in large quantities. On 1 June the Costa Rican freighter *Lion Heart* was unloading at Dodge Island in Miami. Customs officials searched a trailer lashed to the deck. Inside they found 1,065 pounds of the white powder.[54] It was the first major coke seizure from a ship, and perhaps the first case involving drug smuggling by maritime container. Cocaine concealed in otherwise legitimate cargo was almost impossible to detect at sea by boardings. If prior intelligence was available, it was usually better to let the ship arrive at her destination and then search the cargo dockside. No matter how it came, cocaine was arriving in ever-increasing quantities. The market was glutted. Wholesale prices plummeted 50 percent, from $60,000 a kilo in 1981 to $30,000 in 1983.[55]

The total weight of marijuana seized by the United States in 1983 was 3.1 million pounds. Of that total, 75 percent was seized in the Caribbean-Bahamas-Florida region, 26 percent in the Atlantic north of Florida, 7 percent in the Gulf of Mexico, and 2 percent along the Pacific coast. The Coast Guard seized 2.4 million pounds, or almost 80 percent of the total. Marijuana was still very much a maritime item. Of the vessels seized in 1983, 75 percent were taken in the Caribbean-Bahamas-Florida region, 9 percent in the Atlantic, 4 percent in the Gulf, and 2 percent in the Pacific. By general type, the seizures were 57 percent pleasure craft, 33 percent fishing vessels, 7 percent small cargo vessels, and 3 percent unclassified. Cocaine seizures by the Coast Guard in 1983 came to a little over 46 pounds, only 0.01 percent of the total seized (5,254 pounds).[56] The figures tell the story. At the end of 1983, marijuana was a maritime problem; cocaine was not.

A Supreme Court decision was rendered in 1983 that impacted the drug war. The Court upheld the right of Customs and the Coast Guard to stop, board, and inspect the papers of any vessel within their jurisdictions and to use necessary force to compel compliance. *U.S. v. Villamonte-Marquez* challenged the government's right to such boardings under the Fourth Amendment, which guaranteed protection from unreasonable searches and seizures. The case involved the 1980 Customs boarding of the 40-foot French sailboat *Henry Morgan II* in the Calcasieu River ship channel near Lake Charles, Louisiana. Customs officers had no suspicion of illegal activity when they boarded for a documentation check. (Customs authority to check documents is contained in 19 U.S.C. 1581a.) The officers smelled marijuana, and bales were visible in the cabin through an open hatch. The boat was seized and the people on board arrested. On 17 June 1983 the Supreme Court ruled that the suspicionless boarding of the vessel in waters under federal jurisdiction for the purpose of checking her documents was reasonable and consistent with the Fourth Amendment. In the *Villamonte-Marquez* ruling, the court obliquely upheld 14 U.S.C. 89a authorizing Coast Guard officers to stop, board, and inspect a vessel's documents. The signal SQ3 (Stop, I am going to board you) was thus found to be compatible with the Constitution.[57]

The years 1982–83 marked a unified stand by the United States against drug trafficking. First came the vice president's South Florida Task Force, organized to coordinate federal efforts in the area most impacted by the flourishing drug trade. Then the Organized Crime Drug Enforcement Task Forces were created to go after kingpin traffickers and their money on a nationwide basis. Success of the SFTF and concern on the part of elected officials in other parts of the country prompted the administration to expand the concept along all our borders. The National Narcotics Border Interdiction System was born. NNBIS, led by Vice President Bush with the able assistance of Adm. Dan Murphy, was able to bring Department of Defense and national foreign intelligence community assets into the drug war. Until this point, the fragmented drug interdiction strategy had been defensive and reactive. Agencies deployed their resources to meet drug-smuggling threats; there was little interagency planning or coordination. NNBIS brought the direction and staff necessary to organize and implement sustained offensive operations against international drug traffickers.

6

The Offensive
Part One, 1984

When you are occupying a position which the enemy threatens
to surround, collect all your forces immediately, and menace
him with an offensive movement!

NAPOLEON I, *MAXIMS OF WAR,* 1831

I t was time for the United States to take the offensive in the drug war. Bad news was the order of the day in 1984. Negative press and congressional criticism of the government's conduct of the war were influencing public opinion. People were demanding dramatic solutions. President Reagan was still popular with the electorate, but he was feeling the heat as he prepared his campaign for reelection. Reagan had already done more than his predecessors in raising barriers against narcotics, but critics said he was fighting the war on the cheap, with press releases. NNBIS officials got the word through the chain of command to come up with something innovative. They planned a Caribbean offensive for the fall. DEA already had an imaginative plan in the mill.

The first offensive strike of the drug war was a DEA special operation to locate cocaine-processing facilities in Colombia. Few were privy to the plan. There was extensive coverage in the press of the results, but the methods were obscured for security reasons. A small battery-powered device called a platform transmitter terminal (PTT) was essential to the project. Civilian PTTs (used to monitor movements of ocean currents, icebergs, wildlife, etc.) are tracked by environmental satellites. The transmitter in this case was the kind used by the joint NOAA/Coast Guard National Data Buoy Program for oceanographic studies. Units report their positions five or six times a day, depending on the location of the orbiting satellite. Accuracy is to within a few hundred feet. PTT tracking is done by an elaborate system that feeds data to a NOAA office in Maryland. The transmitters can also be tracked by a local user terminal (LUT) with a range of about 3,000 miles. A LUT was used in this effort.[1]

How could a miniature environmental satellite beeper help in an assault on drug traffickers? Cocaine hydrochloride, the usual form in which cocaine is sold, is mainly produced in factories deep in Colombia's interior. There are chemicals called precursors used in the process. Ether is one, and it is usually imported from the United States or Western Europe. DEA's project Operation Chemcon kept track of large shipments of precursors. Agents managed to insert a small transmitter into a drum of ether bound for Colombia. The tagged 55-gallon drum went by cargo ship to a Colombian port, the only maritime part of the operation. Beeping away, it slowly moved into the equatorial jungles of Caquetá Province in the southern part of the country.

On 8 March 1984 it stopped at the remote village of Tranquilandia on the Yari River.

The DEA attaché in Bogotá reported its arrival to the antinarcotics unit of the Colombian National Police. On the morning of 10 March about sixty Colombian officers descended on Tranquilandia by helicopter and engaged in a firefight with defenders of the cocaine complex. After the workers had been subdued and arrests had been made, the antinarcotics police were attacked by men in fatigue uniforms. Police estimated there were at least a hundred. The assault teams drove the "fatigues" back into the jungle and secured the complex. Patrols fanned out into the surrounding countryside. Five other refining complexes were found. When the unit counted its take, it turned out to be the largest cocaine seizure in the world. The total was 13.8 tons, believed to be a quarter of the annual U.S. consumption. That record stood for five years.

Besides the complexes, several airstrips were found and seven aircraft were seized. Six submachine guns, numerous small arms, and documents linking the refineries to the Medellin cartel were taken. Intelligence showed that the complexes were protected by the oldest and best-organized communist guerillas in the country, the Revolutionary Armed Forces of Colombia (Fuerzas Armadas Revolucionarias de Colombia, or FARC). Deserters reported that FARC levied a 10 percent protection charge on the factories. The FARC aspect of the raid got the attention of the Colombian government. This was a national security problem. In the United States a DEA spokesman warned that if cocaine prices did not go up, or if coke did not become scarce, we had a real problem. They did not, and the magnitude of our cocaine epidemic became apparent.[2]

On 30 April, Rodrigo Lara Bonilla, the courageous Colombian minister of justice, was assassinated in Bogotá. Lara had called for a counterattack against the drug traffickers who were taking control of his country. His tragic death changed Colombia's attitude toward the drug menace. President Belisario Betancur declared a state of emergency and gave extraordinary powers to the police and military. Until now Betancur had refused to extradite traffickers to the United States, but he now pledged to enforce the 1979 extradition treaty.[3] Minister Lara's supreme sacrifice cleared the way for better cooperation between our government and Colombia but further inflamed the media and Congress into a frenzy of criticism for the antinarcotics effort.

May was an exceptional month for gloom. On Capitol Hill, Deputy Treasury Secretary R. T. McNamara and Customs Commissioner William von Raab told Congress that the responsibility for detecting smuggler aircraft should be given to the Defense Department. They estimated that Customs was apprehending only one out of every one hundred smuggler planes penetrating our borders. Congressman Glenn English (D., Oklahoma) agreed.[4] Before the month ended, the public heard that the cocaine kingpin Pablo Escobar Gaviria had been elected to the Colombian Congress as an alternate deputy.[5] They also learned that the cocaine-processing industry had spread to the Amazon basin of Brazil. The bad news in May recognized the expanding cocaine threat and the ability of air smugglers to evade interdiction. The only information in the media blitz about maritime smuggling was a small item concerning the seizure of cocaine in the Brazilian port of Belém, at the mouth of the Amazon.[6] Cocaine in Belém meant maritime shipments, probably by containers.

The news was bad not only on the national and international scene, but locally. With the federal enforcement presence in 1982, drug violence in South Florida had subsided; Miami's Cocaine Cowboys were no longer brazenly shooting it out in the streets, and residents had become complacent. Then on 4 March two campers showed up at the Monroe County sheriff's department substation in Key Largo with a bizarre tale. The campers said they had been held at gunpoint for over an hour by four heavily armed men dressed in camouflage. They thought the gunmen were off-loading a drug boat.[7] No one could decide whether to believe them. The incident was forgotten by authorities, but not for long.

On the morning of 20 June a National Marine Fisheries Service agent and park ranger Bennie Davis of John Pennekemp Coral Reef State Park were checking land observation points on Key Largo. At 0930, when the men arrived at Garden Cove, they saw two people waving frantically from a small outboard boat speeding toward them. Crashing into the shallows, the mariners gave a hurried report. They had just landed three fellow fishermen found huddled in the mangroves near Point Willie, about 2.5 miles from park headquarters. The wet and shaken fishermen said they had been captured the previous afternoon by gun-toting smugglers. Customs and Marine Patrol were notified by radio. The park ranger and the NMFS agent rushed to Point Willie in a park boat. They found three Customs Patrol officers, a Florida Marine Patrol officer, and a Monroe Country deputy sheriff pulling up to shore. On park property the officers found a large hollowed-out space under the mangrove canopy. Sixty bales of marijuana (about 3,600 pounds) were stacked on planks. The smuggler-kidnappers were long gone.

The hostages told a tale of terror. It had started the afternoon of a bright, sunny 19 June. As the first man was casting for bonefish from his boat north of Point Willie, several men, described as "Cubans," waded out from shore. The Cubans drew weapons and took the fisherman captive. The man and his boat were dragged into a concealed hideout. He was tied with cord to the roots of a mangrove tree. At about 1800, two more fishermen drifted into the shallows. They too were captured and bound to the tree. When darkness fell, one of the Cubans told the hostages to prepare to die. The captives said there were from five to seven Cubans. They agreed on one point: a Jamaican, who apparently came with the grass load, was their savior. He begged the Cubans not to kill them. When it was totally dark, the Jamaican surreptitiously untied a hostage, then faded into the night. The freed man helped the others. They crawled through the maze of mangrove roots until they reached the ocean's fringe. They quietly waded a few hundred yards and hid until sunrise. The fishermen lived on Key Largo and did not want to be identified. There was no press.[8]

How the load got ashore so close to park headquarters was a matter for speculation. One of the captured men said he believed that it had been delivered by a shallow-draft lobster boat. Were the smugglers really potential killers, or were their threats only intended to silence the unfortunate fishermen? The Jamaican apparently thought they were serious. Or was he part of the act? The kidnappers of Key Largo were never identified; after the emphatic threat of execution, the witnesses were not anxious to cooperate. Ironically, the senior Customs officer was later indicted for conspiring with others to smuggle drugs. He had been the first officer ashore at Point Willie.

Beginning on 9 September 1984 the *New York Times* ran a series of articles under the heading "World of Drugs." Dire predictions were made about the futility of fighting the drug war, considering the rampant spread of drug abuse in this country. The series, written by Joel Brinkley and others, ended on 14 September. In the last article

Sanctuary officer Bennie Davis at Point Willie where the fishermen were taken prisoner by smugglers in 1984 *(Photograph by NMFS agent Mac Fuss)*

Brinkley mentioned the recent results of an eighteen-month study by the Rand Corporation, predicting that unless we could reduce the demand for drugs, the supply would never diminish. It said that drug abuse education was the best solution.[9] The pundits were right about education as the long-term solution to the problem, but their persistent criticism did little for the morale of the drug warriors in those dark days.

November was a month of bad news from an unexpected quarter: Mexico was back in marijuana production big time. Some said it was a massive intelligence failure, but DEA agent Enrique "Kiki" Camarena and his cohorts at the Guadalajara field office had been reporting pot production in desert plantations for some time. The discovery eventually led to Camarena's brutal murder by Mexican traffickers. The Mexican government, with DEA's prompting, mounted a raid on suspected growing areas in the desert of Mexico's northern state of Chihuahua.

On 7 November the Mexican federal judicial police, supported by army troops, moved in by helicopter with DEA observers. They found five pot plantations, barracks for workers, and huge drying sheds for harvested grass. Thousands of peons and a few overseers were rounded up. Government forces destroyed about 9,000 tons of marijuana, a world record. The Chihuahua pot find was seven times the annual estimate for Mexico and 75–80 percent of the estimated U.S. annual consumption. DEA had to revise its estimate for marijuana sources.[10]

Chihuahua was the second offensive of 1984. DEA agents had entered Mexico in October as part of an opium poppy/marijuana eradication verification program, which led to the 7 November raid. The program was obviously not working. Chihuahua was an air-land operation, but there were maritime implications. Resumption of massive marijuana cultivation by canny Mexican growers showed that they recognized the interdiction losses by their Colombian competitors. It was another case of supply-demand adjustment. The paraquat stigma on Mexican grass had faded. With their historical smuggling expertise and easy access to the United States across a 2,000-mile sparsely populated land border, the opportunity to recapture a part of the pot trade was irresistible, even if they had to grow it in the desert. The Chihuahua raid was a serious setback for the Mexicans, but their pot industry was rejuvenated.

The resurgence of pot production in Mexico was not the only new threat facing the interdiction forces; Belize was now recognized as a source for marijuana. In the past, modest shipments from Belize to the United States had been made by small private aircraft. An extensive and lightly populated coastline and close proximity to the Yucatán Channel began to attract boat smugglers. Cruising sailboats and other small craft became the smugglers' choice for transporting Belizean grass.[11]

The third offensive operation was maritime. It was also the largest and most sophisticated assault against Caribbean drug traffickers to date. Conceived and planned by NNBIS and the Seventh Coast Guard District, Operation Hat Trick was a multimedium, multiagency, and multinational effort intended to block the movement of drugs from Caribbean source countries. Colombia was the focal point of the blockade, because most of the narcotics bound for the United States came from there. The NNBIS staff in Washington handled international initiatives, coordination with agencies, and overall organization. Rear Adm. Richard Cueroni, Seventh District commander and NNBIS Southeast Region coordinator, was responsible for much of the detailed planning. The maritime segment was known as Operation Wagon Wheel. Capt. Stephen Duca, the Seventh District's chief of operations, was the key staffer for planning and execution. The commander of the soon-to-be-established Caribbean Squadron (CaribRon) would be the on-scene boss. CaribRon was a Coast Guard–navy unit led by a Coast Guard officer. The squadron continued functioning long after Hat Trick–Wagon Wheel and was the most important Coast Guard–navy operation since World War II.[12]

Planning for Hat Trick was a closely held secret restricted to a very few people. It was meant to be executed in two phases. Phase I was the deployment of ships and aircraft to reinforce the patrol line in the western Bahamas (code name Backribs) and along the choke points from the Yucatán to Puerto Rico (Spoke Outrider). The line was extended to the Leeward Islands, covering Anegada Passage and the lesser passes through the Virgin Islands (Spoke Tailgate). In Phase II, segments of the patrol force moved slowly south to the coastal waters of Central and South America, with a focus on the Guajira Peninsula of Colombia. Colombia was expected to assist by seizing narcotics stockpiled on shore because of the blockade. Coast Guard surface forces consisted of the icebreaker *Northwind* (WAGB-282) serving as flagship, four high-endurance cutters, six medium-endurance cutters, two surface-effect cutters, two patrol boats, and four buoy tenders. The navy contributed a guided-missile destroyer (DDG), a guided-missile frigate (FFG), and three high-speed hydrofoils (PHMs). Air support included three navy P-3 Orions, a Coast Guard C-130, and a Coast Guard HU-25 Falcon for long-range surveillance. Five Coast Guard H-52 helicopters operated from surface ships. Customs and DEA aircraft supported the surface forces and did air interdictions. Other federal resources were used as available. Florida state and local enforcement agencies took part via Operation Purse String, coordinated by NNBIS Southeast.[13]

The icebreaker *Northwind* (WAGB-282), flagship of Operation Wagon Wheel, November 1984 *(U.S. Naval Institute photograph)*

Operation Hat Trick was to cover the segment of a circle with the center in South Florida and radii extending southwest through the Yucatán Peninsula and southeast through the western Bahamas to the eastern boundary of the Leeward Islands. The arc of the segment swung westward across the Caribbean, touching Colombia and Panama and encompassing the rest of Central America. A chord extended diagonally across the Caribbean from the Leeward Islands to Nicaragua. This was the primary patrol line in Phase II.

The operating area was divided into three zones. The departure zone was near drug-producing nations and transshipment countries and extended seaward from their territorial limits to about 100 nautical miles. It was the main target of Hat Trick Phase II. The arrival zone was the customs waters of the United States (to 12 nautical miles offshore) and our mainland. The transit zone was the area in between, including the passes from the Caribbean. Hat Trick Phase I focused on the transit zone.[14]

Phase I began on 31 October 1984. Capt. Lee Krumm, USCG, was commodore of the Caribbean Squadron and broke his broad pennant in the *Northwind*. Operational secrecy was short-lived; ABC News broadcast the event on 16 November followed by articles in the *Miami Herald* and the *New York Times* on the seventeenth and eighteenth.[15] A congressional aide was the suspected source. By now the smugglers were aware of the operation because of the massive buildup of interdiction resources athwart the sea lanes.

The second phase of Hat Trick began on 22 November, when the patrol line was moved south toward Colombia. Murphy's Law was in force from the start. A continuous deluge of rain swept the marijuana growing areas of Colombia while the last of the fall crop was being harvested. Unpaved roads and mule tracks leading to collection and storage areas were washed away or turned to muddy rivers. Gale-force winds and high seas buffeted the picket ships and kept many grass boats in harbor. Hat Trick struggled on until the end of the year, but the results were disappointing compared with the effort. Thirty-seven vessels and 169 tons of marijuana were seized.[16] It was only a small percentage of the annual take. There were, however, lessons learned in the joint operations. We had demonstrated our resolve to take the war to the enemy. The Hat Trick organization remained in place. Planning started almost immediately for Hat Trick II.[17]

The less-than-spectacular seizures by Hat Trick brought more dismal press. An AP article entitled "U.S. Effort Fails to Make Big Dent on Drug Smuggling from Colombia" was typical.[18] Operations like the Colombian Tranquilandia raid and the Mexican Chihuahua raid had produced impressive drug seizures. Unfortunately, the media used those results to portray the drug war as unwinnable. On the other hand, Hat Trick, which failed to return meaningful seizures because of washed-out roads in Colombia, was also used to show the futility of attempting to interdict drugs. Damned if you do, and damned if you don't.

Beyond the tentacles of the press, DEA could boast that its offensive operations were magnificently successful while the huge Caribbean blockade planned by NNBIS and the Coast Guard was literally a washout. Customs managed to keep a low profile, avoiding both glory and criticism. Commissioner William von Raab, however, was making inroads with Congressman Glenn English (D., Oklahoma) and his subcommittee for more intercept planes and boats.[19]

Von Raab's plea to the congressman was like preaching to the choir; English already had a mission to increase Customs resources.

The bad news climaxed on 26 November 1984 with the detonation of 33 pounds of dynamite hidden inside a Fiat parked just outside the U.S. embassy in Bogotá. A Colombian woman was killed. The blast blew out windows of nearby buildings and knocked down trees. It did not damage the embassy. Colombian officials speculated that the target was Ambassador Lewis Tambs. Drug barons were incensed over President Betancur's agreement to extradite seventy-eight Colombian traffickers. They were also offended by the government's confiscation of over 30 tons of cocaine and the torching of almost 2,000 tons of marijuana. Ambassador Tambs was blamed for much of this official mischief. He stood fast but reduced his staff. Colombian traffickers had threatened to kill five Americans for every Colombian gangster extradited, and embassy personnel were obvious targets.[20] Murderous threats by drug lords had to be taken seriously. They boldly continued to blow up things in their country and kill politicians, policemen, and journalists. Threats against Americans were mostly hot air, with the exception of some assaults on DEA agents operating in-country.

Was there any good news in 1984? There certainly was, despite the negative spin in media accounts. Almost 13,000 tons of marijuana were removed from the pipeline to the United States (including about 11,000 destroyed in Colombia and Mexico), approximately twice our estimated annual consumption. The amount of cocaine seized in Colombia was nearly half what was used annually in this country. A big plus was the Colombian president's agreement to extradite traffickers and his authorization of aerial eradication of pot fields with glyphosate. We were certainly taking a beating in cocaine air smuggling, but the maritime situation was improving. In 1984 the Coast Guard seized more smuggling vessels than in any previous or subsequent year. There were no media events to mark that accomplishment; James S. Gracey, the Coast Guard commandant, simply told Congress that maritime operations had cut down the illegal flow of drugs to the United States.

In 1984, cocaine shipments went to sea in many ways. The 33-foot Canadian-registered sailing vessel *Chinook* bore the largest at-sea cocaine seizure so far. The USCGC *Gallatin* (WHEC-721), patrolling the Windward Passage, sighted the boat heading north on 1 April. Acting on information from EPIC, the cutter stopped and boarded the sailboat. The *Chinook* was stuffed with about 1,820 pounds of pack-aged coke hidden in the chain locker and other compartments. The *Gallatin* took her prize to the naval base in Guantánamo, Cuba, with two arrested U.S. citizens. A Coast Guard C-130 flew the cocaine and the prisoners to Miami.[21]

At his arraignment in Miami, Hewitt Gaynor McGill, forty-three, ex-captain of the *Chinook,* told U.S. Magistrate Herbert Shapiro, "Your honor, I didn't know there was cocaine aboard the vessel." Just as McGill made his statement, the lights in the courtroom began to flicker. Before the power failed completely, Shapiro wagged his finger at the defendant and said, "You see! You see!" "Defendant's Case Has Come to Light" announced the *Miami Herald.*[22] As absurd as it was in this case, the "I didn't know it was there" defense became standard if the contraband was concealed in any way.

Cocaine was bound to come in quantity aboard noncommercial vessels. It was the preferred drug for millions of Americans. Aircraft remained the platform of choice for cocaine smugglers, but some was destined to spill over into the sea routes because of the volume needed to satisfy the insatiable demand. It had probably come in sizable loads aboard pleasure craft and fishing vessels before 1984, but the *Chinook* was the first big load taken at sea. Much hoopla was made over the catch, but it was just a drop in the pond; over 80 percent of the cocaine coming here was the flying kind. The day-to-day drudgery of the drug war afloat was to continue hammering the endless procession of northbound grass boats. Hammer them we did.

New Year's 1984 ushered in a preference in the grass trade for off-shore oil rig service and supply vessels. Oil rig tenders, as they are commonly called, were ideal marijuana transports. The ubiquitous rig tenders—with pilothouse right at the bows, open after deck, low free-board, moderate draft, and interior honeycombed with tanks—were common in all oceans. They frequently sailed outside normal shipping lanes and laid up in backwater ports. With the decline of the offshore oil industry in the Gulf of Mexico, many older tenders were sold for-eign at bargain prices. Astute pot smugglers saw a chance to acquire long-legged vessels with a potential for cheaply installed hidden com-partments in interior tanks.

Less conspicuous than most fishing vessels for long runs, the rig ten-ders usually had more interior storage space. They were certainly less suspicious than the small to medium-sized coastal freighter marijuana

Oil rig tenders with low freeboard and many interior tanks were ideal marijuana motherships. *Top:* Bales accessed through cutout in deck. *Bottom:*
Connecting tanks below with cargo rollers.

(Photographs by DEA agent Bud Baggett)

motherships used in the past. With unobstructed weather decks aft that also served as the tops of interior tanks, it was a simple matter to cut out a large section of deck for easy access to the contraband. Most legitimate rig tenders carried oxyacetylene welding and cutting rigs; the presence of such gear aboard a tender was not in itself suspicious. They also had the advantage of a low freeboard to make quick off-loads to smaller pickup boats tied alongside. Low-profile tenders were less conspicuous. All in all, oil rig tenders were much better suited than coastal freighters for use as marijuana motherships, especially when concealed compartments hid the contraband and provided a legal defense for transport crews. They were occasionally misidentified as crew boats, the much smaller and faster boats used to take personnel to and from the rigs.

One of the first seagoing pot busts of the year was an oil rig tender. The M/V *Adventurer*, a 134-foot Panamanian-registered vessel, was sighted off Freeport, Bahamas, on 24 January 1984 by a Customs plane. Suspicions were aroused by the presence of several fast boats alongside the tender. A Customs flash report sent the night watch at Miami NNBIS scurrying. The *Adventurer* was tagged on the status board. The USCGC *Sea Hawk* (WSES-2), a new 110-foot surface-effect cutter, was the closest interceptor. NNBIS requested that the Seventh District's Rescue Coordination Center, just down the hall in the federal building, direct the cutter to the scene. The *Sea Hawk* flew across the straits to her destination. The *Adventurer*'s master granted a standard request from the *Sea Hawk*'s captain for a consensual boarding. Coast Guardsmen found marijuana residue on the after deck. They also detected a strong odor of marijuana throughout the vessel, establishing probable cause to explore.

In a forward berthing area the boarders found fresh welds and fresh paint on the after bulkhead and fresh paint on the deck. An oxyacetylene rig was in plain view just aft of the pilothouse. Topside, a tank vent and sounding hole that appeared to be just aft of the suspicious bulkhead in the berthing compartment below emitted a strong pot odor. The searchers found fresh paint on the deck covering a soft concrete patch in the berthing compartment. Under the patch was a steel plate spot-welded to the deck. Up came the plate, and there it was: the entrance to a hidden compartment running the length of the vessel. A similar compartment was found on the other side. The *Sea*

Hawk's boarders found 20 tons of grass in the cut-out tanks. The compartments had been fitted with lights and cargo rollers attached to the decks to allow rapid movement of heavy pot bales.[23] Built-in rollers in large hidden compartments would be found in other marijuana-transporting oil rig tenders.

They did not all have fancy hidden compartments. The *Rama Cay* was a 70-foot ex-shrimper, flying the Panamanian flag. She was sighted by a navy P-3 Orion as she rattled into the Atlantic north of Hispaniola. The USCGC *Hamilton* (WHEC-715) was vectored to intercept the shabby profile vessel. The big 378-foot cutter had no trouble overtaking the slow-moving shrimper. After a quick SNO from Panama, the cuttermen boarded on 2 February. They found eight Colombians and what was first estimated as 25 tons of Colombian grass. The patrol boat *Point Barnes* (WPB-82371) relieved the *Hamilton* of her prize and delivered the *Rama Cay* to Miami. The actual weight of the marijuana proved to be only 23,000 pounds.[24] It was not uncommon for early seizure estimates to be high, especially when a boat was crammed full of pot bales. Many grass boats still made no attempt to hide contraband.

A second Panamanian-registered ex-shrimper, the *San Nicholas,* was less docile. She was bound north through the Yucatán at the same time the *Rama Cay* was slipping through the Mona Passage. The *San Nicholas* ran afoul of the *Lipan* (WMEC-85) two days before the *Hamilton* caught up with her prey. Perhaps the ancient *Lipan* was not as intimidating as the sleek *Hamilton;* she was certainly not as fast. At any rate, the master of the *San Nicholas* refused to obey the *Lipan*'s order to stop. He plowed ahead despite the cutter's repeated hails. Then the ill-tempered skipper aimed his rusty 70-foot battering ram straight toward the cutter's middle. The *Lipan* responded by lacing the blue water just ahead of the dangerous shrimper with .50-caliber rounds. Fortunately for the eight Colombians aboard the *San Nicholas,* the *Lipan*'s captain refrained from using deadly force to stop the attempted assault on his ship. When the suspect was finally brought to heel, the *Lipan*'s boarders found nearly 20 tons of pot.[25]

Was it a coincidence that two Panamanian-registered 70-foot ex-shrimp boats loaded with unconcealed marijuana and each crewed by eight Colombians were attempting to break out of the Caribbean by divergent routes at the same time? Probably not. It was either a test of the choke-point patrols or the beginning of the decoy loads that later became fairly common. Boats, grass, and Third World crews were cheap on the starting end of the chain. As barrier patrols grew more numerous, grass smugglers occasionally sent an obvious profile boat with a moldy pot load to occupy patrols while the primary load boat made a run through the passes. Throwaway crews on discard boats were not briefed about the mission; morale would have been a problem.

The Yucatán Channel continued to be the primary route for grass boats despite choke-point patrols. The USCGC *Decisive* (WMEC-629) was in the Caribbean approaches to the Gap on 6 February patrolling south of the *Lipan*'s area. The 119-foot British-flagged coastal freighter *Vera* was bound north. Under the U.S.–U.K. agreement, the cutter did not need an SNO to board the small freighter. The *Vera* obediently came to a stop at the *Decisive*'s signal. As the cuttermen suspected, there were no Englishmen aboard this vessel flying the Red Duster of the British merchant navy; they did, however, find eight Colombians and 15 tons of Colombian pot in the cargo hold. The *Vera* was the twenty-seventh vessel seized by the pot-scouting cutters in the Caribbean and Florida waters since 1 January, a seizure rate just shy of one a day. The marijuana take from the effort was over 227,000 pounds.[26] In the not-too-distant past, the *Vera* would have made a safe passage through the Yucatán while the *Lipan* was occupied with the *San Nicholas*—probably a decoy. Having two whites cruising the Gap was mauling grass smugglers. They were recalculating their actuarial tables.

The Windward Passage was another frequently used marijuana route north. In February 1984 the famous pot-busting cutter *Dauntless* (WMEC-624) was on patrol in the Windward. The monotony of roller-coasting over the white-capped seas was broken on the sixteenth day of the month. Lookouts sighted a 70-foot shrimper butting her way against the brisk winter trades. A closer look showed that the *Capt. Black* had not caught crustaceans lately. There was no response to repeated attempts to communicate with the shrimper. Checks with the Seventh District failed to identify any U.S. or foreign registration. The *Capt. Black* was not going to heed warnings. After the standard procedure of advising the suspected smuggler crew in both English and Spanish to move forward, the *Dauntless* put forty rounds into the stern of the shrimper to disable her machinery. They found almost 30 tons of marijuana and nine more Colombian discards. On the way home the *Dauntless* easily picked off the U.S. 42-foot sports fisherman *Nite Hawk Two* with only 1.5 tons of pot.[27] It was hardly worth a line in the deck log.

In May a navy P-3 Orion was searching east of the Bahamas in the open Atlantic. The aircrew sighted a drifting and apparently disabled motor vessel about 500 miles from Miami. Responding to the sighting report, the Coast Guard sent the cutter *Diligence* (WMEC-616) to investigate. When the cutter arrived on 20 May she found the motor vessel *Bismark,* which claimed to be Colombian. An offer of assistance by the cutter involved a consensual boarding to determine the nature of the casualty. Investigations revealed three facts: the *Bismark* was indeed broke, she was in fact stateless, and her cargo was 30 tons of Colombian grass. With the *Bismark* in tow, the *Diligence* sailed west toward Florida.

The cutter continued to deploy her extended eyes en route to Miami with an H-52 helicopter. On one flight the helo crew sighted the Honduran-registered motor vessel *Rosangle*. It was like a vision from the past. The *Rosangle* was deck-loaded with bales of clearly visible pot; Coast Guard airmen counted forty bales. Since the *Diligence* was fully engaged with the *Bismark,* the Seventh District dispatched the *Lipan* at her best speed to intercept. The tug-turned-cutter made the seizure and took six prisoners.[28] The *Rosangle* had probably been sent out as a decoy to clear the way for the heavily loaded but unfortunately disabled *Bismark*. Documentation of authentic decoys was rare, but this case had all the trappings of a planned event. Some grass boat crews were a little dense, but carrying bales on deck in daylight anywhere near South Florida was sheer idiocy—unless it was meant to be.

In June the *Mrs. White* came through Providence Channel in the Bahamas and into the warm embrace of the *Lipan*. The 156-foot coastal freighter wore the British red ensign. Under the matronly name painted on the stern was "Tortola, BVI" (British Virgin Islands). She was in international waters, 7 miles from the nearest Bahamian island, when the *Lipan* politely asked her to stop. The cutter was authorized to board under the U.S.-U.K. agreement. A discussion of legal authority, however, was unnecessary. A gentleman on the freighter, Jacinto Alava-Solano, said he was the master and invited the Coast Guardsmen to come aboard. It was 3 June 1984, a day that would change the prosecution of drug boat crews.[29]

Petty Officer First Class David Amidon, USCG, led the six-man boarding party from the *Lipan*. Through a seaman-interpreter Amidon got permission from Captain Alava-Solano for the sweep team to check all man-sized compartments to make sure no one was aboard the *Mrs. White* besides the eight-man complement mustered on the foredeck. Chief Engineer Alfonso Galves-Diaz was allowed to return to the engine room. The search party found that the ship was properly loaded with a cargo of cement and lumber. Documents showed that the cargo originated in Barranquilla, Colombia, and was bound for Freeport, Bahamas.

While the search went on, Coast Guardsmen near the bow detected the odor of marijuana from a high vent covered with a plastic bag. Boarding officer Amidon got permission from Alava-Solano to access an unaccounted-for space; the master gave permission, unaware that the borders had detected the odor of pot. In the paint locker the search team noticed a thick layer of paint over a 3-foot-square steel plate tack-welded to the deck. When the plate was removed, they found a compartment stacked with bales of marijuana. After this the search was expanded, again with the master's permission. Marijuana odors were also coming from a sounding tube aft. A hole was drilled in the deck over a space just behind the main cargo hold. A small sounding pipe inserted into the hole came up with bits of marijuana. With the discovery of the second hidden compartment, the vessel was seized and the crew arrested. A prize crew went aboard, and the *Mrs. White* was taken to Miami, where a Customs and DEA dockside search found almost 23 tons of marijuana in the two compartments.[30]

The master and crew of the *Mrs. White* were indicted on federal charges for conspiracy to possess with intent to distribute marijuana (21 U.S.C. 955c) aboard a vessel within the customs waters of the United States (21 U.S.C. 955a) and for possessing with intent to distribute aboard such a vessel (21 U.S.C. 955a and 18 U.S.C. 2). Captain Alava-Solano pled not guilty and was brought to trial in the Southern District of Florida on 15 August 1984. At trial the government surmised that the *Mrs. White* was a British vessel at the time of boarding and that the vessel was within the customs waters of the United States pursuant to the U.S.–U.K. agreement. At the close of the government's case, the defense raised the issue that the British Virgin Islands had denied that the *Mrs. White* was a British vessel. The judge accepted the defense's motion for a directed acquittal. The government immediately reindicted, substituting charges of being on a vessel on the high seas subject to the jurisdiction of the United States (21 U.S.C. 955a). The second trial began on 5 December 1984. Despite Alava-Solano's motion that he was being subjected to double jeopardy, the captain and crew of the *Mrs. White* were convicted as charged.[31]

The defendants appealed their convictions to the Eleventh Circuit. The appeals were filed separately for the master (Alava-Solano) and two groups of crewmen, but they were considered together by the court of appeals. The case was captioned *U.S. v. Vidal-Hungria* (794 F2d 1503), after one of the crewmen. Not until 25 July 1986 did the Eleventh Circuit render its decision. The court upheld the conviction of the captain, Alava-Solano, saying that the defendant could not have loaded, unloaded, and distributed the cargo alone, therefore finding that he could be convicted for conspiring with persons unknown. They did not give merit to his claim of double jeopardy. However, the court found that there was not enough evidence to convict the crew members of conspiracy. Despite the large quantity of marijuana, the court concluded that the government had not proved that individual crewmen had participated in the handling of the marijuana or known of its existence in the hidden and sealed compartments. The convictions of the seven crewmen were reversed.[32]

The Eleventh Circuit thus set the standard for prosecuting drug boat crews. What had been known as the mere-presence theory (*U.S. v. Cruz-Valdez,* 773 F2d 1541) of prosecuting people found on a boat full of grass was set aside in hidden-compartment cases. According to the mere-presence theory, common sense dictated that a person voluntarily aboard a small vessel crammed with marijuana had to know it was there, by virtue of the mere presence of the individual and the contraband on the boat at the same time. Now under the *Vidal-Hungria* decision the government had to prove beyond a reasonable doubt that someone on a vessel with drugs in a hidden compartment knew that the contraband was concealed in the compartment. The master of such a vessel, however, was held to higher standards of accountability than his crew. In *Vidal-Hungria* the appellate court implied that the captain, because of his position, was expected to know what was aboard his vessel and would have had to conspire with someone to get contraband into the compartments. A defendant master could still overcome the *Vidal-Hungria* precedent by showing that he did not know that contraband was aboard his ship despite the knowledge expected of one in his position. After 1986 the government was required to conduct innovative investigations after seizures to charge crewmen from vessels with contraband in hidden compartments. In many cases the crewmen were deported, as they had been in the 1970s. In the meantime, juries could be depended on to find crews aboard grass boats guilty, hidden compartments or no.

Fishing vessels and small boats loaded with pot still assaulted the patrol line off South Florida during the summer, reminiscent of the old Marine Corps ditty, "Hi diddle, diddle, right up the middle." Typical of these were the U.S. shrimper *V&S* and the Jamaican lobster boat *Ocean Queen* with 5 tons each, taken adjacent to the Florida Straits, and a 61-foot U.S. cabin cruiser with 10 tons trying to make a landfall at Fort Lauderdale.[33]

On 22 December 1984 the USCGC *Shearwater* (WSES-3) spotted the 35-foot U.S. lobster boat *Barracuda* making toward the Florida coast over the Great Bahamas Bank. Lookouts noted that the boat was down by the bow, with the stern floating unusually high. The *Shearwater* ordered the *Barracuda* to stop. The boarding party did an extensive search but found no unaccounted-for spaces. A line dragged under the boat from bow to stern passed evenly along the keel without snagging. The cutter and the suspect anchored for the night. Since the master of the vessel was not a U.S. citizen, the commanding officer of the *Shearwater,* as required by law, directed the lobster boat to proceed to Key West under escort. On the night of the twenty-fourth, during passage to the Keys, it was learned that the master was the subject of an outstanding warrant. He was arrested and transferred to the cutter. The boat was meticulously searched in Key West, again with negative results. When a diver inspected the bottom, however, two external containers were found, one bolted to each side of the keel. The boxlike containers were 16 feet long, 32 inches wide, and 21 inches deep. They were tapered at each end, allowing a rope to pass smoothly under the boat. When the *Barracuda* was hauled from the water, 2,008 pounds of highly compressed marijuana were removed. Access to the compartments was under the engine batteries on both sides of the boat. Since the compartments were located closer to the stern than the bow, their buoyancy had caused the vessel to float high aft and low forward.[34] The amount of grass seized in this case was minor. The effort and ingenuity in the method of concealment, however, showed that maritime seizures were being taken seriously by drug smugglers. Only one external-compartment case had been noted before the *Barracuda;* there would be others.

Internal and external hidden compartments made the conviction of drug boat crews much more difficult. The Coast Guard published guidelines to help boarding officers obtain and preserve evidence incriminating crewmen. A good suggestion was to remove crewmen's clothes immediately after arrest. Cutters were advised to carry spare coveralls for prisoners. The analysis of clothing worn on a drug boat could reveal the presence of drug residue and help establish the wearer's knowledge of concealed drugs. The procedure was later expanded to include bedding used by boat crews. Another important fact to document, when possible, was that a vessel carrying concealed drugs could not be used for the purpose claimed. This aspect was especially applicable to fishing vessels with missing or inoperable fishing gear. It was circumstantial evidence, but it carried weight with a jury. Boarding parties were also advised to notice the reaction of crewmen to the discovery of drugs.[35]

The whole process for indicting boat crews was becoming more complex. Seized vessels had to be treated like crime scenes to preserve evidence. A good and standard vessel postseizure procedure was needed. A few people in NNBIS organized a postseizure process in late 1984 in Florida and New York. Detailed postseizure reports first appeared in the interdiction intelligence community in 1985. They were valuable to prosecutors, force commanders, and intelligence analysts. The Coast Guard expanded the process, especially in the Seventh District and the Pacific Area Command.

In the North Atlantic there was a decline in maritime marijuana seizures in 1984. Seizures adjacent to the upper East Coast had been above 26 percent in 1983. Now they declined to approximately 14 percent of the total seaborne grass take, a big reduction.[36] Whether this phenomenon was due to fewer motherships transiting north or smarter smuggling techniques was unknown at the time. It was in fact the beginning of a decline in maritime marijuana deliveries to the Northeast. The reason was probably the increased efficiency of choke-point interdiction operations in the Caribbean. Because of the distance involved and the rough seas of the North Atlantic, vessels transporting grass north had to be larger than the norm.

The largest 1984 northeastern seizure was the stateless coastal freighter M/V *Ramsland.* She was taken by Customs in Boston on 16

November with 36 tons of marijuana. A postseizure analysis by NNBIS New York documented a new grass-smuggling route, via the Canary Islands off the northeast coast of Africa.

In December 1983 the 213-foot *Ramsland* had sailed from the Baltic to Las Palmas in the Canary Islands. She was inactive for ten months. On 19 October 1984 the vessel left Las Palmas. Her master said his next port of call was Calcutta, India. Twenty-six days later the *Ramsland* was in Boston—hardly time for a stop in Calcutta. Charts and navigation notes showed that the ship had come on a more or less great-circle route, loitering for two or three days in three different locations. The dilapidated freighter was seen by a Coast Guard plane 110 miles east-northeast of Boston. As the *Ramsland* neared Boston, she was contacted via radio by the Coast Guard and asked to declare her intentions. The master stated that his vessel was British, en route from Las Palmas to Boston. When the freighter crept into Boston Harbor on 14 November, a boarding party including Customs officers went aboard from the 95-foot patrol boat *Cape Morgan* (WPB-95313). The six crewmen had British passports. The ship contained about 600 cubic yards of gravel covering the hold to a depth of approximately 3 feet. No document of registry was aboard, and the vessel had not given the required twenty-four hours' advance notice of arrival. She was detained for Customs search and clearance.[37]

A query to Britain via the State Department determined that the *Ramsland* was not a British vessel. She was declared stateless and subjected to a full Customs border search. After exhausting all other possibilities, the searchers turned to the gravel pit. Strenuous effort was required to move the gravel to reach the deck. Nothing was found. The only space left was the ship's double bottoms. In the maze of 3-foot-high spaces divided by structural supports, Customs officers found compacted 14-inch-square bales of marijuana crammed into every available cranny. Some were inner-wrapped and marked Product of Colombia. There were 72,000 pounds of Colombian pot. The difficulty in loading the contraband can be imagined from the unloading process, which took eleven days. No one could document how the huge pot cargo got aboard. Transshipment in Las Palmas was probable. The advantage of the plan—to avoid patrols off Florida and approach the northeastern United States from the east, directly across the Atlantic, via a nontraditional mothership route—was obvious.[38]

By 1984, marijuana was being shipped in volume across the Atlantic to Europe. A route from Colombia via the Canary Islands was attractive. Many old laid-up vessels were bought cheaply and used for the temporary storage of pot or to serve as motherships to locations on the North Atlantic rim. A grass boat seized in North Fambridge, England, on 5 October 1984 may have received her cargo via this route. British agents seized 10 tons of pot from an 85-foot yacht attempting delivery 30 miles northeast of London.[39] Large shipments of marijuana to Europe in 1984 showed an expanding market and the pressure on grass smugglers along traditional routes to the United States.

There were no serious fluctuations in Pacific maritime marijuana (including hashish) seizures in 1984. Almost 133,000 pounds were taken from a total of sixteen vessels. Seven seizures totaled 10,000 pounds or more. The two largest seizures of the year were made dockside by Customs in the Los Angeles area. In March the motor vessel *Hyundai #23* was taken with 30,800 pounds, followed by the M/V *Shinkashu Maru* in August with 31,173 pounds. The northern Pacific was relatively quiet. The M/V *Allison,* with about 16,000 pounds of Thai marijuana, was intercepted near Seward, Alaska, by the Coast Guard in May with information provided by DEA and Customs. In August, Customs in San Francisco seized 10,900 pounds of Asian hashish from the *President Monroe.*[40]

A dramatic incident occurred in the drug war at sea off California on the last day of 1984. It emphasized the day-to-day hazards faced by maritime interdiction forces laboring heroically to stem the flow of contraband. The World War II–vintage buoy tender *Citrus* (WMEC-300) was on patrol west of Los Angeles. As an expediency, the *Citrus* had been painted white and pressed into service as a medium-endurance cutter. Her best speed was 15 knots, if the sea was calm.

Early on the thirty-first a navy Orion P-3 saw the 162-foot Panamanian rig tender *Pacific Star* over 800 miles southwest of the City of Angels. Intelligence said the tender was smuggling Southeast Asian marijuana. The *Citrus* went to intercept at her best speed. Despite her handicap, the cutter found the suspect in the closing hours of New Year's Eve. The *Citrus* watched the suspect while an SNO was sought from Panama. When it came, the cutter closed to board. The *Pacific Star* suddenly swerved toward the old cutter. The *Citrus* was rammed hard; the collision caused structural damage above the waterline. While the crew assessed the damage, the smugglers set fire to and scuttled their ship. Now the Coasties were ready for battle. They stormed the vessel and subdued the seven crewmen. Despite the best efforts by the cutter crew to fight fire and control flooding, the *Pacific Star* sank in the deep Pacific. Four hundred 10-pound packages of Thai marijuana floated to the surface and were recovered. The seven arrestees included five U.S. citizens, a Panamanian, and a Filipino. The *Citrus* took her hard-earned prisoners and drugs into San Diego. It was very fortunate that no one was injured in the collision.[41] The scuttling of drug vessels off the Pacific coast was becoming routine.

Approximately 3.7 million pounds of maritime marijuana were seized in 1984, including floating bales. Coast Guard seizures accounted for roughly 2.5 million pounds. Total maritime cocaine seized was approximately 14,000 pounds, with Coast Guardsmen taking almost 2,000 pounds. It was quite an increase over the 46 pounds of coke they got in 1983. Despite the increase in coke, marijuana was still the focus of the sea services' interdiction effort. In 1984, 218 vessels were seized by the Coast Guard, a record that still stands.[42] About 57 percent of the smuggling vessels were pleasure craft, 33 percent were fishing vessels, and 10 percent were coastal freighters, oil rig tenders, or other types. The geographical distribution of seized vessels was 73 percent in the Florida-Bahamas area, 14 percent in the Caribbean, 6 percent along the upper East Coast, 4 percent in the Gulf of Mexico (excluding Florida's west coast), and 2 percent in the Pacific.[43] The drug war at sea continued primarily in southern waters.

The real hooker in 1984 was the sudden increase in marijuana seizures along the southwestern border. Pot originating in Mexico and shipped across the land borders rose to an estimated 24 percent. Border seizures accounted for about 5 percent of the total marijuana for the year. The increase was attributed to expanding cultivation and reduced eradication in Mexico. Still, the Mexican government reportedly seized 2,400 metric tons of grass, which was documented by U.S. participation in the giant Chihuahua raid in November.[44] Processing of cocaine had certainly increased in Colombia, and some traditional grass smugglers were shifting to coke. Their rationale was just as certainly related to marijuana cargo losses at sea. Mexico was picking up the slack. The change showed the effectiveness of maritime interdiction.

The burning and sinking mothership *Pacific Star,* which rammed the venerable cutter *Citrus* (WMEC-300) in the open Pacific
(Official U.S. Coast Guard photograph)

Other signals of change in the drug trade were received in late 1984. It meant little at the time, and the impact has yet to be fully felt or evaluated, but Colombian drug traffickers began to experiment with the cultivation of opium poppies.[45] Recent increases in heroin imports are related to that event. In October 1984, Jamaican authorities seized two maritime containers in Kingston with 20 tons of marijuana. They were ready for shipment to the United States.[46] These seizures further documented the threat of container smuggling, a threat that the U.S. government has so far failed to counter. No one knows the volume of drugs coming that way. The sheer number of maritime containers arriving daily at our ports defies control.

The year 1984 saw dramatic changes in the public perception of drug abuse. Drug use and trafficking were finally recognized by citizens and politicians alike, with much prompting by the media, as a major threat to our way of life and our nation's security. Although the government had not yet developed a strategy for fighting the drug war, we shifted from a defensive to an offensive posture. Despite the washout of Hat Trick–Wagon Wheel, the seagoing interdiction forces were learning their trade.

7

The Offensive
Part Two, 1985

When once the offensive has been assumed, it must be sustained to the last extremity.

NAPOLEON I, *MAXIMS OF WAR,* 1831

An offensive spirit permeated interdiction efforts in 1985 despite rampant media defeatism. The plodding grass boats were joined by go-fast cocaine boats, which assaulted South Florida with increasing regularity. Air drops and transshipments from airstrips in the Bahamas were a big part of the coke flooding the United States. Planning for forward deployment of interdiction forces in the nearby islands moved apace with plans for a renewed air and sea blockade of Colombia. The drug threat was expanding, but more interdiction resources were available. Coordination of the antinarcotics effort was improving daily with the leadership of the vice president via NNBIS.

Drug-related events and media reviews monopolized headlines in 1985. On 5 January the Colombian national police put four traffickers on a plane for Miami under the U.S.–Colombia extradition treaty. They were the first. A few days later the infamous cocaine smuggler Carlos Lehder made his television debut at a jungle hideaway. Lehder declared that he would use his millions to destabilize the Colombian government. In wild rhetoric he denounced the United States and proclaimed, "Cocaine is the Latin American atomic bomb." He vowed to use the weapon to destroy the United States and the "oligarchic monarchy" of Colombia.[1]

Two leading periodicals ran extensive articles exposing the futility of the drug war. In February *Time* magazine's cover story declared, "U.S. finds itself mired in a violent, losing battle." It was a frightening piece, illustrated with photos and charts.[2] Not to be outdone, *U.S. News and World Report* wrote a month later, "Flood of Drugs—A Losing Battle." The lead-in announced, "The mighty United States government, despite exposing its agents to hair-raising personal risks and spending millions of dollars, is losing an uphill battle to throttle production of narcotics around the globe." It was just as persuasive and well documented as the *Time* story, with breakdowns of drug sources.[3] The media was defining the drug war, just as it had done with the war in Vietnam.

Early in 1985 OVP/NNBIS finalized a plan to disrupt drug shipments through the Bahamas. A February White House meeting between Vice President George Bush and a Bahamian minister set ground rules. The Bahamas granted U.S. interdiction the unprecedented authority to sweep the islands with air, land, and sea forces in search of drugs. The only caveat was that Bahamian constabulary troops would lead land sweeps and accompany sea and air units. NNBIS Miami coordinated the efforts of federal, state, and local law enforcement agencies to intercept drug loads flushed out of the islands.[4]

Operation Blue Lightning began on 2 April 1985. It was the fourth major offensive of the drug war. About eight hundred U.S. and Bahamian personnel took part in the sixteen-day operation, deployed in eighty-five vessels, thirty aircraft, and six radar facilities in and around the 470-mile-long island chain. They netted 5,500 pounds of cocaine and 33,872 pounds of marijuana, made fifty-eight arrests, and seized twenty-five boats, two aircraft, and two vehicles with trailers.[5]

This display of force had to have a deterrent effect on smugglers using the islands. The results were not spectacular, considering the effort, but they were certainly not shabby. Lessons learned led to the formation of the Blue Lightning Strike Force, institutionalizing the tactics used. It was essentially a Customs-coordinated endeavor using state and local assets for operations along Florida's coast. It later expanded to other areas of the Southeast.

Throughout the year NNBIS planned for Operation Hat Trick II, a continuation of the original sea-air effort of 1984 to block drugs from Caribbean sources. The second run was the largest and most diversified counternarcotics strike to date. It was also the fifth major offensive of the drug war. All military services supported the Coast Guard, Customs, and DEA. The governments of Colombia, Panama, Venezuela, Jamaica, and some of the lesser Caribbean island nations cooperated. This operation would be pulsed at unannounced intervals, to keep smugglers off balance. The Coast Guard and the navy would be the primary maritime interdiction forces, while Customs and all military services would do air interdiction. The State Department and DEA would work with the foreign countries going after stockpiled drugs delayed in shipment because of air-sea blockades. Caribbean choke points were targeted, but there was no gradual movement of patrol lines toward Colombia as in the first effort. Winter storms that disrupted drug movements and patrol operations had been duly noted. Vice President Bush stated in a news release, "The real success of this operation, however, does not rest with thousands of pounds of drugs seized. It depends on our commitment to continue the fight."[6]

Hat Trick II started on 1 November 1985, again coinciding with the fall harvest of marijuana in Colombia. A three-month concerted effort resulted in the seizure of almost 1.7 million pounds of pot and

22,000 pounds of cocaine, and the arrest of thirteen hundred drug traffickers.[7] Blue Lightning and Hat Trick demonstrated a transition from a reactionary posture by individual agencies to a coordinated multiagency, and occasionally a multinational, offensive strategy. It brought to bear the full range of local, state, and federal law enforcement capabilities, supported by military and intelligence-community assets whose objective was to apprehend drug smugglers and disrupt traffic from the Caribbean.[8] Within those perimeters, Hat Trick II was a resounding success.

No sooner was Hat Trick II up and running than another disaster occurred in Colombia. On 6 November, M-19 guerillas (the communist Nineteenth of April Movement) assaulted and captured Colombia's Palace of Justice in Bogotá. The next day Colombian military forces stormed the building. By the time the dust settled, there had been almost one hundred fatalities, including eleven Supreme Court justices and most of the M-19 raiders. A fire had destroyed the judicial archives. Government officials speculated that drug traffickers had financed the raid to destroy extradition records. There was controversy in the United States and Colombia over whether Nicaraguan Sandinistas had played a role in supplying the M-19 troops with weapons.[9] There is no record of any high-level discussion as to whether the Hat Trick II operation had caused or in any way contributed to the M-19 attack. The coincidence of this occurring six days after the start of Hat Trick, however, is provocative.

Inshore maritime forces around Miami were busy from the beginning of the year through the whole of Blue Lightning and much beyond. Cocaine air drops in and around the Bahamas became more prevalent. Inshore seizures increased. On the afternoon of 5 April a Miami Beach shore patrol boat with a Customs officer embarked intercepted a 28-foot Fibra runabout in Government Cut. The suspect was escorted to the Customs dock on the Miami River. A search found 775 pounds of cocaine in a hidden compartment. Three Miami men were arrested.[10] That night a Customs boat stopped a 35-foot Hatteras cruiser approaching Government Cut. The boarding officer noticed loose screws in a cabin deck. Under the deck were 577 pounds of cocaine in gift-wrapped boxes and Tupperware containers. Two people were arrested.[11] These were now routine seizures.

The Coast Guard was anxious to score in the cocaine game. Around midnight on 8 May the USCGC *Cape Shoalwater* (WPB-95324),

A U.S. Customs Blue Thunder interceptor hunts go-fast coke runners off Miami. *(Official U.S. Customs photograph)*

patrolling just off Miami Beach, saw an unlit speedboat heading toward Bakers Haulover Cut. Air Station Miami scrambled a helicopter piloted by Lt. Jim Sellers, equipped with night-vision goggles. At 0115 the crew spotted the suspect about 2 or 3 miles from the cut. The Coast Guard helo followed the boat at a steady 50 knots. The suspect was a 29-foot Mirage, the *Goza Now*, with three men on board. Loudspeaker hails had no effect. Lieutenant Sellers asked Group Miami Beach for surface support. He continued in hot pursuit as the *Goza Now* blasted into Biscayne Bay. A concerned citizen in a nearby fifth-floor condo called the Coast Guard to report that a helo had just flown by *below* his vantage point!

It happened that a Coast Guard TACLET was on training operations in Biscayne Bay with two small boats. Lt. Jerry Lober, the TACLET CO, saw the helo making south over the bay at very low altitude with the go-fast right below it. Lober joined the chase with a rigid-hull inflatable.

Just north of Venetian Causeway, after an 8-mile chase involving wild passes under three bridges, the suspect suddenly slowed. Three occupants dove from the Mirage and swam to the causeway, leaving their unmanned boat spinning in a tight circle. Lieutenant Sellers and his crew saw two of the men jump into a waiting car and speed away. The third ran along the causeway toward some bushes. Shortly after the suspects abandoned ship, the Coast Guard inflatable arrived. Machinery Technician First Class John Catanzaro, with the help of Boatswain's Mate Second Class Mike Fleming, made the tricky maneuver of lassoing the Mirage and shutting down her engines. By now several Miami-Dade Police Department land units had arrived. Lieutenant Lober went ashore to confer with the locals. In the middle of their hurried conference, a woman walked up and pointed to where she had seen a man hiding in the bushes. Two policemen apprehended the wet suspect. He told them he had been fishing and fell in. The suspect was cuffed. Now the Coast Guardsmen had time to examine the large cardboard boxes that filled the go-fast. They had assumed it was pot; instead they found 1,909 pounds of cocaine. It was the largest Coast Guard cocaine seizure, 89 pounds more than the previous record amount taken from the sailboat Chinook in April 1984.[12]

Every month brought new records for maritime-related coke seizures. DEA, Customs, and locals raided a waterfront house in Juno Beach, Palm Beach County, on 27 June after watching suspects unloading duffle bags from a speedboat behind the house. The bags held nearly 2,000 pounds of coke. Agents arrested ten people in the sunrise raid and confiscated two boats and four sports cars. A federal official said that this coke bust was the largest in Palm Beach County and one of the biggest in Florida. An interesting aspect of the raid was another attempt by two suspects to flee in a speedboat. They were arrested by officers who followed them in a helicopter.[13]

Not all cocaine boat intercepts ended peacefully. In the early hours of 1 August a Customs boat on patrol east of Alligator Reef Light sighted a suspect 32-foot Bertram ocean racer. As Customs patrol officers Clark Grindstaff, Bruce Meader, and George Carberry closed the range they saw people tossing duffle bags. After the bags were jettisoned, the boat turned toward the interceptor and repeatedly attempted to ram. The patrol officers blasted the big Mercury engines of the unruly Bertram with shotgun rounds and a few 9 mm pistol rounds. When the engines stalled from too much ventilation, the three men in the racer surrendered. They were unharmed, attesting to the good aim of the sharpshooters in their wildly swerving interceptor. By daylight, thirty-four duffle bags with an estimated 2,000 pounds of coke had been retrieved. This seizure was one of year's largest.[14]

A foreign pilot who had flown approximately a dozen loads from Colombia told about how cocaine got to boats in the Bahamas. By the time he decided to talk to law enforcement officials, Albert (a fictitious name used to protect the individual) had become a born-again Christian. Albert said he flew 300- to 900-kilo loads of coke for a smuggler who lived in Bucaramanga, Colombia. He described the system in detail, even supplying the radio frequencies and call signs used by the organization.

Albert told the investigators that pilots received messages to call Richard in Medellin to arrange schedules. They stayed at the Intercontinental Hotel and were met by a representative of the organization. Private air transport took them to a 4,000-foot airstrip on a big farm near Puerto Wilches. The pilots were assigned aircraft and given instructions. Usually they flew to Puerto Estrella or to a place near Cabo de la Vela on the tip of the Guajira Peninsula for coke loads. Once airborne, they would set a course overland to Punta Espada, which juts into the Gulf of Venezuela. From there the flights went east on the radio beacon to Aruba. Then they flew north-northwest at an altitude of 10,000–12,000 feet to a designated island in the Bahamas. Flights usually started at dusk in Colombia and arrived in the Bahamas between 2300 and 0100. When they landed, the coke was unloaded to waiting boats, usually two boats per aircraft load. Albert claimed that the maritime part of this operation was controlled by a Bahamian who lived in West End, Grand Bahamas. The boats sped to West End for final instructions from this man. Albert made deliveries to Hog, Whale, and Treasure Cays in the Berry Islands, northern Bahamas. He thought the loads were ultimately delivered to a waterfront house in Dania, Florida. He was paid $150,000 per delivery.

Albert's information was dated by the time of his Second Birth, but the people he identified did exist. One was a well-known DEA fugitive. Albert offered to fly a controlled load to the Bahamas but would not agree to advance notification of Bahamian authorities. That was contrary to the OPBAT interdiction protocol, so an opportunity was missed. The pilot went back to his evangelical work without fully compensating for his admitted sins.[15]

Cocaine was the interdiction priority in 1985, but marijuana seizures continued unabated. The interdiction of two spiny-lobster boats about 80 miles northwest of Key West in late May is representative. The USCGC *Cape Fox* (WPB-95316) spotted them while patrolling off Florida Bay. The boats were inbound from Gulf waters too deep for lobstering and headed toward the Everglades. First the small cutter went after the 50-foot *Angelita* and stopped her with no trouble. Ten tons of pot were in plain view. While the *Cape Fox* was involved with the *Angelita,* the second boat ran. A prize crew was put aboard the seized boat, and the cutter took off on a stern chase. Under normal conditions big lobster boats could outdistance small cutters, but the *Ocean Lady* was loaded to the gunnels with grass bales. The *Cape Fox* overhauled the lobster boat for another 10 tons of pot. Eight people were arrested.[16] The two lobster boats had probably received their large loads from a mothership in the Gulf.

The interceptions occurred not far from what was coming to be known in the interdiction community as Route 26. Intelligence and Gulf seizures showed that smugglers were avoiding Yucatán Channel choke-point patrols by running close inshore by the Mexican coast. Motherships then went to the general vicinity of the large NOAA weather/oceanographic buoy moored in deep water at 26° north and 86° west, or approximately 270 miles west of Marco Island, Florida. The big buoy was well lit and offered a good radar return. Smugglers called the NOAA buoy the Coke Machine (referring to the drink rather than the white powder, since these were grass men). Off-loads by the buoy were taken to the Florida coast along the 26° north line. This part of the Gulf of Mexico was now a major conduit for sea-borne marijuana entering the United States.[17] Approximately seventeen seizures of 10,000 pounds or more were made on Route 26 in 1985. The total volume seized exceeded 350,000 pounds. Only two big seizures occurred in other parts of the Gulf that year; both were off Louisiana.

Coast Guard and Customs inshore patrols were thin along the Florida end of Route 26 in 1985. Down south the cutters and navy ships dwarfed and intimidated smuggler boats with big guns. Not so in the shallow waters off southwestern Florida and the Everglades. On the night of 25 August a 41-foot Coast Guard utility boat, manned by a mostly teenaged crew, was told to intercept the 68-foot shrimper *Lanasa II.* The 41-boat did the job handsomely 15 miles off Venice. Twenty tons of grass were packed into the shrimper's hold. Six smugglers were arrested without incident.[18]

Some ploys used to bring marijuana into the Gulf were bizarre, such as the case of the Japanese-built 120-foot stern-trawler *Argana*

Fast lobster boats were prime grass movers along Route 26.
(Author's collection)

II. On 6 June 1985 a Coast Guard C-130 out of Air Station Clearwater was patrolling the Caribbean between Jamaica and Central America. Near Rosalind Bank the crew sighted the *Argana II* making to the northwest toward Yucatán Channel. Some of the flight crew who had flown fishery patrols from Alaska recognized the distinctive Oriental trawler as a type used in the North Pacific. This boat was unlike any fishing vessel found in the Gulf or the Caribbean; it was hard to imagine a craft that would have attracted more attention. The C-130 pilot reported the trawler as a possible smuggler.

The cutter *Steadfast* (WMEC-623) was not far away. At 1642 on 7 June the *Steadfast* had the *Argana II* in sight about 30 miles east of Misteriosa Bank, still heading northwest. The cutter, abeam of the trawler, started preboarding interrogation. The trawler's master gave his name as Kang Soo-Jin from Korea. There was no home port painted on the vessel, and no flag flying. "Morocco" was painted on life rings. Captain Kang said that his vessel was registered in Morocco and that he was bound from Cartagena, Colombia, to Mexico to fish in Mexican waters. According to Kang, the owners had told him they were in the process of getting a Mexican fishing permit. Kang agreed to a consensual boarding. In the fish hold, along with only 1,500 pounds of miscellaneous fish and plastic ice bags, the boarders found a freshly painted fiberglass bulkhead across the forward end of the hold; it was obviously a recent addition. They requested permission to drill into the bulkhead, which the captain granted. There was an odor of marijuana. At this point Kang admitted that marijuana was on board. He said the vessel was actually registered in Colombia, not Morocco. Coast Guard headquarters assimilated the vessel as stateless and directed the *Steadfast* to seize. Kang and sixteen Colombian crewmen were arrested.

Approximately 23,000 pounds of marijuana were removed from the *Argana II*. She was fully equipped with fishing gear, but it was mostly inoperable. There was no polish on the trawl-door metal skids, showing no recent contact with the bottom. Trawl fittings were rusted in place and could not be released. The most damning evidence was the fish in the hold: many were species of reef fish, which could be caught only on ocean bottoms that would tear a trawl to pieces. Any defense claiming ignorance of contraband in a concealed compartment would have been seriously compromised, because the vessel could not have been used for the purpose stated. Faced with this evidence, all hands from the *Argana II* pled guilty.[19]

Detecting dysfunctional vessels was good intelligence. An example was the astute observation by a young Florida Marine Patrol officer on the 59-foot fishing vessel *Laura Lee*. Officer Jeffrey F. Russo made a routine inspection of the boat at Cortez, Florida, in October 1985. He saw engine exhaust pipes running through the vessel's large fish boxes, with little insulation. The officer figured that any ice placed in the boxes would melt quickly, causing catch spoilage. Russo reported his suspicions to NNBIS. After an investigation by U.S. Customs, the boat was placed on EPIC lookout. On 24 November the USCGC *Decisive* (WMEC-629) sighted the *Laura Lee* in the Yucatán Channel. The boarding team found a small amount of cocaine and almost 40,000 pounds of marijuana crammed into every available space. Officer Russo was commended for a job well done.[20]

Hat Trick II began with deep deployments by the cutters and their navy counterparts in the Caribbean. On 10 November the *Gallatin*

The *Argana II* might as well have carried a sign "grass boat."
(Author's collection)

(WHEC-721) drew the first real blood in the war at sea. The 378-foot cutter sighted the 60-foot Colombian motor vessel *El Toro* 170 miles off Colombia's coast. The vessel's name was painted on boards hung over the sides. Capt. Donald Ramsden considered the northbound vessel suspicious. He requested permission from the Colombian government to stop and board the suspect, then laid his ship on a parallel course with *El Toro* and waited. An SNO was received at 1245. In English and Spanish, the freighter was told to stop. Instead the suspect swerved toward the cuter and rammed. Negligible damage was done. The *Gallatin* gave the usual warning, then opened fire with a .50-caliber machine gun. Finally someone on the target waved a white towel. The boarding party found an estimated 28 tons of pot and one crewman with a minor shrapnel wound in his foot. He was transferred to the cutter for treatment before the boat sank. This was the first injury from the use of deadly force by a Coast Guard cutter in the drug war.[21]

As patrol nets tightened again in the Caribbean passes, some big grass boats went further south to reach the Atlantic. The Colombian 140-foot coastal freighter *Island Express* was intercepted skirting the

Bahamas on 14 December by the USCGC *Dauntless* (WMEC-624). The master said he was bound from Puerto Rico to Miami for repairs. He allowed Coast Guardsmen to board for a documentation check. They found approximately 60 tons of marijuana in the freighter's hold.[22] It was one of the biggest pot seizures of the year. The *Dauntless* was still setting records.

Occasionally the sea war took a humorous turn. Early in 1985 Lt. Bill Baker, operations officer at Coast Guard Group St. Petersburg, received an agitated call from the police chief in Fort Myers Beach. The chief wondered if Baker knew where all the Chinese invading his town were coming from. This was news to Baker. He admitted he did not have a clue but promised to check on it. Lieutenant Baker phoned his contact in the Immigration and Naturalization Service's Tampa office. The harassed INS agent, one of two responsible for an area as large as Baker's, asked if the Chinese were causing any trouble. Baker told him that as far as he knew, they were not. The agent said he would get to the problem when he could. Overrun with drug smugglers on Route 26, Baker told Petty Officer Ernie Caamano to get a note out to the troops about the Chinese. He then promptly forgot about the matter and returned to more pressing issues.

The Chinese tale continued with one of Group St. Pete's three 82-foot patrol boats, the *Point Swift* (WPB-82312), commanded by Senior Chief Boatswain's Mate Mark McKenney. Chief McKenney was a decorated veteran of Operation Market Time's sea blockade of North Vietnam. One night in March, McKenney was patrolling off Fort Myers Beach looking for grass runners. A suspicious radar contact materialized as a large sailboat creeping toward shore. As the blacked-out cutter cautiously neared the target, McKenney and his crew saw people on the sailboat toss something overboard. The *Point Swift* managed to retrieve a package. The content was either marijuana or hashish; the record is not clear. Chief McKenney illuminated his patrol boat and closed with the target at top speed. He ordered his executive petty officer, Dave Gray, a taciturn Outerbanker from North Carolina, to stand by to board.

The Coast Guardsmen saw that the target was the *Clorox,* a dilapidated U.S.–registered sailing vessel. Petty Officer Gray jumped aboard with an armed boarding party. Gray disappeared down the companionway. A few minutes later his head popped out of the hatch. "Any more dope, Dave?" shouted McKenney over the throbbing engines. "No, Chief, but the damn boat's fulla Chinamen," replied Gray. The mystery of the Chinese invasion of Fort Myers Beach was solved. The *Clorox* was bringing them from Jamaica for a handsome fee. The drug-smuggling evidence was shaky, but Gray's testimony as a rope expert was enough to make the charges stick. He convinced the jury that the line tied to the contraband package had been cut from a length found on the boat. There was plenty of evidence for INS to charge the crew of the *Clorox* with smuggling aliens.[23]

Seizures off the Middle Atlantic States and the New England and Canadian coasts declined further in 1985. Some interesting cases did occur. The ex-Japanese longline fishing vessel *Fatuk* was of Panamanian registry. Now a refrigerated cargo vessel, the 148-foot *Fatuk* was first seen by a Coast Guard aircraft 40 miles southeast of Montauk Point, Long Island, on 22 February. She was reported as a possible doper. Later on the twenty-second the vessel was boarded by the USCGC *Point Jackson* (WPB-82378) with Customs officers embarked, just inside Narragansett Bay, Rhode Island. The British master rightly claimed a cargo of frozen shark. He alleged that the cargo originated in Dakar, Senegal, and showed documents including a bill of lading, a certificate of origin, and a certificate of sanitation, all photocopies and written in French. A search was hampered by an ammonia leak in the refrigeration system. No drugs were found, so the *Fatuk* was allowed to proceed to a dock in Providence.

Coast Guard and Customs investigators visited the vessel again on the twenty-fifth. The Customs officers had brought a dog team. The dogs were not taken into the hold with the frozen shark carcasses because of the leaking ammonia. This search was more extensive, but still no contraband. Since no violations were found, the *Fatuk*'s crew were allowed to come and go freely. Customs decided to post a watch on the vessel just in case. Within a few days the British master, the chief mate, and the Costa Rican chief engineer disappeared. Only the crew of five Koreans and one Costa Rican remained. No one claimed the cargo. Customs decided to off-load the frozen shark before the refrigeration system failed completely. The off-load started on 28 February. After about a ton of shark carcasses had been removed, Customs officers found a plastic tarp. Beneath the tarp were bales. There were about 80,000 pounds of frozen shark and 52,620 pounds of marijuana. The ship was seized, and the six crewmen were arrested. Prosecution of the crew was declined, and they were deported. A postseizure analysis of charts, documents, papers, and logs aboard the *Fatuk* by NNBIS New York showed that the whole voyage was an elaborate sham. The shark cargo was perhaps the most ingenious part of the scheme. It was of real value and in demand; it was also extremely difficult to search at sea. The interdiction forces were alerted to be wary of vessels bearing sharks.[24]

The *Fatuk* was the first of three identical ex-longliners with cargoes of allegedly African-caught fish that were documented smuggling marijuana to the United States. The second was the M/V *Saja,* seized later in 1985 after successfully off-loading pot in the Columbia River. The *Yoko Maru* was the third, seized in the Gulf of Mexico in 1987. All had Oriental crews and ammonia leaks. After the third seizure in 1987, investigators identified an organization in Europe that controlled these vessels and possibly others. It was one of the most sophisticated groups encountered in the sea war. The *Fatuk* seizure showed the extreme measures that smugglers used to import multi-ton pot loads to the Northeast in 1985.

A second case illustrating these extravagant measures was the 71-foot trawler *Master Mike.* On the morning of 21 August the fishing vessel *Terry II* found a partially sunken vessel floating 1.5 miles west of Great Island, Wellfleet, Massachusetts. The stern was awash, but the name *Divino Criador* and a documentation number could be seen. The *Terry II*'s master notified the Coast Guard. A few hours later, divers found bales of marijuana. When some were removed, the main beam documentation number revealed that the sunken vessel was actually the *Master Mike.* Later that day the real *Divino Criador* was located fishing northeast of Race Point, Massachusetts. The smugglers had picked a legitimate vessel similar to the load boat to disguise the pot delivery to Boston. An enforcement sighting of the smuggler would bring a registration check showing that the vessel was a legitimate fisherman. It was a good plan. The *Master Mike* had been listed in the law enforcement database as a suspect since 1978.

The Coast Guard raised and dewatered the *Master Mike* and brought her to Fairhaven, Massachusetts. She contained about 39,700 pounds of marijuana. NNBIS New York did a postseizure analysis. Charts and waterlogged notes indicated that the smugglers had left Santa Marta, Colombia, on 5 August 1985 with about 45,000 pounds of grass. Chart tracklines and navigational notations showed that the vessel had left the Caribbean via Anegada Passage, east of the British

Virgin Islands. The analysis further showed that the smugglers had come north by Bermuda to the area of Nantucket Shoals. On the seventeenth they came alongside the F/V *Merlin* fishing southeast of Nantucket. A white male aboard the *Divino Criador* asked the *Merlin's* master to call for him via the marine operator to Tony in North Truro with the message "Master Mike will be on 13 at 8 P.M." Using another boat to make the contact call was clever. The call, however, was recorded in the marine operator's log, and the telephone number led to Tony's name and address.

The smugglers' intelligence had been faulty. During the weekend of 16–19 August the Coast Guard and the navy held a joint mobilization drill in Boston Harbor. The exercise included boarding vessels in the area. The *Master Mike,* a.k.a. *Divino Criador,* barely avoided two Coast Guard patrols. It became apparent to the smugglers that reaching their primary off-load site on the Neponset River near Boston was highly unlikely. Also, the weather was deteriorating. Another fishing vessel was used to make a partial off-load from the smuggler and remove the crew before scuttling on the twentieth. On 22 August rangers from Cape Cod National Seashore found forty-one bales of marijuana in the sand dunes north of Herring Cove Beach. The bales were similar in size, shape, weight, and packaging to those recovered from the *Master Mike*. A Colombian passport was also found on the beach near the cove. Six people were indicted.[25]

The last big North Atlantic seizure of the year, a record, occurred off North Carolina on 4 September 1985. The case was a classic of pinpoint shoreside intelligence. Special Agents Stanley Jacobsen of the FBI and Daniel Dunn of Customs recruited a well-placed informant in a smuggling organization that was using a fuel barge to transport over 50 tons of Colombian marijuana to Norfolk, Virginia. The plan was for a Honduran tug to tow the barge north to a point off New Jersey, where an American tug would take the pot-laden barge into Norfolk. The tug exchange would defeat suspicions that the tow had come north from Colombia. As an added safety measure, the second tug would be known locally and would approach Norfolk from the north. The smugglers thought it unlikely that an air sighting would identify the barge, one being much like another. The FBI and Customs planned to make the seizure in Norfolk.

A navy P-3 patrol plane made a routine report of the first tug with the barge off North Carolina. A Coast Guard C-130 overflight at low altitude identified the *Capstan* with her tow but spooked the smugglers. They changed course for Bermuda. The informant told agents that a coded radio call from the tug confirmed the alternative plans. This would not be an in-port seizure after all. The agents contacted the Coast Guard. The venerable cutter *Taney* (WHEC-37) was dispatched to make the intercept off North Carolina. The last Pearl Harbor veteran still in commission found and captured the tug and tow without incident. A lookout for the second tug, the *Eagle,* was set in Norfolk. When the *Eagle* arrived from a voyage on the high seas with no rational explanation of her purpose, the master and crew were identified and later indicted for smuggling. The *Capstan* and the barge were brought into Jacksonville, Florida, to keep prosecution in the Middle District of Florida, where the case originated. A search of the fuel barge found approximately 165,000 pounds of marijuana. All hands aboard both tugs and the barge were convicted in federal court.[26]

Seventeen vessels with 101,394 pounds of pot were seized for drug smuggling in or adjacent to the Pacific Ocean in 1985. There were no important cocaine seizures. Only four vessels were found with major marijuana loads.[27] One that succeeded was the sister ship of the ammonia-leaking *Fatuk,* seized three months before in Rhode Island. On 23 May 1985 the M/V *Saja* arrived in Astoria, Oregon, with 65 tons of black grouper, allegedly from Africa. The ex-longliner had a crew of eleven South Koreans. She also had an ammonia leak. After discharging her fish in Astoria, the boat went 25 miles up the Columbia River to a remote dock in Bradwood, Oregon. The ship's crew left for parts unknown. On 31 May the vessel was boarded by Coast Guard, Customs, and National Marine Fisheries Service officials. A strong odor of ammonia from a leaking refrigeration system hampered the search, which was negative. At this late juncture, a striking resemblance between this vessel and the pot-smuggling *Fatuk* was obvious. The abandoned vessel was later seized by Customs and forfeited to the federal government.[28]

An investigation of the *Saja* incident by Customs in Portland, Oregon, located a crewman who related the following: In January 1985 he was offered a job in Korea by a seaman broker for a position on a ship transporting fish to South America. He flew to the Canary Islands and boarded the vessel *Wha Yang*. The name was changed to *Saja* en route to Dakar. The crewman claimed that the fish were loaded from another vessel. They sailed to Curaçao, Netherlands

Antilles, and then to a point off the Colombian Guajira Peninsula where they picked up about 40,000 pounds of marijuana. It was stored in a refrigerated compartment, which was sealed. From Guajira the ship went through the Panama Canal and then north to Astoria. After the fish were off-loaded, they went up the Columbia River to a dock facility where the marijuana was off-loaded to trucks after dark. The crewman's story was substantiated. He was helpful in identifying several people involved in the venture.[29]

By and large the 1984–85 offensives and the interdiction buildup in southern waters had a positive impact on the maritime marijuana smugglers but little visible effect on cocaine imports, which traveled mostly by air. Cocaine seizures from private vessels went from 11 percent in 1984 to 28 percent in 1985, a sizable increase. Many maritime coke seizures were from go-fast boats making final runs from the Bahamas after picking up loads from aircraft landing in the islands or from air drops in the water.[30] Cocaine seized by the Coast Guard rose from 1,967 pounds in 1984 to 6,547 pounds in 1985.[31] The cocaine seized by the Coast Guard was still only about 6 percent of the total for that year. A study by the General Accounting Office showed that U.S. Customs was the primary seizing agency for cocaine (66 percent) and the Coast Guard was primary for marijuana (65 percent).[32]

In 1985 the National Narcotics Intelligence Consumers Committee concluded that marijuana use in the United States was declining. The committee predicted that supplies of Colombian marijuana would continue to decrease, partly because of eradication efforts and stepped-up interdiction at sea. The committee noted, however, that the decrease of Colombian marijuana would be partially offset by an increase of Mexican marijuana. For the first time since the mid-1970s the estimated percentage of total marijuana imported from Mexico (40 percent) exceeded the figure for Colombia (38 percent). In 1985 about 3.2 million pounds of marijuana destined for the United States were seized from all types of conveyances. Maritime seizures accounted for about 90 percent of the total, most of it from Colombia.[33] Coast Guardsmen took slightly over 2 million pounds of the marijuana seized in 1985, roughly at the 65 percent level figured by the GAO. They also seized 165 vessels.[34]

Coast Guard marijuana seizures declined again in 1985. No one knew if this was because smugglers were getting smarter or because there was less product in the pipeline. One hard fact remained:

interdiction programs and their funding were traditionally justified to Congress by weight of drugs seized and estimated interdiction rates, and the GAO had estimated the rate for marijuana at a paltry 8–10 percent. The Coast Guard was getting nervous. Seizure statistics were on the slide, and the price of grass in the United States remained constant. Interdiction rates were a guess at best. You had to know how much you missed in order to evaluate how well you were doing, but information on misses was hard to come by.

In August 1985 the Seventh Coast Guard District in Miami considered new ways to measure effectiveness. The factors were based mainly on the response of smugglers. The indicators included a decline in American and Cuban-American crews aboard smuggling vessels and an increase in Colombian crews, a decrease in vessel efficiency, and more use of expensive hidden compartments. These were positive indicators that interdiction efforts were having a telling effect. Deliberations in the Seventh District and Coast Guard headquarters brought an interdiction goal statement the next year that read, "Since 1986, the Coast Guard's stated goal concerning interdiction has been to eliminate the maritime routes as a significant trafficking mode for the supply of drugs to the United States by increasing the risk-route denial."[35] The Coast Guard with navy support was on the road to denying the sea lanes to grass smugglers.

According to Capt. Stephen Duca, USCG, the crusty Wagon Wheel planner, the Coast Guard had already proposed a marijuana interdiction rate of 75 percent as its standard goal. The reasoning was that a 75 percent removal rate with concurrent boat losses and incarcerations would deter shipments and raise costs to a point where marijuana smuggling would no longer be economically feasible. Captain Duca said that the administration refused to accept the proposal for spurious reasons.[36] Why such an ambitious objective was refused is unclear, unless it was related to the difficulty of measuring how much was missed. There were ways of using smuggler-defendant interviews to estimate drug loads safely delivered, but the system was fragmentary at best in 1985 and was never fully developed.

Perhaps the best indicator of marijuana interdiction accomplishments by the end of 1985 was the reemergence of Mexico as the primary source. In 1983, Mexico's contribution to pot consumption in the States was only about 9 percent. By 1985 it was above 40 percent. Although many Colombian producers and traffickers were shifting to

MAP vessel with sea-based aerostat *(Official U.S. Coast Guard photograph)*

cocaine, the traditional Colombian suppliers did not relinquish their reign without reason. Crop eradication in Colombia may have been contributory, but marijuana and ship losses at sea were the main cause. Even with questionable seizure-to-effort ratios, our offensive posture in 1984–85 was a strong deterrent to smuggling organizations using sea and air routes to the United States. Land avenues, like those afforded by Mexico, must have been inviting alternatives to cartels.

A major threat to grass boaters were the highly visible aerostats in the Yucatán. The first mobile aerostat platform (MAP) vessel was used in 1984–85 to test a concept called maritime interdiction surveillance teams (MISTs). The sea-based aerostat (SBA) system had the technology to implement MIST tactics centered around the MAP vessel. An SBA is a ship-tethered radar balloon that operates at heights up to 2,500 feet. The ship's radar horizon is thus greatly increased. The Coast Guard developed a target information system (TIPS) to process SBA radar information and to display targets digitally. TIPS displays were transmitted over a protected high-frequency radio circuit to other ships. A cutter with an embarked helicopter served as the MIST command and control ship. The helo investigated SBA targets. MAP vessels were civilian charters with Coast Guard detachments to operate the detection equipment. Other cutters supported the MIST command and control ship as chase craft when available.[37]

When the balloon went up from the MAP vessel, there was no mistaking its mission; SBAs were visible for many miles. They were highly sensitive to lightning and had to be recovered quickly when thunderstorms approached. The MAP vessels and MIST units were, however, a large deterrent to smugglers using Caribbean sea lanes of communications (SLOCs). In a few years SBAs would be familiar sights in the Caribbean passes.

Not as visible as floating aerostats but just as important to interdiction efforts were the new Coast Guard Island-class patrol boats. The boats began coming from builders in 1985. They are 110 feet in length and capable of speeds in excess of 26 knots. The first, the USCGC *Farallon* (WPB-1301), was delivered in November 1985.[38] Forty-nine were eventually commissioned. With a complement of two officers and fourteen enlisted personnel and a range of almost 2,000 miles, the fast little cutters were ideal chase boats for MIST units covering the Caribbean SLOCs.

To improve tactics further, drug interdiction games were initiated at the Naval War College at Newport, Rhode Island, in the fall of 1985 as an annual event. The initial games were sponsored by the Coast Guard Atlantic Area Command. The first two were mostly tactical maritime exercises, using the expertise and facilities of the War College to evaluate interdiction operations in the Atlantic and Caribbean. Only a few representatives from other federal drug enforcement agencies attended as observers. War-gaming of interdiction operations would be expanded in the future. Sponsored by NNBIS, they would test the full range of air, sea, and land tactics and evaluate options for control, coordination, communications, and intelligence support. The results are classified.

The mere presence of the U.S. Navy in a drug-hunting configuration along the sea lanes was in itself a strong deterrent to maritime smugglers. Navy support was more than just a flag-showing exercise. By 1985 the gray ships and aircraft had directly contributed to the arrest of 266 smugglers and the seizure of forty-three smuggler vessels, 962,274 pounds of marijuana, and 46 pounds of cocaine.[39] The little but impressive high-tech guided-missile patrol hydrofoils (PHMs) operating out of Key West were on their way to earning the sobriquet *el Terror Gris* (the Gray Terrors) in the drug trade.[40] Interceptions by the speedy, spider-legged ships accounted for almost half of navy interdictions between 1983 and 1985.[41] The formidable might of U.S. sea power was not lost on the smugglers. Only a fraction was used, but the boat smugglers were running scared.

8

The Ebb
1986

Signal JM: You are running the risk of going aground at low
water.

INTERNATIONAL CODE OF SIGNALS

The Sea of Grass ebbed in 1986. Coast Guard marijuana seizures fell below 2 million pounds for the first time since 1977.[1] Many knowledgeable people felt that our efforts were not deterring the marijuana trade. Because of budget constraints, Coast Guard ship and aircraft interdiction hours declined 18 percent and 28 percent, respectively.[2] A General Accounting Office study published in 1987 reported that only small amounts of drugs bound for the United States were interdicted. The GAO blamed inadequate resources, security, and intelligence. The study also concluded that smugglers were responding successfully to changes in the interdiction system.[3]

The GAO analysts were correct about cocaine air traffic, and to some extent about cocaine sea traffic. They were dead wrong when it came to the grass boaters. José Martinez, the Cuban refugee who picked up the floaters on Cay Sal Bank in 1977 and became a major marijuana off-load operator, took so many hits that he would soon retire with his amassed fortune.[4] Grass was still coming north in quantity, but smugglers were feeling the heat from maritime interdiction.

Input from the likes of José Martinez was unlikely in 1986. There was no motivation for smuggler-defendants to talk about their operations. First- and even second-time smugglers usually got off with maximum sentences of five years, and most served much less time. Organizations frequently paid for their silence. It was better to do time in a serene federal prison and keep the option for reemployment. Many improved their education or pursued physical-fitness programs. Some got their teeth fixed.

Things changed in 1987, when mandatory minimum sentences were implemented in the federal court system. Defendants were now subjected to ten years or more without parole if convicted of smuggling quantities of drugs (i.e., 5 kilograms or more of cocaine or 1,000 kilograms or more of marijuana). Under Rule 11 of the Federal Rules of Criminal Procedure, they could cooperate with the government before trial to reduce their sentences or, under Rule 35, after their conviction. Substantial assistance and approval by the prosecution was required in either case. Agreements mandated the identification of major violators, testimony before a grand jury for indictments, and testimony as a witness at trial.[5]

Regardless of what we knew, did not know, or could have known about marijuana trafficking in 1986, the cocaine situation drove the machine. With our national fixation on sports, the cocaine-related deaths of basketball star Len Bias and pro-football star Don Rogers caused a public outcry for the curtailment of drug abuse. The illegal drug industry here was earning over $100 billion annually. President Reagan vowed, "The time has come to give notice that individual drug use is threatening the health and safety of all citizens." Polls showed that drug abuse was the number one public concern.[6] Almost overnight the press shifted from negative articles about the unwinnable war to a clarion call to arms. We recognized the enemy, and it was us.

On the heels of the polls and the press came the politicians. It was an election year. Drug fever swept Washington. The White House and Congress seemed to be in a bidding war to see who could propose the most for the suppression of drug use. President and Mrs. Reagan addressed the nation on live TV to enlist all citizens as volunteers in the fight. The House wanted the full weight of the military to be used to halt the flow of drugs in forty-five days; calmer heads in the Senate modified the bill and dropped the forty-five-day limit.[7] A new focus was demand reduction and cocaine interdiction. Not much was said about marijuana. The war at sea continued, but not in the limelight.

The National Drug Enforcement Policy Board, chaired by Attorney General Edwin Meese III, finally started to develop a national drug enforcement strategy, with much prompting by congressional critics. The board had been created by amendment to legislation. It was a substitute for the drug czar that Congress had wanted and the president had threatened to veto. The amendment was attached to the Comprehensive Crime Control Act of 1984 and was signed into law on 12 October. The board remained dormant until 1986. Since the president had established the Organized Crime Drug Enforcement Task Forces (coordinated by the attorney general) and had given responsibility for interdiction coordination to the vice president via NNBIS, the Drug Enforcement Policy Board's deliberations were not a White House priority. They were for Congress, however.

An interdiction strategy working group wrestled with the issues of measuring interdiction effectiveness and the roles of agencies, especially the Coast Guard and Customs. There was fear of being accused of the body-count mentality associated with the Vietnam War. Air interdiction was prioritized because of the highly publicized cocaine threat. The working group recommended that Customs be primary for interdicting drugs and apprehending drug smugglers at and between U.S. ports of entry. (The agency was already doing that.) The Coast

Guard would be primary at sea. (It already was.) The Department of Defense would help as it could. NNBIS would continue to coordinate but not command. Overall responsibility for detecting smuggler aircraft was not determined. Interdiction measures were vague.[8]

Congress, working on its own drug strategy, framed the Anti–Drug Abuse Act of 1986. Congress was not pleased with the White House effort, especially with regard to air intelligence and interdiction. Congressional critics faulted EPIC, the El Paso Intelligence Center, for not providing timely tactical information to enforcement agencies. Legislators proposed an All Source Intelligence Center, endorsed by the Policy Board. One congressional aide characterized the proposed center as "a kind of law enforcement CIA." The method proposed in Congress for improving air interdiction was to appropriate $25 million to establish three C3I (command, control, communications, and intelligence) centers to be operated mostly by Customs. Congressional planners would not consider NNBIS centers for air interdiction coordination. They viewed NNBIS as an agency that obtained military support for civilian enforcement. Despite its published mission statement and track record, it was not recognized for its real-time application of intelligence in coordinating interdictions.[9] The main problem Congress had with NNBIS was its White House origin. If the new C3I centers were to function independently of NNBIS, some entity would have to coordinate the coordinators. The vice president was the head of NNBIS; the only one left was the president, and he did not wish to assume the responsibility of drug czar.

Strategy plans were not limited to the United States. In April the Organization of American States, prompted by the Reagan administration, sponsored a drug conference in Rio de Janeiro. For the first time this problem was addressed at the hemispheric level. Latin American countries were worried about drug use at home. Before the Rio conference they had written drugs off as a U.S. problem. Now they wanted to join us in developing a drug control strategy, the Inter-American Commission for Drug Control. A decision on financing the commission was deferred because the United States felt that funds should come from the United Nations fund for drug abuse control.[10] The Rio conference was a public relations event, but it gave drug enforcement agencies more entrées to Latin American nations.

Capt. John E. Lacouture, U.S. Navy (Ret.), called for a military solution. His article "Isn't It Time to Declare War on the Drug Invaders?"

appeared in the *Proceedings* of the U.S. Naval Institute. Captain Lacouture proposed a sea and air defensive barrier around the United States. He predicted that with military assets, a 95 percent seizure rate could be realized.[11] The solution proposed by the navy captain was doable but unrealistic. The Pentagon could not commit the suggested resources without adversely affecting military readiness, specifically prohibited in the Posse Comitatus amendment. As Capt. Stephen Duca, USCG (Ret.), pointed out in a later *Proceedings* article, we were waging a war of attrition, a long holding action that would tie up military assets for years.[12]

The armed forces were providing serious support for the drug war. Lt. Gen. R. Dean Tice, former director of the Department of Defense task force on drug enforcement, outlined their contributions during congressional testimony in February 1986. Navy E-2Cs were flying aerial surveillance, and U.S. Marine Corps OV-10s were performing air interdiction missions for Customs in the Florida-Caribbean area. Navy P-3s flew long-range maritime surveillance over the Caribbean, and navy S-3s did the same over the Pacific near California. Navy ships gave almost a full year for the deployment of Coast Guard law enforcement teams. The navy had also given three P-3s equipped with air force F-15 radars to Customs. The Marine Corps had supplied radar surveillance and personnel intrusion detection equipment along the Mexican border. Air force AWACS planes flew both air and sea surveillance on an as-available basis. Air force B-52 bombers made surveillance reports a part of their maritime mission. Air force C-130s reported suspected maritime smugglers on flights to and from Panama. The air force continued to support Operation Bahamas and Turks/Caicos. During special operations such as Blue Lightning and Hat Trick, the army supplemented air force OPBAT units with two Black Hawk helicopters. Army OV-1D Mohawk aircraft helped Customs along the Mexican border. Sophisticated equipment, including communication encryption devices, were lent to civilian drug enforcement agencies. The National Guard assisted state agencies in locating marijuana farms. Even the Civil Air Patrol helped Customs.[13]

A boost to military and intelligence community involvement in the drug war was given by a national security decision directive (NSDD) issued by President Reagan on 8 April 1986. NSDD 226 was kept secret until Vice President Bush made an announcement at a press conference on 7 June 1986. Titled "Narcotics and National Security,"

the NSDD recognized the threat to U.S. national security from international drug trafficking. The NSDD also identified the drug trade as
a source of financing for insurgent and terrorist groups. Vice President
Bush emphasized that it was now "U.S. policy to aggressively join
with other nations to halt the production and flow of illegal drugs, to
reduce the ability of terrorists to derive support from drug trafficking,
and to strengthen the ability of individual governments to confront
and defeat this insidious threat." He explained that the NSDD "man-
dates that narcotics control objectives should be fully integrated into
this nation's foreign assistance planning efforts."[14]

It was appropriate for Bush to announce the NSDD. He had been
instrumental in enlisting the aid of the Department of Defense and the
intelligence community in the drug war. The weight of the NSDD
would enhance the ability of NNBIS to bring more military and intelligence support to the drug control initiative. It also paved the way for
critical funding of counternarcotics programs within the intelligence
community.

In May 1986, U.S. officials accused Mexico of aiding and abetting
drug traffickers. William von Raab, the vocal and pragmatic commissioner of Customs, said that Mexican officials were doing nothing
to slow the production and flow of drugs through their country to the
United States. Even John Lawn, the reserved and soft-spoken administrator of DEA, admitted that the Mexican government was doing little to curb drug trafficking. Drug enforcement officials believed that
one-third of the Colombian-refined cocaine consumed here came
through Mexico. Representatives of the State Department's Bureau of
International Narcotics Matters said that Mexico's drug problem had
grown so rapidly in the past eighteen months that it had popped off
the charts.[15]

Around the wardrooms and messes of the interdiction fleet, some
Vietnam vets compared the smugglers' migration to land routes
through Mexico with the North Vietnamese response to the Market
Time blockade. Had we created a Ho Chi Minh Trail for drugs through
Mexico because of effective maritime and air interdiction efforts in the
Caribbean?

By June, Governors Bob Graham of Florida and Mark White of
Texas were calling for the administration to use the military to help
shut down drug smuggling. Graham claimed we had lost control of

our borders. Officials of big cities, especially Los Angeles, Houston, Miami, and New York, also petitioned the White House. Many police officials admitted that they had had little success controlling drugs at the retail level. They called on the federal government to do more to interdict drugs at the wholesale stage.[16] Once again the pressure was on the White House.

On 14 August 1986 Vice President Bush, as head of NNBIS, and Attorney General Meese approved the implementation of Operation Alliance to coordinate the attack against drug traffickers along the entire 2,000-mile land border with Mexico. The principal architect of Alliance was Francis A. Keating II, assistant secretary of the treasury for enforcement (and later governor of Oklahoma). The Drug Enforcement Policy Board and NNBIS did much of the planning, assisted by the Treasury and Justice Departments. Keating co-chaired the special Southwest Border Committee with John Lawn, administrator of DEA. Other members of the committee were Commissioners von Raab of Customs and Alan Nelson of Immigration and Naturalization. They created a joint command group headed by Alan Eliason, chief of the U.S. Border Patrol. More than twenty federal and state law enforcement agencies took part in Alliance. In its first year of operation, it was claimed, Alliance doubled cocaine seizures along the border.[17] With the Alliance buildup on the border, smuggler aircraft avoided flying into U.S. airspace entirely. They landed on the Mexican side, and cocaine loads were divided up for transport in small units by expendable human "mules," a practice known as trampolining.[18]

Alliance did not take many resources from maritime operations; it was an air-land effort. Some maritime assets were needed to cover land border sea flanks, but they were there anyway. Alliance did not stop the migration to the west. The Mexican Ho Chi Minh Trail was a reality.

In 1986, Operation Hat Trick III became more of a concept than a special operation. Hat Trick's umbrella would encompass Alliance, Caribbean operations, and any special operations by NNBIS. It became a year-round effort focused as much on strategy as on tactical operations. Priorities were to improve intelligence, security, and communications. All aspects of Hat Trick, including planning, were tracked by Lt. Col. Ron Layton, U.S. Air Force, project officer in the OVP/NNBIS. Pulsed operations in the Caribbean were covered under

Hat Trick III–Checkmate. Rear Adm. Howard B. Thorsen, USCG, the NNBIS Southeast Region coordinator and Seventh District commander, was responsible for coordination.[19]

Much of the deep Caribbean work was done by the Caribbean Squadron. Capt. John Lockwood, USCG, took command of CaribRon in late 1986, just as Operation Checkmate came on line. Coast Guard junior officers with teams of seven to nine petty officers were assigned to each navy combatant. The LEDET officers-in-charge, although junior to the ship's CO, decided which contacts were to be boarded. They had to know their business as well as be diplomats of a high order. Coast Guard rigid-hulled inflatable boats (RHIBs) were used for boardings. Open-ocean boardings, down where the trades blow strong for a good part of the year, were demanding and required exceptional seamanship.[20]

CaribRon–Checkmate evolved into a continuous effort in the Caribbean. Navy ships remained under the operational control of parent commands but came under the tactical command of ComCaribRon. The deployed squadron usually consisted of a cruiser or destroyer as flagship, several frigates and Coast Guard cutters, and an oiler. Navy amphibious ships and patrol hydrofoils also participated, along with Coast Guard sea-based aerostats. Long-range air support came from navy P-3s and Coast Guard C-130s. Local air surveillance was the responsibility of embarked navy LAMPS (light airborne multipurpose system) and Coast Guard helicopters. Depending on the mission, air support was also given by U.S. Customs aircraft, air force E-3 AWACS planes, navy E-2C Hawkeyes, Coast Guard HU-25 Falcons, and Royal Dutch Air Force Fokker F-27 aircraft. Joint operations sometimes included navy or Coast Guard vessels from Colombia, Honduras, Jamaica, and Venezuela.[21]

CaribRon traditionally concentrated on the departure zones adjacent to drug-producing countries and the southern transit zone. The squadron was thus the most forward-deployed segment of the three-tiered interdiction screen covering the southern approaches to the United States. Coast Guard assets patrolled the transit zone, which included the choke points at Yucatán, the Windward, Mona, and Anegada Passages, and the eastern passages exiting the Caribbean. Coast Guard patrol boats, Customs marine interceptors, and state and local marine enforcement assets covered the contiguous arrival zone. This tiered coverage was known as defense in depth.[22]

Crewmen aboard the patrol hydrofoil USS *Taurus* (PHM-3) stand by as their ship moves in to stop a suspect merchant vessel.
(Official U.S. Navy photograph by PH2 Mark Kettenhofen)

Coverage of the arrival zone off South Florida was facilitated in early 1986 with the opening of Customs' new Blue Lightning Operations Command Center (BLOCC) in the Miami federal building. BLOCC got its name and mission concept from Operation Blue Lightning, which had been staged in the Bahamas and South Florida in April 1985. Customs' effort to promote greater state and local agency involvement in coastal interdiction eventually resulted in the term *command* being dropped from the center's name. The mission of BLOC, as it came to be spelled, was to coordinate but not command the interdiction of suspect vessels in near-shore waters by federal, state, and local marine resources. Information was received from aerostats and from radars installed on the tops of high buildings and towers.

Customs felt that it needed a center with advanced radar capabilities to use in combination with its newly acquired high-speed interceptor boats. A similar center was opened in Houston later in the year.[23]

The BLOC concept was of questionable utility in sorting unknown targets, but it was very useful in tracking known ones. The NNBIS coordination center was just down the hall in the same building, staffed in part by detailed Customs personnel. There was no overall plan to say who was responsible for what. If NNBIS and BLOC talked to each other, everything was fine. However, they did not always do so. What had started out a few years before as a presidential plan to coordinate all interdiction activities via NNBIS was falling apart. Why did that happen? Because of partisan politics between the White House and Congress.

An issue needing a competent command decision was who would own and operate the fast boats used to catch cocaine smugglers. The interdiction forces needed them to counter the threat of cocaine runners coming from the Bahamas. They also needed to interdict fast boats retrieving air drops offshore for delivery along the Florida coast. Congress gave the money to Customs. The Coast Guard, however, would have been a better choice. It had the historical expertise and the command and control structure to operate the boats. It also had the capabilities and facilities to train operators and maintain the equipment. If additional inshore surface radar was needed, the Coast Guard had trained people who knew how to operate and maintain that equipment. Customs had little or none of these. Its boarding authority was limited to the 12-mile contiguous zone. The Coast Guard's authority was not so limited.[24] The decision to build a Customs boat fleet and radar system was made by legislative appropriation. The Coast Guard did receive a few go-fast interceptors later on, when there was no real need for them.

A similar argument could be made against the building of a Customs air interdiction force. The Coast Guard had an existing and highly trained air arm for its maritime mission. It also had the structure for training pilots and aircrews and maintaining the aircraft. The operative words are *maritime mission*. There was a rational basis for building a Customs air fleet. Air smuggling was moving west from a maritime environment to a land environment. Only the air force and the army had existing expertise, training, and equipment to operate air interdictions in and over the wastelands of our southwestern border, but they were prevented from hands-on enforcement by Posse Comitatus. The expansion of Customs air capabilities was a reasonable decision, even if it had to be done by legislation.

In March 1986 the General Accounting Office, the watchdog of Congress, began another audit of NNBIS. The stated purpose was to determine how NNBIS fit into the overall federal drug interdiction effort. It was as though the GAO had never heard of NNBIS. Guidelines to NNBIS personnel for cooperating with GAO auditors were transmitted from the Office of the Vice President on 18 March 1986. The message said personnel should give auditors what they needed to accomplish their work, but certain restrictions would apply. GAO auditors must provide security clearances and demonstrate a need to know for access to sensitive intelligence. No special intelligence could be given, except to auditors assigned to Fort George Meade.[25] Consequently, the extremely important special intelligence contribution made by NNBIS—especially in the Southeast Region, where most smuggling occurred—was denied to the auditors. These restrictions were necessary to retain the support and cooperation of the intelligence community, but they did not help the NNBIS cause. Classified intelligence received and "washed" by the Miami NNBIS center was unique and not available in any other drug intelligence system; the judicious use of this information had played an important part in the downfall of the marijuana boats. The GAO's audit of NNBIS was not favorable.

During this period Congress also became concerned about the drug interdiction agencies' duplication of seizure statistics. To give an accurate count of the different drugs seized, the Federal Drug Seizure System (FDSS) was implemented in September 1986. EPIC was charged with keeping the FDSS records. The first agency to take custody of any drugs was responsible for obtaining a federal drug identification number (FDIN) from EPIC. FDINs were required only if the drugs were to be transferred to another agency or exceeded certain weights. Almost all Coast Guard drug seizures required FDINs.[26]

Despite all the machinations topside, the field grunts continued to fight the war with determination and growing skill. One marvelous aspect of the drug war was that field agents, officers, and Coast Guardsmen got along with each other regardless of agency turf battles. They hardly noticed what went on between the administration and Congress.

Drug boat cases were getting harder to prove. The use of hidden compartments had become the norm. On 25 July 1986 the Eleventh Circuit Court of Appeals reversed the conviction of seven crewmen from the coastal freighter *Mrs. White* seized in 1984 with a multi-ton load of pot in concealed compartments (*U.S. v. Vidal-Hungria,* described in chapter 6). The Eleventh Circuit found the following persuasive in deliberations:

The vessel was a cargo ship carrying a legitimate cargo.
Marijuana was stored in hidden, sealed compartments.
There was no evidence that the crew had participated in loading the marijuana; clothing tests for marijuana residue were negative.
No crew member made an inculpatory statement.
The vessel did not attempt to elude when approached by the Coast Guard cutter.

In hidden-compartment cases, the mere-presence theory of prosecution was set aside. It would now be incumbent on the Coast Guard and investigating agencies to prove beyond a reasonable doubt that persons aboard a drug boat knew that contraband was in the hidden compartment. The *Vidal-Hungria* decision thus became the standard for prosecutions in hidden-compartment cases.[27] Good boarding procedures, with proper preservation of evidence, and good postseizure procedures were a must.

A unique, if insignificant, hidden-compartment seizure took place in 1986. The 52-foot sailboat *Navesink* arrived at Clearwater, Florida, from the Caribbean in mid-January. Customs was suspicious. A search of the interior of the boat was negative. However, a very small cable ran down through the swing-keel well, attached to a cleat in the cockpit; its purpose could not be explained. The boat was hauled out of the water at a nearby boatyard. In place of the swing-keel was a hinged metal plate. When the small cable was released in the cockpit, the plate swung down. Out dropped sealed packages containing 250 pounds of hashish oil, a potent derivative of hashish. It was an ingenious but simple method for hiding contraband in such a way that it could be jettisoned at any time. The boat's occupants denied any knowledge of the concealed compartment or the hash oil. They were arrested and the boat was seized, but it would be a tough case to prove.

A local newspaper ran a small article about the arrest and listed the names of the boat and the crew. A few days later a woman called the Clearwater Coast Guard station saying she had information about the seizure. She was passed to another agency as a possible crank caller.

The lady was cranky—about her ex-husband, the owner of the *Navesink*—but her information was right-on. She had read the news account and decided the time had come to get even. The yachtsman-smuggler had promised her a settlement of $10,000 when they first separated. He never paid. According to the ex-wife's story and testimony, she and the defendant had divorced seven years earlier after she objected to his drug smuggling. Two years after the divorce, she tried a reconciliation and lived on the boat with him. She was there when her ex-husband and another man drew plans and discussed the construction of a concealed compartment in the boat's keel that could be opened from the cockpit by releasing a cable. She decided to leave him for good. For a man who had been such a successful smuggler for so many years, he was abominably naive about the wrath of a woman spurned. The *Navesink*'s owner paid the price in jail.[28]

One of the first sizable pot seizures of 1986 was a score for the partially completed Blue Lightning Operations Center. Using computer-enhanced signals from an aerostat radar balloon on 21 February, watch standers noted unusual activity by three surface targets in the lower Gulf on Route 26. The three targets were together, then took off in different directions. One went slowly southwest and the other two at a much greater rate of advance toward the coast. What looked like an off-load probably was. The two suspect boats headed for the Everglades. Customs contacted one of its high-speed boats lurking along the dark coast and gave her a vector to intercept. Customs also requested a Coast Guard 41-boat from the Fort Myers Beach station for backup.

Three Customs officers aboard a 36-foot go-fast boat intercepted the leading inbound target at 0415. It was the 58-foot stone-crab boat *Aiakatsi* with two men aboard. The officers smelled marijuana as they pulled alongside the crabber. As they prepared to board the suspect, the second inbound target came bearing down on them as if to ram. A quick maneuver by the operator of the powerful interceptor took them out of harm's way. Now they were faced with a dilemma: chase the newcomer, or stay with the bird in hand. They opted for the former and took off at high speed. They soon identified the 45-foot crab boat *Fast and Easy.* She was certainly fast, but not easy to catch. Three men aboard the fleeing boat began to toss bales. The 41-boat was coming on, but far away. Alerted by NNBIS, an audacious U.S. Park Service ranger and a park technician in a small boat were in position to try to block the fleeing smugglers. The Customs officers were running out of options. They fired warning shots across the bow of the crab boat. The smugglers were wild, but not crazy; they stopped. Leaving the surrendered crab boat in the care of the park personnel and a Customs man, the interceptor sped back to the *Aiakatsi.* The boat was drifting, but the retreating night had taken the two occupants to parts unknown. In total there were 28,250 pounds of marijuana on the two crabbers. It was a good night's work. BLOC had proved that it could deliver.[29]

Meanwhile, the third BLOC-detected target, the presumed mothership, was fading off the scope into the Gulf. The Customs people had no assets or authority to reach that far, so they went down the hall to NNBIS. The NNBIS watch put the cutter *Dependable* (WMEC-626) on the chase via the Seventh District. The cutter found the suspect about 80 miles offshore. It was the 420-foot Honduran coastal freighter *Karia.* The freighter's master consented to boarding, claiming he was en route to Tampa, Florida. Coast Guardsmen found two empty hidden compartments. Accesses were welded shut. Marijuana residue in the compartments was sufficient evidence to seize the ship and arrest the crew.[30] It was a good operation despite the physical separation of the two coordination centers.

Like the *Fast and Easy,* some smuggler boats were hard to stop if their crews were determined to resist. But a boat without a crew was even harder. On 6 April the 95-foot patrol boat *Cape Fox* (WPB-95316) sighted the 45-foot sports fisherman *Profiteer* about 75 miles northwest of Key West. The Coast Guardsmen decided to investigate; perhaps it was the vessel's name. As the small cutter approached the suspect, the crew were astonished to see the two occupants leap into the ocean. They saw nothing wrong with the boat. The two men floundered in the water while the *Profiteer* continued on her way at about 14 knots. The Coast Guardsmen hastened to rescue the swimmers. Then the *Cape Fox,* not the fastest cutter in the inventory, set out to corral the runaway. Her crew called for assistance. The much faster surface-effect cutter *Sea Hawk* (WSES-2) responded, and the chase was afoot.

At one point the pursued and the pursuers charged through a group of about thirty shrimp boats. The shrimpers frantically dodged the weaving flotilla, flashing blue lights. Repeated attempts to lasso the crewless vessel or foul her propeller failed. The *Profiteer,* periodically changing course on her own, headed for shoal water near the Tortugas. The seemingly possessed sports fisherman circled twice without grounding, then took off again for deep water. The chase ended 60 miles west of Tortugas when the *Profiteer* made another unexpected turn and crashed into the steel side of the *Sea Hawk.* The roundup lasted eleven hours.

The runaway fiberglass boat was seriously damaged and in a sinking condition; the cutter had minor dents. Marijuana bales were found crammed into the cabin of the wrecked boat. The load was estimated at 12,000 pounds. Attempts to tow the waterlogged boat were futile. A bale of pot was removed for evidence, then gunfire sent the derelict to the bottom in deep water. The *Cape Fox* took the marijuana and the two swimmers, now prisoners, to Key West. The hard-driving *Sea Hawk* went back on patrol.[31]

Demonically possessed drug boats were rare; so were ghosts. The new Island-class cutter *Manitou* (WPB-1302) met one of the latter on the night of 12 May about 50 miles east of Great Abaco on the far side of the Bahamas. Maneuvering to approach a night sighting, Lt. Chris Able, the *Manitou*'s CO, thought the vessel's lines were familiar. The suspect stopped when hailed and submitted to boarding. It was the 125-foot motor vessel *Sun Bird* with a crew of thirteen Colombians and two Brazilians. When the cutter drew alongside, the raised name *Crawford* could be seen under many coats of paint. The name meant nothing to the young lieutenant, but he was sure there was something familiar about the little ship. The *Sun Bird,* a.k.a. *Crawford,* was loaded with pot. A Coast Guardsmen went into the engine room to make sure the machinery was sound for the trip to Miami, and there he found the identification plate proclaiming that the ship was the United States Coast Guard cutter *Crawford.* Lieutenant Able's feeling of déjà vu was well founded; he had undoubtedly seen photographs or paintings of the famous Buck-and-a-Quarter-class cutter. The *Crawford* was born during the Rum War and had been a mainstay of the Prohibition fleet. She had served as an escort for Caribbean convoys during World War II. The old cutter was decommissioned in 1947 and donated to Woods Hole Oceanographic Institute for a research vessel in 1955.[32] No one knew how this faithful steel servant of the U.S. government found herself in the employ of drug smugglers. It was a sad day for the old ship. Almost 20 tons of marijuana were removed from spaces that had once housed the rum warriors, lifesavers, and U-boat hunters of the old guard.

In May 1986 Joseph W. "JoJo" Birchfield tried to reopen the old Steinhatchee terminus from a Tallahassee halfway house. He had to be in the house every night, and his use of the phone was limited. JoJo hired neat and handsome Dan Dunn to manage the planned delivery of 82,000 pounds of pot in the ex–oil rig tender *D'Milu's One*. Dunn was actually an undercover agent of U.S. Customs. In his first meeting with Birchfield's crew, Dunn told them to get haircuts and discard their gold neck chains. The motley crew complied with the soft-spoken agent's demands. Dunn was a capable manager. One off-load boat he procured belonged to Customs. Customs and DEA planned to take down the whole gang at the off-load. For one reason or another the investigating agencies did not file a Category I lookout on the vessel, which would have precluded boarding at sea. An existing Category III lookout made it open season for the interdiction forces.[33]

On the afternoon of 29 May *D'Milu's One* was sighted by a Georgia National Guard aircraft on a drug-hunting patrol in the eastern Gulf. The cutter *Vigorous* (WMEC-627) made the intercept. The vessel appeared to be fully loaded, but the master claimed that no cargo was aboard. He agreed to a boarding and a search. There were freshly painted raised steel plates welded to the main deck on both sides forward. There was also a padeye welded to the overhanging bridge deck above each plate. From a central alley below, holes were drilled into the spaces under the plates. A leafy substance on the drill bit tested positive for THC (tetrahydrocannabinol), the unique chemical substance found only in marijuana. The *D'Milu's One* was seized. False name boards with the name *Blanco I* were found in the concealed compartments, along with almost 80,000 pounds of pot. The ship's dog was seized, paroled, and adopted.

JoJo Birchfield was disgusted; he had been defeated by the Georgia National Guard. Dan Dunn was not happy either; he would have to continue his association with Birchfield until the next year, when JoJo

"Guajira Dog" aboard the *D'Milu's One* was seized (a yellow tag around the neck identified him as seized property), paroled, and adopted.
(Author's collection)

and two of his crew were arrested for conspiracy to import marijuana. Dunn could not testify at the trial of *D'Milu's One*'s master. The trial ended in a hung jury. A good defense lawyer used the hidden-compartment defense. The government reindicted, but the master pled guilty before the second trial.[34]

On 8 July DEA's station in Barranquilla, Colombia, reported the departure of the ex–oil rig tender *South C. Express*. Information indicated that metal boxes had been built into the fuel tanks to hold marijuana. The vessel had been on previous lookouts. On 29 July U.S. Customs in Fort Myers, Florida, reported that two suspect off-load boats had left at noon. Intelligence predicted that a 20,000-pound off-load would be made by an unknown mothership in position 24° north and 87° west, or about 315 miles southwest of Naples near the Campeche Bank. NNBIS Miami, connecting DEA's report from Barranquilla with Customs' report from Fort Myers, requested that the Coast Guard fly a covert patrol to locate the mothership. A Coast Guard C-130 found the *South C. Express* on 30 July approximately 90 miles south of the suspected off-load position. The USCGC *Courageous* (WMEC-622) was on barrier patrol north of the Yucatán Channel. The *Courageous* intercepted the *South C. Express* on 30 July about 70 miles north-northwest of the Yucatán Peninsula. The master consented to boarding, claiming he was bound for Coatzacoalcos, Mexico, on a salvage mission. Permission was given for the boarding party to drill into some suspicious tank spaces. Marijuana was found, and the ship was seized. The Colombian master and eleven Colombian crewmen were arrested and taken to Tampa.[35]

A postseizure inspection was made at Tampa on 3 August by an NNBIS representative and DEA agent Bud Baggett. Among other things, a chart was found in the master's stateroom with a track line running from Santa Marta, Colombia, to a position 24° north and 87° west. There was no doubt that the *South C. Express* was the mothership delivering marijuana to the boats that had left Fort Myers on 29 July. In all, 21,620 pounds of pot were removed. The amount matched information in the intelligence report. When the *South C. Express* arrived in Tampa, it was unknown how the grass had been loaded into the compartments. Then an interior inspection of the most forward portside compartment found a steel plate over a cutout in the overhead. Tapping on the plate could be heard in a stateroom just above. The 3-inch-deep layer of cement covering the stateroom deck was removed, revealing the access hatch to the hidden compartments. Loading 10 tons of marijuana, bale by bale, through the small cutout must have been a horrendous task. After the grass was loaded, the officers' staterooms and the connecting passageway had to be covered with cement so that the deck in the stateroom with the hidden access would not be higher than the rest.[36]

The interception of the *South C. Express* was a classic example of the efficiency of a regional coordination center matching departure and arrival intelligence to tag a suspect for seizure. DEA- and Customs-generated intelligence was used to put the Coast Guard in the right place at the right time. It would have been better to let the pickup boats start unloading before closing in on the target to arrest the U.S. off-loaders. There was a possibility, however, that partially loaded pickup boats would escape and deliver what they had to the coast. The pros and cons of controlled deliveries are still hotly argued. DEA and Customs usually supported controlled deliveries, and the

Top: Interior of concealed compartment aboard the *South C. Express* showing cutout in overhead above bales of marijuana. *Bottom:* Cement deck removed from stateroom above gave access to hidden compartments containing 21,620 pounds of pot. *(Author's collection)*

Coast Guard usually opposed. It was more a matter of who got the statistics—the body-count mentality of the drug war.

Six days before the seizure of the *South C. Express,* the *Vidal-Hungria* decision on hidden compartments had finally been rendered by the Eleventh Circuit. The U.S. attorney's office in Tampa refused to consider prosecution of the crewmen; they were deported. The master, Armando Soto-Rivera, was indicted and tried in Tampa. Customs would not expose its informant, who could have testified about the significance of the 24° north, 87° west, off-load position. Assistant U.S. Attorney Walter Furr, the prosecutor, was also concerned about Coast Guard graffiti on the inside bulwarks of the rig tender's weather deck. Ens. Vincent Delaurentis, the boarding officer and custody crew commander, had let his people paint the cutter's name in large red letters on the raised plating. Furr believed that the artwork might be used by the defense to show that the Coast Guard was overzealous in sweeping drug boats from the seas. Delaurentis could not defend the graffiti. Regardless, the jury did not buy Captain Soto-Rivera's lack-of-knowledge defense or his story about going to salvage a vessel in Mexico to tow her back to Colombia. He was sentenced to ten years in prison on 25 November 1986.[37]

The saga of the *South C. Express* did not end in Tampa. An OCDETF investigation in Tulsa, Oklahoma, four years later produced the indictment of José Rafael Abello-Silva on cocaine air smuggling charges. Abello was arrested in Colombia by local narcotics police and was extradited under the U.S.–Colombian treaty. He was allegedly a top cocaine transportation expert in the Medellin cartel. Abello's ex-partner was arrested in Panama and also brought to Tulsa. He became a government informant. Boris Olarte Morales testified that he and Abello purchased the *South C. Express* for $170,000 to send a load of pot to the Gulf for delivery in Florida. He also told how Abello converted to cocaine smuggling in 1987 after losing his grass boat.[38] Abello is a good example of how the more astute maritime grass smugglers shifted to cocaine air smuggling after 1986 because of losses at sea.

A sizable part of the maritime marijuana sent to the United States in 1986 was destined for off-load in the Gulf of Mexico. The cocaine interdiction buildup along the east coast of Florida was a factor. Vessel seizures in the Caribbean en route to the Gulf were also a serious problem for grass boaters. It was common to route motherships through Mexican waters close to the Yucatán Peninsula to avoid Yucatán patrols. The competency of mothership crews, mostly Colombians, had so deteriorated through attrition that many off-load rendezvous failed.

Shrimper-smuggler Harold King's experience was common. Ambrose Weldon and associates bought a shrimp boat for King. He fished as he pleased but was on call for off-loads. In the summer of 1986 King attempted to make five pickups from motherships between the NOAA buoy (the Coke Machine) and Mexico along Route 26; not one was successful. Later in the year he took his wooden-hulled boat to the Campeche Bank, where he met two old tugs moored alongside each other, flying the Mexican flag. The seas were rough. After taking on only 2,000 of the 30,000 pounds he expected to receive, King's wooden boat was severely damaged by the rolling tugs in the rough water. He called in another boat to take the load. They took it but never paid him a finder's fee. It was a bad year for King; the next would be worse.[39]

A partial solution to the problem of getting motherships through the Yucatán was to use Mexican boats and crews. They had a better chance of coming through the waters just offshore. Mexico's navy seldom boarded Mexican boats. The 1982 nationalization of the Mexican fishing fleet helped, leaving some two thousand Mexican shrimpers suddenly underemployed. Much of the fleet was inactive because the profit motive had been removed. Boats could be used to pick up a grass load in the Caribbean from a Colombian, Panamanian, or stateless vessel that would be suspect running the Yucatán. The Mexican F/V would then transit the territorial sea to a point in the Gulf where the load was transferred to U.S. boats for the final run to Florida. The Mexican 70-foot shrimper *Churumbel* was seized by the USCGC *Courageous* (WMEC-622) on 2 August 1986. The *Churumbel* was intercepted off Rosalind Bank, between Jamaica and Honduras, carrying 46,000 pounds of pot. Crewmen claimed they were bound for the Gulf for an off-load. The vessel and crew were turned over to the Mexican Navy.[40]

Off-loading from motherships could be dangerous; suspect drug boats sometimes disappeared with little notice. The 68-foot wooden shrimper *Lady Virgo* was a smuggling lookout in 1986. On 11 May, Coast Guard Group Galveston, Texas, got a call from the alleged owner. He said that the vessel was overdue on a voyage from St. Petersburg, Florida, to Freeport, Texas, having gotten under way on or around 16 April. The Coast Guard broadcast a notice to "All shipping—Gulf of Mexico" requesting a sharp lookout for the lost shrimper. She was not reported. The *Lady Virgo* would have joined the ranks of the eternal missing except for a man known as Roger. Group St. Petersburg got a phone call on 22 May from a person with information on the missing shrimper. He was interviewed but demanded confidential-informant status before telling his story. A DEA task force in Naples, Florida, complied.

Roger was on crutches. He said he had injured his foot aboard the boat, and the owner refused compensation. According to the limping crewman, the *Lady Virgo* did depart in mid-April, but not for Texas. She was bound for 26°30' north, 84°00' west, approximately 100 miles west of Fort Myers, to pick up 30,000 pounds of marijuana from an unknown mothership. Before reaching the pickup point, the old shrimper started taking on water, fast. Soon she was sinking. No Mayday was sent; instead the smugglers called a contact in Naples on a designated frequency for assistance. Before anyone could get there, the *Lady Virgo* took a dive in 50 fathoms. Roger and two companions floated on a hatch cover for hours before they were rescued by the contact in a go-fast boat. He felt that it was a miracle they were found at all. Roger identified the people who had hired him for the off-load. He got even with the miserly owner who had put him on the beach with a crippled foot.[41]

As marijuana seizures declined, cocaine seizures at sea increased. The Coast Guard topped the 10,000-pound mark for coke in 1986.[42] Most of it was from the Caribbean-Florida area. It was about half of the total seized from private vessels in 1986, but only one-fifth of the amount seized from aircraft. The real maritime cocaine threat was from containerized cargo usually carried on large merchant ships. A new record coke seizure was made by a U.S. Customs contraband enforcement team (CET) on 17 October at West Palm Beach, Florida. The CETs were trained to search cargo. A rusty corrugated-metal container was unloaded on 9 October from the freighter *Malargo I* of La Guaira, Venezuela. The ship left. The CET officers noticed that the inside of the 40-foot container seemed much shorter than the outside; there was a false interior wall at one end. A total of 4,620 pounds of coke packed in small boxes was removed. Customs and DEA had no reason to suspect the crew of the ship that had transported the container to Florida.[43]

The fall marijuana harvest in Colombia brought the gray ships prowling the Caribbean. During November, Coast Guard LEDETs operating from navy ships seized four grass boats in the deep Caribbean, a larger number of navy-assisted seizures than in any previous month. On 14 November, 50 miles north of the Guajira Peninsula, the USS *McCloy* (FF-1038) intercepted the 45-foot fishing vessel *Rose Marie 10*. The master refused a consensual boarding. The suspect crew struck their Honduran flag and broke out Colombian colors and proceeded to jettison bales. The *McCloy* requested and received an SNO to board and seize the *Rose Marie* as a stateless vessel. Again the frigate ordered the suspect to stop, but the order was ignored. When bursts of .50-caliber machine-gun fire over the bow proved fruitless, the *McCloy* got permission to use disabling fire. The navy gunners fired into the vessel until she stopped. When the smoke cleared, the *Rose Marie* was in a sinking condition, the result of scuttling rather than machine-gun fire. One member of the smuggler crew was seriously injured, with a gunshot wound in the right arm and a shrapnel wound to the head; he was flown to Puerto Rico for treatment. This was the fourteenth time disabling fire had been used on a smuggler boat, but the first time a crewman had been seriously wounded. Some of the marijuana bales were removed as evidence. The boarding party estimated the total grass cargo at 10 tons.[44]

The lethal frigate was not done yet. A few days later, in roughly the same area, the *McCloy* sighted the 110-foot motor vessel *Sea Wanderer*. She was declared stateless. Perhaps the word had gone out among the smugglers coming from the Guajira to beware the slim gray frigate with the number 1038, for the *Sea Wanderer* meekly submitted to a search. The LEDET quickly found a bonanza: close to 50 tons of pot in the hold. It was the largest marijuana seizure of the year.[45] The load's destination was unknown, but its size was noteworthy. Only one other marijuana seizure of that magnitude would occur again on the Atlantic side. Well done, the *McCloy*!

Marijuana motherships had serious problems getting out of the Caribbean to Atlantic routes north in 1986, but some were still running the choke-point gauntlets. The 158-foot U.S. oil rig tender *Breton Seahorse* arrived in Melville, Rhode Island, on 13 April, from Morgan City, Louisiana. There was no reason to believe that the vessel had been foreign. Customs questioned the master, who was vague about the purpose of his voyage. Surveillance was established. Crew

The USS *McCloy* (FF-1038) bagged more pot than any other navy ship and was the first to draw blood in the drug war. *(U.S. Naval Institute photograph)*

members were apparently conducting countersurveillance. Two 20-foot containers were loaded onto the boat. Spying and counterspying continued until the rig tender suddenly got under way on 15 May. The Coast Guard was notified, and an aircraft covertly surveilled the vessel as she moved offshore but lost the target during darkness. A plane located her on 17 May, and she was intercepted by the USCGC *Cape Henlopen* (WPB-95328) about 100 miles east-southeast of Montauk Point, Long Island. The boarding party smelled an odor of marijuana coming from a vent pipe, but the interior access was blocked by the deck-loaded containers. The *Breton Seahorse* was escorted to Woods Hole, Massachusetts, where Customs, DEA, and Coast Guard investigators did a complete search. When the containers were removed, access was gained to compartments holding nearly 26 tons of marijuana; gravel was mixed with the bales. Five U.S. citizens aboard the rig tender were arrested. They refused to comment about the grass and the gravel.

The day before the rig tender was seized, the USCGC *Unimak* (WHEC-379) boarded the 265-foot Panamanian cargo vessel *Jane K* in the area of the tender's seizure. The boarding party spent three hours on the freighter without finding contraband; the *Jane K*'s cargo was gravel. On the seventeenth, the *Unimak* was told to relocate the gravel carrier. The cutter found the ship again. This time the boarders dug into the gravel cargo and found marijuana residue. The *Jane K* was seized and her thirteen-man crew arrested. The ship was taken to Boston. Using a small bulldozer in the ship's hold, the searchers uncovered a broken bale buried in the cargo. A lab analysis showed that the gravel on the cargo ship was identical to that on the rig tender. Intelligence analysts believed that the *Breton Seahorse* had received her cargo from the *Jane K* on the night of 15 May when the Coast Guard lost sight of the rig tender.[46] Scuttlebutt in the Seventh District said that northeast cutters were being issued shovels to improve their seizure rates.

Pacific seizures were low in 1986. Marijuana seizures were about 54,000 pounds, down about one-half from the previous year. Cocaine seizures were a little over 1,000 pounds, up from the year before but not as high as in 1983–84. On the basis of confidential-informant reports, analysts believed that at least nine shipments of marijuana were successfully delivered in 1985 and in 1986, higher than any previous or subsequent year. With the huge area available to Pacific smugglers and the lack of choke points close to the United States, major Pacific drug seizures are traditionally based on intelligence. Analysts calculated that seizures declined after three or four years of successful interdictions. The periodic declines are thought to be due to the effort required by the few shoreside investigators to prepare cases for trial. The effectiveness of good informants usually decreases after seizures based on their information. When the smuggling organization folds or lies low, the informant obviously has little information.[47]

January brought the first sizable maritime cocaine seizure on the Pacific side. Intelligence said that the 179-foot coastal freighter *Eagle I* was coming to the West Coast with drugs. NNBIS Long Beach issued a lookout to navy ships and aircraft transiting the eastern Pacific. Despite the vastness of the search area, the USS *Belleau Wood* (LHA-3) sighted the suspect off Everett, Washington. The Coast Guard was alerted.[48] The patrol boat *Point Countess* (WPB-82335) made radar contact with the suspect ghosting past Neah Bay at the entrance to the Strait of Juan de Fuca on the night of 18 January. The ship tried to cross the line into Canadian waters, but the *Point Countess* blocked the move. The cutter *Confidence* (WMEC-619) came to support the 82-footer. The *Eagle I* was escorted to Port Angeles for a search by Customs, the Coast Guard, and DEA. After two days of diligent effort, the searchers found almost 500 pounds of cocaine in a welded-closed concealed compartment. The Colombian master and first mate were indicted. Intelligence indicated that the *Eagle I* was supposed to off-load the coke near the Oregon coast, but bad weather interfered. A secondary off-load was apparently planned for the straits or somewhere in Puget Sound. Drug enforcement officials thought Puget Sound might become a new entry point for cocaine because of enforcement pressures in the southeastern United States.[49]

Almost 85 percent of the Pacific marijuana seized in 1986 came from two vessels. In April the motor vessel *Line Island Trader* was intercepted by the Coast Guard in the vicinity of Kingman Reef, Line Islands, Central Pacific, with about 10,000 pounds. The next month the motor vessel *Panamco II* was seized about 700 miles west of the California-Oregon border with 35,351 pounds of Thai marijuana. The two seizures were based on prior intelligence developed by DEA or Customs.[50]

The logistics of transporting multi-ton cargoes of Far Eastern marijuana across the Pacific were formidable. In 1986 a reliable informant told how it was done. Negotiations for the load and payment took place between November and February. Payment was usually made in Hong Kong by courier. The selected vessel was loaded in Thailand in March–April after the crop was harvested. Route choices were based on weather, the proximity of friendly ports, and pirate activity. The source suggested that Cebu in the Philippines was a good port with few enforcement problems. The most common route was north of the Philippines (via Luzon Strait) to about 40° north and then eastward on the great-circle route. About midpoint the smuggler sent a position report to alert the off-load organization on the U.S. West Coast. The longitude of Hawaii was the usual place for the midpoint report. Communication frequencies and coded messages were prearranged. Any off-load changes were usually reconciled at midpoint. The source provided typical radio frequencies used. The loads usually arrived off southern California in June and off the Pacific Northwest in July and August. The informant's scenario seemed to be accurate. The peak

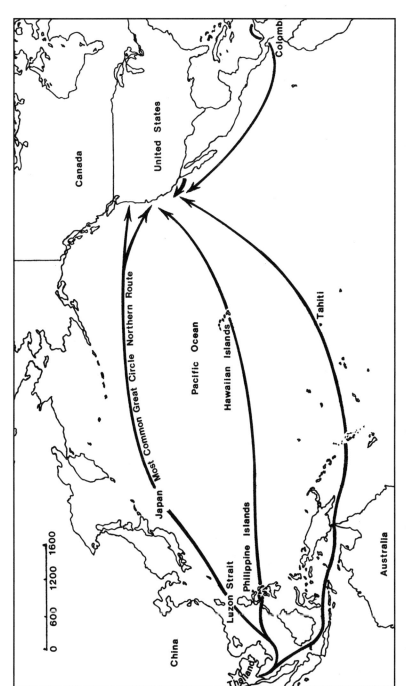

Typical marijuana routes to the western United States

months for marijuana seizures in the Pacific were indeed July and August.[51]

Marijuana boats coming out of the Gulf of Thailand usually entered the Pacific via the Luzon Strait between the Philippines and Taiwan. An examination of major cases involving Southeast Asian marijuana seizures showed vessel track lines invariably transiting the strait. There was a Pacific choke point, albeit one 200 miles wide, but it was too far from the United States to be of practical value.[52] Navy ships with Coast Guard LEDETs could have been used in the Luzon Strait, perhaps with aerostats, but the few marijuana vessels coming that way were not worth the cost of maintaining such a distant choke-point patrol.

The declines in marijuana seizures at sea in 1986 were the result of good interdiction tactics and a slightly reduced market here. About 2.3 million pounds were seized that year, 87 percent of it from vessels. Most was Colombian marijuana. Production was down in Columbia but up in Mexico. Domestic production of marijuana was now at 18 percent, compared with 12 percent in 1984. Overall, wholesale prices of marijuana in the States were higher than in recent years.[53] Marijuana prices in the Northeast were rising rapidly; by October they had jumped 50 percent or more in many cities. DEA in Hartford, Connecticut, reported that wholesale pot prices had almost tripled in two years, to as much as $1,000 per pound.[54] Drug prices taken out of context mean little, but when considered with other indicators they are useful. For example, consider that most of the pot smoked in this country at the time was seaborne. If Mexico and our domestic sources were increasing production and the price was going up, it had to be because of losses at sea. The signs were there.

9

Back-strapped
1987

Being set on the idea of getting to Atlantis,
*   you have discovered of course only the Ship of Fools*
*   is making the voyage this year.*

    W. H. AUDEN, "ATLANTIS"

T he tide was going out for the grass boaters. The wind was still fair for the market, but they could not stem the ever-stronger strengthening current of the forces arrayed against them. In the words of the old sailors, they were "back-strapped." The anti-narcotics effort was in the same fix. Interdiction forces were frustrated by bureaucracy.

Ambrose Weldon's heir to the Gulf off-load organization emphatically stated that his losses exceeded 80 percent in 1987. Colombian suppliers no longer sent motherships through the Yucatán. Grass loads came in Mexican vessels after pickups from motherships off the Belize-Mexico border. He had to negotiate with Cuban intermediaries to arrange off-loads from Mexican boats within the 200-mile range of his high-speed crab boats. The off-load manager said that it was getting harder and harder to find reliable help because of arrest attrition. By the end of the year they had no assets. They could no longer pay support to dependents of jailed smugglers to keep them from cooperating with the government. Things fell apart.[1]

Rear Adm. Howard B. Thorsen, USCG, NNBIS Southeast Region coordinator and Seventh District commander, estimated that the overall marijuana interdiction rate was between 20 and 50 percent, and up to 60 percent for some smuggling organizations. He explained that smugglers had been forced to change their methods of operation and had resorted to using ingenious and expensive hidden compartments. He claimed that this was proof that at-sea interdiction was hitting smugglers where it hurt.[2] Weldon's man would certainly have agreed with the admiral but would have disputed his conservative estimate. Weldon's man knew; he operated in the admiral's area of operations.

About 2.4 million pounds of marijuana were seized in 1987, a slight increase over 1986. Approximately 78 percent was from commercial and noncommercial vessels. For the first time in a decade the sea-seizures percentage of marijuana dropped below the high 80s. Land seizures rose to about 14 percent, more than double the previous year's figure, showing a trend away from maritime shipments. Cocaine seizures totaled about 150,000 pounds. Maritime coke seizures rose to almost 43 percent of the total, the highest of any year. Cocaine land seizures also increased, to about 14 percent. Almost half the maritime coke came from containers on commercial vessels. Approximately 376 vessels were seized in 1987, an increase of 23 percent over 1986.[3]

In 1987, Coast Guardsmen seized nearly 1.2 million pounds of pot—50 percent of the total and 65 percent of the maritime pot. They seized approximately 14,700 pounds of cocaine that year—about 10 percent of the total and 23 percent of the maritime coke. Coast Guard vessel seizures totaled 139.[4] Marijuana statistics held steady, with a decline in maritime and an increase in land-border seizures. Cocaine seizures rose along with the take from vessels. Coke by sea was definitely on the increase. So was coke by land across the Mexican border.

National periodicals lost interest in the drug war in 1987. Coverage of narcotics-related events and drug war exposés declined by 37 percent from the previous year.[5] The media focused on Iran-Contra, Oliver North, the Persian Gulf, a stock exchange tumble, and the alleged affair of a popular TV evangelist.

Fickle blow the winds of the free press. They did report the arrest and extradition of the infamous cocaine kingpin Carlos Lehder of television fame. A U.S. plane flew Lehder out of Bogotá on 4 February. Extraditions continued intermittently until 28 May 1987, when the Colombian Supreme Court split on a finding to an extradition treaty challenge. It was a frivolous technicality related to the signing of the treaty by an interim president in 1986 and a resigning after the fact by President Barco. After a 12–12 high court vote, an alternate was brought in to break the tie. It was the end of the U.S.–Colombian extradition treaty. Medellin was victorious.[6]

Meanwhile, the long-awaited national drug strategy had rolled off the press in January. *National and International Drug Law Enforcement Strategy* (the "Green Book") was the first important document of the National Drug Enforcement Policy Board. The strategy was replete with motherhood statements (e.g., "The ultimate goal of both supply and demand reduction efforts is the elimination of drug abuse and trafficking"). The major components of the strategy were intelligence, interdiction, prosecution, and controlled-substance regulation; the document was ambiguous when designating lead agencies for each component. A threat assessment was given for cocaine, opiates, cannabis (marijuana and hashish), and dangerous drugs (amphetamines, etc.). There was a special section on the southwestern border.[7] From the perspective of the operating agencies, there was little new in the Green Book.

Under interdiction and border control, the strategy's objective was "to reduce the amount of illegal drugs entering the United States by

targeting the transportation link between drug supply and demand."
A need for flexibility in interdiction was stressed. "Clearly," the document stated, "the response to the trafficking of a multi-ton shipment
of marijuana from Colombia differs considerably from the response
to smuggling a few kilograms of cocaine across the Southwest border." Begging the question? Perhaps. The strategy rejected quantifiable measures of interdiction, such as pounds seized; the Policy Board
felt that such measures did not show the importance of deterrence,
which discouraged smugglers from even attempting a venture. Deterrence, of course, was impossible to quantify.

The strategy defined the roles of the agencies involved in interdiction—actually the traditional missions of those agencies. NNBIS was
recognized as the coordination mechanism for regional and special
operations such as Hat Trick and Blue Lightning. The Policy Board
kept the role of coordinating the functions of the expanding C3I centers, EPIC, and NNBIS. The strategy encouraged the development of
regional detection and response capabilities, specifically the Joint
Marine Interdiction Command Center (JMICC) in Miami, precursor
of the Blue Lightning Operations Center (discussed in chapter 8). The
strategy did not explain how BLOC and NNBIS would coordinate
their work in the same area.[8] Apparently the Policy Board would
coordinate the coordinators. Hard questions were left unanswered by
the Green Book, but at least we had a document that would pass as
a national drug enforcement strategy. It was more a mission statement
than a plan to fight the drug war.

In March President Reagan issued Executive Order 12590, expanding the duties of the Policy Board to include drug prevention and
treatment efforts and making it responsible for supply and demand
reduction. The name was changed from the National Drug Enforcement Policy Board to the National Drug Policy Board (NDPB). It now
had the full spectrum of drug reduction responsibilities.[9] The administration wanted the board's mandate to counter the effort by some
congressmen to legislate for a drug czar. Blanks in the strategy gave
Congress fuel for the fire.

On 22 May 1987 the Policy Board issued a directive defining the
role of lead agencies in drug control. Congress found it inadequate. A
report by the Committee on Government Operations, *The National
Drug Policy Board: A Failure in the War on Drugs,* proclaimed that
the federal government had failed to designate a single head of the

Vice President George Bush presides over a meeting of the National Drug Interdiction Operations Oversight Group in Washington on 9 April 1987. Capt. Howard Gehring, NNBIS director, is at the vice president's left.
(Official White House photograph)

drug war, a failure that the committee said had plagued the nation's antidrug effort for more than twenty-five years. The committee said that the Policy Board's directive did not give sole responsibility to lead agencies and provided no command authority. It also found that lead agencies were already charged with those very responsibilities: "They are doing what they already were." Much of what the committee members said was true, but they knew that the Policy Board could not establish a single command authority. They implied that Congress should institute a federal reorganization to place all major drug enforcement agencies in a single department under the direction of a cabinet-level secretary.[10] This was another call for a drug czar. Congress still refused to accept NNBIS in a coordination role. At an interdiction oversight meeting in April, Vice President Bush told the group that Congress still did not understand NNBIS's mission.[11] He could have said that Congress was out to destroy NNBIS and the Policy Board because it wanted a drug czar.

NNBIS conducted an internal audit at the request of Capt. Howard Gehring, the director. It was completed in February 1987. The evaluation team leader was Philip D. Brady, deputy assistant to the vice president, assisted by representatives from Customs, the Coast Guard, DEA, and the Department of Defense. The audit was as critical as anything done by the General Accounting Office, but it showed a much better understanding of the system's intelligence capabilities. The evaluation found that many participating agencies had not met their original commitments in personnel, and that some personnel were being arbitrarily withdrawn for other duties. NNBIS regions were faulted for not giving agency managers detailed mission statements to use in selecting qualified personnel. The auditors also found that the rigid regional organization design, based on the South Florida Task Force, was not applicable in some areas. Flexibility was recommended for region-specific missions that should be threat-driven, using a form-follows-function organization.

NNBIS intelligence functions were emphasized in the evaluation report, perhaps because of the backgrounds of two team members: Bill Duncan of Customs and Rich Kobakoff of DEA. The team stressed that NNBIS was not an intelligence collector but was responsible for regional analysis of intelligence from all sources to promote coordinated interdiction and joint planning. NNBIS regions, they said, must concentrate on defining essential "elements of information" to guide collectors in getting information of greatest utility. They emphasized the need for regional advisers from the national foreign intelligence community to "collect and sanitize" intelligence products and ensure that their release did not compromise sources and methods. They found confusion in the regions about the relationship between NNBIS and EPIC for the intelligence mission; a statement of the relationship was recommended.

In addition to the discrepancies and opportunities identified systemwide, the NNBIS evaluation team made specific recommendations for improving the operations of the six NNBIS regions. They also recommended that the western Pacific district (Hawaii) be upgraded to a region because of area-specific smuggling problems.

The NNBIS regional evaluation did much to focus the mission of NNBIS.[12] There was still a lot to be done, but after almost four years of operational experience, NNBIS had become a national asset in the drug war. It was unfortunate that the drug enforcement strategy did not name NNBIS as primary coordinating body for interdiction. It was more lamentable still that Congress would not recognize or support NNBIS and felt that it had been superseded by the National Drug Policy Board, which Congress held in even lower esteem. NNBIS had forced the agencies to recognize the enemy and to plan attacks via threat assessments and operation orders. Despite its limitations and its critics, NNBIS was doing a good job in coordinating the vast interdiction effort.

The year brought confusion to the drug warriors. Administration officials were distracted by Iran-Contra. They had done well until now. Reagan had placed more emphasis on the drug problem than any other president. The South Florida Task Force, NNBIS, the Organized Crime Drug Enforcement Task Forces, military involvement, the national security decision directive, and many other drug initiatives had been implemented on his watch. Direct involvement by Vice President George Bush gave leverage to make things happen. Congressional involvement was admirable, but efforts to manage through legislation were creating a plethora of overlapping entities and functions. It was hard to figure out who was doing what. Congress wanted a drug czar, and it got a committee: the National Drug Policy Board. Things were now managed by a very large committee with subcommittees to work out details. The results were chaotic. We now had a diluted NNBIS; Congress-sponsored C3Is and JMICCs, which were greatly needed but overlapped the responsibilities of NNBIS; and renewed battles between Customs and the Coast Guard over missions. With all this political and bureaucratic meddling, the drug warriors were just as back-strapped as Weldon's crew. The long-awaited strategy did not straighten out the mess.

Retired Coast Guard captain Stephen Duca called it the ad hoc drug war. He described the current setup as being beset with "Byzantine inefficiencies." Captain Duca objected to the division of responsibility between Customs and the Coast Guard for interdiction. He argued that the Coast Guard had the command and control structure to do the entire job, and Customs did not.[13] Duca's thesis was parochial, but it had merit. Richard Young, a naval reserve rear admiral and civilian lawyer, agreed with the Coast Guard captain. In an article co-authored with two other naval reserve officers, Admiral Young faulted the Policy Board for designating Customs the lead agency in interdiction. They argued that the Coast Guard, with its two centuries of experience and much broader jurisdiction than Customs, was the logical choice to run the show. They pointed out that the budding Customs C3I system was not coordinated with the Coast Guard maritime defense zones (MDZs) created in 1984 to upgrade our littoral defense, or with the air force sector operations control centers (SOCCs). The naval reservists wanted the Coast Guard designated the lead agency for surface and air interdiction in the maritime environment.[14]

Coast Guard captain Donald Naples asked for the Coast Guard's transfer from the Department of Transportation to Justice. His thesis was that the primary law enforcement mission of the Coast Guard was much more compatible with the Justice Department than with Transportation.[15] Captain Naples did not say how this would affect cooperation with Customs, where the real problem lay. Considering the times, Naples had a better argument for returning the Coast Guard to the Treasury. Coordinating the activities of the two principal drug interdiction players would have been much easier with both in the same department.

All these treatises on the drug war were published in the prestigious *Proceedings* of the U.S. Naval Institute in the same year. Whether or not readers agreed with the authors' positions, there was a signal that something had gone awry. In Washington no one paid any attention; if anyone did, the articles were written off as Coast Guard or military propaganda. The most basic primers on organization call for clear lines of command or management to meet goals. If Customs were given the C3I capabilities, at considerable expense, it should have been given complete control of air interdiction resources, including available Coast Guard assets. It was unthinkable to give primary control of maritime interdiction to any agency but the Coast Guard. The Coast Guard should have been given control of all maritime assets, including Customs boats and the BLOC units. The activities of both sides, including the use of military assets, should have been coordinated by NNBIS. Let the Policy Board deal with agency heads and politicians and stay out of operations. There were a lot of could-have-beens in 1987 that would have cleared the fog of battle.

The Wharton study came to town in the summer of 1987. Customs commissioned Wharton Econometrics of Pennsylvania to determine the impact of federal, state, and local law enforcement efforts against drugs. The study showed that interdiction was much cheaper than investigation as a means of removing drugs. The study assumed that drug removal was the major objective. In fact, that objective was not as important as the removal of traffickers. With respect to the falling prices of cocaine in spite of increased seizures, the study concluded that price declines were due to increased supplies in producing countries. Abundant supplies kept prices down despite increased enforcement. The analysis indicated that a 10 percent increase in federal law enforcement expenditure would result in a 3.5 percent reduction in cocaine consumption and a 1.5 percent fall in marijuana use. Wharton concluded that interdiction was the cheapest way to go.[16] There was no universal agreement, but the findings sounded good to the interdiction forces.

It was time to expand the El Paso Intelligence Center. The Policy Board's strategy document had designated DEA the lead agency for intelligence. DEA managed EPIC, a multiagency effort. In the summer of 1987 EPIC was designated the National Tactical Drug Intelligence Center by the Policy Board. It would still be known as EPIC. Money was appropriated for a new building with expanded data-processing capabilities at Fort Bliss, Texas. Recommendations on how to improve EPIC were made by the operating agencies and NNBIS to the Policy Board. Some were adopted, but most were not. EPIC's staff felt that they had a good handle on how to develop and disseminate tactical drug intelligence. They did the same work as before, but they did more and they did it faster. Drug intelligence centers were springing up like mushrooms. Besides traditional intelligence functions conducted by the line agencies at headquarters, regional, and district levels, there were intelligence components at each NNBIS region and developing intelligence units at JMICC/BLOC and the air C3Is. More would come. All were needed, but definitive guidelines establishing a rational division of labor was missing.[17] Loose ends and uncoordinated changes were the epitaph of 1987.

The opposition was also adjusting to changing times. Marijuana prices were going up, and cocaine prices were coming down. Commercial-grade marijuana went as high as $1,400 a pound in 1987. Coke dropped as low as $12,000 a kilo. Marijuana land seizures along the Mexican border increased from 66 metric tons in 1986 to 146 metric tons in 1987.[18] It was not all Mexican pot. Near-record prices in the United States sent Colombian marijuana literally flying to Mexico for importation to the States. Mexican authorities documented about 50 tons of Colombian grass passing through their country in ninety days. Cocaine had been routed through Mexico for at least three years, but this was the first evidence of Colombian marijuana coming that way.[19] It was another indication of marijuana losses at sea and the impact on maritime grass smugglers.

CaribRon's activities in the deep Caribbean, coupled with the more frequent deployment of cutters in the passes and all along the sea lanes, were having an obvious deterrent effect on smugglers. Capt. John Lockwood, USCG, Caribbean Squadron commander, reported rising numbers of vessels that, having been "rigged" (overflown and identified) by squadron aircraft, jettisoned their contraband in anticipation of boarding.[20] In the past, boat smugglers had been apprehensive when circled by a Coast Guard aircraft, but they realized that the plane could be looking for a distressed or overdue vessel. It was a different ball game now. To be rigged by a gray aircraft anywhere in the Colombian Basin seemed like the kiss of death. But as Commodore Lockwood said, deterrence was a hard thing to sell.

By the end of 1986 Ambrose Weldon and his crew had decided to send their shrimp boats to Colombia again. Harold King commanded the first. They were frustrated with incompetent mothership masters and failed meetings. An old wooden shrimp boat was procured and outfitted at a Florida west coast port. (The vessel's name is omitted to prevent the identification of Ambrose Weldon and Harold King.) Unbeknownst to the smugglers, Customs had obtained a court order to place a transponder on the boat's mast. It failed shortly after the shrimper left for Colombia and was found by the crew. They deep-sixed the transponder and gave the boat a new name. However, they did not paint out the vessel's U.S. home port—a big mistake.

About 20,000 pounds of pot were loaded in Colombia. No attempt was made to conceal the cargo. The northbound transit was as close to the Central American coast as possible to avoid Caribbean patrols. Transit of the Yucatán was inside Mexican waters. The plan called for the boat to proceed to a point off the Texas coast before coming to Florida along a route used by shrimpers between the Texas-Louisiana and Florida fishing grounds. Unfortunately, King almost collided with a blacked-out cutter on Campeche Bank. A Spanish-speaking crewman told the cutter they were Mexican. It might have worked, but the cutter's searchlight illuminated the U.S. home port painted on the stern. King's long smuggling career was over.

Harold King made his last run aboard this shrimper. *Left to right:* PO Ernie Caamano, unidentified Customs agent, Lt. Bill Baker, and the author.
(Author's collection)

King and his crew went to trial. He had no concealed-compartment defense. The high-powered attorney Weldon provided did little. He tried to discover the information Customs had used for probable cause to install the transponder on the boat before she left Florida; this would have benefited Weldon, but not King. In any case, the lawyer's attempts failed. King and the others were convicted. King got twenty years. He petitioned Weldon to make expense payments to his wife and his girlfriend but was informed that the organization was broke. King then tried to save himself with a belated Rule 35. He called a Customs agent, a DEA agent, and an NNBIS representative, all involved in his prosecution, and invited them to visit him in prison; King was covering the ballpark. After conferring with the appropriate assistant U.S. attorney, the three complied. The agents spent two days at the drab lockup recording King's history. They came away with enough information to nail Weldon and others, and a commitment by King to testify before a grand jury and at subsequent trials. King had his Rule 35.[21]

About the same time that Harold King was being hauled in with his load of grass, authorities in Naples, Florida, turned Willard Wooten, the burly and gray-bearded grass smuggler we met in 1976 at Everglades City. (Wooten died in the crash of a home-built aircraft in Collier County, Florida, on 26 March 1989.) He was documented as a confidential informant and agreed to continue his smuggling activities under the direction of state's attorney investigator James Decker. Decker found Wooten through an unusual investigative technique. When Decker's boss told him to go out and investigate smugglers operating just south of Naples, the former state trooper had no clue where to start. He teamed up with Jack Larson of the Florida Department of Law Enforcement (FDLE), and the two intrepids knocked on doors of a half-dozen suspected smugglers to see if they wanted to cut their losses. Amazingly, two agreed to talk. They incriminated Wooten.

Wooten was given the code name Popeye. His primary job was to operate a high-speed chase boat and provide countersurveillance for off-loads. He also had the dangerous task of trying to rescue delivery boat crews in the event of interception. Popeye got off-load information approximately twelve hours before deliveries. He usually gassed the chase boat at a marina and notified his wife from a pay phone that he would not be home for a while. Wooten also called Decker from the pay phone with the off-load intelligence. Popeye mostly operated alone, but sometimes he took county undercover investigator Art McLellan along as crew for the chase boat. Decker would notify Lt. Bill Baker, the operations officer at Coast Guard Group St. Petersburg, and NNBIS. He also notified Customs, DEA, and FDLE. Through this local ad hoc agreement, Wooten's reports were collated with offshore target information held by the NNBIS center in Miami. The seizure rate of grass boats in the coastal waters of the eastern Gulf of Mexico increased dramatically in 1987. Many U.S. citizens involved in off-loads were arrested. With mandatory minimum sentences in place, some of these arrestees opted for a Rule 11.[22]

Information given by King and others produced enough testimonial evidence to indict five off-load organization members. One was Ambrose Weldon, who had just started serving his original sentence. If convicted again, Weldon faced a life sentence under new sentencing guidelines for conducting a continuing criminal enterprise. He too opted for a Rule 11. The house of cards began to fall. To contend with the massive amount of information from cooperating defendants, the U.S. attorney's office in the Middle District of Florida established an Organized Crime Drug Enforcement Task Force, or OCDETF, unit. Operation Peacemaker was born.

The end was in sight for the last major marijuana off-load enterprise on the Atlantic-Gulf side of the United States. During 1987 thirteen vessels carrying almost 300,000 pounds of marijuana were seized in the final approaches to Florida's west coast. Others were intercepted in the Yucatán Channel by choke-point patrols.[23] All of this caused Weldon's lieutenant to claim that the off-load organizations' losses exceeded 80 percent in 1987. Many losses were directly attributed to Popeye, who played his dangerous and lonely role on dark nights in the Gulf waters adjacent to his beloved Everglades. Willard Wooten paid his debt, perhaps with his life.

The pacification of Everglades City was a real challenge. Most of the little town's population felt they were getting an unfair share of attention and harassment by drug warriors. They did not welcome outsiders, especially the Feds. Capt. Brian Sonner, the Coast Guard group commander whose area included Everglades City, was concerned about a possible deadly confrontation between his troops and the townspeople. Sonner knew that when his 41-boats had to probe the Ten Thousand Islands separating the town from the Gulf, the crews instinctively mounted machine guns and went to battle stations. He felt that something had to be done to open the town to an intermittent Coast Guard presence. He decided to lead a parade in full uniform. On the morning of 9 September, Captain Sonner stood on the deck of a polished 41 with no weapons showing. The boat slowly glided up the Barron River to the Sportsman Hotel, the social center of Everglades City.

By prearrangement, a civilian agent and a uniformed captain of marines stood on the dock solemnly awaiting Sonner's arrival. Capt. David Matthews, USMC, was persuaded to take part in the Admiral Perry–type expedition because he was familiar with Everglades City. They hoped the town's inhabitants would believe that the marines had landed. The 41 boat moored in front of the quaint old two-story wooden hotel. The trio ate lunch on the hotel veranda, attracting many stares from the regulars. Coincidentally, Florida's state representative Mary Ellen Hawkins was visiting this outpost of her constituency. Captain Sonner exchanged polite words with the representative and briefly explained the purpose of his visit. After lunch Sonner paid an impromptu visit to the mayor of Everglades City and the Collier County sheriff's substation. Mission accomplished! After releasing the 41-boat to return to her Fort Myers station, Captain Sonner left with the agent and the marine. Everyone in town knew he had been there, but no one was sure why. A confidential informant said there was wild speculation about the purpose of the Marine Corps representative.[24] The opening of Everglades City was at least a start in reducing tensions.

Local and state enforcement agencies were sharing intelligence more freely along the Gulf coast and elsewhere by 1987. The Miami NNBIS center had representatives from the Florida Department of Law Enforcement to handle state and local liaisons. Now we had the Customs-sponsored Blue Lightning strike forces composed of state and local agencies. The strike forces gave intelligence to the Blue Lightning Operations Center in Miami. Customs analyzed the data, collated that information with its own, and sent intelligence reports back to participating agencies.[25] Customs sometimes provided radios and radar transponders to state and local patrol boats so that they could be identified on BLOC's radar. Patrol officers could act as Customs officers if authorized by BLOC. The state and local people had a forum of their own. It was a good concept, and it improved coordination and intelligence exchange for inshore operations. Unfortunately, there was no formal mechanism to mesh the Blue Lightning system with NNBIS. The new strategy did not address these issues. It was another case of loose ends.

By the end of 1987, Blue Lightning radars placed atop condominiums and other tall buildings covered the Florida coast from Fort Pierce on the Atlantic, around the Keys, and up to Pensacola. They could detect boats about 17–20 miles from shore.[26] BLOC watch standers saw a lot of boats but had no idea what they were unless specific intelligence said that a boat was expected at a certain time, or she was a high-speed craft heading for shore at night from the Bahamas, or she behaved like a mothership. NNBIS Miami had suspect sightings and certain types of special intelligence, but no coastal radar system. If the two were combined under one roof—technically it was one roof, since they were in the same building—and one authority, it would have been a potent coordination center. But as Steve Duca said, it was an ad hoc war.

The new interdiction gadgets were wasted on multi-ton grass boaters. For them, as for NNBIS, time was running out. They were still coming north in 1987, but in reduced numbers. Harold King and others like him had grown disgusted with the performance of foreign-crewed motherships and were making a desperate attempt to go all the way to Colombia with American-flagged fishing boats. Not since the mid-1970s had U.S. smugglers risked bulk deliveries through the choke points. Smugglers were fully aware of the dangers, but some old-timers were confident because of past successes. A few were willing to take the chance just to prove themselves again. It was still a game.

Elvin "PeeWee" Young was an old-timer. He took the big 72-foot steel-hulled shrimper *Lady Hamilton III* to Panama in February and loaded over 30,000 pounds of grass. Young was northbound through the Mexican side of the Yucatán Channel on the evening of 15 March. He was well offshore. So was the cutter *Dependable* (WMEC-626). Repeated radio calls to the shrimper were ignored. A home port of New Orleans was clearly printed on the transom. When the cutter came up to the shrimp boat, Young stopped. He and his two American crewmen came on deck. Young readily admitted that his vessel was of U.S. registry. After the *Dependable*'s boarding party made a security sweep, they went to the main hold hatch. When they started removing the cover, Young told the Coasties he could save them some trouble; he admitted that the hold was full of marijuana. When PeeWee Young and his crew were brought to the Coast Guard station in St. Petersburg, they seemed relieved. For lack of a better place, the three prisoners were initially processed in the NNBIS office and handcuffed to the office furniture. Secretary Linda Mulik was uneasy. A crew member stared at her continually; he looked like Charles Manson. Young's demeanor seemed to say, "I gave it my best shot, but you got me." The old grass boaters' heyday was coming to an end.[27]

Human intelligence paid for by DEA was commonly collected in source countries. Reports to the United States by convicted smugglers were not routine. In early 1987 a Colombian from a seized drug boat decided to cut his losses. He had previous drug-smuggling convictions and realized his jeopardy. He agreed to make an open guilty plea, with no promise of a reduced sentence, and to testify against the other people on the boat. They were convicted. The agents involved in the case petitioned the U.S. attorney for a Rule 35 and parole for the man based on his cooperation and his promise to provide more intelligence

The crew of the *Lady Hamilton III* being processed. Customs officer John Henderson is on the phone. *(Author's collection)*

from his home in Colombia. Skeptics said he would never be heard from again. The agents persevered and managed to convince an assistant U.S. attorney that the man had valuable smuggling connections in Colombia. After an intense briefing by one of the agents at the Krome Detention Center in Miami, the man was released on parole with a plane ticket home and instructions on how to make telephone reports.

Much to the doubters' surprise, the converted smuggler made his first report a week after his release. He said the *Mercedes* was leaving a Colombian port with a load of marijuana for an unknown destination. The information was entered into the intelligence system through EPIC and the NNBIS center in Miami. The USS *John L. Hall* (FFG-32) intercepted the suspect on 19 July at Quita Sueño Bank, about 125 miles east of Nicaragua. The boat was scuttled by the crew of five Colombians, but enough marijuana residue was recovered to arrest the people on board. They were handed over to Colombian authorities. The valuable source sent intelligence reports well into 1988.[28]

Navy assistance to Coast Guard drug interdiction peaked in 1987. LEDETs assigned to navy ships seized twenty vessels, approximately 117,000 pounds of marijuana, and 1,600 pounds of cocaine. Navy P-3 aircraft sightings aided the seizure of four additional vessels with about 73,000 pounds of pot. The USS *McCloy* (FF-1038) accounted for two of these, with a total of 31,500 pounds. The USS *Semmes* (DDG-18) made the largest navy-supported grass take of the year. Navy hydrofoils scored seven seizures, with the *Gemini* (PHM-6) accounting for four. The hydrofoil *Hercules* (PHM-2) made the largest navy-assisted coke seizure that year, with a little over 1,000 pounds.[29]

Maritime marijuana still seeped through the old Bahamas route in 1987. An example was the 225-foot Colombian coastal freighter *Don Julio*. NNBIS Miami developed intelligence that sent the cutter *Bear* (WMEC-901) to Eleuthera Island on 3 June. The target vessel was located inside Bahamian waters by the newly commissioned 270-foot Famous-class cutter. The Coast Guard requested and received permission for the *Bear* to enter Bahamian territorial waters. The *Don Julio* and the 45-foot Bahamian boat *Lady Christina,* tied alongside the freighter, were captured by the cutter. A boarding party from the *Bear* found 11 pounds of cocaine and 64 tons of pot. It was the largest maritime marijuana seizure of the year, and the last of that magnitude on the Atlantic-Gulf side of the United States. The *Don Julio* was one of the last classic marijuana motherships.[30]

The Coast Guard made its largest coke seizure so far just off the northwest coast of St. Croix, U.S. Virgin Islands. Three Coast Guard auxiliary volunteers were searching for a man lost while diving from a pleasure boat on 8 May. They sighted a fishing vessel anchored or aground in a shallow reef area. The auxiliarists figured the boat might be smuggling illegal aliens. They called the regulars to investigate. The USCGC *Ocracoke* (WPB-1307) was in the area. The *Ocracoke* found the 28-foot *LaToto* out of Riohacha, Colombia. The fishing vessel was in U.S. waters, so there was no legal problem about searching her. The *Ocracoke*'s team found 2,791 pounds of cocaine. Five Colombians were arrested. It was the largest coke seizure for the Coast Guard since the hair-raising air sea chase in Biscayne Bay in May 1985. The next morning the determined auxiliarists also found the body they had been searching for.[31]

This was the last big year for multi-ton loads of marijuana in the Gulf of Mexico. Besides the thirteen vessels seized in the vicinity of

Route 26, two were intercepted north of Tampa Bay and a few in the northern Gulf. About seventeen vessels were taken by choke-point patrols in the Yucatán with approximately 170,000 pounds. Also, two big floater finds were made west of Fort Myers in June, with over 37,000 pounds consigned to the fishes.[32] The floaters had been jettisoned by smugglers spooked by patrols. Such finds were common, but not to the tune of the $11 million cast adrift. Times were hard.

By this time few Gulf seizures exceeded the routine 20,000-pound pot loads of the past. One that did was the 66-foot U.S. shrimper *My Girls*. She was intercepted by the USCGC *Point Steel* (WPB-82359) 30 miles west of Cape Romano on 8 May. She was not on the lookout list. The *Point Steel*'s CO, Lt. (jg) Gregory Shaffer, grew suspicious because the people on board were up and about; shrimpers usually sleep during the day and fish at night. Shaffer decided to send a boarding party. They found approximately 24 tons of marijuana. Every compartment, including the cabin and pilothouse, was filled with bales—a total of 588. As far as Shaffer was concerned, this was a typical cold hit with no prior intelligence. In fact, the ubiquitous Popeye with the undercover as crew had met the load boat during the night. He told them to sit tight until he could arrange an off-load. He called Jim Decker, who called the Coast Guard.[33]

The trial of the three people arrested aboard the *My Girls* was anything but typical. Assistant U.S. Attorney Jeff Downing called an NNBIS agent to serve as an expert witness to describe a hypothetical mothership off-load in the Gulf. The agent had been an expert at ten previous drug boat trials in the same jurisdiction, giving the same testimony. In this case, a smart former assistant U.S. attorney was the lawyer for one of the defendants. He was able to ask the witness specific questions on cross-examination that would have required the disclosure of classified information, although no such information had been used in locating the grass-loaded shrimper. The witness refused to answer the attorney's questions. The defense immediately made a motion for a mistrial. The trial judge rejected the motion but ordered the testimony struck from the record. At the conclusion of the trial, the three defendants were convicted. They immediately filed an appeal based on the government's failure to raise the issue of classified information pretrial, as prescribed by the Confidential Information Procedure Act. The Eleventh Circuit Court of Appeals, however, upheld

The rig tender *Triton Express* detected by FLIR from a Customs aircraft off Louisiana *(Photograph by Customs agent J. Thomas Maher)*

the convictions without comment.[34] A lesson was learned about the use of experts who based their opinions, even indirectly, on classified information.

Drugs were rarely if ever identified on a vessel at night by an aircraft. A Customs aircrew from the naval air station at Belle Chasse, Louisiana, merited that distinction on the night of 12 May. They were alerted to a possible marijuana off-load somewhere in the Gulf near the coast. A Customs Citation 550 aircraft, equipped with forward-looking infrared radar (FLIR), was searching the area for the suspect vessel *Triton Express,* a 123-foot oil rig supply vessel. Just after midnight, air interdiction officer Tom Maher advised pilot Mike Berry that he had a target on the scope. When the Citation approached the target, Maher saw that the FLIR image showed a vessel with a pilot-house forward and a large box or stack of something on the aft deck. According to Maher, the FLIR image of the stack or box glowed, which meant that something was generating a lot of heat. Plant material like marijuana generates heat.

Discrete air surveillance was flown for over three hours as the suspect headed for the coast. When the vessel entered Hero Canal near Belle Chasse, not far from the Customs plane's home base, the aircrew updated the land troops with the possible off-load site. The boat put in at a dock on the canal. Customs officers closed in and collared the off-load crew and their trucks. The three-man crew was also arrested. The *Triton Express* had arrived with almost 38,000 pounds of heat-producing grass. It was puzzling that they did not try to conceal the load inside the spacious hull.[35]

The last of the old-time profile pot boats came into the Gulf in May. How she got through the choke-point patrols was a marvel. The *Claribel* could best be described in marine insurance terms as a constructive total wreck. She could move on her own power but was worth only the value of her scrap metal and electronic equipment. The engine room was literally coated with fuel oil from various leaks, making the deck as slippery as glass. Wood decks in the hold were so rotten that when the contraband was eventually unloaded, planks had to be laid to prevent workers from falling through to the bilge. The 65-foot boat appeared to be an old anchovy purse seiner, once common on the west coast of South America. The *Claribel* was loaded with 30,320 pounds taken on near Riohacha, Colombia. Positions stored in the memory of the vessel's LORAN C. unit indicated that the boat had entered the Gulf very close to the Yucatán Peninsula. When the *Claribel* was sighted by the cutter *Decisive* (WMEC-629) on 19 May, she was headed east toward Florida on Route 26. When the *Decisive* approached the rust-streaked boat, her crew could smell marijuana from a distance. The *Claribel*'s master claimed Costa Rican registry, but he agreed to a consensual boarding. In a matter of minutes the boarding party found marijuana; bales were just stacked in the hold. The *Decisive* took her prize home to Panama City, Florida.[36]

The *Claribel*'s load belonged to two Cuban-American former freedom fighters, who organized and financed many multi-ton shipments of marijuana to Florida. After losing radio contact with the vessel, they met the off-load manager and other interested parties in a central Florida town for a status conference. Two people in the group were experienced private pilots. They chartered a plane to fly over the Coast Guard stations along the west coast looking for their errant mothership; nothing. Out over the Gulf they went; the *Claribel* could not be found.[37] They might have figured she went down with all hands, but these were eternal optimists. The *Decisive*'s homing instinct created a mystery for the smugglers that lasted several days.

The 195-foot Honduran cargo vessel *Carmiel* had everyone guessing in the spring of 1987. In March, DEA put the vessel on lookout. Aruba Customs had been suspicious of the vessel back in 1986 when she was commanded by Roberto Suarez (a fictitious name for an individual wanted by Interpol), a Spanish national involved with the trawler *Argana II* seized in 1985. The USCGC *Bear* (WMEC-901) sighted the freighter on 12 May coming north through the Yucatán. The *Bear* sent a boarding party, but they could not do a thorough search of the cargo hold; she was carrying 400 tons of cement in 50-pound bags. The *Carmiel*'s captain said he was bound for Tampa. He expected to arrive there the next day. The *Bear* reported the suspect's position and intentions and resumed patrol.

Coast Guard and Customs units were alerted along the Florida west coast, but the *Carmiel* did not show up. Finally, a week later on 19 May, the USCGC *Point Swift* (WPB-82312) found the freighter about 90 miles west of Fort Myers. Her average rate of advance from where she was boarded by the *Bear* had been 1.4 knots! The freighter captain told the boarders he had engine trouble but was still bound for Tampa. They also took a look at all the cement and left. Three days later the *Point Swift* found the *Carmiel* again, anchored just outside U.S. customs waters off the mouth of Tampa Bay. Just then, Popeye reported that he was expecting a mothership loaded with cement over pot. The Coast Guard decided that it was time to request an SNO from Honduras. It was received, and the *Point Swift* escorted the freighter to a commercial dock at Port Manatee on the south side of the bay. Customs and Coast Guard searchers, assisted by Manatee County sheriff's deputies with drug-sniffing dogs, began a complete search of the cargo hold. After some of the cement was removed, giving access to the deck, the searchers found 38,500 pounds of marijuana in the ship's double bottoms and some in a concealed compartment just aft of the forepeak.

The *Carmiel*'s deck log and port documents showed that she had been loaded with cement in Limón, Costa Rica, in April. When the ship sailed from Limón on 14 April, the master was Philip Dufour (a fictitious name for an individual wanted in Canada). He declared for Bermuda. A ship inspection report showed the next port as Canada. An older document had a signature in the space for the captain to sign; the signature appeared to be the same as that of Roberto Suarez on documents from the seized *Argana II*.

The ship actually went to Santo Domingo, Dominican Republic. Departure documents showed that the ship left Santo Domingo on 5 May and listed the master who was aboard at seizure. His destination was Tampa, Florida. Nothing on the seized *Carmiel* explained what had become of the vessel after the *Bear* boarded her on 12 May. A postseizure inspection produced photographs of people not on the *Carmiel* at the time of seizure. The pictures were tucked into books on a shelf in the captain's stateroom. Others were developed from exposed film found in a crewman's baggage.

The *Carmiel*'s captain admitted that he had been directed to make an off-load to boats off the Florida west coast before he entered Tampa. A few months after their arrest, the *Carmiel*'s master and chief engineer decided to plead guilty before trial and cooperate with U.S. investigators. They told of a voyage in 1986 to Tampa with cement as a cover for a successful multi-ton marijuana delivery to pickup boats. They could access the double bottoms by moving only one pallet of cement, but the off-load was much more difficult. Documents showed that the ship was in Tampa in December of that year. Both men identified the master at the time as Roberto Suarez. The captain said Suarez told him the cement cargo was used to prevent U.S. airborne heat detection devices from picking up the heat generated by marijuana. Reports of FLIR's capabilities, somewhat exaggerated, were spreading throughout the smuggling community.

The ship's officers told how the cargo on the *Carmiel*'s last voyage had been taken on. The chief engineer said the original plan had been to deliver the pot somewhere in Quebec after transiting north by Bermuda. He said Philip Dufour, a French Canadian, was master when the ship left Costa Rica. The officers claimed that the load's owners suspected that Dufour was planning to steal the vessel and the pot cargo, so they replaced him in Santo Domingo. The delivery was changed to the Gulf. The *Carmiel*'s captain then explained the mystery of the missing week. After the boarding by the *Bear* in the Yucatán, he proceeded north until he thought the cutter was beyond radar range, then turned around and went back through the pass. He knew they would be intercepted if they kept going. Near the Cayman Islands, he got a radio call from a man named Alberto who told him to deliver the load or lose his head. He turned the ship around again,

A Canadian smuggler and friend identified by the master and chief engineer of the freighter *Carmiel* *(Author's collection)*

made an undetected passage through the Yucatán, and was found by the *Point Swift* on 19 May not far from his planned off-load point.

The information from the *Carmiel*'s postseizure analysis and the debriefing of the vessel's master and chief engineer provided documentation of this smuggling venture and identified new techniques. Testimonial evidence from the officers could have been used against Roberto Suarez and Philip Dufour, but these two remained at large. What was relevant was the captain's and chief engineer's identification of the people in the photos found on the ship. They identified one man as Dufour, a second Canadian as Norman, and a Canadian female as Julie or Judy. This information, with the photos, was passed to DEA agent Ted Handoga in Montreal and by him to the Royal Canadian Mounted Police. In September the RCMP and DEA learned that Dufour had purchased an 87-foot Canadian fishing vessel, the *Charlotte Louise*, and a building on a dock at Rimouski, Quebec. The vessel was placed on lookout, and surveillance was established on the dock. On 28 October the RCMP seized the *Charlotte Louise* with

1,057 pounds of hashish when she returned to Quebec. Norman and Julie/Judy, whose photos had been found on the *Carmiel,* were aboard the *Charlotte Louise.* Philip Dufour was not. Postseizure analysis was good for more than historical notation.[38]

The crab boat *Nella,* transporting approximately 20,500 pounds of grass, was Popeye's last roundup. Wooten got the word on 4 October to take the chase boat the next day to a position about 90 miles west of Captiva Island. He was to search for enforcement units and then go to a point about 55 miles east-northeast to meet an unidentified load boat. The rendezvous was scheduled for the night of 6 October. Popeye was to escort the grass boat to a position just off Little Gasparilla Pass. He got radio frequencies on the 40- and 2-meter bands and the call signs for his boat, the load boat, and a shore station. Finally, Wooten was given the pad code NEW YORK CITY for the operation, but he made a mistake copying the numbers that corresponded to the letters of the code; later this caused a crisis. The code would be used by the load boat to give updated positions, since the schedule was flexible. Popeye passed the plan to his handler, Jim Decker. At 0800 on 5 October a patrol aircraft sighted the *Nella* near the Coke Machine and identified her as the possible load boat.

A small coordination crew gathered in Decker's Naples office on the afternoon of 6 October. An antenna was rigged from the office window for the radio monitor, and a guard was set on the appropriate frequencies. A mobile land unit equipped with a 2-meter monitor was positioned at the north end of Pine Island, near the expected off-load point by Little Gasparilla Pass. In the late afternoon a station was heard calling the unidentified load boat's code on the specified 40-meter frequency. That evening the Coast Guard stationed a 41-foot utility boat about 20 miles west of the pass. The weather was clear and the sea moderate. The Charlotte County sheriff's department put a 33-foot Donzi go-fast equipped with radar between the 41-boat and the pass. Customs sent a 38-foot Scarab to the expected off-load location. The officers were actually some miles to the south. The Scarab was not equipped with radar. Radio calls were heard on the 40-meter frequency between 1600 and 1700. More calls were intercepted by the Pine Island mobile unit on the 2-meter frequency, but not at Naples. These intercepts meant that the activity was to the north of Naples, reinforcing the hope that Wooten's off-load position was correct. The team in Decker's office had no direct radio communication with the three interdiction boats. Updates from radio intercepts were telephoned to the agencies involved and relayed by radio to the enforcement boats.

About 1730 someone called an unidentified station on the 40-meter frequency, giving two series of six letters with the advice "Figure it out" followed by "When can you be there?" According to the pad code from Popeye, the position was in the Atlantic! Something was obviously wrong. A frantic rearrangement of the numbers for the code letters gave a different position. To everyone's relief, the new position matched exactly the suspected off-load location. The answer "Will be there two, two-thirty" assured all hands that the seizure of the unknown grass boat was in the bag. Land units took up positions on shore.

Around 2330 the Pine Island mobile unit heard calls between the chase boat and the shore station. Everyone was getting tense. Just before 0200 Popeye called the Pine Island unit on a separate pre-arranged 2-meter emergency frequency with amazing news: "Where the hell is everybody, the load boat is unloading to mullet boats right where they said they would." The invisible boat, known to be approaching a known off-load position, had arrived on her announced schedule without being seen. After frantic calls, all units converged on the off-load position. The Charlotte County Donzi sped to the scene. Sgt. Ron Bellomy found mullet boats going at high speed in all directions. Three were apprehended. The shore troops got two trucks, one partially loaded with pot, and detained four wet men in nearby mangroves who said they were bird-watching. The Customs Scarab was sent south to look for the load boat. As the Customs agents approached Captiva Island, they came within BLOC radar range. BLOC gave them directions to a target proceeding south about 1.5 miles offshore. The Customs boat intercepted the target at 0330. It was the *Nella* with two people aboard. Enough marijuana residue was found for Customs to seize it. Sea and shore units eventually found most of the *Nella*'s pot cargo.

An afteraction assessment showed how the *Nella* had passed through the patrol line. This operation was a case of outstanding intelligence but very poor radio communications on the part of the enforcement agencies. The intelligence team gave the arrival time within fifteen minutes and the location of the off-load within 0.5 mile. They had only a general idea of where the patrol units were and no direct radio link with the interceptors. Decker's crew was in telephone contact with agency shore stations and NNBIS Miami. In hindsight, the Naples contingent should have had direct telephone contact with BLOC, but Naples was accustomed to dealing with NNBIS. Information passed between NNBIS and BLOC was unknown to Naples. The need for a multiagency secure radio system and a single command or coordination system to control near-shore interdiction was thus further documented.[39]

The last known 20-plus-ton load of marijuana bound for the Gulf managed to get past the Yucatán Channel choke-point patrol on 28 October 1987. Ammonia leaks in freezer spaces curtailed the search of the 148-foot ex–longline fishing vessel *Yoko Maru No. 77* by the LEDET from the USS *Hercules* (PHM-2). The South Korean master showed the boarding party a Sierra Leone registration certificate and apparently correct cargo and sanitation documents. He said he was transporting frozen fish from Cádiz, Spain, to a fish company in Tampa. His logbook and chart rhumb lines across the Atlantic and through the Caribbean were complete with satellite navigator positions. The eight-man Korean crew had seaman papers from Sierra Leone. There was a cargo of frozen fish aboard the vessel. The circumstances were nearly identical to those of the *Fatuk* case in Rhode Island and the *Saja* case in the Columbia River in 1985. The *Yoko Maru No. 77* passed through the net, but the LEDET report stated the belief that the vessel was transporting contraband in a hidden compartment even though the search was negative.

A few hours after the *Yoko Maru* cleared the Yucatán, Customs agent John Ryan in Fort Myers reported that a major marijuana off-load would take place at a position 112 miles west of Charlotte Harbor on the night of 30 October. Ryan's intelligence said the mothership would be about 200 feet long, superstructure aft, low amidships and with a high bow; except for the length, the description fit the *Yoko Maru*. Ryan also gave the name and description of a pickup vessel. NNBIS messaged a description of the expected mothership, the name and description of the pickup boat, and coordinates of the off-load position to appropriate action commands. NNBIS then alerted the USS *Semmes* (DDG-18) cruising the southern Gulf with a LEDET aboard. Although the *Hercules'* boarding report was there, the NNBIS watch had not yet made a connection between the *Yoko Maru* and the mothership reported by Ryan.

A surveillance plane sighted the *Yoko Maru* on the afternoon of 30 October near the area of the expected off-load. The description of the *Yoko Maru* fit the description of the expected mothership. The *Semmes* picked up the target on radar and began to shadow. Around 1730 the target loitered in the vicinity of the expected off-load. The destroyer moved in. After obtaining consent from the master, the *Semmes* LEDET, commanded by Lt. (jg) Chris Buckridge, USCG, boarded the *Yoko Maru*. The master was very cooperative. He gave the boarders the same story he had given the *Hercules'* people. Despite the strong odor of ammonia in the main deck freezer flats, the LEDET persevered. A large inaccessible space was found on the lower portside. When the captain was queried about the space, he said one of the crew knew more about that than he did. The crewman showed the boarders a manhole, covered by boxes of freezer-burned frozen fish. This area had the strongest ammonia smell. After ventilating the space, the Coast Guardsmen removed the cover. Below was a 30-by-15-by-13-foot freezer with 44,160 pounds of very cold marijuana. After the contraband was found, the Korean master cooperated. The LEDET took the *Yoko Maru* to Port Manatee for processing. As usual in seizures made by naval vessels, the *Semmes* remained over the horizon. Inshore boaters and dockside idlers seldom saw the gray ships.

The *Yoko Maru*'s documents were bogus, including the logbook and navigation tracks. The vessel had come from Dakar, Senegal (like the *Fatuk* and *Saja*), to Aruba. Then she went to Riohacha, where the pot was loaded and the hidden compartment sealed. She sailed on 23 October for the off-load position in the Gulf. All radio frequencies and codes were thrown overboard before the vessel was boarded by the *Semmes*. The captain cooperated, but the crew pled innocent and went to trial. This was a reverse of the usual hidden-compartment case, where the master was charged and the crew dismissed. They were all convicted except for the cook, who got a directed acquittal.

An OCDETF investigation followed in Boston, using evidence from the three ammonia-leaking longliners. Ten people in the United States were indicted. A major smuggling enterprise was identified with participants in Spain, West Africa, Colombia, and the United Kingdom. This was one of the most sophisticated smuggling operations uncovered so far.[40]

Marijuana traffic through the Mexican Bypass was brisk in 1987 but later declined because of the collapse of smuggling organizations along Florida's west coast. The *Nella* and others got their loads from Mexican intermediate transports for final delivery across the Gulf by Route 26. Alacran Reef on the Campeche Bank was a favorite place for transshipments. Small islands and rock outcrops provided protected waters for those with local knowledge. One of the last Mexican vessels seized near the Yucatán Peninsula was the shrimper *Carmita Aracely,* intercepted on 19 November by the Mexican Navy. The old vessel was broken down and drifting. Marijuana debris was found in the fish hold. When the boat was towed to a Mexican port, almost 9,000 pounds were found in a hidden compartment next to the engine room. It was believed that 20,000 pounds had been off-loaded to two boats out of Naples, Florida, before the *Carmita* was seized.[41] The Bypass in Mexican waters was a protected and productive route for Florida grass smugglers until they could no longer make pickups. Operation Peacemaker saw to that.

Cocaine was a different story. Maritime seizures in and around Florida more than doubled in 1987.[42] About one-half of the volume, however, was transported in maritime containers and generally immune to seizure at sea. The main risk to the smuggler was the loss of direct control of multimillion-dollar cargoes while en route. If a small coastal freighter was carrying one or two containers on deck, it was possible for boarding parties to search them, depending on the contents. Large merchant ships transporting multiple containers, however, were almost impossible to search at sea. Interdiction of cocaine or marijuana in containers was the province of Customs freighter search teams. With about twenty thousand commercial containers entering our ports each day, it was an impossible task without good intelligence.[43]

Northeastern maritime seizures for the year were down to almost nothing. With a little over 1 percent of the pot seized and none of the cocaine, the area north of South Carolina seemed abandoned by smugglers. A small revival in seizures took place the next year, but the routine transportation of multi-ton loads of marijuana through the northern Atlantic ended in 1987. The 90-foot stateless motor vessel *Wamandai* with 22,000 pounds was one of the last motherships seized. A Coast Guard C-130 from Elizabeth City, North Carolina, found the suspect 105 miles southeast of Bermuda on 2 September. A marathon air surveillance began that lasted until 5 September, when the cutter *Gallatin* (WHEC-721) finally arrived after being released from a navy exercise.[44] This was definitely one for the Airedales.

Marijuana sea seizures on the Pacific side in 1987 almost doubled, to about 99,000 pounds. This was just a little over 4 percent of the maritime take. About 89 percent of the pot came from only five vessels, not an unusual ratio in the Pacific. Three of the seizures were in the Pacific Northwest.[45] Almost all the Pacific marijuana seized in 1987 originated in Southeast Asia. For the first time the Philippines was documented as a source of marijuana. West Coast narcotics intelligence analysts believed that the lack of known marijuana imports from South America was related to diminished stocks in Colombia.

Pacific maritime coke seizures in 1987 faded to almost nothing. The Pacific narcotics-smuggling situation was expected to remain fairly static through 1988.[46] To everyone's surprise, however, the 1988 threat estimate for the West Coast turned out to be vastly conservative.

The Coast Guard's proposed goal of a 75 percent maritime marijuana interdiction rate, which had been rejected by the National Drug Policy Board, was apparently a valid threshold. Seizures exceeding 75 percent made pot smuggling economically unfeasible. Ambrose Weldon and other indicted smugglers admitted they were at that point or beyond by the end of 1987. An effective interdiction rate was thus verified by the opposition. If you want to know how much you missed, you have to ask the other side. Smugglers will agree to cooperate only if mandatory minimum sentences remain in effect. What was lacking in 1987, and still is today, is a procedure to extract and verify enough interdiction information from the prison population to make the data quantitatively valid. A system for debriefing extensive numbers of offenders in U.S. custody was proposed in a later drug strategy, but it was never fully implemented.[47]

The *Washington Post* noted that the tide of the battle against drugs appeared to turn in 1987. The *Post* reporters conducted polls and consulted experts outside of government. They found that illegal drugs were still the biggest problem facing the country but that marijuana use among high school seniors was at a ten-year low. The *Post* survey also showed a big drop in cocaine use in 1987. Crack cocaine, however, was a virulent problem. The article suggested that in the future, 1987 might be hailed as the year of the turnaround in the war on drugs. The authors passed on the warning that the measurable decline in drug use was small compared with the magnitude of the problem. They also acknowledged that the data did not cover the high school dropouts or older drug users whose problem was most severe. The most promising find was the changing attitude toward drugs.[48]

In June 1987 the United Nations convened a drug control conference in Vienna. Attorney General Edwin Meese led the U.S. delegation. It was the first time leaders from around the world had expressed a united commitment to reducing illegal production and use of drugs. The conference, Meese said, signaled that a turning point had been reached in the war on drugs.[49] Ambrose Weldon and a host of grass smugglers would have certainly signed off on a turning-point declaration; they were more than convinced. If nothing else, 1987 was a year of change in the drug war.

10

Silence and Eddies
1988

There was a strange stillness. The birds, for example—where had they gone? . . . It was a spring without voices.

RACHEL CARSON, *SILENT SPRING*

T he pot world was turned upside down. To the interdiction forces along our southeastern perimeter, the early months of 1988 must have seemed like Rachel Carson's "spring without voices."[1] Hardly a chirp was heard. Where was the fleet of marijuana motherships? Herbicides in Colombia were a contributing factor, but it was the skill of the drug warriors and their ability to interpret the smuggler songs that killed the migration. Florida pot seizures decreased by an amazing 96 percent that year.[2] There were more surprises to come.

In *The Sea around Us,* Carson describes the locus of the second major pot aberration of 1988: "Drifting toward America, the Japan Current forms the northern wall of the great North Pacific eddy."[3] On the other side of the continent, where the Japan Current traces the great-circle route from Southeast Asia to our rugged Northwest, there was a marijuana eruption. Pacific seizures shot up an astonishing 344 percent. It was the great Pacific grass eddy.

Overall maritime pot seizures were less than one-half of the previous year's figure, down to about 867,000 pounds. But marijuana seizures on the Mexican land border were almost double. Marijuana seizures from all sources totaled a little over 1.4 million pounds in 1988, a decrease of about 40 percent from 1987. Cocaine seizures were approaching a quarter-million pounds, with about 32 percent coming from ships and boats. Volume was going up, but the percentage of seaborne coke was beginning to slide.[4]

Coast Guard pot seizures dropped to about 438,000 pounds in 1988, the first time since 1976 that the Coast Guard took less than a million pounds. With the increase in land border pot seizures, the Coast Guard's share of the take declined to about 31 percent, far less than the traditional 65 percent. Vessel seizures increased slightly, to 150, but 78 of these were for minor amounts of drugs (called zero-tolerance seizures).[5]

Colombian multi-ton marijuana smuggling ended in 1987.[6] The eastern Silent Spring of 1988 was a time of delayed comprehension. No authority made so bold as to declare a victory at sea. Cocaine was such a raging threat that the defeat of the grass boaters was treated as insignificant. Coast Guard officials could have declared the Caribbean supply lines secure, but they were seeing an unprecedented rise in Pacific seizures and a possible need to shift resources to the west. A declaration of victory on the eastern front would hardly help them justify existing resources or any additional assets. They also saw the looming specter of cocaine replacing pot as the primary seagoing drug. It took eighteen years of herculean effort to drive the big grass boats from our southern and eastern seas. The accomplishment deserves more than a passing note.

There was little coverage of the maritime pot industry's demise. A *U.S. News and World Report* article that summer criticized Vice President Bush as a reluctant drug czar but did credit the South Florida Task Force, and NNBIS by implication, with ending large marijuana shipments to the area. In the next line, the article qualified the accomplishment by declaring that "smugglers quickly shifted to cocaine that is more easily concealed."[7] Some grass smugglers did shift to cocaine, but the broad generalization was very wide of the mark. Many incarcerated pot smugglers could have set the record straight, but they were not consulted; good news about the drug war was not a popular media item.

Media coverage focused on the Medellin cartel, which some pundits said had evolved from a criminal organization to a multinational conglomerate with private armies and a foreign policy of its own. Gen. Paul Gorman, U.S. Army (Ret.), the former commander of the U.S. Southern Command, told a Senate subcommittee in March that drug trafficking constitutes "a clear and present danger to the very survival of democracy in certain countries which have long been friends and allies of the United States."[8] Author Tom Clancy developed "clear and present danger" into a rattling good tale of U.S. military intervention in the drug war.[9] A proposed peace treaty by some members of the Medellin cartel may have resulted from Clancy's book.

Colombia's attorney general, Carlos Mauro Hoyes, was assassinated in January. Edwin Meese, the U.S. attorney general, met with President Virgilio Barco Vargas to discuss a possible Organization of American States multinational police force to help shore up Colombia's antidrug effort. President Barco did not reject the proposal outright—a strong indication of how close he came to accepting a UN-type peacekeeping force.[10]

Colombia did not dominate the drug news in 1988. Panama's Gen. Manuel Antonio Noriega was federally indicted in February in Miami and Tampa for drug trafficking. The indictments alleged drug ties between Noriega and Cuban president Fidel Castro.[11] After the Noriega indictments, a federal grand jury in Miami indicted seventeen people for air-smuggling Colombian cocaine through Cuba using Cuban military facilities. No Cuban officials were named.[12] Much national headline press resulted from the long trial of Carlos Lehder in Jacksonville, Florida. Lehder was finally convicted on 19 May after a seven-week trial.[13] The extinction of the grass fleet was ignored.

The west coast of Florida was the last major arrival zone for marijuana deliveries to the eastern continental United States. Operation Peacemaker was in full bloom by 1988. It ensured that no roses sprang from the ashes of the recent seizure frenzy. The Organized Crime Drug Enforcement Task Force, or OCDETF, unit established by the U.S. attorney's office in the Middle District of Florida prosecuted historical marijuana-smuggling cases after grand jury testimony by Ambrose Weldon, Harold King, Willard Wooten, and other cooperating defendants. They identified people, vessels, businesses, and residences used in the smuggling ventures and supplied a host of intelligence on operating procedures, routes, and countersurveillance methods.

Customs special agent David Weatherly was the prime mover for investigations out of the Tampa office, with Customs investigator Michael Noonan and DEA special agent Richard Crawford. Gentle but determined Assistant U.S. Attorney Theresa Flynn coordinated their work and managed the indictments. Flynn became the nemesis of a crowd of Gulf coast grass smugglers. A second unit of Peacemaker was coordinated by Assistant U.S. Attorney Douglas Frazier from an office in Fort Myers with the help of AUSA Susan Deltuvia. Jim Decker, Jack Larson, Paul Kilcoyne of Customs, and Dennis Perry of DEA were the primary investigators for Peacemaker South. By the end of the year the OCDETF unit had indicted over 160 people, seized twenty vessels for ongoing or historical drug violations, and confiscated almost $100 million in other property and assets.[14] The Florida west coast arrival zone was pacified. Operation Peacemaker was a sterling example of what could be accomplished when seizures produced American defendants who cooperated if faced with mandatory minimum sentences.

On the national scene, the General Accounting Office gave the National Drug Policy Board a passing grade for doing what Congress intended. The GAO auditors admitted that the NDPB was a forum for drug enforcement officials to stop interagency disputes. They also saw that a national drug enforcement strategy was in place. The GAO felt that the Policy Board had not developed budgetary priorities as authorized but qualified the criticism by explaining that the board lacked the information necessary to make budget decisions.[15] Considering the GAO's past criticisms of the administration's antidrug programs, this evaluation of the NDPB was a glowing testimonial.

In March the Policy Board drafted a report that defined lead-agency responsibilities for implementing the national strategy. The thick, phone-book-sized report rehashed the strategy. The board's Interdiction Committee was to review and approve plans.[16] Meanwhile, the Coast Guard and Customs had worked out a memorandum of understanding to implement maritime interdiction coordination. Even the use of the Blue Lightning Operations Center was addressed. The Coast Guard had to use BLOC as primary coordinator with Customs and state/local agencies in the arrival zone.[17] Drug-fighting plans and coordination were finally coming together.

The Policy Board's 1988 lead-agency report gives some indication of NNBIS's decline. NNBIS was not even mentioned in the introduction to the interdiction section. In the air interdiction section, Customs and the Coast Guard, which shared the lead-agency role, were to coordinate planning for use of assets and support with NNBIS and other agencies. In the same section, the new C3I centers east and west were told to coordinate and execute operational activities and focus intelligence. Only in the last part of the air section were the agencies admonished to work closely with NNBIS to achieve national objectives. They were also advised to plan special operations through NNBIS, which had "an established in-place coordination process for working joint, multi-agency operations with all appropriate entities: National Security Council (NSC), DoS [Department of State], DoD, FBI, DEA, EPIC, and other federal, state and local agencies." It was hard to reconcile this acknowledgment of NNBIS's prowess with the report's failure to identify it as a coordination entity.

Even more glaring was the sparse mention in the section on maritime interdiction, an arena in which NNBIS had a much stronger role than in air interdiction. There was no acknowledgment that NNBIS had coordinated joint operations such as Hat Trick. NNBIS was cited only at the end of the maritime section. There the report said that the Coast Guard commandant was to give semiannual evaluations of maritime efforts to the Interdiction Committee of the NDPB for review;

these assessments were to be part of the "routine semi-annual assessment of the jointly coordinated national and international interdiction operations completed through NNBIS."[18] Gerrymandering interdiction plans around an existing NNBIS was difficult. Why it was done at all by an instrument of the executive branch is baffling. Perhaps it was a sop to the drug-czar hawks in Congress. More likely it was an attempt to establish the credibility of the NDPB to defuse the drug-czar movement.

Whatever progress the NDPB made in attempting to nail down the responsibilities of the various agencies in the drug war was shattered by Congress in the fall of 1988. In the fiscal year 1989 Defense Authorization Act, the Department of Defense was designated the lead agency for "detection and monitoring" of both air and maritime drug-smuggling targets approaching the United States. After years of resisting greater involvement in drug fighting, with much of the senior echelon believing it to be an impossible war of attrition without clear political objectives, DoD was dragged into the fray. It had supported the effort for some time, but now it had a leadership role. In typical no-nonsense military fashion, the Joint Chiefs of Staff developed a plan to meet the requirements of their new mission. The plan identified five commanders-in-chief (CinCs) with drug mission responsibilities: CinCLant (Atlantic), CinCPac (Pacific), CinCSouth (Southern Command), CinCNorAD (North American Air Defense Command), and CinCFORCE (U.S. Forces Command). CinCLant, CinCPac, and CinCFORCE elected to establish joint task forces (JTFs) to be commissioned in Key West, Alameda, and El Paso to detect and track drug-smuggling targets. The plan called for CinCSouth to support Latin American counternarcotics forces. CinCNorAD was to support the overall air interdiction program.[19] The NDPB would have to rewrite the manual of responsibilities.

Military hardware and expertise would be welcomed by interdiction forces and would be well suited for the detection and monitoring mission. First, the military operations and intelligence types assigned to the JTFs would have to learn the ropes. The problem was the number of people and units involved. South Florida is illustrative. With the addition of a military JTF in Key West, there would be four separate groups identifying and tracking drug smugglers in the Miami-Keys area: the military JTF for air and marine targets, the Customs–Coast Guard C3I for air targets, the Customs BLOC for inshore maritime targets, and the veteran NNBIS Southeast center for marine and air targets. Only NNBIS was created by the executive branch to coordinate the civilian agencies and the military and intelligence community. The other centers were a result of congressional management through appropriation. Only in America!

By the time the pendulum had swung to the point of multiple tracking centers with associated assets, multi-ton pot loads were almost history. Only a few years before, watch commanders at NNBIS Miami, like young Coast Guard lieutenants Dennis Hughey and Paul Guinee, were forced to rely on Everglades Park rangers in johnboats to intercept off-loads. Now that the assets were there to do a decent if disorganized job, the main maritime targets were gone. Even the high-speed coke boats were fading. All eyes were on coke planes and the Mexican border; that was the new battleground.

At the beginning of the year, conservatives in and out of government demanded drug use accountability. Many advocated tougher treatment of users. They pointed out that federal and state laws regarding drug use and possession were seldom enforced because law enforcement had few resources to track down smugglers and dealers. We had, claimed the Republican leadership, decriminalized the use and possession of drugs by failing to enforce the laws adequately. These critics acknowledged that programs to hold users more accountable would have little effect on hardened addicts.[20]

The move toward a national zero-tolerance policy began with a memorandum from Attorney General Meese on 30 March 1988 to all U.S. attorneys. His memo, headed "Continued Zero Tolerance/User Prosecution Initiative," called for use of the 1986 federal law on simple possession, with a $1,000 mandatory minimum fine for first offenses, to prosecute people caught with "personal use amounts of drugs." Meese urged U.S. attorneys to follow the lead of Pete Nunez, of the Southern District of California in San Diego, who had been prosecuting personal-use cases for months.[21]

On 11 April, without fanfare, the Reagan administration implemented a zero-tolerance policy for the seizure of conveyances found with measurable amounts of drugs. The Coast Guard began seizing vessels under the new policy. The seizure of the 133-foot $2.5-million yacht *Ark Royal* for one-tenth of an ounce of pot got the boating public and the media stirred up. On 7 May the cutter *Tampa* (WMEC-902) stopped the U.S. yacht in the Yucatán Channel for a routine choke-point inspection. The first trace of marijuana was found in a trash can. A little more was in a stateroom dresser. The *Ark Royal* was duly seized as per instructions.[22]

Many other publicized zero-tolerance seizures came in short order, including that of a well-known research vessel. Criticism by legitimate boaters and members of Congress brought policy modification on 23 May to exclude vessels on the high seas.[23] Further modification exempted U.S. fishing vessels. Other changes followed. By the end of 1990, zero tolerance was history. It was a noble experiment with no public support. To many veteran drug warriors accustomed to seizing tons of drugs, the experiment was actually embarrassing. Were it not for zero tolerance, the number of vessels seized for drugs by the Coast Guard in 1988 would have been reduced by almost half.[24]

Along with the flurry of efforts to hold drug users accountable for their failings, there arose a new drug legalization movement. These movements seem cyclic, with varying degrees of scientific and political support. In 1988 there were some impressive backers. They did not condone or encourage drug use but felt that the best way to curtail abuse was to treat drugs as a public health problem. It was also an election year. Baltimore mayor Kurt Schmoke, formerly a federal prosecutor, was a visible and convincing advocate. He called for a national debate on the issue at the U.S. mayors' conference in April. For drug dealers, said Mayor Schmoke, "going to jail is just part of the cost of doing business. It's a nuisance, not a deterrent." According to Schmoke and others, legalization would take much of the crime out of cities; the government could regulate the sale of drugs at low prices. It would be like the repeal of Prohibition.[25]

These arguments had been used before to support the legalization of drugs, but now they were coming from mayors and big-city police officials who were frustrated with drug violence. When Schmoke spoke of jail time as just a cost of doing business, he obviously was not talking to traffickers who were getting ten years plus mandatory minimums in federal courts. When the issue arose at a congressional hearing in June, Senator Alfonse D'Amato (R., New York) cast scorn at the "half-assed commentators" who favored legalization. Even the members of the liberal House Democratic Caucus conveyed their feelings to the party platform committee, saying, "Legalization . . . has never worked anywhere. It would send the wrong message to the

American public and violate U.S. international treaty obligations. Legalization is surrender."[26]

Despite the dramatic decline in Atlantic, Gulf, and Caribbean seizures, there were some interesting cases in 1988. The only notable volume maritime marijuana seizure on this side was a rare case where drugs were detected in containers at sea. The USCGC *Decisive* (WMEC-629) boarded the 150-foot Panamanian-registered coastal freighter *Sabrina* just after she cleared the Windward Passage on 11 February. After the cutter got an SNO, deck containers were inspected. They held a total of 57,333 pounds of marijuana.[27] This load was probably going to the mid-Atlantic or New England coast. Maritime containers with pot cargoes were intercepted that year in New York, New Jersey, Maryland, Louisiana, and Florida.

The most dramatic decline in maritime grass smuggling occurred along Route 26 in the eastern Gulf, the last major pot pipeline to the east. In 1988 only one vessel was seized near the Coke Machine. On 27 April, NNBIS Miami was informed that a vessel planned to offload marijuana somewhere near the NOAA buoy the next day. Intelligence from local agencies in Naples–Fort Myers indicated that a load boat was broken down near the buoy. Coast Guard Group St. Petersburg sent the 82-footer *Point Swift* (WPB-82312), Master Chief Boatswain's Mate Duane Jones commanding, to investigate. When Lt. Bill Baker, group operations officer, asked the Seventh District people about the suspect hovering by the Coke Machine, they said it was news to them.

On the twenty-fifth, Master Chief Jones reported to Baker that a navy LAMPS helo had just flown by. "What's up?" asked Jones. He was told to stand by. Someone up the line had decided it would be good PR for a new 270-foot cutter conducting trials with the navy SH-60 LAMPS helo to make a drug bust. It took a while to get the *Escanaba* (WMEC-907) from the Yucatán barrier over to the hot side of the NOAA buoy. Meanwhile, Jones was kept on the cool side in a backup position. As planned, the LAMPS found the 40-foot drifting lobster boat–longliner *Luz Maria* (a.k.a. *Luz Marina*), which was seized by the *Escanaba*. Before he was boarded, the master admitted he had a cargo of grass. It was about 15,000 pounds. The *Point Swift* escorted the *Luz Maria* to the coastal buoy tender *White Sumac* (WLM-540), which took the drug boat to Fort Myers.[28] The ratio of interdiction assets to smuggler targets had reached the point where commands with reliable intelligence could pick and choose who made the seizures. Times had really changed.

The Florida Gulf coast, a prime target for pot smugglers, got a cocaine jolt in the spring of 1988. The M/V *Amazon Sky* came to St. Petersburg on 19 April with nine thousand cedar planks. Intelligence said a huge load of cocaine was concealed in the wood. Customs surreptitiously verified the claim by drilling a few of the planks during a routine inspection. DEA and Customs, with local assistance, decided to let the cargo go to a warehouse to implicate owner Michael Tsalickis of Tarpon Springs, a longtime smuggling suspect. The warehouse was raided after Tsalickis and two Colombians were videotaped selecting seven hundred planks for special treatment. A total of 7,228 pounds of cocaine were found packed inside hollow planks. Tsalickis and his pals were convicted, and the *Amazon Sky* was seized.[29]

If the *Amazon Sky* had been intercepted at sea, searching for cocaine in planks packed in the hold would have been impossible. Finding cocaine in concealed compartments on fishing vessels and yachts was hard enough. In a case like this, choosing the ground was important. The objective was to link Tsalickis irreparably to the cocaine, which would have been doubtful with a sea seizure. It was risky letting that much coke get off the ship, even though the amount was not yet verified. The risk paid off.

By the summer of 1988, many maritime smugglers had decided that the danger of running the Yucatán, Windward, and Mona Passages was just too great. An alternative was to smuggle narcotics into Puerto Rico and the U.S. Virgin Islands in smaller loads for shipment to the States. Some had done this for years. This route had a distinct advantage: once the load was safely ashore in the Commonwealth or island territories, it was technically in the United States. The owner need not be too concerned with Customs inspecting packages or containers. Small vessels with modest drug cargoes began targeting our Caribbean islands in ever-increasing numbers. Some nondescript smuggling craft making the run from Colombia had very low freeboards, presenting a poor radar target. Most were painted gray, green, or light blue with white trim to blend in with the choppy seas common in the trades of the central Caribbean.[30] The "stealth" boats had arrived.

The *Grace Caroline* was one of the first. The light blue 40-foot vessel was sighted by the USCGC *Attu* (WPB-1317) on the morning of

The *Grace Caroline* being intercepted in the Caribbean by the boarding party of the USCGC *Attu* (WPB-1317). This was one of the first low-profile "stealth" boats. *(Official U.S. Coast Guard photograph)*

29 August 1988 about 20 miles south of Cabo Rojo, Puerto Rico. The suspect was visually detected at a range of 5 miles. There was no radar contact until the range closed to 3.5 miles. The boat sat low in the water and appeared to be heavily loaded. The hull was steel, but only a foot was above the waterline. The color scheme blended in well with the sea. The *Attu* pulled alongside the homemade-looking craft. A spokesman readily responded to questions from a Spanish-speaking petty officer. The man said the vessel was bound from Aruba to St. Martin with an unknown cargo. After the preliminaries, Lt. Dane Egli, CO of the cutter, requested a consensual boarding, which was granted. The *Attu*'s boarders found seven Colombians on the small vessel and approximately 6,500 pounds of pot. The pot bales, stacked from deck to overhead, filled the forward part of the boat. An SNO request resulted in the vessel being assimilated as stateless because Colombia had no record of a *Grace Caroline*. The *Attu*'s CO seized the boat, arrested the crew, and took them into Ponce for processing.[31]

Two weeks later the *Attu* found another low-rider near Vieques, an island just east of Puerto Rico. The *Agapi* was manned by four Colombians and carried a little over 7,000 pounds of grass.[32] So began the brisk but limited marijuana trade by small low-profile boats running from the Guajira to Puerto Rico and the Virgin Islands. The trade still exists, but cocaine has replaced marijuana.

Evidence was mounting against Cuba. José Martinez, retired from his off-load business because of growing problems in getting shipments through the passes, had a visit from an old smuggler associate in late 1988. "Juan Valdez" invited Martinez to ride in a go-fast boat to a coastal military base in Cuba to discuss transshipping multi-ton grass loads through the island. Martinez overcame his anticommunist convictions, at least for the duration of the trip. After an uneventful boat ride, the free-enterprise diplomats met with a senior Border Guard officer at the base east of Havana. Plans were made for Martinez to send a good-sized fishing boat to the base, where it would be repainted, given a Cuban flag and guide, and allowed to meet a vessel coming from Colombia. Another plan promised safe passage for a ship from Colombia to Cienfuegos on the south side of Cuba. The pot cargo would be off-loaded and transshipped by truck across the island. On the north side, Martinez could pick up his cargo with small boats. The officer even offered to send a Border Guard patrol boat to check Nicholas Channel for U.S. Coast Guard cutters. It was all academic: Martinez was arrested on indictment for historical smuggling ventures after he and his friend returned to Florida. This was at last the end of José Martinez's smuggling career, which had begun with the floaters by Elbow Cay in the spring of 1977.[33]

Before Martinez made his trip to Cuba, an indicted air smuggler was spilling his innards to investigators and Assistant U.S. Attorney Thomas Mulvihill in Miami about cocaine air shipments through Cuba in 1987. Reinaldo Ruiz identified people and places, including some encountered by Martinez. The highest-ranking official named was Col. Anthony (Tony) de la Guardia of the Ministry of the Interior.[34] Mulvihill, known as the Cuban Desk in the Miami office, found other indicted sources who were willing to talk about Cuba. After the information was processed and verified by intelligence agencies, the State Department confronted Cuban officials. Evidence showed official Cuban involvement in drug trafficking through, around, and over the island. The scandal broke in June 1987 when Cuban war hero

Gen. Arnaldo Ochoa Sanchez and five other officers were arrested by the Castro government for corruption and drug trafficking.[35] Eventually, seven other military officers or government functionaries were arrested. Ochoa and others were executed. Fidel Castro's involvement in narcotics trafficking through his fortress island remains an enigma.

Before leaving the pot-holed road to the Southeast for the Pacific battleground, we should note a major cocaine seizure by Customs in Miami. On 20 December a search team found 4,792 pounds of coke aboard the 300-foot Panamanian-registered freighter *Santo Domingo Express*. This shipment was not concealed in a cargo; it was hidden in a ballast tank. The captain was arrested.[36] The ship had been used to deliver the load from Colombia via Aruba to the United States. Previous maritime cocaine shipments approaching this size had been concealed in bulk cargoes (lumber and fertilizer) or in maritime containers. The *Santo Domingo Express* load was the first known multi-thousand-pound cocaine shipment sent north in a ship dedicated for that purpose.

Drug seizures in the Pacific varied considerably from year to year, but they usually accounted for about 4–5 percent of all seizures. Most maritime seizures were based on prior intelligence because of the vast area and the lack of any choke points within reasonable distance of the United States. There were not enough major loads coming from Southeast Asia to make distant-patrol deployments worthwhile. Marijuana seized off the West Coast traditionally came from Colombia, although Far Eastern pot seizures were more common off the Northwest and British Columbia. Then came 1988.

Pacific maritime marijuana/hashish seizures in 1988 soared to 463,688 pounds—the largest figure ever, though small compared with the Caribbean total. About 97 percent came from eight vessel seizures, with an average load of 56,000 pounds. Big loads carried by a small number of vessels were typical of Pacific pot smuggling. The Coast Guard seized 303,279 pounds.[37] This was an unprecedented 69 percent of the total 437,879 pounds seized by the Coast Guard in 1988, down from over a million pounds in 1987.[38]

Action in the Pacific started early. In January the 158-foot Panamanian-registered coastal freighter *Christina M* left Rabaul, New Britain, in the Bismarck Archipelago. The vessel had been in port undergoing repairs from a grounding. Roosevelt Augustus Rodney, a resident of Panama, commanded the black-hulled freighter. The

Christina M met a vessel at sea during the first week of February and took on about 41,000 pounds of Thai marijuana. Rodney followed the less traveled equatorial route rather than the great circle toward Hawaii. He came under the control of a clandestine radio station in the vicinity of Honolulu. On or about 17 January, two fishing boats got under way from Oxnard Harbor just above Los Angeles to meet the mothership off Hawaii. They were the 58-foot *Venture Three* and the 41-foot *Eagle B*, two old wooden trollers. Coded instructions were given by off-load manager Robert Singer from a temporary command post in Honolulu. A benchmark position north of Hawaii and known only to key players was used as a reference point. This was a sophisticated plan that probably would have gone undetected but for the human element.

On 24 January a Customs Service confidential informant (CI) was approached by Singer. He was asked to provide another off-load boat capable of transporting 20,000 pounds of pot. The CI agreed. Customs furnished a seagoing rig and an undercover crew. The CI's information said an unidentified pickup boat met the *Christina M* on 29 or 30 January to take on a load. The *Venture Three* and *Eagle B* met the *Christina M* about 650 miles east-southeast of Hawaii on 3 February. The *Venture* was down to 50 gallons of fuel. The *Christina M* tried to fuel the troller but managed to knock a hole in her engine room, and the *Venture* started to sink. The *Christina M*'s people were able to get about 5,000 pounds to the *Eagle B* along with fuel and groceries. The decrepit troller left for California, and reinforcements were called.

The 62-foot ex-shrimper *New Triton* quickly got under way from Sausalito, hard by the Golden Gate. She met and fueled the *Eagle B* about 1,300 miles from the coast. Before they met the mothership, the *New Triton* developed engine problems, forcing them to divert to Hawaii. The smugglers' problems were epidemic. Things seemed to be looking up when the undercover boat got to the mothership on 17 February. A little over 17,000 pounds were loaded onto the boat, which ostensibly set course for California. Once clear of the *Christina M,* the Customs people headed for Pearl Harbor, arriving there on the twenty-first. A Coast Guard C-130 flew the pot load to San Francisco to use in the game's final play.

There was now enough evidence to move in on the *Christina M*. An SNO came from Panama on 18 February. The oceangoing Coast Guard buoy tender *Mallow* (WLB-396) was pressed into service to establish radar contact and shadow the mothership. The next day a C-130 from Coast Guard Air Station Barbers Point verified the *Christina M*'s position.

Seizure day was 19 February. The *Mallow* made radio contact with the freighter. The *Christina M*'s master first denied the *Mallow*'s skipper, Lt. Comdr. Christian Bohner, permission to board his ship. Rodney claimed he was bound for Panama and told Bohner he would have to follow him all the way there if he wanted to board. About that time the U.S. Navy frigate *Ouellet* (FF-1077) with a Coast Guard LEDET arrived on the scene. Bohner told Rodney, "We have the authority to stop you, and with the USS *Ouellet*, we have the means. Stop your vessel at this time." Rodney did. Boarding parties from the buoy tender and the navy ship went aboard the *Christina M*. They found 21,660 pounds of Thai marijuana still in the hold. The vessel was seized. Captain Rodney and seven crewmen were arrested. An American, William Snyder, seemed to be in charge of the load.

Meanwhile, back in Honolulu, Robert Singer did not know that the *Christina M* had been seized. He told the CI that an electrical problem on the freighter had probably caused the radio to fail. Not until 23 February did a small notice about the seizure of an unidentified vessel appear in the *Honolulu Advisor*. Singer figured out that the silent *Christina M* was the subject of the report and went back to California.

While all this was in progress, the *Eagle B* struggled toward California. By now the old troller was taking on water at a rate that threatened to overwhelm her pumps. Singer radioed the four smugglers on the troller that the mothership had been seized. He told them to keep a good lookout for enforcement units. Actually, the smugglers were being tracked toward the U.S. coast. On 25 February the high-endurance cutter *Morgenthau* (WHEC-722) closed in. No matter how good their lookout, there was not much the crew could do. Considering that the *Eagle B* sank after boarding, the pot runners had to be philosophical; they could have drowned. That same day the buoy tender *Mallow* towed the *Christina M* into Pearl Harbor. Case closed? Not quite.

A DEA confidential informant in California reported that a group of smugglers were waiting for the arrival of two boats near Sand Hill Bluff north of Santa Cruz. A connection was made between the *Christina M* and the Santa Cruz gang. The load delivered to Honolulu by Customs' undercover boat and flown to San Francisco by the

Coast Guard was used once more. On 1 March, DEA and Customs made a controlled delivery of the 8 tons to the smugglers. Nine people were arrested, including Robert Singer, the Honolulu-based off-load master.[39] This case was an excellent example of cooperation and shared intelligence among Customs, the Coast Guard, and DEA. It also demonstrated the great difficulty of off-load operations in the vast Pacific.

Calvin Robinson, meanwhile, probably got his idea from the East Coast and Gulf operators who first tried the barge scam. Robinson, a burly 6 feet 6, was forty-seven years old. He had spent over a third of his life in jail and was under serious scrutiny by the drug cops. A snitch reported that Robinson and his kin took the tug *Ruby R* to Hawaii and picked up a big load of hash. The police department in Napa, a small town north of Oakland, received an anonymous letter about Robinson's smuggling capers. It outlined the *Ruby R*'s voyage and said another was planned by Dredge Masters Associates, Robinson's company. Napa's chief passed the note to Customs. A full-scale investigation of Calvin Robinson and Dredge Masters Associates began.

The next break came in February 1988. Calvin Robinson's stepson, Wesley Bastin, twenty-six, told a Customs confidential informant that he would soon work on another Robinson job and get a lot of money. Surveillance of Bastin now became routine. In March, Diana Robinson Rauch, Calvin's sister, purchased the 72-foot tug *Intrepid Venture* and a 110-foot barge. By April, DEA was involved in the Robinson case, which had been elevated to the status of an OCDETF investigation. The *Ruby R* and *Intrepid Venture* were watched.

On 6 May the *Intrepid Venture* left her moorings near Rio Vista on the Sacramento River. On board were Calvin Robinson, his son William Robinson, his stepson Wesley Bastin, and his nephews, the brothers John and Frank Robinson. The younger Robinsons ranged in age from twenty-three to twenty-six.

The Robinson tug headed down the river for the long run through Suisun and San Pablo Bays for the Golden Gate. En route, the big tug picked up the 110-foot barge with six 20-foot containers strapped to its deck. The barge had numerous fuel tanks and cargo compartments below deck. The senior Robinson advised the San Francisco Vessel Traffic System (VTS) that his next port of call was Eureka. By 13 May, investigators were getting nervous; the *Intrepid Venture* had disappeared. DEA asked for a lookout on the tug through EPIC. Customs

The smuggler tug *Intrepid Venture* tows a barge with 112,129 pounds of hash and pot on board. *(Official U.S. Coast Guard photograph)*

and DEA coordinated closely with the Coast Guard and NNBIS to try to find the wayward tug. The next day special intelligence said the tug and barge were about 1,100 miles due west of San Francisco. An air search had no immediate results. On 22 May a navy aircraft found the Soviet stern trawler *Poseydon* making erratic course changes and speed adjustments. On the twenty-third a Customs P-3, returning to Naval Air Station Alameda, sighted the *Intrepid Venture* with barge in tow near the Farallon Islands. They were headed for San Francisco Bay.

The USCGC *Cape Romain* (WPB-95319) and two utility boats from Coast Guard Group San Francisco got under way with a few Customs officers for the intercept. The *Intrepid Venture* was boarded without incident just as she entered the bay. Tug and barge were taken to the Coast Guard base at Yerba Buena Island in the shadow of the Bay Bridge. An extensive search detected a huge concealed compartment on the barge accessed by cutting through the deck. Inside were 85,900 pounds of Southwest Asian hashish and 26,229 pounds of Thai marijuana. This was the largest hash seizure so far. The combined load of 112,129 pounds put the *Intrepid Venture* seizure in the elite and verified 100,000-plus class with the *Don Emilio* and a half-dozen others. The Robinson crew and the tug's owner, Diana Rauch, were arrested.

Markings in Farsi (a dialect of the Middle East) on most of the hashish packages translated into "Turkestan." Could it be the Soviet Union's Turkestan just north of Iran? No one knew where the *Intrepid Venture* had loaded the hash and pot, except that it was somewhere in the Pacific off San Francisco. A connection between the Turkestan markings and the sighting of the Soviet trawler by the navy P-3 in an area where the tug was believed to be is provocative but totally speculative. The Robinsons were vague about where they got the huge load. Calvin Robinson, who had once been a cellmate of convicted Soviet spy Christopher Boyce at Lompoc Federal Prison, defended himself at trial and was convicted on all counts.[40]

A break in the investigation leading to the largest West Coast marijuana seizure occurred in April 1988. DEA undercover agents posed as off-load boat operators and penetrated the Brian Peter Daniels smuggling organization. Daniels was thought to be one of the biggest pot brokers delivering to the Pacific coast. He was a U.S. citizen who had lived in Thailand for years. DEA held a coordination meeting with Customs and the Coast Guard in Seattle and laid its information on the table.

Case agent Larry Brandt told the story. The motor vessel *Encounter Bay* would deliver approximately 70 tons of marijuana somewhere off the Washington coast in June. The pot cargo would be loaded near Da Nang, Vietnam. Other meetings were held as new information developed. The mothership was a husky 189-foot ex–oil rig service and supply vessel registered in Panama. Off-load to fishing vessels would occur between 2 and 4 July about 400 miles west of Cape Flattery. Samuel Colflesh, a former U.S. Special Forces trooper, would be in charge of the delivery. Colflesh had developed a sophisticated operational plan code-named Denver. Coded position reports from the mothership would be sent via a commercial communications satellite. The DEA investigators put strict limits on the distribution of the

Operation Denver plan, to protect their sources. They wanted the Coast Guard to intercept the vessel before she got to the off-load site, making it appear that the intercept was part of a random patrol. DEA hoped to nail down its case against Daniels with evidence from the seizure and arrest him before he left the States.

The Thirteenth Coast Guard District in Seattle established a multi-agency command post to coordinate operations with DEA. Interception responsibilities were assigned to the USCGC *Boutwell* (WHEC-719), Capt. Cecil Allison commanding, with Coast Guard and navy air support. The Pacific Area commander, the Thirteenth District's boss, kept a gentle hand in the operation by detailing Lt. (jg) Kevin Conroy and Radioman First Class Tom Primeau, two PacArea intelligence people with a record for producing exemplary postseizure reports. Patrol aircraft flew search patterns over the approaches to the expected off-load position. On 28 June the *Boutwell* deployed from Seattle to take up a position west of the *Encounter Bay*'s destination. More intelligence originating from an OCDETF investigation in San Diego indicated that another 20 tons of Thai marijuana from Daniels were en route to the West Coast in an old wooden ship. At that point the second vessel was thought to be headed for southern California and of no concern to this operation. The departure intelligence was correct, but the destination forecast was wrong. The *Lloyd B. Gore,* an old wooden Canadian tug measuring 119 feet, crossed the Pacific about a month behind the *Encounter Bay.* She was actually destined for Vancouver Island, British Columbia.

Meanwhile, the *Boutwell* was in position. On 30 June the radio watch picked up an unidentified station calling Yellow Leader on the suspected primary frequency. The bearing was right for a vessel approaching the cutter from the west. A Coast Guard C-130 soon had a visual sighting of a target meeting the *Encounter Bay*'s description more than 100 miles northwest of the cutter. As he headed for the intercept, the *Boutwell*'s captain got an SNO to board the Panamanian vessel. The subject was sighted at 1400, and the SNO was received an hour and a half later. The *Boutwell* closed with the rig tender, now positively identified as the *Encounter Bay,* and tried to make radio contact. Repeated calls were ignored, as were signals to heave to. A navy P-3 flying cover made five very low level passes across the fleeing vessel's bow, with no response. The *Boutwell* fired warning shots.

First the cutter lay bursts of .50-caliber machine-gun rounds across the tender's bow. Then a 5-inch main battery round failed to get results. Captain Allison was given permission to use disabling fire.

At 1745 Allison advised the *Encounter Bay* on Channel 16 that he intended to use disabling fire. For the first time, the target's master responded. He demanded a telex copy of the Coast Guard's authority to board his vessel. Captain Allison told the speaker to move his people forward because the cutter was going to fire. At 1859 the *Boutwell* fired .50-caliber rounds into the aft part of the tender. After sixty rounds the *Encounter Bay* began to lose way. The cutter was informed by radio that the tender would stop involuntarily for boarding.

In fact they had no option; their engine had been damaged by the *Boutwell*'s fire. The boarding party found deck containers full of marijuana. Bales covered with tarps and plywood sheets were also stacked between the forward containers. The containers and the temporary covers were painted the same as the vessel's hull, making the deck cargo difficult to discern from a distance. The vessel was seized at 2018 local time by Lt. T. J. Rogers, the boarding officer, about 600 miles west of Cape Flattery.

Eighteen people were on the *Encounter Bay:* a New Zealander, an Englishman, two Thais, eight Indonesians, three Singapore residents, and three Americans. One American was Samuel Foy Colflesh, age thirty-two, ex–Green Beret, author of Operation Denver, and alleged owner-captain of the *Encounter Bay*. When the pot cargo was finally weighed, it was 144,000 pounds—the largest single marijuana seizure ever made on the Pacific coast. DEA's plan to expeditiously lay hands on Brian Daniels in the United States came to naught. He was arrested in Zurich, Switzerland, on 25 July 1988 and extradited to the United States to stand trial. Robert Colflesh, Samuel's twin brother who operated the smuggler's radio station in Seattle during the attempted delivery, was arrested in Thailand on 5 August and was also extradited.[41]

Daniels pled guilty to operating a continuing criminal enterprise and was sentenced to twenty-five years. He might have received a reduced sentence under a Rule 35 for cooperation but chose not to. The Colflesh brothers also pled before trial and were sentenced to ten years each. Five years later, the persistent OCDETF investigator Fran Dyer and his associates in Seattle facilitated the British arrest of Michael Forwell, an Englishman and majority owner of the *Encounter*

USCGC *Boutwell* fires on the mothership *Encounter Bay*, carrying 144,000 pounds of marijuana—the record Pacific seizure.
(Official U.S. Coast Guard photograph)

Bay's load. Forwell's wife was also indicted for money laundering related to the Pacific drug operation.[42]

As the Daniels investigation progressed, more specific information on the other 20-ton pot shipment coming from the Far East became available. By 19 June a source in Hong Kong reported that part of Daniels's big load had gone to a wooden vessel, 130–50 feet in length and capable of no more than 5–7 knots. The source said the boat resembled a minesweeper with the pilothouse forward. OCDETF agents in San Diego turned an indicted individual involved in the 20-ton shipment on 28 July, who told them that the load was "safe, somewhere in Canada."

Agents accompanied the turncoat to Vancouver on 3 August to meet with officers at the Royal Canadian Mounted Police. The RCMP made a connection with the U.S. agents' information and the master of the *Lloyd B. Gore*, which had cleared Customs at Vancouver on or about 1 August. This individual had long been suspected of drug smuggling. The RCMP inserted an undercover agent to work with the

American informant. The Canadian was supposed to have access to a barge and trucks to move the load to the United States. With the help of information obtained by the spies, the load, weighing 45,200 pounds, was found on 12 August by RCMP officers and U.S. Customs agents in Sperm Bay, off Flamingo Inlet on the southern end of Queen Charlotte Island. Landing the cargo was done by high-line in the isolated and uninhabited cove. After off-loading, the smugglers went to Vancouver Island and cleared Customs. When the hidden pot was found in Sperm Bay, the RCMP arrested the *Gore*'s crew and two other Canadians involved in the venture and seized the vessel on a warrant.[43] So ended the flow of Daniels's marijuana, which had been following the Japan Current to North America for about fifteen years.

By the end of the year many interdiction people had come to believe that Far Eastern pot smugglers were taking up the slack where the Colombian sources had left off. Some, however, said it was just another three- to four-year Pacific cycle. The 1988 Pacific eddy in the Sea of Grass was a little of both. Daniels and others saw pot demand holding steady, supplies shrinking, and prices going up with declining Colombian imports. Intelligence obtained by Customs and DEA with help from state and local agencies was probably better than it had ever been on the West Coast. A worthy epitaph to that phase of the drug war was the degree of cooperation among the key agencies. Customs and DEA were involving the Coast Guard early in the development of major cases. The Coast Guard, in turn, was accepting the responsibility for protecting confidential sources by maintaining tight security of CI- and undercover-agent-generated information. NNBIS was playing a stellar role by enlisting the support of the military and the intelligence community to help find smuggler boats in the vast Pacific Ocean.

Management of the drug war was a big political issue in the presidential campaign of 1988. Vice President Bush, the Republican candidate, revealed in a speech in May his plan to make his vice president responsible for all aspects of the antidrug effort. Said Bush, "The vice president will have the power and the authority from the president that is required to do the job."[44] It never happened. Congress passed the Anti–Drug Abuse Act, which established an Office of National Drug Control Policy (ONDCP) in the Executive Office of the President. Congress had its drug czar at last.

President Reagan's chance of sustaining a veto was slim. He signed the bill into law on 18 November, a few days after Bush was elected president. Subtitle A of the law mandated the disestablishment of NNBIS, the National Drug Policy Board, and the White House Drug Abuse Policy Office.[45]

On 13 December 1988, Bush met for the last time with the key drug interdiction people, including the NNBIS headquarters staff, regional coordinators, and staff directors. Bush thanked all hands for their efforts and dedication. He assured everyone that he would somehow retain the expertise developed by NNBIS. Bush did not criticize the drug-czar concept in the presence of the fifty-five or so senior drug warriors, but he did express doubt that anyone selected for the job could do what Congress expected.[46]

Personnel detailed to NNBIS were recalled by their home agencies for other assignments. Regional centers were closed or reduced in size. Ad hoc Coast Guard–Customs groups took over some interdiction coordination responsibilities. What had taken five years to build into a workable interdiction coordination mechanism was thrown away.

11

A Victory at Sea
1989

Not with rolling of drums,
Not with music and songs,
Not with laughter and weeping,
Or cheering of passionate throngs;
But silently, as is fitting
Grey ghosts passing from sight.

DYSART MCMULLEN, "SHIPS THAT SAIL IN THE NIGHT"

On she came, pushing white water eastward across the indigo Gulf. Miguel Gonzalez-Uribe, master of the 105-foot Honduran tug *Turtola,* was optimistic. It was midmorning, 4 April 1989. Clear skies and calm seas would ease his work. Gonzalez would turn forty in eighteen days. With luck, he would be home in Venezuela for his birthday and a lot richer.

Gonzalez and his five-man crew had withstood a boarding and space-accountability search the day before by the U.S. Coast Guard cutter *Diligence* (WMEC-616). The boarding officer examined the tug's valid registration certificate and noted telex messages about pending engine repairs in Tampa, Florida. Searchers missed the 20,000 pounds of marijuana cleverly concealed in the forward center and wing fuel tanks. Alacran Reef was now 80 miles astern of the twenty-eight-year-old ex-U.S. tug. She was on a course of 055° true that would take her to an off-load position 110 miles west of the Everglades. Miguel Gonzalez would meet a group of go-fast boats to take his pot cargo and dash for shore. The smuggler captain did not know he was headed for a major Coast Guard drug interdiction exercise. No one knew the *Turtola* would be the last known marijuana mothership to reach an off-load position near the U.S. coast. After nearly twenty years, the procession of grass boats was coming to an end. The *Turtola* was a dinosaur in her own time.[1]

In January, DEA special agent Andrew Perez, based in Barranquilla, Colombia, put the *Turtola* on lookout. Perez's information was good. He described the tug and predicted that the pot would be hidden in a forward section near fuel tanks. Before Perez's report, Lt. Comdr. Mike McCoy of the Seventh Coast Guard District had put on lookout a Florida-registered 37-foot Midnight Express go-fast bearing number FL9362EM, expected to pick up a load of grass at sea. The go-fast and the tug were destined to meet with considerable impact.

On 17 March, Captain Gonzalez left Panama towing the derelict tug *Colosa.* Gonzalez declared for Coatzacoalcos, Mexico, on the Bay of Campeche. Tugs were common in that offshore oil industry port. The *Colosa* was a good cover for the *Turtola*'s run through the Yucatán. Alas, the derelict was not up to the trip. Three days into the tow and abeam of Swan Island, 100 miles off the Honduran coast, the *Colosa* gave up her struggle and sank. An engineer was injured trying to save the tug. The captain put into Puerto Cortés to get medical help for his man. Gonzalez left again for Mexico on 23 March, figuring that a Honduran tug with a departure record from Puerto Cortés would get him by any Coast Guard patrols in the Yucatán Channel. Perhaps there was no contraband on the tug to cause the captain concern. Coatzacoalcos was a good choice as a next port of call. It may have been an essential way point.

The *Turtola* did not stop long enough to take on grass between Panama and Mexico. She came through the Yucatán Channel hard by the Mexican shore and arrived in Coatzacoalcos on 27 March. The only chart on the tug for that port showed a track line extending 3 miles past the port channel and turning right up to the beach. Six days were spent in or around Coatzacoalcos for no apparent reason. Possibly they were loading pot from lighters off the beach west of the town.

Organizers of the *Turtola* delivery could not have picked a worse time for an off-load near the NOAA buoy on old Route 26. Coast Guard Patrol Boat Squadron One (BoatRonOne) was exercising in the area. The squadron consisted of three new 110-foot Island-class boats (the *Manitou, Matagorda,* and *Maui*) supported by the 82-foot *Point Thatcher* (WPB-82314) and a floating aerostat (AS-1). It was the most formidable force ever to occupy the pot grounds by the Coke Machine. Nothing of consequence had been seized there since the *Luz Maria* in the same month the year before.

On 1 April, the day before the *Turtola* cleared the Mexican port, intelligence sources indicated that there was a mothership in the western Gulf near Alacran Reef. It was believed that the ship would off-load west of Naples. Date and time of delivery were unknown. The *Diligence* was dispatched to Alacran and intercepted the tug on 3 April. After the boarding, the *Turtola* was written off as a suspect.

On 4 April the off-load crew was gathering at a motel in Naples. They had come in twos and threes from the Miami–Fort Lauderdale area. They came in cars and trucks, towing at least six big go-fast boats including four Midnight Expresses. One was McCoy's suspect, FL9362EM. Some of the smugglers were Americans, and some were Cubans. There were no locals or members of the old off-load crews who had traditionally worked this area. Most of those had been indicted by Peacemaker or were already serving time. Only one of the group of eighteen to twenty-four people was competent in the use of LORAN. The LORAN-literate member stayed up late on the night of 4 April trying without much success to teach the others how to use the equipment; actually, only two or three of the boats were even LORAN-equipped. The smugglers had neither a communications plan nor an escape plan. No one in the group knew much about this section of the coast. Most of the boats intended to make for stash houses in the Keys after taking on their consignment of pot. This was an amateur crew compared with the old southwest Florida off-loaders led by the likes of Ambrose Weldon.

Mounting intelligence on 5 April, including a report by local agencies that some strange go-fast boats were preparing to depart from Naples, pointed to an off-load somewhere near the NOAA buoy. NNBIS Miami requested Coast Guard and Customs air surveillance. When they could not locate a prospective mothership between the Yucatán Peninsula and the buoy, attention was again focused on the *Turtola,* whose whereabouts were now unknown. The *Matagorda* (WPB-1303) and *Maui* (WPB-1304) were on station near the Coke Machine. The *Manitou* (WPB-1302) and *Point Thatcher* (WPB-82314) were further inshore.

Two aircraft types used in the *Turtola* case were new and unique. One was a motorized glider. The Coast Guard had two Schweizer RG-8A motorized gliders from the Department of Defense. The slender, two-place aircraft are powered by a reciprocating engine and carry sophisticated communications equipment and forward-looking infrared radars (FLIR) with video gear.[2] The other unique aircraft were two Nomads, new Customs acquisitions frequently called Nightstalkers. Built in Australia, the Nomad is a high-winged, twin-engined reconnaissance plane admirably suited for maritime work. It is also equipped with FLIR.[3] These units would all play a key role in the pending action.

At noon on 5 April the aerostat (AS-1) detected a suspicious target 84 miles southeast of the NOAA buoy. A Coast Guard C-130 got close enough to identify the target as the *Turtola.* The *Matagorda* and *Maui* were ordered to shift their positions to the east to block the tug. The patrol boats were directed to remain covert, staying beyond visual range of the target. The hope was that some of the off-loaders could be taken down with the transport. The suspect disappeared from the aerostat's radar, but she was on a course toward the Florida coast. The patrol squadron tightened their perimeter and settled down to wait.

In midafternoon the pickup boats got under way. There were six known go-fast boats. The Midnight Express FL9362EM was typical.

Three neophyte smugglers launched the boat from a ramp in Naples. They had a LORAN unit none of them could operate. They were told to go southwest and meet a red go-fast coming out of Marco Island. A few minutes after they reached the open Gulf, a 36-foot red Mirage roared up alongside. A Latin male, the only LORAN operator, jumped aboard the Midnight and tried to punch some way points into the machine, without success. Disgusted, he told the Midnight crew to follow him out. The boats barreled off into the setting sun. They had 100 miles to go, but with a moderate sea and boats that make 50-plus knots, it took only a few hours. After sunset they joined four other boats and drifted together. They could see the lights of the mothership they were to meet less than a mile away. At 2030 they started a slow approach to their destination.

Not far away to the northwest lay the blacked-out *Matagorda* and *Maui*. A few miles further out the inbound aerostat AS-1 acquired another suspicious target making to the northeast. They suspected that it was the first target, first detected at noon. The *Maui* had to go to the aerostat for refueling. The *Matagorda* and the recently arrived power glider RG-8A were vectored to the new target. A little after 2100 the almost silent RG-8A found the drifting and lighted *Turtola* with the go-fast boats approaching. The people on the tug and the off-load boats had no clue that the blue-gray aircraft was circling a few hundred feet above. A Customs twin-engine Nomad equipped with night-seeing FLIR and video gear was also approaching. At 2115 the *Matagorda* was 3 miles away from the *Turtola*. The cutter's radar was painting the tug and eight smaller targets. District Seven via Boat-RonOne directed the *Matagorda* to close with the suspect under the right-of-approach doctrine to determine the vessel's nationality and registration.

As the crew of the Midnight Express FL9362EM jockeyed around the tug to pick up their bales—and, they hoped, $10,000–20,000 each—they were caught in a minor traffic jam. Four boats were already alongside. One was loaded but still tied to the tug. A second was being loaded. Trying to get a place at the side, the inexperienced FL9362EM operator collided with the tug and gouged a furrow in their boat. They fell off downwind to regroup.

At that moment the approaching *Matagorda*, at a range of about 1 mile, energized her rotating blue light and illuminated the Coast Guard ensign. All hell broke loose aboard the tug and on the go-fast boats. The *Turtola*'s captain rang for full ahead—where to, he was not sure. Throttles on the small boats were slammed against the stops. High-performance engines screamed in the night as white water boiled. Panic reigned. Two go-fast boats tied to the tug did not bother to cast off. The operators just two-blocked throttles and broke the lines. Boatswain's Mate First Class Joe Cross, the *Matagorda*'s officer of the deck, reported that about eight contacts around the tug exploded like a fireworks display on the radar screen and took off in all directions.[4] Lighting up that far away from the unsuspecting targets was premature. No explanation for the cutter commander's decision was given in his afteraction message or in any of the follow-up seizure reports.

The *Matagorda* and her semirigid boarding boat (RHIB) made straight for the erratically steering tug. When the cutter came alongside, the *Turtola* swerved toward her in an attempt to ram. Repeated hails and calls to stop on VHF Channel 16 were ignored. The *Matagorda*'s CO had his gunner fire about a dozen M-60 rounds across the bow of the tug. Gonzalez responded. He called the cutter, saying the Coast Guard now had his attention and he intended to stop. Boatswain's Mate Cross instructed the captain to get everyone on deck and stand by to be boarded. Cross saw one crewman putting on a life jacket; he surmised that the tug was being scuttled and so reported. By this time the *Matagorda*'s boarding team was alongside. Gonzalez gave them permission to come aboard.

Lt. (jg) R. E. Kane, the *Matagorda*'s boarding officer, accompanied by the *Turtola*'s captain, began to inspect the tug. Kane detected a strong odor of marijuana. As they walked forward on the weather deck, Kane looked through an open porthole. He saw a hole cut into the messroom deck, and under the cutout he saw bales. Gonzalez shrugged his shoulders and admitted he had a problem with that compartment. Field tests showed that the bales contained marijuana.

While this was taking place, the *Matagorda*'s chief machinery technician and the tug's engineer were securing valves in the engine room to stop a halfhearted scuttling attempt. At 2245 the USCGC *Maui*, topped off with fuel, joined the party. Her CO put a three-man support team on the tug, then raced to join the *Point Thatcher* in an attempt to intercept the fleeing go-fast boats tracked by the aerostat. At 0112 on 6 April the *Matagorda* was authorized to seize the tug after an SNO was granted by Honduras and affirmed by the com-

Fred Schellenberg (*left*) and the author with the *Turtola* in the background, April 1989 *(Author's collection)*

mandant of the Coast Guard. Lieutenant Kane officially seized the *Turtola* and made an entry in the ship's log. He directed the *Maui*'s senior man to arrest the tug's master and five crewmen. The spoils of war were thus divided between the two cutters.

Meanwhile, on-scene aircraft were doing their best to track the escaping go-fast boats. The Customs Nomad, Omaha-1, picked a go-fast running to the northeast and bird-dogged the doper with FLIR and video running. FL3254FR, the red Mirage with the LORAN man, was chased into the arms of a Coast Guard 41-foot utility boat about 30 miles off Captiva Island. One floating bale of pot was enough for them to detain the boat and crew of three. The Coast Guardsmen towed the go-fast into Station Fort Myers Beach, where Customs and DEA agents took over. They had probable cause to seize the boat and arrest the crew. A Coast Guard helicopter found FL9362EM about 35 miles northeast and approximately 70 miles west of Naples. The

Manitou, coming down from the north on a flank bell, took charge of the go-fast, which made no attempt to run. Boarders found traces of marijuana, probably from a previous adventure. It was enough for them to seize the Midnight and arrest the three people.

The last go-fast collared in this caper was FL9980EY, also a 37-foot Midnight. She was tracked by the second Customs Nomad, Nightstalker 64, to Marathon in the Florida Keys. Customs officers were waiting at Bonefish Marina on Grassy Key when the boat eased in during the wee hours of the morning. A new marijuana trace detector, an aerosol known as Cannibispray, was used on the boat with positive results. The boat was seized, and the three crewmen were identified, released, and later indicted.

Nearly 20,000 pounds of uniquely packaged marijuana were stored in the 20-foot-wide, 6-foot-long, and 14-foot-deep concealed compartment in the *Turtola.* Cofferdams and swash bulkheads created a 6-inch void around the compartment to defeat drilling and borescoping done to detect the contraband. To access the sealed compartment, it was necessary to chip away about an inch of deck cement and cut through the steel plate. This work was obligingly done by the tug's crew before the Coast Guard boarded. Vinyl tile had covered the messroom deck. As each tile was removed, it was numbered on the bottom for quick reinstallation. The cement over the cutout was greenish-colored and crumbly; it seemed fresh and recently poured. The compartment had probably been modified for the pot cargo months or years before but just recently sealed.

Sophisticated marijuana packaging was new to the Florida coast. Compacted blocks measuring 12 inches by 9 inches by 4 inches and weighing about 7 pounds (3 kilograms) had been heat-sealed in doubled clear-plastic wrappings. Eight blocks were wrapped with cardboard and secured with plastic straps. Cartons were wrapped with black plastic and covered with burlap-looking plastic. Outer covers were labeled "Acetato De Celulos En Escamas; De Celanese Mexicana, S.A." (roughly meaning oiled cellulose acetate packaged by a Mexican company). The marijuana was in excellent condition. Identical packaging had been used by San Diego smugglers in an attempted small-boat delivery just off the U.S.–Mexican border. The origin of the *Turtola's* marijuana has not been identified. It could have come from Colombia, Belize, or Mexico. Outer coverings with Mexican markings made no sense unless the bales had at some time been transported overland through Mexico. If the cargo had been loaded and sealed in Colombia, Panama, or Honduras, the Mexican labels would have been a wasted effort. The grass had probably been transported by truck to Coatzacoalcos and loaded aboard the tug while she loitered in or around the Mexican port.

The case was prosecuted by Assistant U.S. Attorney Mark Jackowski, who had indicted General Noriega in the Middle District of Florida. At trial in September the *Turtola*'s Miguel Gonzalez pled guilty in U.S. district court before the government could complete its case. After the government's case, the judge granted a directed verdict of acquittal to one tug crewmen. Four other tug crewmen and six go-fast crewmen were convicted on all counts. Six other off-loaders were indicted and convicted in the *Turtola* venture. DEA was still investigating the case in 1994 and anticipated more indictments.[5]

The *Turtola* follow-up investigation was given to DEA agent Sam Murad, who served as the case agent at trial. Murad worked for five years on follow-ups to the tug seizure, which ended in the dismantling of one of the last Florida off-load organizations. The *Turtola* case, like the highly successful Peacemaker operation, showed the great advantage of capturing American off-load crews in sea seizures. Cooperation by defendants faced with mandatory minimums eliminated whole smuggling organizations.

The *Turtola*'s attempted off-load identified the depth of incompetence to which Florida grass smugglers had fallen. The absence of LORAN knowledge and navigation skills was truly remarkable. It is doubtful that the off-loaders would have found the *Turtola* at all if the tug had not displayed lights, an unheard-of dereliction among the old-timers on Route 26. There was no countersurveillance before or during the operation. Most important, no one was in charge! The command problem was exacerbated by the fact that at least two independent groups of off-load boats were involved, and that the people who planned the operation did not participate.

There were a few grass motherships intercepted in 1989 before the *Turtola*. The largest at-sea seizure of the year was made by a Coast Guard LEDET from the navy oiler USS *Platte* (AO-186) on 19 March about 55 miles east of Great Abaco Island, Bahamas. With the master's permission to board, the LEDET found over 50,000 pounds on deck and in a fuel tank on the 160-foot Honduran freighter *Esso Bonaire III*.[6] Marijuana on the deck meant that an off-load was pending.

None of the seized vessels had reached an off-load point near the United States.

The first known marijuana mothership attempt after the *Turtola* occurred in April about 120 miles west of Fort Bragg, California. Approximately 20,000 pounds of Colombian grass were dumped at sea by an unidentified fishing vessel. Deliveries of Southeast Asian marijuana across the Pacific did not continue as the 1988 seizures had indicated. U.S. Customs did intercept 50,000 pounds of Far Eastern hashish aboard the ex–research vessel *Lady Bridgid* in St. Helens, Oregon, on the Columbia River. Vessel seizures on the West Coast dropped to less than half the previous year's figure.[7] The Pacific eddy disappeared without fanfare. The off-load organizations had been neutralized.

An interesting and daring seizure was made on 5 May by the USCGC *Diligence* (WMEC-616) 200 miles out in the open Atlantic east of Cape Canaveral. Undoubtedly smarting after having failed to find the load on the *Turtola,* the cutter's crew were not about to let the 150-foot U.S. motor vessel *Venture* escape. The *Diligence* was serving as a safety picket off the cape for the launch of the space shuttle *Atlantis.* When the *Venture* hove into sight around sunset, cutter lookouts watched a small boat speed away and disappear over the horizon. The *Diligence* closed with the *Venture,* but repeated radio and loud-hailer calls and flashing-light signals got no response. The cuttermen saw no sign of life on the boat, which was moving at an estimated 10 knots. Thirty rounds of .50-caliber machine-gun fire laid over the runaway's bows had no effect. Finally the cutter's captain matched his speed with the suspect's and laid his ship right alongside. A fearless *Diligence* crewman jumped aboard the moving craft in the dark. He found the ship abandoned and stopped her engine. Boarders discovered 11,000 pounds of pot on the motorized Flying Dutchman.[8] There was another smuggler like Harold King who would not approach an off-load site without a chase boat.

In the Caribbean at least three grass boats with moderate loads were seized after the *Turtola* in 1989. On 12 May the USCGC *Vashon* (WPB-1308) intercepted the 60-foot *Melpo Jr.* off Puerto Rico with 13,000 pounds. On 11 June the USCGC *Dauntless* (WMEC-624), the famous drug buster, detected the 50-foot *Horizonte* 40 miles southwest of Isle of Pines, Cuba. Boarders found approximately 12,000 pounds of pot in plain view.[9] The 65-foot U.S. motor vessel *Miss*

Mothership quantity of cocaine from the seized coastal freighter *Barlovento,* July 1989 *(Official U.S. Coast Guard photograph)*

Beverly Ann was run to a stop off Cozumel, Mexico, by Her Majesty's Frigate *Alacrity* (F-174) and the Royal Fleet Auxiliary Service tanker *Brambleleaf* (A-81). According to the press report, the Royal Navy units were not participating in antidrug operations. The Seventh Coast Guard District said the British ships had approached the suspect at high speed to cover the approach of a cutter.[10] The USCGC *Petrel* (WSES-4) came up and made the boarding. Over 14,000 pounds of pot were found on the boat. Two U.S. citizens and one Colombian were arrested. None of these vessels made it to their off-load positions.

Major at-sea cocaine seizures in 1989 came after the *Turtola*. On 5 July the 160-foot Panamanian coastal freighter *Barlovento,* a sister to the *Esso Bonaire,* was intercepted by the surface-effect cutter *Shearwater* (WSES-3) in the Yucatán Channel. The USCGC *Sitkinak* (WPB-1329) came to help. Boarders did not find dope, but the ship was loaded with 200 tons of difficult-to-search bagged cement. Lt. Ken Savoie, the *Shearwater*'s CO, requested an SNO to bring the coaster in for a more detailed cargo space investigation. Panama's government in exile, which was opposed to the renegade Noriega regime, granted the SNO. On 6 July the *Barlovento* was escorted to Key West, where an extensive search was initiated by Coast Guard, DEA, and Customs investigators with their sniffer dogs. After eight hours of laborious work, the searchers discovered a hidden compartment between the fuel and water tanks in the freighter's double bottoms. A total of 3,359 pounds of cocaine was removed from the compartment.[11] Substitute coke for marijuana, and we have a repeat of the cement-carrying coastal freighter *Carmiel*. Some interdiction folks thought we might be seeing the dawn of cocaine motherships in the tradition of the late grass carriers.

The Mexican Navy scored a record cocaine seizure on 8 August about 100 miles southwest of Cabo San Lucas, Baja California. Patrols intercepted the 286-foot Panamanian cargo vessel *Sea Point* with over 5,000 pounds in her cargo hold and ballast tanks. It was the largest Pacific at-sea cocaine seizure so far. Pacific coke seizures greatly increased in 1989, to over 25,000 pounds. Most of that came from a merchant vessel seized by Peruvian Customs as she departed Peru.[12]

The coastal freighter *Nerma* was a cocaine mothership in the grass tradition. DEA agents in Colombia developed intelligence on the shipment long before the reasonably well-kept 236-foot freighter was laden with 3,000–6,000 pounds of cocaine off the coast of Venezuela. A lookout was established. The *Nerma* was sighted by a Coast Guard aircraft midmorning on 9 September northbound about 3 miles off Burrows Cay, Berry Islands, Bahamas. A Coast Guard patrol plane maintained discreet air surveillance until it was relieved by a Customs aircraft at midnight. About 0300 the Customs aircrew saw four high-speed small boats approach the ship and start to off-load what appeared to be bales and barrels. The activity was video-recorded. One speedboat was observed making contact with the 42-foot Grand Banks cruiser *J. J. Lorick*. Soon the 110-foot patrol boats *Manitou* (WPB-1302) and *Maui* (WPB-1304) arrived. The *Manitou* went after the freighter, and the *Maui* chased one of the go-fast boats. Other units came to help.

The *Manitou*'s boarders found bales of cocaine floating near the *Nerma* and other bales still on the ship. The *Maui* had to fire forty-three rounds of machine-gun fire across the bow of one fleeing speedboat to stop her. Two other go-fast boats were apprehended, but one got away. In all, 1,172 pounds of cocaine were seized from the mothership and the go-fasts or found in the water. Agents and officers figured that about five or six times that much had been lost in the ocean. Seven Danes were arrested aboard the freighter and seven U.S. citizens or resident aliens aboard the go-fasts. Within forty-eight hours investigators had tracked the *Lorick* to the Miami River. Another 1,540 pounds of coke were found on the husky cruiser, for a grand total of 2,712 pounds. Three more people were arrested.[13] The specter of cocaine motherships replacing marijuana motherships loomed large.

The *Barlovento* and *Nerma* were just warmups for the finale that came in October. As with the *Nerma,* there was a lookout on the 173-foot oceangoing tug *Zedon Sea.* The USCGC *Cushing* (WPB-1321) intercepted the big tug on 2 October about 165 miles east of Tampico, Mexico, in the Bay of Campeche. In containers on deck, under bags of cement, Coast Guardsmen found 11,455 pounds of cocaine, the biggest maritime coke seizure so far. The tug was escorted to New Orleans. The week before, authorities in Los Angeles had found 20 tons of cocaine in a warehouse, the largest coke seizure ever.[14]

Marijuana smuggling did not die with the motherships and their multi-ton loads, but the volume of seaborne grass was greatly reduced. Pot shipments of a few hundred pounds continued to arrive along our coasts. An example is a 37-foot sloop that was intercepted near Florida in 1989 with 200 pounds of Belizean grass. There was nothing special about the *Celia* (a fictitious name); she was like thousands of other midsized sailboats swarming the Florida Gulf coast and the hundreds venturing south to the Caribbean. Her owner was skilled in fiberglass work and was a competent sailor. In early 1987 he met the amiable John O'Barry (a fictitious name for an individual who cooperated with the government in describing smuggling techniques and routes), an avid diver and spear fisherman. O'Barry had use of a small spread on the Mexican Caribbean coast. He also had contact with marijuana growers in Belize just south of his outpost. O'Barry and the boat owner had common interests—boats, tropical seas, sailing, diving, Margaritas, a little grass smoking—and an aversion to steady employment. What they needed was enough money to maintain a carefree lifestyle. They were not greedy. One had a boat, and the other had a base. Two modest grass trips a year would give each a minimum stipend of $100,000.

The *Celia*'s company had simple but effective operational security. Only the two partners participated in the whole evolution, from pur-

chasing the raw material directly from small growers in Belize to sell-
ing the product from a private home to a clientele of friends. There
was no radio base or any radio communications whatsoever during
transit, except, of course, in dire emergency. Instead they exploited
loose talk by the opposition. Prior to sailing for Mexico, the gregari-
ous smugglers frequented a sailors' bar near the Coast Guard station
at their home port. At the expense of a few beers, they engaged young
Coasties in conversation and occasionally got good information on
cutter deployments in the Caribbean. They already knew that the
Yucatán Channel was occupied by hungry patrols.

The *Celia*'s usual route was directly to Cape Catoche at the northeastern corner of the Yucatán Peninsula. On the empty run south they
kept mental records of Coast Guard, U.S. Navy, and Mexican Navy
ship sightings for future reference. As they sailed south from the cape,
they stayed close inshore to avoid the steady Yucatán current that had
carried Ambrose Weldon north in his south-pointed shrimper. A rest
stop was made at O'Barry's hacienda on the southern coast of Quin-
tana Roo, peopled for most of the year by Mayan spirits. After sufficient R and R the sailors continued south almost to the Belize border,
entering Chetumal Bay via an almost unknown pass near Reef Point
at the north end of Ambergris Cay. Crossing the bay to Corozal
Town, Belize, the part-time smugglers contacted their sources and
negotiated the purchase of 200–300 pounds of quality hand-picked
grass. The small cargo was brought aboard in flour or bean bags to
fool any observers.

Homeward bound, the *Celia*'s crew first did a binocular search of
Chetumal Bay for Mexican naval units running to or from their base
north of Corozal. Leaving the hidden pass by Reef Point, the *Celia*
went eastward through a channel in the barrier reef. In the Caribbean
the sailboat made north far enough offshore to pick up the strong current. Rounding Cape Catoche as close inshore as prudent and beyond
reach of the probing Yucatán Channel patrols, the *Celia* was put on a
northerly course leading to the central Gulf. O'Barry's idea was to
penetrate the Gulf along the line between the Seventh and Eighth
Coast Guard Districts, which he felt would be less intensely patrolled.
The theory had merit. At 26° or 27° north, the *Celia* came to a northeast course and headed for home. A daytime landfall was planned to
avoid suspicion.

Top: The sailboat *Savage Shrimp* was caught returning from a race to Jamaica with 347 pounds of pot. *Bottom:* The contraband was cleverly sealed in a compartment between the aft end of the cabin and the lazarette. *(Author's collection)*

O'Barry and his friend sailed right up to a temporary anchorage just across the channel from the Coast Guard station. The small grass cargo was off-loaded in sail bags by dinghy to a residential park in plain view of the station. Once ashore, the two men walked up the street to a relative's house and got a car to transport the valuable pot to a refrigerator in O'Barry's house. Who would ever suspect these bronzed sailor men of landing marijuana in broad daylight at the back door of the Coast Guard station?

The *Celia* made two successful deliveries in 1987 and two in 1988. The smugglers were certain they could go on indefinitely as long as they followed their proven plan, did not expand beyond a market of trusted friends, and did not boast about their accomplishments. It would have worked, except for DEA resident Les Tuell's sharp-eyed spies, operating out of Mérida, Mexico. A beer stop was the smugglers' undoing. DEA placed the *Celia* on lookout even though its information was speculation. A number of overflights by surveillance aircraft while they crossed the Gulf convinced the smugglers that they had been had. By the time they were boarded near their destination by the USCGC *Point Countess* (WPB-82335), O'Barry had convinced his partner that it was best to confess and cooperate.[15] Casual smuggling represented by the *Celia* case is extremely hard to detect and control. It will be with us as long as demand for the product exists.

At-sea interdiction of marijuana motherships put a huge strain on the industry, and in some cases forced the survivors to seek other work. Shoreside operations such as Peacemaker along the Gulf coast of Florida and some Pacific operations directed against Brian Peter Daniels and others were the *coup de grâce*.

The impact on little Everglades City, the last big marijuana import center, is instructive. U.S. District Judge Elizabeth Kovachevich handed out forty-year sentences to indicted smugglers who refused to cooperate with the government and were convicted at trial. Few who went to trial were acquitted. The many who did cooperate faced a life of fear. One was killed by a car bomb, and others had their boats burned. All were labeled rats, and they and their families were threatened. Some moved away. Others went into the Federal Witness Protection Program and were given new identities and transported to distant places. Those who went to jail left a generation of children without fathers. The dubious compensation for their offspring was local recognition of their fathers as outlaw heroes. As one wife said, "My husband, he's got his pride and his honor, I guess."[16] It was a terrible price to pay for two decades of gold chains and wild, exhilarating nights on the Gulf. National publicity should have been given to Everglades City as a deterrence to drug smuggling. It was not. Exposing the wages of sin for drug trafficking in Cuba overshadowed the end of Everglades City.

The highly publicized trial of Gen. Arnaldo Ochoa Sanchez, hero of the Cuban Revolution, and other officials charged with corruption and drug trafficking began in Havana on 25 June. Col. Tony de la Guardia of the Interior Ministry and his identical twin Patrico, a brigadier general in the army and a close associate of Ochoa, were tried along with the general and other lesser officers.[17] Their convictions were preordained. As expected, nothing came out of the trial to implicate Fidel Castro in drug trafficking. The general was executed on 13 July. Others reportedly met the same fate.

After the Ochoa trials, Gen. José Abrantes, interior minister and Tony de la Guardia's boss, was arrested for corruption with three top Interior Ministry officials. Abrantes died in jail of an apparent heart attack.

According to Andres Oppenheimer's *Castro's Final Hour*, Castro had long sanctioned drug trafficking when it could be justified as a national security measure, such as a deal with Colombian smugglers for shipment of weapons to M-19 guerillas in return for landing privileges. After five months spent in Cuba interviewing relatives of Ochoa and the de la Guardia brothers and a few former Interior Ministry intelligence officers, Oppenheimer concluded that Castro moved swiftly to prevent a perceived disclosure by the United States of Cuba's role in drug smuggling. He further believes that Castro used the opportunity to purge the military and the secret Interior Ministry of disaffected officers who were a threat.[18]

Oppenheimer observes that it is hard for the Castro regime to avoid using oppressive methods to control growing discontent as the socialist world disintegrates. He believes that the drug/corruption trials and Ochoa's execution marked a dramatic break in the bond of mutual tolerance between the government and the people.[19] If Oppenheimer's prediction of Castro's approaching final hour is correct, and if Ochoa's execution was a primary cause for Fidel's slide, U.S. exposure of officially sanctioned drug trafficking through Cuba should be recorded as the bullet that terminated the bearded leader. On the practical side, Cuba was no longer a safe haven for transiting pot boats.

A good indication of the decline in marijuana imports was the expansion of the domestic pot industry. By 1989 at least 25 percent of the marijuana consumed in the United States was home-grown. Some observers believed that the domestic pot industry was generating $16 billion in annual sales. A case in the Midwest involving the so-called Cornbread Mafia showed the extent of organized pot cultivation. Focusing on Marion County, Kentucky, authorities targeted a group using twenty-five farms in nine midwestern states. Seventy-five members were prosecuted, and 182 tons of sinsemilla seized.[20]

Expanding domestic production of pot concurrent with diminishing maritime deliveries showed that grass boaters had not retired for lack of gainful employment. The National Institute on Drug Abuse's National Household Survey on Drug Abuse in 1988, however, declared that the number of current drug users in America had fallen to 14.5 million from 23 million in 1985, a striking reduction of 37 percent.[21] Drug use was declining, but there was still a brisk market for marijuana in 1989. With wholesale pot prices bumping $1,000 per pound and sinsemilla street prices up to $300 per ounce, there was a big profit motive for importing marijuana. The decline of the grass boats in this market environment was a testimonial to maritime interdiction and shoreside investigations that dismantled the off-load organizations.

Combined interdiction forces seized about 425,000 pounds of shipborne marijuana in 1989, a reduction of over 50 percent from 1988. The Coast Guard seized almost 215,000 pounds, or about 51 percent of the total. By contrast, Coast Guardsmen seized 32,896 pounds of cocaine in 1989, over twice as much as in 1988 and a record that stands.[22]

Media claims regarding the failure of interdiction—"the Reagan administration's primary strategy against Latin drug trafficking"— totally ignored the passing of the marijuana motherships.[23] Myopic or politically motivated media pundits concentrated solely on the cocaine menace. It may have been more important, but the sea interdiction forces were deprived of the recognition they deserved. Spectacular at-sea coke seizures like the *Zedon Sea* with 11,455 pounds ran up the maritime statistics, but most large coke shipments rode in cargo holds or in containers carried aboard vessels not dedicated to drug smuggling. Concurrent with the increase in sea coke seizures, the drug war was moving ashore.

Intelligence community support of the drug war had been progressing for some time, but it was escalated in the spring of 1989. William H. Webster, director of the Central Intelligence Agency, commissioned the Counter Narcotics Center (CNC) at the CIA.[24] Analysts from different parts of the agency were assigned to the center along with Coast Guard commander Dick White, redetailed from NNBIS. Much of the work performed by the CNC was already being done by the CIA, but now efforts would be concentrated and focused under one director. The CNC was a conduit for passing intelligence developed by the national foreign intelligence community (NFIC) to the law enforcement community after appropriate cleansing to protect certain sources. The CNC still functions and does good work. The old problem of protecting NFIC sources from court discovery has been mitigated by policy so that actionable information can be used as leads for investigations.

The administration still talked about a National Drug Intelligence Center (NDIC) to coordinate the collection and production of all drug-trafficking intelligence (an all-source center). Battles went on between the White House and Congress and among the various agencies about where the NDIC would be located and who would run it. The NDIC was supposed to serve as the "exchange point for classified drug intelligence between the law enforcement community and the foreign intelligence community, providing guidance for domestic and foreign drug intelligence collection, assessing interagency intelligence efforts and promoting information sharing among various law enforcement agencies."[25] A modest NDIC was eventually established in 1993 under the Justice Department, concentrating on strategic intelligence.

A brief but positive event occurred on 26–27 July 1989 at the Defense Intelligence Agency College, Bolling Air Force Base, Washington, D.C. The Coast Guard's Intelligence Coordination Center, commanded by Capt. J. C. Trainor, sponsored a Post-Seizure Intelligence Collection Conference. The center's Analysis Division chief, Lt. Comdr. Raymond Brown, organized the two-day session to promote effective collection of intelligence from seized vessels and cooperating defendants.[26] This was a much-needed opportunity for the few postseizure collectors to meet and exchange ideas with experts in the intelligence community. Unfortunately, the conference took place just as the primary maritime drug transporters were becoming extinct.

Military involvement in interdiction increased in 1989. As the lead agency responsible for detection and monitoring, the Department of Defense established major drug joint task forces in Key West and in Oakland, California. Their mission was to detect, sort, intercept, and track smuggler targets approaching the United States. JTF4 in Key West, responsible for finding and tracking drug planes and ships coming from the Caribbean, received the initial emphasis. Vice Adm. James C. Irwin, USCG, was the first commander of JTF4. He reported to the commander-in-chief, U.S. Atlantic Command (CinCLant).[27] JTF5 on Alameda Island, responsible for the Pacific, received fewer resources. Its first commander was Rear Adm. William P. Leahy, Jr., USCG. Under CinCPac, JTF5 had the advantage of being co-located with the Coast Guard Pacific Area, a command long experienced in developing intelligence on Pacific smugglers.[28] JTF6 was responsible for the southwestern land border and came on line later, but it had few if any maritime concerns. Personnel assigned to the JTFs were from all branches of the military services.

Navy captain Larry Fairchild, the JTF6 chief of staff, reportedly made a comment reflecting the views of the few law enforcement liaison people detailed to the JTFs. Captain Fairchild said the first DEA agent attached to the unit told him, "You know, working with DoD is a lot like having a gorilla in love with you."[29] The civilian agencies were concerned that the DoD Goliath might attempt to take over the drug war. It never happened. In theory, JTFs would detect and pass on identified targets to the Coast Guard or civilian enforcement agencies, assuming that military detectors could decide if the target was a smuggler; they usually could not without input from law enforcement. It also assumed a free flow of information between the different agencies, which seldom happens voluntarily.

Only under the NNBIS umbrella, with some remarkable exceptions in certain Pacific cases, did interagency communications in the drug war occur on a regular basis. NNBIS was finished. The final entry in the log did not come until 1201 EST 8 April 1989. At that moment all remaining personnel detailed to the National Narcotics Border Interdiction System were transferred to the Office of National Drug

Control Policy (ONDCP) by order of John Sununu, the White House chief of staff.[30] The steadying hand of George Bush had been withdrawn. He was respected by the great majority of law enforcement and military people. They tried to get along with each other in an attempt to please the World War II combat veteran. It is debatable how well another vice president would have done in his place.

It was poetic justice that the marijuana motherships that NNBIS had done so much to sink passed into history at the end of the vice president's experiment. The *Turtola* was brought in as a prize by Boatswain's Mate First Class Bill Weaver, USCG, on 7 April, one day before NNBIS was stricken from the list. It was appropriate that this event took place before the watch ended for the most effective counternarcotics coordination mechanism developed so far in the long and seemingly endless drug war.

Many objected, on political and procedural grounds, to having the vice president run what some felt was a separate department without the advice and consent of Congress. That was a valid concern. The administration countered with the position, written into the NNBIS plan, that the vice president did not command anything; he just coordinated and inspired. That was also true. In practice—a fact known to both the ruling party and the loyal opposition—when the vice president of the United States suggests something to the secretary of a line department, it usually gets done with alacrity. It was not a direct chain of command, which the military and many others asked for, but it was the closest we got. The continuation of an OVP/NNBIS coordination system coupled with the resources of the JTFs would have been a potent interdiction weapons system. NNBIS would have been the bridge between the military/intelligence community and the law enforcement community just as it had been for the past six years.

William J. Bennett was appointed director of the ONDCP by President Bush in the second week of 1989. After confirmation by the Senate, he had 180 days to deliver a national drug control strategy. An arch-conservative and former Reagan secretary of education, the outspoken Bennett was considered a good choice. Observers called him "pugnacious" and "two-fisted."[31] The forty-five-year-old former educator would place much emphasis on the education of young people. At a Washington meeting of the American Society of Newspaper Editors in June, Bennett told them, "If we did education right, the drug problem would only be on the periphery, on the fringe of our society—and if we can see a re-affirmation, a re-invigoration of these institutions whose job it is to raise and nurture our children, we'd have less of a problem."[32] Statistics show that drug use declined during Bennett's watch as drug czar, with occasional cocaine use down by 29 percent.[33]

Control and coordination of the supply reduction agencies, mainly Customs, the Coast Guard, DEA, and now DoD, would take more than a bully pulpit, for which the new drug czar was justly famous. Bennett had cabinet status, but he was not a member of the cabinet and had no direct authority over the agencies.[34] He was required to certify the adequacy of each department's budget report to implement the drug control strategy, but he had no veto power over initial submission. If Congress had given the drug czar budget authority, it would have been a different story. Control of money means power.

Title I (Coordination of National Drug Policy) of the enabling legislation (the Anti–Drug Abuse Act of 1988) was amazingly vague on operational coordination, which was one of the avowed purposes of the law and of the whole drug-czar concept. Only in the discussion of high-intensity drug areas was coordination of operations even mentioned. Only the coordination of policy was required. The Interdiction Committee, which served as a forum under the old National Drug Policy Board to facilitate interagency coordination, was renamed the Border Interdiction Committee (BIC).[35] The BIC would help to iron out differences at the headquarters level, but there was nothing in the new law or the later strategies for the NNBIS-type day-to-day coordination of regional field operations or special operations. It seemed that Congress deliberately intended to expunge all traces of NNBIS when framing the Anti–Drug Abuse Act of 1988.

Interdiction operators, accustomed to working under the NNBIS system and procedures established by Operation Hat Trick, were adrift in a sea of confusion. ONDCP retained and conditionally absorbed the NNBIS centers in Miami, Houston, Long Beach, and Honolulu for an undetermined transition period. The moment, however, was gone. Agencies quietly took back their people and the money that went with them. They also slowly withdrew into their own shells. The Coast Guard and Customs agreed to common guidelines in areas such as South Florida, and the navy–Coast Guard Caribbean Squadron continued to do business as usual. Military joint task forces were joint for the military but had only token representation from the civilian enforcement agencies. The JTFs did assume the military-asset-scheduling responsibility developed by NNBIS, but large-scale multinational operations like Blue Lightning and Hat Trick went by the board.

A military detailee to ONDCP with a strong background in his service's counternarcotics work put it this way: "NNBIS had finally got its act together in 1987. We had a national strategy by the Drug Enforcement Policy Board with all its limitations. DoD was showing support. Coordination was good—joint ops near regular. NNBIS was the synergist that got things moving. Then came the law that created ONDCP. It said all the things that NNBIS was doing should be absorbed by ONDCP but they never were. The senior staff at ONDCP just ignored the functions. Coordination just faded away. We were back to where things were in the 1970s."[36]

Bennett and the shakedown crew at ONDCP did a good job of producing the required national drug control strategy within the 180 days of the drug czar's confirmation, as required by law. It was actually the second national strategy. The first, the "Green Book" published by the National Drug Policy Board in 1987, had been limited to enforcement or supply reduction. The new "Red Book" was transmitted to Congress by the president on 5 September 1989. It contained quantifiable goals concerning user or demand reduction. With the exception of some agency assignments in data processing and responsibilities at the Mexican border, the new strategy was no more specific than the 1987 rendition on who would do what and when.[37] The temper and confusion of agency managers would surface at Newport, Rhode Island's, historic Naval War College on a bright November day, two months away.

ONDCP sponsored the war games this year as NNBIS had in previous years; it would be the first and last time. Appropriately, this exercise was a policy seminar rather than an operational game. Navy commander George Heim served as the ONDCP project officer. With the assistance of some old NNBIS hands and the War College Gaming Department, Commander Heim put together a comprehensive series of three scenarios. They combined elements of the real-world drug-smuggling situation with some innovative make-believe. Heim's imagination created hypothetical policy issues associated with the entire national drug supply reduction effort. The objective of the seminar was to identify and analyze major issues impacting strategy, policies, and operations. Over 180 representatives of the different agencies and military services, including some from state and local organizations, participated in the three-day exercise beginning on 31 October. An ONDCP Control Cell was charged with recording, analyzing, and reporting the issues raised and the results of the deliberations. Naval War College gaming experts kept the seminar on track.[38]

Participant agencies (State, Defense, Justice, Treasury, Transportation, etc.) were represented by principal surrogates and staffers who identified issues and discussed them during the first two days. Agencies would develop their policy postures in separate discussions. Agency principals would arrive on the third day for an executive session to decide department/agency positions on issues raised by the surrogates/staff during the initial sessions.

To the great chagrin of the working troops, the so-called executive session degenerated into a barroom brawl. Principals had their own agendas. They trashed the scripts prepared by their surrogates. Most felt they could not address contentious issues, even when couched in hypothetical terms, without prior approval by top departmental policymakers. Parochial feelings bubbled over. There was a total disconnect between the first two days of the seminar and the last day. Nothing of substance was decided. People wanted to know how Czar Bennett was going to run their lives. George Heim and his Control Cell felt badly used. Stan Morris, ONDCP deputy director for supply reduction and former chief of the U.S. marshals, had a hard time keeping the peace. Many of the principals behaved like petulant small boys. They could have played the game according to the scenario. With a little luck, they might have found ways to establish a new drug-fighting coordinating mechanism.[39]

The unsightly show at Newport was a symptom of the havoc wrought by Subtitle A of the new law, ironically titled the National Narcotics Leadership Act of 1988. Bennett was a leader, albeit one without much interest in law enforcement. He did make a desperately needed difference in drug demand reduction. After all, Bennett was an educator of tested mettle. But there was not much the czar could do about controlling supply reduction, even if that had been his burning ambition. He did not have the authority to go with the responsibility. Only the ONDCP staff was subject to Bennett's command. Later drug czars have not equaled William Bennett in style and visibility.

What if Congress had created a Department of Drug Control with an absolute chain of command from the secretary down? Let us suppose it had been built around the Drug Enforcement Administration, the only federal agency solely responsible for drug control. How many Coast Guard cutters would have gone to the new department? What resources would have been left to the Coast Guard to do the other critical things like saving lives and property, maintaining aids to navigation, inspecting merchant ships, controlling oil spills, protecting fisheries, and the like? What about the Treasury? Would most of Customs have gone to the new agency? Who would have stayed in Customs to collect tariffs and duties? These are just the obvious problems to be faced in designing a counternarcotics department. A super joint task force composed of military and civilian agency personnel and equipment, with the person in charge reporting directly to the president, would have worked for the short term, but it could not possibly have been of sufficient size to have staying power. Expecting a person with less than full cabinet status to do the job was absurd.

Did it matter? The drug war was displaced from media focus, and therefore public concern, on 7 November 1989. On that day at 2317 the gate was opened at Checkpoint Charlie in Berlin. After forty years, the cold war was over. Communism was crumbling all over the world. There would be a peace dividend. We could start thinking about the state of the economy and the deficit. The Department of Defense took another look at the antidrug mission; after all, the drug war was the only one left. The Coast Guard was concerned that the navy would try to take over its drug interdiction mission, and maybe put the service out of business completely.[40]

Events kept most of the military occupied, despite the Bear's retreat. At 0030 on 20 December, Eighty-second Airborne troops and army rangers jumped into Panama City, Panama. If arresting Manuel Noriega for drug trafficking was a primary mission, it was the grandest drug bust in our history. Desert Shield–Desert Storm would come in due course. There would be a great increase in military counternarcotics involvement with the JTFs, but it would come slowly. During the summer President Bush had signed a new national security decision directive permitting the deployment of U.S. military personnel in the coca-growing jungles of Peru's upper Huallaga Valley.[41] That war story is in the making.

By the end of 1989 the great marijuana fleet was finished. Two boats that could qualify as grass motherships were seized in following years, but neither got anywhere close to an off-load position: the *Halycon* was taken in August 1991 in the Gulf of Panama with 22,700 pounds, and the *Maria B* with 18,000 pounds was captured in the mid-Caribbean in early 1992. There were, of course, some merchant vessels with pot in their cargoes intercepted in U.S. ports after 1989.[42] Two hashish seizures occurred after 1989 in what appeared to be mothership operations. The 120-foot Honduran tug *Nina I* was seized by the USCGC *Seneca* (WMEC-906) on 20 February 1990 with 8 tons of Middle Eastern hash well out in the Atlantic en route from Tripoli, Lebanon, to an unknown destination.[43] The largest hashish seizure ever made took place on 1 July 1990 about 600 miles west of Midway Island in the Pacific. An OCDETF investigation on the West Coast identified the St. Vincent–registered 343-foot merchant ship *Lucky Star* trying to deliver a multi-ton load of Afghani hash somewhere between California and Canada. A Coast Guard LEDET from the USCGC *Rush* (WHEC-723) on board the navy destroyer USS *Ingersoll* (DD-990) made the midocean seizure. Over 75 tons of hashish were found in zippered canvas bags stacked in the hold.[44] None of these cases had the trappings of the *Turtola*, caught in the middle of an off-load; they did not get that far.

Defeat of the grass boats happened after a prolonged war of tonnage attrition all along the marijuana maritime supply lines by U.S. forces and investigative operations ashore that dismantled off-load organizations. The continuous and steadily improving intelligence from source countries on departing ships and boats, and later special intelligence on vessels in the transit zone, were decisive. It was a victory at sea not proclaimed by the operating agencies for fear of losing people, ships, and aircraft to another peace dividend. The media either ignored the event or were distracted by other world events. Adm. Paul Yost gave the victory this short note in his final State of the Coast Guard Address as commandant: "We've practically shut down the marijuana traffic across the Caribbean."[45]

The victory over the grass boats will not soon be forgotten by the men and women who fought the battles at sea and along our shores. Their devotion and sacrifices need to be remembered. That is the goal of this record.

Epilogue

By 1990 the Sea of Grass was only a few floating patches of weeds. While the maritime forces searched for nonexistent marijuana motherships, *Government Executive* magazine denounced drug interdiction as an expensive failure. No mention was made of the vanquished multi-ton grass haulers.[1] Drug enforcers and military detection experts nervously watched their scopes for seagoing targets. Many speculated that the smugglers were using new techniques or routes to get pot to this country. Jailed kingpin grass smugglers said there were no more grass boats, but no one in authority was ready to admit that the motherships were extinct.

The Coast Guard seized just over 62,000 pounds of marijuana in 1990, an amazing drop from 214,625 pounds in 1989.[2] The Seventh Coast Guard District, sitting athwart the marijuana supply lines from the Caribbean, got only 29,079 pounds that year.[3] The total Coast Guard seizure weight was little more than a single shipload of three years earlier. An astonishing 74 percent of the marijuana taken in 1990 was seized on land at or near the Mexican border. At the end of 1990 DEA reported a severe shortage of marijuana and increasing prices, despite the finding of the National Household Survey that the use of pot was declining.[4] By 1993, wholesale pot prices had risen to $1,500–2,000 per pound.[5] That was three to five times more than the *Turtola*'s smugglers could have gotten for their load in 1989.

An example of maritime interdiction capabilities in the early 1990s came from a report in the March 1991 Eighth Coast Guard District's *Guardian*. An occurrence took place in January in the Gulf of Mexico off Destin, Florida, between Pensacola and Panama City. Shoreside intelligence said a go-fast boat would pick up marijuana from another boat offshore. On the morning of 2 January a go-fast was sighted. The Coast Guard, Customs, and the Florida Marine Patrol were involved in the chase. The boat and her two-man crew were arrested. A few packages (not bales) of marijuana were seized. Seven marine units and six aircraft took part in bringing to bay a smuggler boat with two occupants.[6] This operation was a terrific deterrent to would-be boat smugglers, but it was a mighty slim body count.

Florida is still a smuggler target, but nothing like what it was in the 1980s. An interesting 1992 case reported by Customs marine enforcement officer Ken Hysell shows that the once flamboyant Florida smugglers had fallen on tough times. A cocaine air drop was picked up by four men in a go-fast boat off the coast of Cuba. The load was stashed on an island. Three days later the go-fast returned to get the load. They were surprised by a Cuban patrol boat. Shots were fired. After a short and one-sided firefight, the smuggler boat was destroyed and the four crew members were killed. A smaller boat accompanying the first was intercepted after the smoke cleared. This boat, manned by a single operator, was clean. The operator was shown the floating debris and bodies and told to leave Cuban waters immediately. Radio news announcements about the incident were made in Cuba the next day. The shootings were confirmed by a confidential informant.[7] Things were changing. In September 1993 Cuba surrendered a cocaine go-fast and two smugglers to U.S. authorities; it was a first.[8]

By the end of 1990 as much as 70 percent of the coke entering the United States was coming across our Mexican border. Interdiction operations along the Caribbean-Florida routes were believed to be responsible for the westward movement.[9] Trampolining continues. Smuggler aircraft land near our border and off-load cargoes at isolated and safe Mexican landing strips. Cocaine loads are broken down into small units for transportation across the border by cars, trucks, or Mexican "mules."[10] This route is still the main source of cocaine smuggled into the United States.

Major at-sea cocaine seizures, although intermittent, have continued. The *Sea Chariot*, a 225-foot freighter registered in the Caribbean

A navy P-3 Orion rigs the suspect freighter *Sea Chariot* in the eastern Pacific.
(Official U.S. Navy photograph)

island of St. Vincent, was intercepted in the eastern Pacific on 22 April 1993 by the guided-missile cruiser USS *Valley Forge* (CG-50). The cruiser's LEDET made a consensual boarding and found about 11,000 pounds. This seizure ranked with the *Zedon Sea*, intercepted in the Gulf of Mexico in October 1989. Like the *Zedon Sea*, the *Sea Chariot* was carrying coke in deck-loaded containers. A postseizure analysis discovered that the ship was bound from Esmeraldes, Ecuador, to Manzanillo, Mexico.[11] It appeared to be a trial attempt to get volume cocaine from Colombia into Mexico for shipment to the United States.

A drug port of entry still open in the Caribbean after the westward smuggler migration of 1989–90 was the U.S. Virgin Islands and Puerto Rico. Low-profile stealth boats became more common as cocaine gradually replaced pot. Determined smugglers built "drug subs" in their latest effort to break the blockade. They range in size from 17 to 30 feet in length and are built of wood and fiberglass. The waterproof cockpits hold two people, who get air through a snorkel protruding 6 feet above the water. Power is provided by a 100-plus-horsepower marine diesel engine. The semisubmersibles have a range of approximately 600 miles and a reported capacity of a metric ton.

Radar detection is extremely difficult. The first such boat was discovered in early 1993 off the Colombian island of Providencia when its engine failed. A second boat washed ashore empty in the Dominican Republic. A third was captured by the Colombian Navy in December 1993 with cocaine aboard. DEA estimates that up to twenty of these unique vessels may be operational.[12] Maritime challenges still exist.

One victory in the apparently endless battle to reduce the supply of cocaine in the States was the fall of the Medellin cartel. Pablo Escobar was killed by Colombian police on 2 December 1993.[13] Unfortunately, Medellin has been replaced by the Cali cartel, but it too shows signs of collapse. A few years ago experts believed that it was impossible to make any headway against the Medellin gang. Critics say the fall of Medellin means nothing; Cali will just carry on. Despite the naysayers, an encouraging trend was the increase in coke prices that occurred in early 1993. Wholesale prices went up several thousand dollars per kilo, indicating a reduction in availability.[14] Customs claims to have reduced by nearly three-quarters the number of smuggling aircraft crossing our border with Mexico.[15]

Typically, news articles proclaimed, "Half-billion spent in futile attempt to stop airborne drug smugglers." In one article Arnold S. Trebach, president of the Washington-based Drug Policy Foundation, was quoted as saying, "As soon as the air interdiction program appears to be effective, smugglers find new ways to beat it."[16] The same headlines and opinions persisted fifteen years ago, when there seemed to be no end to the marijuana motherships. Many Coast Guard and Customs officers looking at the future from that time and place agreed. We persevered, committed more resources, ignored defeatist media advice, and prevailed against the grass boats. That should be a lesson.

Focus on the drug war declined further when our troops took up defensive positions behind President Bush's "line in the sand." In 1990, Middle East military deployments and public attention to Desert Shield–Desert Storm pushed drugs further off the front burner. For a time the Pentagon almost forgot about counternarcotics. The desert war and the military's lapse of interest in drug fighting were short-lived. When the desert war ended, military seniors scurried back to the drug war to offset pending cuts.

Bill Clinton won the White House in 1992. In the first issue of the Interim National Drug Control Strategy under the new Clinton administration, the loss of media and public focus on the drug problem was recognized. The report said that although citizens may think the decline in drug use by young people signals the end of the crisis, such a "conclusion is as dangerous as it is wrong."[17]

In early 1993 President Clinton's slashing of the White House staff, called symbolic by some, took a heavy toll on the Office of National Drug Control Policy. The ONDCP was targeted for a cut from 146 people down to 25.[18] It never got that far, but what morale was left in the office went by the board. The drug czar, Florida's former governor Bob Martinez, certainly lost his ability to focus. Clinton appointed former New York City police chief Lee Brown to the post. The new strategy targeted hard-core users and source countries. Demand reduction was the main thrust. Interdiction was hardly mentioned.[19]

People are more concerned today with violent crime than with drugs. Many ignore the causal relationship between the two. There is a movement to do away with mandatory drug sentences. They did much to bring down the vast marijuana off-load organizations. U.S. Attorney General Janet Reno told Seventh Circuit judges that the federal government cannot build enough prisons to hold the population of convicted drug traffickers and smugglers. Reno said she would consider recommending the elimination of mandatory sentences for low-level drug crimes.[20]

Drug use by our nation's youth has continued to decline. There were almost 6 million casual cocaine users in the mid-1980s; that number dropped to 1.3 million in 1992. Our primary drug problem today is the increasing use of cocaine, especially crack, by hard-core addicts. A recent and disturbing statistic is the increase in marijuana use by eighth- and ninth-graders and high school students in 1994.[21] Whenever we become complacent about the drug problem, things seem to fall apart.

When Adm. J. W. Kime took over as commandant in May 1990, he emphasized that all Coast Guard missions were equally important. "Balance will be our watchword," said the admiral. The new commandant intended to restore the service's environmental programs. Media focus was on the huge *Exxon Valdez* oil spill. Kime said candidly that the Coast Guard had overemphasized drug interdiction and military readiness to the detriment of other missions. Admiral Kime, formerly commander of the West Coast Eleventh District and NNBIS Pacific Region coordinator, was well aware of the effect declining drug seizures would have on his service. He welcomed the massive assistance provided by the Department of Defense but cautioned that the new emphasis on air smuggling and the land border might leave the sea lanes open.[22] Rear Adm. W. T. Leland, USCG, articulated the maritime interdiction dilemma in his December 1992 *Proceedings* article on total quality management: "Support for increased effort wanes quickly when we are not able to photograph tons of cocaine being unloaded from seized vessels and aircraft. Deterrence has an easily defined cost but people debate its value."[23]

With the Clinton administration's change in the drug strategy and drastically declining maritime seizures, the sea interdiction forces began to crumble. The floating Fat Alberts went in May 1992; the Coast Guard aerostats that did such a good job blocking the Caribbean choke points were decommissioned and transferred to the army.[24] In 1993 the navy laid up its six guided-missile patrol hydrofoils (PHMs), the Gray Terrors to the boat druggies.[25] These little ships had accounted for 28 percent of the navy's drug seizures. January 1994 marked the end of the only Coast Guard cutters developed specifically for drug interdiction; three surface-effect cutters based in Key West were mothballed.[26] Those fast and strange black and white craft had glided over the surface of southern waters to capture many grass boats. In February 1994 the navy and the Coast Guard disestablished the Caribbean Squadron, which had been the mainstay of deep Caribbean drug patrols for the past ten years.[27] Customs too was not spared. By the end of 1995 it had decommissioned most of its interceptor boats.[28] A Coast Guard flag officer recently said that we have seen "a systematic dismantling of a splendid operational capacity to detect and interdict drugs."

Some maritime drug warriors took on a green tinge in the 1990s. Riverine warfare in the source countries followed a gradual shift in U.S. policy from transit-zone to source-country efforts. In 1992, Coast Guard international maritime law enforcement teams (IMLETs) with DEA agents deployed on the rivers of Bolivia to train and support Bolivian naval personnel and national police raiding cocaine-processing facilities. Firefights with the enemy were not unusual.[29] U.S. Marine Corps and navy personnel deployed about the same time and for the same purpose on rivers in Colombia to train and support Colombian Marine Corps forces organized in riverine combat elements (RCEs). Colombian forces have suffered heavy causalities in

The "Gray Terrors" of Hydrofoil Squadron Two head for Little Creek and decommissioning, June 1993. End of an era!
(Official U.S. Navy photograph by PH2 Douglas Mooney)

their battles with cocaine producers.[30] The river wars continue. It is too soon to estimate their effectiveness, and too far from salt water for consideration here.

There has been a recent change in the interdiction structure to coordinate the few forces left and provide a direct but limited chain of command. On 29 September 1994 the military joint task forces (JTFs) were renamed joint interagency task forces (JIATFs). More civilian enforcement people were added. Coast Guard commandant Robert F. Kramek is the U.S. interdiction coordinator. He will give policy guidelines to the JIATFs. Task force commanders, now called directors, are still subordinate to their commanders-in-chief but report to Dr. Lee Brown, the director of the Office of National Drug Control Policy. JIATF directors have tactical control of the assets assigned to them—a positive development.[31] Unfortunately, the command structure becomes fuzzy above the task force level. The JIATFs have to satisfy the Coast Guard commandant, their respective CinCs, and the drug czar. Time will tell if the new system is workable.

Our victory at sea in the drug war has left the old sea lanes open. It was a hard-fought twenty-year battle that proved we can reduce the supply side of the drug equation if we put our minds and resources to the task. Formidable reductions in the maritime shipment of drugs, especially marijuana, by dedicated vessels were accomplished. Adequate resources and perseverance were the keys. The drug war must be won in the minds and hearts of our children. In the meantime, we should maintain a barrier to the flow of mind-altering narcotics into our country. It is the right thing to do. We should reduce sea interdiction forces to a level consistent with the threat, but our remaining guns must be returned to battery. We secure the watch at our peril.

Notes

Newspaper articles, news releases, unpublished reports, agent notes, personal communications, and government memoranda and messages are cited completely in the notes. Books, periodical articles, and published government reports—all of which are described completely in the bibliography—are cited here in abbreviated form. Newspapers and statistical sources are further abbreviated as follows:

MH: Miami Herald
NNBIS, "Seizures": NNBIS Northeast Region, "Drug Related Vessel Seizures" (New York, 1984)
NYT: New York Times
SPT: St. Petersburg Times
USCG, *Digest:* U.S. Coast Guard, *Digest of Law Enforcement Statistics* (Washington, D.C., various years)
USCG, *General Statistics:* U.S. Coast Guard, *General Law Enforcement Interdiction Statistics* (Washington, D.C., 1986)
USCG, "Statistics, Pacific": U.S. Coast Guard, Pacific Area, "Narcotics Statistics, Pacific Region, 1971–1989" (Alameda, Calif., 1989)

PREFACE
1. "Nixon's Plan to Fight Menace of Drugs," 60–62.
2. "Pot: Year of Famine," 36–37.
3. Taft, "Role of DoD," 6–9.

PROLOGUE: THE FIRST ONE HUNDRED YEARS

1. Lyle, "Logistics of Junk," 59–67.
2. Messick, *Grass and Snow,* 10.
3. Scheina, "Marriage," 13–15.
4. Green, *Smugglers,* 58.
5. Shannon, *Desperados,* 34–35; Green, *Smugglers,* 47–52.
6. Lyle, "Logistics of Junk," 59–67.
7. Jeffee, *Narcotics,* 27–28.
8. Messick, *Grass and Snow,* 17; Tully, *Secret War,* 163–68.
9. Shannon, *Desperados,* 36; Messick, *Grass and Snow,* 17.
10. Green, *Smugglers,* 85, 90–107.
11. Art Beauchamp, "Florida Dope Ring Crippled," *SPT,* 22 Mar. 1961, B1.
12. Schulz, "Smugglers of Misery," 45–54.
13. Galloway, "Vietnam Story," 36–48; Messick, *Grass and Snow,* 19.
14. Manheimer, Mellinger, and Balter, "Marijuana Use," 1544–45.
15. Green, *Smugglers,* 88.
16. Messick, *Grass and Snow,* 10–16.
17. Shannon, *Desperados,* 60–61.
18. "Drug Generation," 107–10.
19. Gollan, "Great Marijuana Problem," 74–80.
20. Schulz, "Smugglers of Misery," 45–54.
21. "Pot: Year of Famine," 36–37.
22. Shannon, *Desperados,* 53–55.
23. Tully, *Secret War,* 30–36.

CHAPTER 1. IT BEGINS, 1970–1973

1. "Blooming Traffic in Drugs," 41–44.
2. "Alarming Rise in Dope Traffic," 43–45.
3. Tully, *Secret War,* 233–42. Reprinted by permission of Harold Matson Co., Inc.
4. "France, Another Connection," 39.
5. Beck, "Bubble Trade," 38–47.
6. Shannon, *Desperados,* 26–27.
7. Based on interviews with business and government representatives in Jamaica conducted by author in 1980 while on assignment as a consultant for the United Nations.
8. Shannon, *Desperados,* 82–83.
9. Ibid., 79.
10. Based on author's prison interview with an indicted smuggler, 1987.
11. Based on author's recollection and notes for the period 24 Jan. 1972–18 Jan. 1973.
12. Laliberte, "Drug War at Sea," 55–57.
13. Dennis Sneiger, "Unlucky Boat's Pot Cargo Found," *Ft. Lauderdale News,* 15 June 1973, 1; personal communication with Comdr. David E. Henrickson, USCG (Ret.), 28 July 1994.
14. Larzelere, "Away the Prize Crew," 52–59.

15. Excerpts from agent Jorge E. Picon's patrol report, "Enforcement Fisheries Patrol, Bahama Islands, 23–27 September 1973," in author's collection.
16. How, "Coast Guard Approaching the Century's End," 92–107.
17. Adams, "Enforcing Unpopular Laws," 92–93.
18. James Savage et al., "Key West, Smugglers Island," *MH*, 16–21 Mar. 1980 (series).
19. NMFS Rep. to NNBIS, in EPIC, *Fishing Vessel Identification Guide*, 1, 44.
20. Based on author's prison interview with an indicted smuggler, 1988.
21. Based on author's recollection and notes for the period 1970–74.
22. Based on author's interview with an indicted smuggler, 1989.
23. Ibid.
24. Rodrigues, "Jamaica Defense Force Coast Guard," 6–7.
25. Based on author's prison interviews with the son of a convicted smuggler in 1984, while the individual was serving time on a federal conviction.
26. Green, *Finest Kind*, 226–27.
27. "Biggest U.S. Pot Haul Made in State," *SPT*, 7 Mar. 1973, 1A, 3A.
28. Ibid.
29. "U.S. Charges Seven in Massive Pot Seizure," *SPT*, 8 Mar. 1973, 1A, 17A.
30. Ibid.
31. Elaine Randolph, "Jurors Find Steinhatchee Seven Guilty," *SPT*, 10 Oct. 1973, 1B, 4B.
32. Jan Gowdown, "Steinhatchee Drug Trial, Twenty Years for Six, Ten for One," *SPT*, 30 Oct. 1973, 1B, 4B.
33. "Florida Based Factions Involved in Maritime Drug Smuggling," EPIC SR-08-80, May 1980, introduction only.
34. "3,000 Pounds of Pot Seized off Everglades," *SPT*, 8 Nov. 1973, 2B.
35. Douglas, *Everglades*, 2.
36. "25–30 Tons of Pot Seized, Eleven Charged in Nation's Largest Marijuana Bust," *SPT*, 25 Dec. 1973, 1B, 17B.
37. "State Grand Jury Eyed in Big Pot Haul," *SPT*, 28 Dec. 1973, 6B.
38. Messick, *Grass and Snow*, 24–39.
39. NMFS, *Fishery Statistics of the United States, 1969*, 199.
40. Mueller and Adler, *Outlaws of the Ocean*, 72.

CHAPTER 2. CROSSCURRENTS, 1974–1976

1. Canney, "Rum War," 21–39.
2. Messick, *Grass and Snow*, 63–65.
3. Shannon, *Desperados*, 68–69.
4. Based on the following *SPT* articles: Allan Cowan, "Attorneys Clash on Bond," 10 June 1974, 1B, 2B; Caroline Heck, "A Simple Fisherman Goes on Trial," 10 Dec. 1975, 1B, 2B; and Lucy Morgan, "Drug Charges Aren't New to This Family," 29 Aug. 1991, 1A, 2A.
5. Based on the following *SPT* articles: Caroline Heck, "Lawyer Says Pot Client Drowned," 7 Jan. 1975, 1B; Lucy Morgan, "Is Mystery Man in Drug Probe Really Dead?" 8 Mar. 1981, 1B; and Lucy Morgan, "With Stansel's Disappearance State's Drug Case Came Unraveled," 8 Mar. 1981, 4B.

6. Mueller and Adler, *Outlaws of the Ocean,* 72.

7. Thompson, *Fisheries Department: Annual Report,* 14.

8. Thomas E. Ricks, "Inside Dope, the Cocaine Business, Big Risks and Profits, High Labor Turnover," *Wall Street Journal,* 30 June 1986, 1:6.

9. Author's interview with retired Customs Patrol supervisor Richard P. Keating,1992; seizure statistics from Mueller and Adler, *Outlaws of the Ocean,* 30, 72.

10. Satchell et al., "Narcotics: Terror's New Ally," 30–37.

11. Michael Isikoff, "Drug Flights Unabated over Cuba," *Washington Post,* 28 June 1989, A20.

12. Editorial José Marti, *Narco Tráfico.*

13. Based on author's prison interviews with the son of a convicted smuggler in 1984, while the individual was serving time on a federal conviction.

14. Messick, *Grass and Snow,* 63–69.

15. Rosenberg, *Spivey Assignment,* 243, 281–85.

16. White, "Most Bitter Winter," 164.

17. NNBIS, "Seizures," 7–12.

18. Ibid.

19. Mills, *Underground Empire,* 134–41.

20. Morganthau et al., "Black Tuna Gang," 47; "Tuna Catch," 28.

21. USCG, "Statistics, Pacific," 2, enclosures 1–3.

22. Based on author's interview of Willard Wooten, 1987, and background information on Wooten provided by investigator James Decker of the Collier County state's attorney's office.

23. Seizure of M/V *Ea* described in a briefing book by Richard Keating, deputy district director of Customs Patrol, with reference to U.S. Middle District Court civil case 76-586 T-R.

24. "Florida Based Factions Involved in Maritime Drug Smuggling," EPIC SR-08-80, May 1980, A20, A21, B118.

25. Bergin, "Yacht Piracy," 36–38, 76, with companion article by Gibbs, "Piracy and Boat Theft: Rebuttals and Solutions."

26. Siler, "Tradition of Excellence," 35–37.

Chapter 3. The Flood, 1977–1978

1. White, "Most Bitter Winter," 164.

2. Messick, *Grass and Snow,* 89–102.

3. Lucy Morgan, "Ship That Disappeared in '77 Discovered at Bottom of Gulf," *SPT,* 21 May 1992, 1A, 3A.

4. Messick, *Grass and Snow,* 125–36.

5. Lucy Morgan, "Ship That Disappeared in '77 Discovered at Bottom of Gulf," *SPT,* 21 May 1992, 1A, 3A.

6. "Fire, Not Smugglers, Sent Boat to Bottom, Say Experts," *SPT,* 7 Aug. 1992, 5B.

7. Messick, *Grass and Snow,* 102–4.

8. Based on author's prison interview with an indicted smuggler, Apr. 1989.

9. Based on author's interviews with an indicted smuggler, June 1988.

10. Shannon, *Desperados,* 80–82.
11. Mills, *Underground Empire,* 139–41.
12. NNBIS, "Seizures," 6–7.
13. Lester, "Coast Guard Goes to 'War,'" 4–10.
14. "Florida Based Factions Involved in Maritime Drug Smuggling," EPIC SR-08-80, May 1980, B8, B24, B26, B27, B35, B52, B53, B62, B81.
15. Baker, "Naval and Maritime Events, 1977," 250.
16. Personal communication with Comdr. William Baker, U.S. Coast Guard Institute, Oklahoma City, Okla., 16 Feb. 1994, concerning the *Cigale* seizure.
17. Taken from the following articles in the *SPT*: "Pot Laden Freighter Seized," 15 Apr. 1978, 5B, and "Marijuana Smugglers Get Burned," 22 June 1978, 1B; and from the following in the *St. Petersburg Evening Independent:* "20 Tons of Pot Seized," 23 May 1978, 1A, and "Two Boats Seized," 3 June 1978, 6C.
18. Messick, *Grass and Snow,* 137.
19. Ibid., 106.
20. Ibid., 107.
21. Baker, "Naval and Maritime Events, 1978," 229.
22. Philipson and Llerena, *Freedom Flights,* 198–99.
23. Larzelere, "Coast Guard and the Southeastern Frontier," 146–47.
24. "Florida Based Factions Involved in Maritime Drug Smuggling," EPIC SR-08-80, May 1980, B85, B9, B15.
25. NNBIS, "Seizures," 6.
26. NDEPB, *National and International Drug Law Enforcement Strategy,* 22.
27. Eddy, Sabogal, and Walden, *Cocaine Wars,* 78–82, 131–45.
28. Messick, *Grass and Snow,* 52–54.
29. Seizure statistics for 1975 from "Battle against Drugs Takes to Seas," 69–71. Those for 1977 from Lester, "Coast Guard Goes to 'War,'" 4; and Baker, "Naval and Maritime Events, 1977," 250. Those for 1978 from Larzelere, "Coast Guard and the Southeast Frontier," 146–47; NNBIS, "Seizures," 8–9; and USCG, "Statistics, Pacific," enclosures 2 and 3.

CHAPTER 4. HIGH WATER, 1979–1981

1. "Dealers and Police Note a Marijuana Shortage in U.S," *NYT,* 27 Dec. 1979, A17.
2. Baker, "Naval and Maritime Events, 1979," 220–22.
3. Philipson and Llerena, *Freedom Flights,* 199.
4. Larzelere, "Coast Guard and the Southeastern Frontier," 146.
5. "Florida Based Factions Involved in Maritime Drug Smuggling," EPIC SR-08-80, May 1980, B59.
6. Based on author's prison interview with a convicted smuggler, July 1987.
7. Baker, "Naval and Maritime Events, 1979," 53, 64.
8. NNBIS, "Seizures," 5; Baker, "Naval and Maritime Events, 1979," 52–53.
9. USCG, "Statistics, Pacific," enclosures 2 and 3.
10. "Biggest Haul of Them All," 20–21.

11. Based on the following articles in the *San Francisco Chronicle:* Kevin Leary, "Coast Guard's Pot Hunt," 3 Aug. 1979, 5; and George Draper, "Marijuana Mother Ships' Confusion over Sunk Vessel," 4 Aug. 1979, 6.

12. USCG, "Statistics, Pacific," 3.

13. USCG, *General Statistics,* 2.

14. Caffrey, "Strategy of Enforcement," 2–5.

15. DiCarlo, "International Initiatives," 6.

16. Statement by Alvah Chapman in House of Representatives, *Review of the Administration's Drug Interdiction Efforts,* (hereafter cited as House, *Review of Efforts*), 95–99.

17. Based on author's prison interviews with convicted smugglers between 1984 and 1990.

18. "Bayou Bypass," 16; USCG, *General Statistics,* 9.

19. Baker, "Naval and Maritime Events, 1980," 224.

20. Tony Schwartz, "Venezuelan Boat Seized Near L.I. with Marijuana," *NYT,* 25 Mar. 1980, B2; NNBIS, "Seizures," 5.

21. NNBIS, "Seizures," 4–5; "Vessel Carrying 20 Tons of Marijuana Seized," *NYT,* 26 Sept. 1980, B5 (*Roon Diep* spelled *Roundiep* in article).

22. NNBIS, "Seizures," 4–5.

23. USCG, "Statistics, Pacific," 4.

24. William Cooney and Maitland Zane, "Pot Raid—Cargo Seized," *San Francisco Chronicle,* 12 Sept. 1980, 1, back page.

25. Statement by Rear Adm. D. C. Thompson in House, *Review of Efforts,* 292, with data from USCG, *General Statistics,* 2.

26. Smuggler operational security measures based on author's interviews with indicted and/or convicted smugglers between 1984 and 1990.

27. Smuggler organization, divisions of labor, and additional security measures based on author's interviews with indicted and/or convicted smugglers between 1984 and 1990 and with law enforcement personnel.

28. USCG, *General Statistics,* 2.

29. Statements by William J. Anderson and Dominick L. DiCarlo in House, *Review of Efforts,* 32, 147–51.

30. Based on author's recollection and supervisory notes concerning Special Agent Ronald Dearmin's alleged violation of the NMFS firearms policy on 25 Feb. 1986 and personal communication with NMFS agent Dearmin on 9 Oct. 1993.

31. Statement by Rear Adm. D. C. Thompson in House, *Review of Efforts,* 292.

32. Brelis, "Searching for Colombian Gold," 26–27.

33. "Twenty-six aboard Freighter Jailed after Chase in Florida Straits," *NYT,* 24 June 1981, A14.

34. "Law Enforcement Monograph One," U.S. Coast Guard, Seventh District, Miami, 24 Aug. 1984, 2.

35. Jewell, "Saying No in the Caribbean," 76–78.

36. Robert Pear, "155 Indicted as Two Year Federal Drug Inquiry Ends," *NYT,* 13 Mar. 1981, A12; "Why the Crackdown," 8.

37. NNBIS, "Seizures," 3, 8.

38. "Coast Guard Saves a Honduran Vessel Carrying Marijuana," *NYT,* 21 July 1981, B7; NNBIS, "Seizures," 4.
39. Shawn G. Kennedy, "Hashish in Sunken Ship Found off Jersey Shore," *NYT,* 26 Oct. 1981, 6B.
40. USCG, "Statistics, Pacific," 4–5, enclosure 3.
41. "Cocaine Haul from Land, Sea Totals 371 Pounds," *SPT,* 17 Dec. 1981, 1B, 16B; Daniel J. Vargas, "Smuggler Enters Guilty Plea in Drug Case," *SPT,* 13 July 1991, 6B.
42. Mermelstein, *Man Who Made It Snow,* 116–19.
43. Taft, "Role of DoD," 7–9.
44. Statement by Alvah Chapman in House, *Review of Efforts,* 94, 104.

CHAPTER 5. BATTLE LINES, 1982–1983

1. White House, *Reagan Record,* 5; statement by Charles F. Rinkevich in House, *Review of Efforts,* 175–209.
2. Statement by Charles F. Rinkevich in House, *Review of Efforts,* 181.
3. Shannon, *Desperados,* 94–97.
4. Statement by William Anderson in House, *Review of Efforts,* 36–44.
5. Statement by Larry Orton in ibid., 496–99.
6. Juliana, "Battlefront America," 10–15.
7. Statement by Congressman Glenn English in House, *Review of Efforts,* 1.
8. Statement by Florida governor Bob Graham, "Strategies for Drug Control Efforts," in ibid., 80–87.
9. Bush, "National Law Enforcement," 4.
10. Statement by Rear Adm. D. C. Thompson in House, *Review of Efforts,* 291–92.
11. Statement by Charles F. Rinkevich in ibid., 180; USCG, *General Statistics,* 7.
12. Ibid.
13. Christmann, "Naval Air Tags Smugglers," 47; USCG, *General Statistics,* 7.
14. Statement by Rear Adm. D. C. Thompson in House, *Review of Efforts,* 295.
15. Christmann, "Naval Air Tags Smugglers," 48.
16. Kelly, "Feds vs. Drug Runners," 54–55.
17. NNBIS, "Seizures," 3; "Second Marijuana Ship Seized off New England," *NYT,* 24 July 1982, 6; "New York Drug Seizures Rise with Florida Route Cut," *NYT,* 18 Aug. 1982, B4.
18. NNBIS, "Seizures," 2–3.
19. Garcia, Alva, and Yang, "Running Pot," 20; Mueller and Adler, *Outlaws of the Ocean,* 110–13; "Three on Boat Held as Smugglers," *NYT,* 24 Aug. 1982, A16.
20. Mueller and Adler, *Outlaws of the Ocean,* 103; Garcia, Alva, and Yang, "Running Pot," 20.
21. NNBIS, "Seizures," 8–11.
22. USCG, "Statistics, Pacific," 5.
23. Scheina, "U.S. Coast Guard in 1982," 81; Mueller and Adler, *Outlaws of the Ocean,* 184.
24. Laliberte, "Drug War at Sea," 57; USCG, *General Statistics,* 2.

25. NNICC, *Narcotics Intelligence Estimate, 1983,* 9.

26. From author's notes summarizing marijuana and cocaine seizures by land, sea, and air for 1981–91 from various sources including EPIC and Coast Guard reports.

27. Shannon, *Desperados,* 110, 117–19, 413.

28. Mermelstein, *Man Who Made It Snow,* 145–47.

29. Ibid., 150–53.

30. Ibid., 147, 153–55, 211–13, 233–34, 278.

31. Michael Isikoff, "Drug Flights Unabated over Gulf," *Washington Post,* 28 July 1989, A20.

32. "U.S. Drug Charges Cite Four Cuban Aides," *NYT,* 6 Nov. 1982, 1, 6.

33. Statements by Charles F. Rinkevich and James Lucas in House, *Review of Efforts,* 198, 403; Shannon, *Desperados,* 483.

34. Statement by Alvah H. Chapman in House, *Review of Efforts,* 88–105.

35. "Everglades City Shifts from Fishing to Drugs," *NYT,* 15 Aug. 1982, 27.

36. "Twenty-eight People Arrested in Everglades City," *SPT,* 8 July 1983, 1B, with subsequent articles.

37. Statements by Congressmen Glenn English and by Ronald Coleman et al. in House, *Review of Efforts,* 1–589.

38. "The President Announced Today the Formation of the National Narcotics Border Interdiction System," White House, Office of the Press Secretary, 23 Mar. 1983 (photocopy).

39. Based on author's recollection and notes concerning the early days of NNBIS.

40. Schowengerdt and Hart, "National Narcotics Border Interdiction System," 25–27.

41. Shannon, *Desperados,* 96–102.

42. Based on author's prison interviews with an indicted kingpin smuggler and two convicted smuggler vessel captains, 1987 and 1988.

43. "Law Enforcement Monograph One," U.S. Coast Guard, Seventh District, Miami, 10 May 1984, 1.

44. Based on author's recollection and notes concerning space-accountability searches.

45. "Law Enforcement Monograph One," U.S. Coast Guard, Seventh District, Miami, 10 May 1984, 2.

46. Ibid., 3–5.

47. Mueller and Adler, *Outlaws of the Ocean,* 90–91; USCG, *General Statistics,* 7, 9.

48. "Boat Crews Avoid Arrest in Drug Seizures," *SPT,* 25 Apr. 1983, 11B.

49. Mueller and Adler, *Outlaws of the Ocean,* 90–91; USCG, *General Statistics,* 7, 9.

50. Grubb and Scheina, "U.S. Coast Guard in 1983," 219.

51. NNBIS, "Seizures," 9, 10.

52. Ibid., 1–2, 8–9; "Marijuana Found aboard Freighter," *NYT,* 17 Sept. 1983, 24.

53. USCG, "Statistics, Pacific," 5–6.

54. "1,065 Pounds of Cocaine Seized on Ship in Miami," *NYT,* 2 June 1983, A19.

55. "Snow Blizzard," 23.

56. USCG, *General Statistics*, 2; "Maritime Smuggling Trends, 1983–1984 (9 Mos.)," EPIC, El Paso, Tex., 15 Oct. 1984 (photocopied interim report using graphs).

57. Whipple, "Is 'SQ3' Unconstitutional?" 143–45.

CHAPTER 6. THE OFFENSIVE: PART ONE, 1984

1. PTT equipment description based on industry and government brochures describing the Argos Satellite System in author's files (e.g., "Argos Location and Data Collection Satellite Systems," Service Argos, Inc., Landover, Md., 1987); and on discussions with NOAA personnel at the National Data Buoy Program and the National Environmental Satellite Data and Information Service in 1987–88.

2. Shannon, *Desperados*, 160–61; "Cocaine Valued at $1.2 Billion Reported Seized in Colombia," *NYT*, 21 Mar. 1983, A1, A4.

3. Hewitt et al., "Cocaine Assassination," 48.

4. Joel Brinkley, "U.S. Is Seen Losing War on Cocaine Smuggling as Planes Get Through," *NYT*, 8 May 1984, A12.

5. Alan Riding, "Colombia Starts to Feel Side Effects of Drug Trade," *NYT*, 20 May 1984, E2.

6. Marlise Simons, "Cocaine Industry Has Spread to the Amazon Basin," *NYT*, 27 May 1984, L12.

7. "Held at Gunpoint, Campers Report," *MH*, 7 Mar. 1984, 18.

8. Based on an incident report, "Marijuana/Hostage Incident; Key Largo, Fla., 19–20 June 1984," filed by author with NNBIS Miami on 6 July 1984.

9. Joel Brinkley, "Rampant Drug Abuse Brings Calls for Move against Source Nations," *NYT*, 9 Sept. 1984, L1, L12; Joel Brinkley, "The War on Narcotics: Can It Be Won?" *NYT*, 14 Sept. 1984, A1, A12.

10. Shannon, *Desperados*, 220–23; Lamar, Diederich, and Wippman, "Bust of the Century," 26.

11. Based on an interview with an indicted smuggler at the author's office, 1989.

12. Jennifer L. Schenker, "U.S. Navy to Blockade Drug Lanes?" *MH*, 17 Nov. 1984, 1A; Duca, "Ad Hoc Drug War," 91 (Duca's curriculum vitae); Lockwood, "Blocking Caribbean Drug Traffic," 101.

13. Based on author's recollection and unclassified Hat Trick briefing notes recorded on 10 Nov. 1984.

14. Duca, "Ad Hoc Drug War," 88; Lockwood, "Blocking Caribbean Drug Traffic," 101.

15. Jennifer L. Schenker, "U.S. Navy to Blockade Drug Lanes?" *MH*, 17 Nov. 1984, 1A; "U.S. Planes to Increase Patrols Near Colombia," *NYT*, 18 Nov. 1984, L33.

16. Brigham, "U.S. Coast Guard in 1984," 60.

17. Based on author's recollection and unclassified Hat Trick briefing notes recorded at OVP/NNBIS during 1984–85.

18. "U.S. Effort Fails to Make Big Dent on Drug Smuggling from Colombia," *SPT*, 25 Nov. 1984, 2B.

19. Joel Brinkley, "Few Smuggling Boats Are Caught, Officials Say," *NYT*, 10 Aug. 1984, A10.
20. "Drug Bang," 46.
21. Fred Strasser, "Cutter Halts Cocaine Boat in Largest Sea Haul Ever," *MH*, 3 Apr. 1984, 1B.
22. "Defendant's Case Has Come to Light," *MH*, 15 Apr. 1984, 1B.
23. "Law Enforcement Monograph One," U.S. Coast Guard, Seventh District, Miami, 10 May 1984, 5; "Three Pot-Laden Ships Seized by U.S.," *MH*, 28 Jan. 1984, 1B.
24. "Coast Guard Brings in Vessel Hauling 25 Tons of Marijuana," *MH*, 6 Feb. 1984, 3B; USCG, *General Statistics*, 7.
25. "Shrimp Boat Halted by Fire, Guard Reported," *MH*, 7 Feb. 1984, 1B.
26. "Pot-Laden Freighter Towed to Key West," *MH*, 12 Feb. 1984, 2B; USCG, *General Statistics*, 6.
27. "Two Pot-Laden Boats Towed to Key West," *MH*, 21 Feb. 1984, 7A; USCG, *General Statistics*, 9.
28. "Two Ships, 18 Tons of Pot Seized," *MH*, 26 May 1984, 3B; USCG, *General Statistics*, 7.
29. "Freighter Seized with Drugs," *NYT*, 6 June 1984, A24; USCG, *General Statistics*, 6; 794 F2d 1503, 1503–5.
30. 794 F2d 1503, 1506–9.
31. Ibid., 1509–16.
32. Ibid., 1513–16.
33. "Fishing Boats Seized with Pot," *MH*, 6 June 1984, 1D; "Three Arrested, 10 Tons of Pot Seized," *MH*, 17 June 1984, 3B.
34. Based on author's recollection and field notes.
35. Ibid.
36. "Maritime Smuggling Trends, 1983–1984 (9 Mos.)," EPIC, El Paso, Tex., 15 Oct. 1984 (photocopied interim report using graphs).
37. "M/V *Ramsland*, NNBIS NE Post Seizure Analysis," NNBIS Northeast Region, New York, Feb. 1985, 6–8.
38. Ibid., 7–8.
39. "Marijuana Worth $6 Million Seized on Yacht in England," *NYT*, 6 Oct. 1984, L2.
40. USCG, "Statistics, Pacific," 6–7.
41. Brigham, "U.S. Coast Guard in 1984," 60, 64; USCG, "Statistics, Pacific," 7; USCG, *General Statistics*, 7.
42. USCG, *General Statistics*, 2.
43. "Maritime Smuggling Trends, 1983–1984 (9 Mos.)," EPIC, El Paso, Tex., 15 Oct. 1984 (photocopied interim report using graphs).
44. NDEPB, *National and International Drug Law Enforcement Strategy*, 38–39.
45. Alan Riding, "Shaken Colombia Acts at Last on Drugs," *NYT*, 11 Sept. 1984, A12.
46. "Jamaicans Seize Marijuana in Harbor Worth $35 Million," *NYT*, 31 Oct. 1984, A2.

CHAPTER 7. THE OFFENSIVE: PART TWO, 1985

1. Shannon, *Desperados,* 192–94.

2. Iyer et al., "Fighting the Cocaine Wars," 26–33.

3. McBee, "Flood of Drugs," 52–57.

4. "Draft Interdiction Strategy," Office of the Vice President, Washington, D.C., 25 Apr. 1986, 3.

5. Howard Kurtz, "Bahamian, U.S. Agents Seize $100-Million in Drugs," *SPT,* 20 Apr. 1985, 1.

6. "Draft Interdiction Strategy," Office of the Vice President, Washington, D.C., 25 Apr. 1986, 3; news release by Vice President George Bush about Hat Trick II, 11 Nov. 1985.

7. White House, *Reagan Record,* 18.

8. "Draft Interdiction Strategy," Office of the Vice President, Washington, D.C., 25 Apr. 1986, 3–4.

9. Shannon, *Desperados,* 195–97.

10. "Three Nabbed, Cocaine Seized on Boat," *MH,* 6 Apr. 1985, 3D.

11. "577 Pounds of Cocaine Seized," *MH,* 8 Apr. 1985, 6B.

12. Waldschmidt, "TACLET, Helo Set Record"; Jeff Leen and Peter Hamm, "Coast Guard, Town Seize Tons of Cocaine," *MH,* 9 May 1985, 1D.

13. Keith Lawrence, "Palm Beach County Drug Raid Nets 2,000 Pounds of Cocaine," *SPT,* 20 June 1985, 8B.

14. Brian Duffy, "Customs Fires on Drug Boat in Pennekamp Park," *MH,* 2 Aug. 1985, 2D.

15. Based on author's interviews with a confidential informant, 1987; and personal contacts with personnel of DEA, Customs, and NNBIS.

16. "Two Fishing Vessels with 20 Tons of Pot, Eight Crewmen Seized," *Key West Citizen,* 28 May 1985, 1.

17. Based on author's interviews with indicted and/or convicted smugglers between 1984 and 1990.

18. "Coast Guard Seizes 20 Tons of Pot, Arrest Six," *SPT,* 27 Aug. 1985, 6B.

19. Based on author's recollection, notes, and inspection of the vessel *Argana II,* St. Petersburg, Fla., 11 June 1985; and his subsequent preparation for the trial of the master and crew.

20. Taken from author's 22 Oct. 1985 report to NNBIS Miami with information provided by Florida Marine Patrol officer Jeffrey Russo on the suspect F/V *Laura Lee.*

21. Arnold Markowitz, "U.S. Sinks Dope Ship Near Colombia," *MH,* 13 Nov. 1985, 11A.

22. "Coast Guard Seizes Marijuana Freighter," *MH,* 15 Dec. 1985, 5A.

23. Personal communications with Comdr. William B. Baker, USCG, 11 Feb. 1993, and Mr. Ernie Caamano, ex-BM2, USCG, 7 Sept. 1993.

24. "M/V *Fatuk,* Post Seizure Analysis, NNBIS NE, July 1985," NNBIS Northeast Region, New York, July 1985, 1, 3, 7, 9–11.

25. "F/V *Master Mike* Post Seizure Analysis, NNBIS NE, Dec. 1985," NNBIS Northeast Region, New York, Dec. 1985, 1, 5, 8–15.

26. Personal communications with Special Agents Stanley Jacobsen, FBI (Ret.), and Daniel Dunn, U.S. Customs Service, 5 Sept. 1993.
27. USCG, "Statistics, Pacific," 1989, 7–8.
28. "M/V *Fatuk* and 'Sister Ship' M/V *Saja*," NNBIS Northeast Region, New York, 3 Mar. 1986; Tony Meyers, "Firm Buys Abandoned Load of Grouper," *Daily Astorian*, 17 Feb. 1986, 3.
29. Personal communication with Special Agent E. Neil Van Horn, U.S. Customs Service, Portland, Ore., Mar. 1988.
30. NDEPB, *National and International Drug Law Enforcement Strategy*, 29.
31. USCG, *General Statistics*, 2.
32. GAO, *Drug Smuggling*, 39.
33. NNICC, *National Narcotics Intelligence Consumers Committee Report, 1985–1986* (hereafter cited as *NNICC Report*), 4, 9, 13–15.
34. USCG, *General Statistics*, 2.
35. Laliberte, "Measuring Drug-Interdiction Effectiveness," 93–94.
36. Duca, "Ad Hoc Drug War," 87.
37. Blowitski, "Lone Rangers Team Up," 113–14.
38. McCarthy, "Coast Guard's New Island," 109–10.
39. Brigham, "U.S. Coast Guard in 1985," 43–44.
40. Watkins, "PHM's," 88.
41. USCG, *General Statistics*, 7.

CHAPTER 8. THE EBB, 1986

1. USCG, *General Statistics*, 2.
2. Duca, "Ad Hoc Drug War," 86.
3. GAO, *Drug Smuggling*, 40.
4. Based on author's prison interview with an indicted smuggler, Apr. 1989.
5. Fuss, "Lies," 68.
6. Based on Lang and Taylor, "America on Drugs," 50; and Duffy et al., "Drugs, New Prime Time," 16–17.
7. "Lining up to Join the War against Drugs," 6; Morganthau et al., "Drug Fever," 39.
8. Based on a memorandum, subject "Draft Interdiction Strategy," from the Interdiction Strategy Working Group to Ken Thompson, NDEPB staff, 25 Apr. 1986, 1–14 (in author's files); GAO, *National Drug Policy Board*, 2, 11.
9. Based on author's recollection and notes from discussions with personnel at DEA, Customs, and OVP/NNBIS, Washington, D.C., 11–12 Apr. 1987.
10. Alan Riding, "Latin Nations Join U.S. Effort to Combat Drugs," *NYT*, 27 Apr. 1986, 8L.
11. Lacouture, "Isn't It Time," 84–85.
12. Duca, "Ad Hoc Drug War," 88.
13. From statement of Lt. Gen. R. Dean Tice, USAF (Ret.), director, DoD Task Force on Drug Enforcement, to Congress, Feb. 1986 (from NNBIS documents).
14. "Opening Statement by the Vice President," Vice President, Office of the Press Secretary, press conference, Houston, Tex., 7 June 1986.

15. Joel Brinkley, "U.S. Aides Accuse Mexico as Drug Trade Surges," *NYT,* 12 May 1986, A4.
16. Morganthau et al., "Can We Stop the Smugglers?" 28–29.
17. Based on author's recollection and notes; and Keating, "Alliance," 44–45.
18. William Safire, "Thataway Posse Comitatus," *NYT,* 28 Feb. 1986, A31.
19. Based on author's recollection and unclassified notes taken at Hat Trick meetings, Washington and Miami, 1986 and 1987.
20. Lockwood, "Blocking Caribbean Drug Traffic," 101–2.
21. Ibid., 102–3.
22. Ibid., 105–6.
23. GAO, *Drug Smuggling,* 30–31.
24. Duca, "Ad Hoc Drug War," 89.
25. Based on unclassified message 181848Z MAR 86 from OVP/NNBIS to NNBIS regions, GAO, and other addresses, subject "GAO Audit."
26. Based on unclassified message 090559Z SEP 86 from commander, Seventh Coast Guard District, to all Seventh District units, subject "Implementation of FDSS."
27. 794 F2d 1503, 1513–16.
28. Based on author's recollection, notes, and inspection of the vessel *Navesink,* 18 Jan. 1986; and interview with owner's ex-wife, 26 Jan. 1986.
29. Based on author's recollection and notes for 21–22 Feb. 1986; and Richard Wallace, "New Drug Command Post Makes First Bust," *MH,* 23 Feb. 1986, 2B.
30. Ibid.; Brigham, "U.S. Coast Guard in 1986," 47; Coast Guard unclassified message 301700Z APR 86 from Group St. Petersburg to commander, Seventh District, subject "Smuggling via Freighters—FL West Coast."
31. Brigham, "U.S. Coast Guard in 1986," 48; Geoffrey Tomb, "Unmanned Pot Boat Takes Cutter on Wild Chase," *MH,* 9 Apr. 1986, 2B.
32. Arnold Markowitz, "Onetime Cutter Seized; Pot Found Aboard," *MH,* 15 May 1986, 6D.
33. Personal communications by author with U.S. Customs special agent Daniel Dunn, May 1986; Lucy Morgan, "Dixie County Drug Smugglers Back in Jail," *SPT,* 4 Apr. 1987, 4B.
34. Based on author's recollection, notes, and inspection of the vessel *D'Milu's One* at St. Petersburg, Fla., 17 June 1986; and subsequent notes prepared as a witness for the master's trial.
35. Based on author's recollection and notes recorded at the U.S. Coast Guard station, St. Petersburg, Fla., 29–30 July 1986, concerning the search for and subsequent seizure of the vessel *South C. Express.*
36. Based on author's recollection, notes, and inspection of the vessel *South C. Express,* Tampa, Fla., 3–4 Aug. 1986.
37. Based on author's preparation for trial as a witness in *U.S. v. Armando Soto-Rivera,* U.S. District Court, Tampa, Fla., 14–16 Oct. 1986.
38. Based on author's preparation for trial as a witness in *U.S. v. José Rafael Abello-Silva,* U.S. District Court, Tulsa, Okla., 10–16 Apr. 1990; and Julie DelCour, "Ex-Partner Recalls Abello Drug Deals," *Tulsa World,* 12 Apr. 1990, A1, A4.

39. Based on author's prison interview with a convicted smuggler, June 1987.
40. Based on author's recollection and notes concerning the seizure of the F/V *Churumbel,* Apr. 1986.
41. Based on Coast Guard unclassified message 1110092 MAY 86 from commander, Eighth District, to Comm. Station New Orleans, subject "Alert F/V *Lady Virgo*—Overdue"; and author's interview of a survivor of the *Lady Virgo,* Tarpon Springs, Fla., 22 May 1986.
42. USCG, *Digest,* 1991, 4.
43. Jeff Leen, "Cocaine Seized on Truck Sets a National Record," *MH,* 30 Oct. 1986, 1A.
44. Brigham, "U.S. Coast Guard in 1986," 45, 51; "Navy Fires at Pot Boat, One Wounded," *MH,* 16 Nov. 1986, 25A.
45. "Coast Guard Gets Biggest Pot Haul," *SPT,* 22 Nov. 1986, 2B; "50 Tons of Marijuana Seized," *NYT,* 24 Nov. 1986, B17.
46. "M/V *Jane K*–M/V *Breton Seahorse* Post Seizure Analysis," NNBIS Northeast Region, New York, Sept. 1986, 5–6.
47. Based on author's recollection and notes concerning discussions with Coast Guard Pacific Area personnel, 1989.
48. Couey and Coletta, "National Drug Interdiction System," 96.
49. Brigham, "U.S. Coast Guard in 1986," 47; Wallace Turner, "Northwest Seen as Growth Area in Drug Smuggling," *NYT,* 22 Jan. 1986, A15.
50. USCG, "Statistics, Pacific," 8.
51. Personal communication with Customs special agent Al Fraga, Honolulu, Hawaii, 3–4 May 1989.
52. Based on author's report "Pacific Smuggling Survey and Agency Cooperation" for the ONDCP, Washington, D.C., 23 May 1989.
53. *NNICC Report,* 9–13.
54. Robert Lindsey, "Marijuana Drive Reduces Supplies and Raises Prices," *NYT,* 4 Oct. 1986, 6L.

CHAPTER 9. BACK-STRAPPED, 1987

1. Based on author's interview with an indicted midlevel smuggler at a U.S. attorney's office in Florida, Oct. 1988.
2. Thorsen, "Waging the War on Drugs," 172.
3. Based on author's notes for a *Proceedings* article published in 1989. Primary sources were various NNBIS and EPIC reports and personal communications with intelligence analysts.
4. USCG, *Digest,* 1991, 4.
5. Statistics extracted from Marra, *Readers Guide to Periodical Literature,* 1986 and 1987, 1319–20, 1325–27.
6. Smolowe et al., "Fall of a Cocaine Kingpin," 37; Guy Gugliotta and Jeff Leen, "Inside the Medellin Cartel," *SPT,* 11 June 1989, 1D, 4D.
7. NDEPB, *National and International Drug Law Enforcement Strategy,* i–xv.
8. Ibid., 13, 81–100.
9. GAO, *National Drug Policy Board,* 8.

10. House of Representatives, *National Drug Policy Board: A Failure in the War on Drugs,* 1, 3, 13–14, 18–19.
11. Based on author's recollection and notes taken at the National Drug Interdiction Operations Oversight Group meeting at Old Executive Office Building, Washington, D.C., 9 Apr. 1987.
12. Based on author's recollection and notes relative to the NNBIS regional evaluations taken at various OVP/NNBIS sessions, Washington, D.C., 1987.
13. Duca, "Ad Hoc Drug War," 90–91.
14. Young, Griffes, and Tomasellin, "Customs or Coast Guard?" 67–73.
15. Naples, "Justice for the Coast Guard," 84–89.
16. Gerald Godshaw, Ross Koppel, and Russell Pancoast, "Anti-Drug Law Enforcement Efforts and Their Impact," Wharton Econometrics, Bala Cynwyd, Pa., 1987, draft executive summary, 1–5.
17. Based on OVP/NNBIS message 141536Z July 87, subject "Request for Comments and Suggestions on How an Expanded EPIC May Best Serve NNBIS"; and subsequent discussions by author with line agency and NNBIS intelligence personnel.
18. *NNICC Report,* 9, 13, 26.
19. Larry Rohter, "Mexico Challenging U.S. on Drugs," *NYT,* 17 July 1987, A3.
20. Lockwood, "Blocking Caribbean Drug Traffic," 104–5.
21. Based on author's recollection, notes, and inspection of the vessel, 23 Jan. 1987; his preparation as a witness for the trial of the master and crew, Mar. 1987; and his interviews of the convicted master at a federal prison, 1987.
22. Based on author's contacts with investigator James Decker of the Collier County state's attorney's office, 1987–88; and a telephone interview with Decker, 13 Dec. 1993.
23. Fuss, "It Worked in Florida," 66.
24. Based on author's recollection and notes taken on 9 Sept. 1987; and an NNBIS file memorandum dated the same day requesting Capt. David Matthews, USMC, to participate in a visit to Everglades City, Fla.
25. "Blue Lightning Strike Force, Florida West Coast Intelligence Groups," Florida Department of Law Enforcement, Florida Intelligence Center, undated, 1–2.
26. "Condo Radar to Scan Seas for Drugs," *SPT,* 19 Feb. 1987, 3B.
27. Based on author's recollection, notes, and inspection of the vessel *Lady Hamilton III,* St. Petersburg, Fla., 19–20 Mar. 1987; and his interviews with the crew.
28. Based on author's interview with an arrested smuggler at a Coast Guard station in Florida, Jan. 1987, and a briefing of this individual at Krome Detention Center, Miami, July 1987, with excerpts from unclassified message 201633Z July 1987 from the USS *John L. Hall.*
29. Brigham, "U.S. Coast Guard in 1987," 172, 174; USCG, *Digest,* 1991, 17–18.
30. Jeff Leen, "Coast Guard Seizes 64 Tons of Pot," *MH,* 5 June 1987, 4C; Brigham, "U.S. Coast Guard in 1987," 180.
31. "Five Jailed in Puerto Rico in Big Cocaine Seizure," *NYT,* 10 May 1987, L23; "Search for Lost Diver Yields Huge Coke Bust," *MH,* 10 May 1987, 9A.

32. Based on a chart prepared by investigator Bruce Meader, U.S. Customs, Tampa, Fla., showing the positions of drug boats seized in the eastern Gulf of Mexico and Yucatán Channel during 1987–89.

33. "*My Girls* Seized," 3; personal communication with Collier County investigator James Decker, 30 Oct. 1994.

34. From author's trial testimony in *U.S. v. Franklin Thomas Norris et al.*, case 87-12-Cr.-FT. M.-17, U.S. District Court, Middle District of Florida, Tampa Division, 29–30 July 1987; and notification by U.S. attorney's office, Tampa, Fla., of the Eleventh Circuit Court ruling in this case (Oct. 1988).

35. Based on a note to author from Customs air interdiction officer Tom Maher, 18 June 1987, describing the seizure of the vessel *Triton Express;* and personal communication with Customs senior special agent Maher, 16 Nov. 1993.

36. Based on author's recollection, notes, and inspection of the vessel *Claribel,* Panama City, Fla., 21 May 1987; and personal communication with Collier County investigator James Decker, 30 Oct. 1994.

37. Based on author's prison interview with an indicted smuggler, June 1988.

38. References to the *Carmiel* and *Charlotte Louise* seizures based on author's recollection, notes, and inspection of the vessel *Carmiel,* Tampa, Fla., 29 May 1987; his interviews of the vessel's captain and chief engineer, Tampa, 18 Sept. 1987; his interview of the captain at a prison, 28 Sept. 1987; and personal communications with DEA special agent Ted Handoga, Montreal.

39. Based on author's recollection and notes taken at Naples, Fla., on the night of 6–7 Oct. 1987; and his afteraction and postseizure report concerning the seized vessel *Nella* completed 27 Oct. 1987.

40. Based on author's recollection, notes, and inspection of the vessel *Yoko Maru No. 77,* Port Manatee, Fla., 31 Oct. 1987; his preparation as a witness in the trial of the crew in Feb. 1988; and his meeting with OCDETF agents from Boston.

41. Based on author's interview with an indicted smuggler at the U.S. attorney's office, Tampa, Fla., 6 Oct. 1988.

42. Arnold Markowitz, "Cocaine Seizures by Coast Guard Doubled in 1987," *MH,* 14 Jan. 1988, 1B.

43. Marshall, "War on Drugs with Real Troops?" 15.

44. Brigham, "U.S. Coast Guard in 1987," 179.

45. USCG, "Statistics, Pacific," 9–10, enclosures 3 and 10.

46. Based on Coast Guard unclassified message 281830Z JAN 88 from Intelligence Coordination Center, Washington, D.C., to commander, Pacific Area, subject "Pacific Region Non-Commercial Maritime Narcotics Trafficking: A Threat Evaluation for CY 1988."

47. "Interrogating the Prisoners," 3.

48. Richard Morin and Jodie Allen, "Are We Shooting Ourselves in the Foot in the War on Drugs?" *Washington Post,* 26 June 1988, C1, C4.

49. "UN Drug Conference Is Convened in Vienna," *NYT,* 18 June 1987, A14.

CHAPTER 10. SILENCE AND EDDIES, 1988

1. Carson, *Silent Spring,* 1–9.
2. Fuss, "It Worked in Florida," 67.
3. Carson, *Sea around Us,* 143.
4. Based on author's notes for the period 1986–90 for a *Proceedings* article published in 1989. Primary sources were various NNBIS and EPIC reports and personal communications by author with intelligence analysts.
5. USCG, *Digest,* 1991, 4.
6. Laliberte, "Measuring Drug-Interdiction Effectiveness," 94.
7. Walsh and Plattner, "Miami Nice," 20–21.
8. Bradley Graham, "Power of Colombia's Drug Traffickers Undermining Government," *SPT,* 2 Mar. 1988, 19A.
9. Clancy, *Clear and Present Danger.*
10. Sandza, "Drug Wars," 35.
11. Philip Shenon, "Noriega Indicted by U.S. for Links to Illegal Drugs," *NYT,* 6 Feb. 1988, A1–5.
12. "Drug Smugglers Used Cuban Base for U.S. Shipments, Jury Charges," *NYT,* 27 Feb. 1988, A6.
13. "Colombian Tied to Drug Empire Is Found Guilty," *NYT,* 20 May 1988, A1, A32.
14. Fuss, "It Worked in Florida," 66–67; personal communication by author with Customs special agent David Weatherly, 26 Nov. 1993.
15. "National Drug Policy Board, Leadership Evolving, Greater Role in Developing Budgets Possible," GAO, Washington, D.C., 12 Feb. 1988, 2–5, 15–19, 27–28.
16. NDPB, *Lead Agency Committee Reports,* 291.
17. "Implementation Guidelines for Maritime Interdiction Plans," U.S. Coast Guard and U.S. Customs Service, signed by William von Raab, commissioner, U.S. Customs Service, 25 Feb. 1988, and P. A. Yost, admiral, U.S. Coast Guard commandant, 26 Feb. 1988.
18. NDPB, *Lead Agency Committee Reports,* Air Plan, 5, 9–10, 13, 20, and Maritime Plan, 5–6, 32.
19. Diaz, "DoD Plays in the Drug War," 76, 78.
20. House of Representatives, *Americans on Drugs,* 2–3.
21. Memorandum of 30 Mar. 1988 from Attorney General Edwin Meese III to all U.S. attorneys, subject "Combined Zero Tolerance/User Prosecution Initiative."
22. "Yacht Seized over 1/10th Ounce of Pot," *MH,* 8 May 1988, 1A.
23. "Zero Tolerance Policy Modified," *SPT,* 24 May 1988, 6A.
24. USCG, *Digest,* 1991, 4.
25. Church et al., "Thinking the Unthinkable," 12, 14.
26. Marshall, "Flying Blind," 1606.
27. USCG, *Digest,* 1991, 25.

28. Based on Coast Guard unclassified message 301903Z APR 88 from commander, Seventh District, to commandant, Coast Guard, subject "Law Enforcement Sitrep One and Final F/V *Luz Marina* Seized"; and personal communication with Lt. Comdr. William Baker, USCG, Coast Guard Institute, 16 Nov. 1993.
29. Curtis Krueger and Milo Geyelin, "Massive Drug Load Seized in Pinellas," *SPT,* 5 May 1988, 1A, 4A; Milo Geyelin, "Pieces in Local Drug Puzzle Point to Cartel," *SPT,* 8 May 1988, 1A, 15A.
30. Based on author's interview with an indicted Colombian smuggler, Tampa, Fla., Apr. 1988.
31. Based on report of the seizure of the M/V *Grace Caroline* by Lt. D. S. Egli, USCG, CO USCGC *Attu,* addressed to commander, Coast Guard Greater Antilles Section, 30 Aug. 1988.
32. Egli, "First B-Class 110," 12.
33. Based on author's prison interview with an indicted smuggler, Apr. 1989.
34. Richard Cole, "Smuggler Whose Case Led to Scandal Implicates Castro," *SPT,* 22 Aug. 1989, 6A.
35. Julia Preston, "U.S. Reportedly Alerted Cuba to Drug Movements," *Washington Post,* 25 July 1989, A20.
36. David Hancock, "Third-Largest Coke Bust Made," *MH,* 21 Dec. 1988, 3B.
37. USCG, "Statistics, Pacific," 10–11, enclosure 3.
38. USCG, *Digest,* 1991, 4.
39. Gene Ayres, "Coast Guard Hits Jack (Pot), 22 Tons of Marijuana Seized," *Oakland Tribune,* 3 Mar. 1988, A1, back page; personal communication with RD1 Thomas Primeau, Coast Guard Pacific Area, May 1988.
40. Based on the following *San Francisco Chronicle* articles: Kevin Leary, "Mammoth Drug Bust on the Bay," 25 May 1988, A1; Edward Lempinen and Bill Wallace, "Sixth Arrest Made in Probe of Drug Tug," 26 May 1988, A1; and Harriet Chiang, "S.F. Jury Convicts Drug Tug Skipper," 23 Feb. 1989, A3.
41. "Pot Laden Ship Towed to Shore," *Sacramento Bee Final,* 7 July 1988, A16; *Seattle Post Intelligencer* articles by Steve Miletch, "Coast Guard's Story on Ship Seizure Changes," 12 July 1988, B1, B3, and "The Huge Pot Deal That Went up in Smoke," 27 July 1988, A1, A4; postseizure report by RD1 Tom Primeau, Coast Guard Pacific Area, Alameda, Calif., 25 Aug. 1988.
42. Personal communication with IRS special agent Fran Dyer, an OCDETF investigator, Seattle, Wash., 17 May 1994.
43. Based on author's recollection and notes taken during a visit to Coast Guard Pacific Area Command, 16–17 May 1989, including discussions on Pacific maritime smuggling with Lt. Christopher Olin, Lt. (jg) Kevin Conroy, and RD1 Thomas Primeau.
44. "Excerpts of Remarks by Vice President George Bush to Hackensack Chamber of Commerce, Hackensack, NJ, Thursday, 26 May 1988," Office of the Vice President, news release, 26 May 1988; notes from author's discussion with Howard Gehring, director, NNBIS, at Old Executive Office Building, Washington, D.C., 29 June 1988.

45. *Anti–Drug Abuse Act of 1988*, Public Law 100-690, 100th Cong., 2d sess.
46. Based on author's recollection and notes taken at National Drug Interdiction Operations Oversight Group Meeting hosted by Vice President Bush, Old Executive Office Building, Washington, D.C., 13 Dec. 1988.

CHAPTER 11. A VICTORY AT SEA, 1989

1. Unless otherwise indicated, all references to the *Turtola* seizure are based on author's recollection and notes taken on 4–5 Apr. 1989; his inspection of the vessel, St. Petersburg, Fla., 17 Apr. 1989; and his interviews with three of the indicted off-load crew.
2. Polmar, "U.S. Coast Guard," 170–71.
3. Personal communication with Customs special agent Tom Maher, Customs Air Branch, New Orleans, 3 Mar. 1994.
4. Personal communications with Coast Guard PO1 Edward A. Rubertas, 3 Mar. and 4 June 1994.
5. Personal communication with DEA special agent Sam Murad, Tampa, Fla., 3 Mar. 1994.
6. Duca, "U.S. Coast Guard in 1989," 194–95.
7. USCG, "Statistics, Pacific," introduction, 11, enclosures 2 and 3.
8. "Atlantic Ocean, Coast Guard Man Jumps off Cutter onto Drug Ship to Confiscate Dope," *MH*, 6 May 1989, 2B.
9. Based on a chart prepared by U.S. Customs investigator Bruce Meader, Tampa, Fla., showing the positions of drug boats seized in the eastern Gulf and Yucatán Channel during 1987–89.
10. Ibid.; "Cocaine Concealed in Truck, Seized at Port of Tampa," *SPT*, 3 Sept. 1989, 5B.
11. Jones, "Anatomy of a Major Drug Bust," 70–71.
12. USCG, "Statistics, Pacific," 11, enclosure 10.
13. Candy, "Another Big Bust in D7," 18; Sean Rowe, "Bust Nets Freighter, Three Speedboats, More Than a Ton of Coke," *MH*, 13 Sept. 1989, 3B.
14. "Coast Guard Stops 11,000 Lbs. of Cocaine in Largest Seagoing Bust," *The Press*, 5 Oct. 1989, 1; personal communication with Lt. Comdr. William Baker, senior Coast Guard representative, EPIC, El Paso, Tex., 1991.
15. Based on interviews with an indicted smuggler at author's office, 1989.
16. Jeffrey Good and Bruce Vielmetti, "Smuggling Has Destroyed Our Hometown," *SPT*, 14 May 1989, 1D.
17. "Cuban Tribunal Weighs Drug Case," *SPT*, 26 June 1989, A6.
18. Oppenheimer, *Castro's Final Hour*, 121–28.
19. Ibid., 162–63, 422–23.
20. Witkin and Cunco, "Inside the High-Flying Pot Industry," 27–28.
21. ONDCP, *National Drug Control Strategy*, 1991, 5.
22. USCG, *Digest*, 1994, 2.
23. Morganthau et al., "Bennett's Drug War," 18.
24. "CIA Gets Anti-Narcotics Unit," *SPT*, 28 May 1989, 7A.
25. ONDCP, *National Drug Control Strategy*, 1990, 83–84, and 1991, 118.

26. Letter from Capt. J. C. Trainor, USCG, commanding officer, U.S. Coast Guard Intelligence Center, to ONDCP, 15 June 1989, concerning Post-Seizure Intelligence Conference.
27. Irwin and Thomas, "Interview: Vice Admiral James C. Irwin," 60.
28. Lahneman, "Interdicting Drugs in the Big Pond," 56.
29. Kitfield, "Drugs," 12.
30. Memorandum by White House chief of staff to C. Boyden Gray, 7 Apr. 1989, subject "Transfer of National Narcotics Border Interdiction System Personnel."
31. "Nominee for 'Drug Czar' Has Tough-Talking Past," NYT, 13 Jan. 1989, D17.
32. William Bennett, "Strategy in the War on Drugs," SPT, 14 May 1989, 4D.
33. ONDCP, National Drug Control Strategy, 1991, 5–13.
34. "Drug Warrior," 20–24.
35. ONDCP, National Drug Control Strategy, 1990, 71.
36. Personal communication with a retired military person who served at ONDCP from 1989 to 1992, 3 Apr. 1992.
37. ONDCP, National Drug Control Strategy, 1989, 1–153.
38. "Seminar Guide, National Drug Policy Seminar," United States Naval War College, War Gaming Department, Newport, R.I., 30 Oct.–3 Nov. 1989.
39. ONDCP, Report of the National Drug Policy Seminar, 1989, 2–5; notes made by author as a member of the National Drug Policy Seminar Control Cell.
40. Abel, "Hunker Down Now!" 58–63.
41. Michael Isikoff, "Secret Part of Drug Plan Seeks Added Military Role," SPT, 10 Sept. 1989, 1A.
42. Personal communication with an intelligence analyst at EPIC, 19 Apr. 1993.
43. "Boardings Yield Drugs, Arrest," 20.
44. Brigham, "U.S. Coast Guard in 1991," 161; personal communication with IRS special agent John Willing, OCDETF coordinator, San Francisco, Calif., 12 Apr. 1994.
45. "Four Star Talk," 14.

EPILOGUE

1. Goldstein, "Drug Wars, Turf Wars," 25.
2. USCG, Digest, 1991, 4.
3. "Drugs, Alien Interdiction," 19.
4. "Marijuana Users Find 'High' Refers to Price," SPT, 23 Dec. 1990, 9A.
5. Personal communications with Customs special agent David Weatherly, Tampa, Fla., 12 July 1993, and with IRS special agent and OCDETF coordinator John Willing, San Francisco, Calif., 6 Apr. 1994.
6. "Marijuana Smugglers Busted," 9.
7. Personal communication with Customs marine enforcement officer Kenneth Hysell, 11 Mar. 1992.
8. "Cuba Turns over Drug Suspects to U.S," SPT, 19 Sept. 1993, 1A, 12A.
9. Witkin and Robinson, "New Frontier," 52.

10. Douglas Jehl and Marjorie Miller, "U.S. Planes Help Head off Drugs at Border," *Los Angeles Times,* 9 Apr. 1990, 1.
11. "Ship Loaded with Cocaine," *SPT,* 10 May 1993, 6B.
12. "Coke and Water," 24; "Drug Smuggler's Newest Vehicle, Homemade Subs," *SPT,* 18 Feb. 1994, 4A.
13. Susan Benesch, "Police Kill Drug King Escobar," *SPT,* 3 Dec. 1993, 1A, 3A.
14. Witkin, "New Assault on Cocaine," 21.
15. "Officials, Drug Seizures a Success," *SPT,* 25 Feb. 1993, 7A.
16. "Half-Billion Spent in Futile Attempt to Stop Airborne Drug Smugglers," *SPT,* 17 Aug. 1992, 9A.
17. ONDCP, *Breaking the Cycle,* 1.
18. Witkin, "How Politics Ruined Drug-War Planning," 29.
19. ONDCP, *National Drug Control Strategy,* 1994, 50.
20. Paul Wilborn, "A New Anti-War Protest," *SPT,* 5 Sept. 1993, 1D.
21. ONDCP, *Breaking the Cycle,* 7; ONDCP, *National Drug Control Strategy,* 1994, 12, 61.
22. Kime, Rainbow, and Armfield, "Interview: Admiral J. W. Kime," 95–96.
23. Leland, "Is TQM . . . ?" 100.
24. "Drug Tracking Blimps Decommissioned," *SPT,* 2 Apr. 1992, 4B.
25. Watkins, "PHM's," 87–88; Baker, "Combat Fleets," 87.
26. David Dahl, "Coast Guard Changes Course," *SPT,* 14 Jan. 1994, 1B, 5B; Baker, "Combat Fleets," 87.
27. Personal communication with Lt. Guy McArdle, USCG, 10 Mar. 1994.
28. Personal communication with Customs supervisor James Connelly, chief, National Marine Support Unit, 5 Apr. 1994.
29. "Jungle Operations," 2–5.
30. Pitts, "Fighting Drugs at the Source," 52–59.
31. Thomas, "Anti-Drug Effort Takes New Twist," 25.

Bibliography

Periodicals are abbreviated as follows:

CGCB: U.S. Coast Guard Commandant's Bulletin
N&WR: U.S. News and World Report
USNIP: U.S. Naval Institute *Proceedings*

BOOKS

Carson, Rachel. *The Sea around Us.* New York: Oxford Univ. Press, 1951.
————. *Silent Spring.* Cambridge, Mass.: Riverside, 1962.
Clancy, Tom. *Clear and Present Danger.* New York: G. P. Putnam's Sons, 1989.
Douglas, Marjory Stoneman. *The Everglades, River of Grass.* New York: Rinehart, 1947.
Eddy, Paul; Hugo Sabogal; and Sara Walden. *The Cocaine Wars.* New York: W. W. Norton, 1988.
Editorial José Marti. *Narco Tráfico, Crimen sin Fronteras.* Havana, Cuba: Publicaciones en Lenguas Extranjeras, 1989.
Green, Ben. *Finest Kind: A Celebration of a Florida Fishing Village.* Macon, Ga.: Mercer Univ. Press, 1985.
Green, Timothy. *The Smugglers.* New York: Waller, 1969.
Jeffee, Saul. *Narcotics: An American Plan.* New York: Paul S. Erickson, 1966.
Marra, Jean M., ed. *Readers Guide to Periodical Literature.* New York: H. W. Wilson, various years.
Mermelstein, Max. *The Man Who Made It Snow.* New York: Simon and Schuster, 1990.
Messick, Hank. *Of Grass and Snow.* Englewood Cliffs, N.J.: Prentice-Hall, 1979.

Mills, James. *The Underground Empire*. New York: Dell, 1986.
Mueller, G.O.W., and Freda Adler. *Outlaws of the Ocean*. New York: Hearst Marine Books, 1985.
Oppenheimer, Andres. *Castro's Final Hour*. New York: Simon and Schuster, 1992.
Philipson, Lorrin, and Rafael Llerena. *Freedom Flights*. New York: Random House, 1980.
Rosenberg, Philip. *The Spivey Assignment*. New York: Holt, Rinehart and Winston, 1979.
Shannon, Elaine. *Desperados*. New York: Penguin Books, 1988.
Tully, Andrew. *The Secret War against Dope*. New York: Coward, McCann and Geoghegan, 1973.

ARTICLES

Able, Christopher A. "Hunker Down Now!" *USNIP,* Dec. 1990, 58–63.
Adams, Michael R. "Enforcing Unpopular Laws." *USNIP,* Oct. 1978, 92–93.
"The Alarming Rise in Dope Traffic." *N&WR,* 2 Sept. 1968, 43–45.
Baker, A. D., ed. "Combat Fleets." *USNIP,* June 1994, 87.
Baker, Brent. "Naval and Maritime Events, 1977." *USNIP,* May 1978, 229, 250.
———. "Naval and Maritime Events, 1978." *USNIP,* May 1979, 229.
———. "Naval and Maritime Events, 1979." *USNIP,* May 1980, 52–64, 220–22.
———. "Naval and Maritime Events, 1980." *USNIP,* May 1981, 224.
"Battle against Drugs Takes to Seas." *N&WR,* 27 Mar. 1978, 69–71.
"Bayou Bypass, the Louisiana Connection." *Time,* 29 Dec. 1980, 16.
Beck, Horace. "The Bubble Trade." *National History,* Dec. 1976, 38–47.
Bergin, Edward J. "Yacht Piracy." *Motor Boating and Sailing,* Mar. 1975, 36–38, 76.
"The Biggest Haul of Them All." *Macleans,* 23 June 1980, 20–21.
"Blooming Traffic in Drugs." *N&WR,* 7 Dec. 1970, 41–44.
Blowitski, Raymond W. "Lone Rangers Team Up." *USNIP,* Apr. 1987, 113–14.
"Boardings Yield Drugs, Arrest." *CGCB,* Apr. 1990, 20.
Brelis, Dean. "Searching for Colombian Gold." *Time,* 11 May 1981, 26–27.
Brigham, Lawson W. "U.S. Coast Guard in 1984." *USNIP,* May 1985, 60.
———. "U.S. Coast Guard in 1985." *USNIP,* May 1986, 46.
———. "U.S. Coast Guard in 1986." *USNIP,* May 1987, 47–48.
———. "U.S. Coast Guard in 1987." *USNIP,* May 1988, 172–74.
———. "U.S. Coast Guard in 1991." *USNIP,* May 1992, 157–63.
Bush, George. "National Law Enforcement: A Personal Perspective." *Investigators' Journal,* Fall 1987, 4.
Caffrey, Ronald J. "The Strategy of Enforcement." *Drug Enforcement,* Fall 1982, 2–5.
Candy, Veronica. "Another Big Bust in D7." *CGCB,* Sept. 1989, 18.
Canney, Donald L. "Rum War, the U.S. Coast Guard, and Prohibition." *CGCB,* Feb. 1989, 21–39.
Christmann, Timothy J. "Naval Air Tags Smugglers." *Naval Aviation News,* May/June 1983, 47–49.
Church, George J., et al. "Thinking the Unthinkable." *Time,* 30 May 1988, 12–19.
"Coke and Water." *N&WR,* 14 Feb. 1994, 24.

Couey, Ralph F., and David R. Coletta. "A National Drug Interdiction System." *USNIP,* Feb. 1987, 95–96.

Diaz, Charley L. "DoD Plays in the Drug War." *USNIP,* May 1990, 76–86.

DiCarlo, Dominick L. "International Initiatives to Control Coca Production and Cocaine Trafficking." *Drug Enforcement,* Fall 1982, 6.

"Drug Bang." *Time,* 10 Dec. 1984, 46.

"The Drug Generation: Growing Younger." *Newsweek,* 12 Apr. 1969, 107–10.

"The Drug Warrior." *Newsweek,* 10 Apr. 1989, 20–24.

"Drugs, Alien Interdiction Keep Seventh District Busy." *CGCB,* Oct. 1991, 19.

Duca, G. Stephen. "The Ad Hoc Drug War." *USNIP,* Dec. 1987, 85–91.

———. "The U.S. Coast Guard in 1989." *USNIP,* May 1990, 190–200.

Duffy, Brian, et al. "Drugs, New Prime Time." *N&WR,* 11 Apr. 1986, 16–17.

Egli, Dane S. "First B-Class 110 Has Hot Patrol in Caribbean." *CGCB,* Oct./Nov. 1988, 12–13.

"Four Star Talk." *CGCB,* Apr. 1990, 14–15.

"France, Another Connection." *Time,* 13 Mar. 1972, 39.

Fuss, Charles M., Jr. "It Worked in Florida." *USNIP,* Dec. 1989, 66–67.

———. "Lies, Damn Lies, Statistics, and the Drug War." *USNIP,* Dec. 1989, 65–69.

Galloway, Joseph L. "Vietnam Story." *N&WR,* 29 Oct. 1990, 36–48.

Garcia, Guy D.; Marilyn Alva; and John E. Yang. "Running Pot Where It's Not as Hot." *Time,* 29 Nov. 1982, 20.

Goldstein, Mark L. "Drug Wars, Turf Wars." *Government Executive,* Jan. 1990, 22–28.

Gollan, Antoni. "The Great Marijuana Problem." *National Review,* 16 Jan. 1968, 74–80.

Grubb, Michael D., and Robert L. Scheina. "U.S. Coast Guard in 1983." *USNIP,* May 1984, 219.

Hewitt, Bill, et al. "The Cocaine Assassination." *Newsweek,* 14 May 1984, 48.

How, A. B. "The Coast Guard Approaching the Century's End." *USNIP,* May 1974, 92–107.

"Interrogating the Prisoners." *Newsweek,* 25 June 1990, 3.

Irwin, James C., and V. C. Thomas, Jr. "Interview: Vice Admiral James C. Irwin, Commander Joint Task Force Four." *USNIP,* Oct. 1989, 60–64.

Iyer, Pico, et al. "Fighting the Cocaine Wars." *Time,* 25 Feb. 1985, 26–35.

Jewell, Paul D. "Saying No in the Caribbean." *USNIP,* June 1991, 76–78.

Jones, Melvin R. "Anatomy of a Major Drug Bust." *USNIP,* Oct. 1989, 70–71.

Juliana, James N. "Battlefront America: The Military Joins the Drug War." *Defense,* Mar. 1983, 10–15.

"Jungle Operations." *CGCB,* Feb. 1993, 2–5.

Keating, Francis A., II. "Alliance: Greater Than the Sum of Its Parts." *Investigators' Journal,* Fall 1987, 44–45

Kelly, Orr. "Feds vs. Drug Runners: Game Gets Trickier." *N&WR,* 4 Oct. 1982, 54–55.

Kime, J. W.; Fred Rainbow; and Follin Armfield. "Interview: Admiral J. W. Kime, Commandant of the Coast Guard." *USNIP,* Sept. 1990, 95–102.

Kitfield, James. "Drugs: The Military's New Unwinnable War." *Government Executive,* Mar. 1990, 10–14.

Lacouture, John E. "Isn't It Time to Declare War on the Drug Invaders?" *USNIP*, Dec. 1986, 84–85.

Lahneman, William J. "Interdicting Drugs in the Big Pond." *USNIP*, July 1990, 56–63.

Laliberte, Daniel A. "Drug War at Sea." *U.S. Naval Institute Naval History*, Fall 1992, 55–57.

———. "Measuring Drug-Interdiction Effectiveness." *USNIP*, June 1992, 93–94.

Lamar, Jacob V.; Bernard Diederich; and Larry Wippman. "The Bust of the Century." *Time*, 3 Dec. 1984, 26.

Lang, John S., and Ronald A. Taylor. "America on Drugs." *N&WR*, 28 July 1986, 50.

Larzelere, A. R. "Away the Prize Crew." *USNIP*, Jan. 1975, 52–59.

———. "The Coast Guard and the Southeastern Frontier." *USNIP*, May 1980, 146–47.

Leland, W. T. "Is TQM . . . ?" *USNIP*, Dec. 1992, 99–100.

Lester, Marianne. "The Coast Guard Goes to 'War.'" *The Times Magazine* (a supplement to *Army Times/Navy Times/Air Force Times*), 1 May 1978, 4–10.

"Lining up to Join the War against Drugs." *N&WR*, 22 Sept. 1986, 6.

Lockwood, John Weldon. "Blocking Caribbean Drug Traffic." *USNIP*, Dec. 1989, 101–6.

Lyle, David. "The Logistics of Junk." *Esquire*, Mar. 1966, 59–67.

McBee, Susanna. "Flood of Drugs: A Losing Battle." *N&WR*, 25 Mar. 1985, 52–57.

McCarthy, Frank N. "The Coast Guard's New Island in the Drug War." *USNIP*, Feb. 1986, 109–10.

Manheimer, D. L.; G. D. Mellinger; and M. B. Balter. "Marijuana Use among Urban Adults." *Science* 166 (1969): 1544–45.

"Marijuana Smugglers Busted." *Guardian* (Eighth Coast Guard District), Mar. 1991, 9.

Marshall, Eliot. "Flying Blind in the War on Drugs." *Science* 240 (1988): 1605–7.

———. "A War on Drugs with Real Troops?" *Science* 241 (1988): 13–15.

Morganthau, Tom, et al. "The Black Tuna Gang: Marijuana Smuggling." *Newsweek*, 14 May 1979, 47.

———. "Bennett's Drug War." *Newsweek*, 21 Aug. 1989, 18.

———. "Can We Stop the Smugglers?" *Newsweek*, 23 June 1986, 28–29.

———. "Drug Fever in Washington." *Newsweek*, 22 Sept. 1986, 39.

"*My Girls* Seized." *CGCB*, 26 July 1987, 3.

Naples, Donald A. "Justice for the Coast Guard!" *USNIP*, July 1987, 84–89.

"Nixon's Plan to Fight Menace of Drugs." *N&WR*, 28 July 1969, 60–62.

Pitts, Darren. "Fighting Drugs at the Source." *USNIP*, July 1994, 52–55.

Polmar, Norman. "The U.S. Coast Guard, Flying Higher and Farther." *USNIP*, Oct. 1989, 169–71.

"Pot: Year of Famine." *Newsweek*, 22 Sept. 1969, 36–37.

Rodriguez, M. L. "Jamaica Defense Force Coast Guard, Fifteen Years of Service, 1963–78." *Seawatch: Journal of the Jamaica Defense Force Coast Guard*, Aug. 1978, 6–7.

Sandza, Richard. "The Drug Wars: A Multinational Force?" *Newsweek,* 18 Apr. 1988, 35.

Satchell, Michael, et al. "Narcotics: Terror's New Ally." *N&WR,* 4 May 1987, 30–37.

Scheina, Robert L. "The Marriage of Fixed-Wing Aviation and the Cutter." *Naval Aviation News,* May/June 1983, 13–15.

———. "The U.S. Coast Guard in 1982." *USNIP,* May 1983, 78–81.

Schowengerdt, L. N., Jr., and T. P. Hart. "The National Narcotics Border Interdiction System." *U.S. Coast Guard Alumni Association Bulletin,* Nov./Dec. 1984, 24–29.

Schulz, William. "The Smugglers of Misery." *Reader's Digest,* Apr. 1970, 45–54.

Siler, Owen W. "Tradition of Excellence, Time of Change." *USNIP,* Mar. 1976, 35–37.

Smolowe, Jill, et al. "The Fall of a Cocaine Kingpin." *Time,* 16 Feb. 1987, 39.

"Snow Blizzard." *Time,* 12 Sept. 1983, 23.

Taft, William H. "The Role of DoD in Civilian Law Enforcement." *Defense,* Mar. 1983, 6–9.

Thomas, Vince. "Anti-Drug Effort Takes New Twist." *USNIP,* Nov. 1994, 25.

Thorsen, H. B. "Waging the War on Drugs." *USNIP,* May 1988, 172–73.

"Tuna Catch: Black Tuna Gang Marijuana Smuggling." *Time,* 14 May 1979, 28.

Waldschmidt, Dan. "TACLET, Helo Set Record." *Coastline* (Seventh Coast Guard District), June 1985, 1.

Walsh, Kenneth T., and Andy Plattner. "Miami Nice: George Bush as Drug Czar." *N&WR,* 11 July 1988, 20–21.

Watkins, Roger D. "PHM's: Ships Prematurely Put Away." *USNIP,* Aug. 1993, 88.

Whipple, Carlyle H. "Is 'SQ3' Unconstitutional?" *USNIP,* Apr. 1985, 143–45.

White, Lawrence A. "The Most Bitter Winter." *USNIP,* May 1978, 164.

"Why the Crackdown on Pot Smugglers." *N&WR,* 23 Mar. 1981, 8.

Witkin, Gordon. "How Politics Ruined Drug War Planning." *N&WR,* 22 Feb. 1993, 29.

———. "A New Assault on Cocaine." *N&WR,* 11 Jan. 1993, 21.

Witkin, Gordon, and Alice Z. Cuneo. "Inside the High-Flying Pot Industry." *N&WR,* 6 Nov. 1989, 27–28.

Witkin, Gordon, and Linda Robinson. "The New Frontier in the Drug War." *N&WR,* 3 Dec. 1990, 52.

Young, Richard; Michael Griffes; and John J. Tomasellin. "Customs or Coast Guard?" *USNIP,* Aug. 1987, 67–73.

PUBLISHED GOVERNMENT REPORTS

El Paso Intelligence Center (EPIC). *Fishing Vessel Identification Guide.* Reference document RD-05-85. El Paso, Tex., 1985.

General Accounting Office (GAO). *Drug Smuggling: Large Amounts of Illegal Drugs Not Seized by Federal Agencies.* Washington, D.C., 1987.

———. *National Drug Policy Board.* Washington, D.C., 1988.

House of Representatives, Committee on Government Operations. *The National Drug Policy Board: A Failure in the War on Drugs.* Washington, D.C., 1987.

———. *Review of the Administration's Drug Interdiction Efforts.* Washington, D.C., 1983.

House of Representatives, Republican Research Committee. *Americans on Drugs: A Republican Strategy.* Washington, D.C., 1988.

National Drug Enforcement Policy Board (NDEPB). *National and International Drug Law Enforcement Strategy.* Washington, D.C., 1987.

National Drug Policy Board (NDPB). *Lead Agency Committee Reports on Strategy and Implementation Plans.* Draft. Washington, D.C., 1988.

National Marine Fisheries Service (NMFS). *Fishery Statistics of the United States, 1969.* Statistical Digest no. 63. Washington, D.C.: U.S. Department of Commerce, National Oceanic and Atmospheric Administration, National Marine Fisheries Service, 1972.

National Narcotics Intelligence Consumers Committee (NNICC). *Narcotics Intelligence Estimate, 1983.* Washington, D.C., 1983.

———. *National Narcotics Intelligence Consumers Committee Report.* Washington, D.C., various years.

Office of National Drug Control Policy (ONDCP). *Breaking the Cycle of Drug Abuse.* Washington, D.C., 1993.

———. *National Drug Control Strategy.* Washington, D.C., various years.

———. *Report of the National Drug Policy Seminar, 1989.* Washington, D.C., 1990.

Thompson, R. W. *Fisheries Department: Annual Report and Review of Activities, 1975.* Nassau, Bahamas: Ministry of Agriculture, Fisheries and Local Government, 1976.

White House, Office of Public Affairs. *The Reagan Record on the Crusade for a Drug-Free America.* Washington, D.C., 1988.

Index

Note: Italicized page numbers indicate photographs.

Abello-Silva, Jose Rafael, 190
Able, Christopher, 185
Abrantes, Jose, 269
Active, USCGC, 65
Adventurer, 136–37
Adventurer III, 11–13
Aerial eradication, 31, 41, 51, 133
Aerostats: decommissioned, 284; described, 167–68; used to deter smugglers, 168
Agapi, 240
Aiakatsi, 183
Aircraft: A-7 Corsair, 96; C-130 Hercules, 130 *passim;* Citation 550, 217; E-2C Hawkeye, 97, 178; E-3 AWACS, 178; F-27 Fokker, 178; HU-16 Albatross, 20; HU-25 Falcon, 130, 178; J2F Duck, 1; LAMPS helicopter, 178, 237; Nomad, 256, 257, 259, 260; OV-1D Mohawk, 175; P-3 Orion, 98 *passim, 281;* RG-8A, 256, 257; SOC-4 Seagull, 1; UH-60 Blackhawk, 175
Alacrity, HMS, 263
Alava-Solano, Jacinto, 139, 140, 141
Albatross. *See* Aircraft
Albazul, 56
Alexander, Nollie, 54
Allison, Cecil, 247

Allison, 145
Amazon Sky, 238
American Civil Liberties Union, 4
American Society of Newspaper Editors, 273
Amidon, David, 140
Anderson, Andy, 84, 85
Andiamo, 8
Angelita, 156
Anti-drug Abuse Act, 174, 250, 274
April 19th Movement, 152
Argana II, 157–58, *159,* 220
Aries, USS, 114
Ark Royal, 235–36
Arrest attrition, 200
AS-1, government contract aerostat ship, 255, 256
Attu, USCGC, 238–40, *239*
AWACS. *See* Aircraft

Baggett, Bud, 188
Bahama Islands: Cay Sal Bank of, 49; Lobster War in, 11; protected smuggling routes through, 11, 28; spiny lobsters of, 34; stash houses on, 25
Bahamian Defense Force, 22
Baker, William, 55, 160, 210, 237
Barco Vargas, Virgilio, 201, 231

Barlovento, 263–64, 265
Barracuda, 142–43
Barrier patrols, 138
Bassols, Gonzalo, 105
Bastin, Wesley, 244
Bay of Pigs, 34
Bayou Bypass, 69–70
Bear, USCGC, 215, 219, 220
Belleau Wood, USS, 195
Bellomy, Ron, 223
Bermuda route, 98–100, 101
Berry, Mike, 217
Betancur, Belisario, 125, 133
Biaggi Act, 72
Bias, Len, 173
Bibb, USCGC, 100
Big L., 11–12
Birchfield, Joseph W., 186–87
Biscayne Freeze, 101
Bismark, 139
Blackhawk. *See* Aircraft
Black Tuna Gang, 38–39
Blow Me Down, 3
Blue Lightning Operations Command
    Center: described, 179–80, 183; radar
    coverage by, 212
Blue Lightning Strike Forces, 151, 212
Blue Seas, 84–85
Boat piracy, 40–41, 48
Boat theft, 40
Bocas, 58
Bohner, Christian, 243
Bolivian Navy, 284
Bongos (canoe-like craft), 20, 76
Bookhultz, Jack, 109
Boucan, Marcel, 8–9
Boutwell, USCGC, 102, 247–48, 249
Boyce, Christopher, 246
Brady, Philip D., 204
Brambleleaf, Royal Fleet Auxiliary Service
    tanker, 263
Brandt, Larry, 246
Break Sea, 85–86
Breed, Alan, 52–54
Breton Seahorse, 193–95
Brinkley, Joel, 127–28
Bristol County Drug Task Force, 100
Brown, Andy, 81–83
Brown, Raymond, 271
Bubble traders, 9
Buckridge, Chris, 225

Bureau of International Narcotics
    Matters, Department of State, 176
Bureau of Narcotics, 1
Bureau of Narcotics and Dangerous
    Drugs, 4, 11
Bush, George, *203;* announcement of
    NSDD by, 175–76; appointment of
    Drug Czar by, 273; comments on
    Operation Hat Trick by, 151; Desert
    Shield decision by, 282; NNBIS director,
    111, 121, 203, 205, 273; plans for fight-
    ing drug war as president, 250; South
    Florida Task Force director, 92, 93, 231
Busick, Peter, 55

Caamano, Ernie, 160
Calabres, 48
Cali cartel, 282
Camarena, Enrique, 128–29
Cannibispray, 260
Cape Current, USCGC, 66
Cape Fairweather, USCGC, 87–88
Cape Fox, USCGC, 155–56, 184–85
Cape Henlopen, USCGC, 194
Cape Morgan, USCGC, 144
Cape Romain, USCGC, 245
Cape Shoalwater, USCGC, 13, 57, 152–53
Cape Strait, USCGC, 70
Capo, David, 47
Capo, Floyd Farrel, 22, 24, 47
Caprice des Temps, 8–9, 86
Capstan, 164
Captain Black, 138
Carberry, George, 154
Cargo carriers, private/common, 40
Caribbean Squadron, 130, 178, 208, 274,
    284
Carmiel, 219–22, 264
Carmita Aracely, 226
Carter, Jimmy, 64
Castro, Fidel, 3, 58, 231, 241, 269
Catanzaro, John, 154
Catchalot II, 44
Cayman, 117
Central Intelligence Agency, Counter-
    Narcotics Center of, 271
Charlotte County Sheriff's Department,
    222, 223
Charlotte Louise, 221–22
Chase boat, described, 74–75, 117
Chase, Michael, 64

Cherokee, USCGC, 99–100
Chiang Kai-shek, 2
Chihuahua raid, 129, 132, 146
Chinook, 133–34, 154
Choke Points: Caribbean, 95, 130, 138, 213, 216; Pacific, 198
Chris Covey, 59
Christina M, 241–42
Churumbel, 191
Cigale, 55
Citation. *See* Aircraft
Citrus, USCGC, 145–46
Civil Air Patrol, 175
Civonney, 118
Clancy, Tom, 231
Claribel, 218
Clifton E. Sprague, USS, 96
Clinton, Bill, 282–83, 284
Clorox, 160–61
Cocaine: air deliveries of, 103, 133, 155, 165; air drops of, 89, 103–4, 150, 152, 280; concealed in lumber, 238; "Cowboys," 69, 126; crack, 227, 283; decreasing use of, 274; demand, 68; go-fast boats and, 150, 165, 280; industry, 60, 126; by merchant ships, 119–20; by noncommercial vessels, 134; by private vessels, 165; precursor chemicals and, 124; prices of, 103, 120, 207, 282; processing facilities for, 124; production of, 68, 124; record seizures of, 125, 154, 192, 264, 265, 270; routed through Cuba, 105, 232, 240; routed through Mexico, 176, 208, 280
Codes, alphanumerical and pad, 72–74, 222, 223
Cohen, Richard, 100–101
Coke machine (NOAA buoy), 156, 191, 222, 237, 255–56
Coleman, Ronald D., 107
Colflesh, Robert, 248
Colflesh, Samuel, 246, 248
Colombian Extradition Treaty, 125, 150, 201
Colombian Marine Corps, 284
Colombian Navy, 282
Colosa, 254
Command, Control, Communications and Intelligence Centers, 174
Comprehensive Crime Control Act, 173
Concealed compartments: beginning use of, 113–16; as external containers,

142–43; ingenious and expensive, 200; standard for prosecution, 182; use of, 136, 141–42, 158, 209; use of cargo rollers in, 137; Vidal-Hungria decision on, 141–42, 190
Conch Kingdom, 17
Confidence, USCGC, 196
Confidential Information Procedure Act, 216
Congressional management, 235
Conroy, Kevin, 247
Container smuggling, 126, 147, 226, 237, 241
Containerized cargo, 192
Contiguous Zone, 180
Contrabandistas, 9
Controlled drug deliveries, 188–90, 244
Coral I, 87–88
Cornbread Mafia, 270
Corsair. *See* Aircraft
Courageous, USCGC, 14–16, 48, 188, 191
Court of Appeals, Eleventh Circuit, 141, 182, 190, 216–17
Crawford, Richard, 232
Crawford. See Sunbird
Cross, Joe, 258
Cuban boatlift. *See* Mariel boatlift
Cuban Border Guard, 240
Cuban patrols, 280
Cueroni, Richard, 130
Cummings, Kevin, 109
Cushing, USCGC, 265

Dallas, USCGC, 114, 118
D'Amatto, Alfonse, 236
Daniels, Brian Peter, 56, 246–50, 268
Darlene C, 59
Dauntless, USCGC, 11–12, 44–45, 84–85, *85,* 138–39, 160, 262; PUC awarded to, 101
David, 66
Davis, Bennie, 126–27, *128*
Deadly force, 116, 137, 159, 193
Dearmin, Ronald, 80–83
Decisive, USCGC, 138, 158, 218–19, 237
Decker, James, 210, 216, 222–23, 232
DeConcini, Dennis, 92
Decoys, 138, 139
Defendant interviews, 166, 227
Defense Authorization Act, 234
Defense, Department of: contributions to drug war, 175; counter-narcotics mission

Defense, Department of *(cont'd.)*
  of, 94, 277; detecting and monitoring
  mission of, 234; directive 5525.5 by,
  90; entry into drug war, 90; Joint Chiefs
  of Staff and, 234; joint drug task forces
  of, 234, 272, 274–75, 285; responsibil-
  ities of commanders in chief, 234
Defense-in-depth, 178
Defense Intelligence Agency College, 271
Defense of necessity (smugglers), 67
De La Guardia, Anthony, 240, 269
De La Guardia, Patrico, 269
Delaurentis, Vincent, 190
Deltuvia, Susan, 232
Dependable, USCGC, 184, 213
Derber, Harold, 30–31, 35–36, 44
Desert Shield/Desert Storm, 282
Diecidue, David, 45
Diligence, USCGC, 139, 254, 255, 262
Disabling fire, 69, 70, 116, 159, 193, 248
Divino Criador, 162–63
D'Milu's One, 186–87
Dominable, 100
Don Alvaro, 65
Don Emilio, 36–37, *37,* 44, 68, 246
Don Frank, 71
Don Julio, 215
Douglas, Marjory Stoneman, 25
Downing, Jeff, 216
Drug abuse: cocaine, 2; decline of, 283;
  demand reduction, 276, 283; education
  as solution to, 4; at elementary school
  level, 4; morphine, 2; public concern
  over, 173; rationalizing as escape, 4–5
Drug culture: beginning of, 3; expansion
  of, 5, 44
Drug Czar: Bob Martinez as, 283; concept
  of, 274; efforts to legislate for, 173,
  202, 203, 205; established by legislation, 250; Lee Brown as, 283, 285;
  William Bennett as, 273–74, 275, 276
Drug Enforcement Administration, established, 26
Drug interdiction: air, 282; capabilities in
  the 1990s, 280; definition of, 26; deterrence by, 202, 208, 280; dilemma of,
  284; effectiveness of, 146, 172, 173,
  270; fragmented strategy of, 121; games,
  168; influenced by Biaggi Act, 72; measures of, 166, 202; rates of, 58, 166,
  200, 227; strategy in 1993, 283; verified by the opposition, 200, 211, 227

Drug legalization movement, 236–37
Drug Policy Foundation, 282
Drug residue, in clothing, 143, 182
Drug seizure summaries, general:
  1966–68, 4; 1975, 61; 1977–78, 61;
  1982, 103; 1983, 120; 1984, 146;
  1985, 165; 1986, 198; 1987, 200;
  1988, 230; 1989, 270
—New England, 52, 98, 100
—Northeast, 59, 66, 98, 101, 143, 226
—Pacific: 1970s, 39, 66–67; early 1980s,
  71, 88–89, 102, 119, 145; late 1980s,
  164, 195, 227, 241
—Southeast (including the Gulf of Mexico
  and the Caribbean), 58, 72, 83–84, 95,
  211, 279
—U.S. Coast Guard: 1973, 28; 1974,
  32–33; 1978–79, 68; 1980, 72; 1981,
  80; 1982, 102–3; 1983, 120; 1984,
  133, 146; 1985, 165; 1986, 172; 1987,
  201; 1988, 230; 1989, 270; 1990, 279
—U.S. Customs: 1975, 34; Louisiana,
  1980, 70
Drug subs, 281
Drug trade: earnings by, 173; end of
  1960s, 5; national attention to, 69
Drug War: 1987 turning point, 228; poli-
  tics, 27; theories for waging, 205–6;
  zones, 131
Duane, USCGC, 101, 118
Duca, Stephen, 130, 166, 175, 205, 212
Duck. *See* Aircraft
DUKW (amphibious truck), 55
Duncan, Bill, 204
Dunn, Daniel, 163, 186–87
Dyer, Fran, 248
Dysfunctional vessels, as indicators of sus-
  picion, 158

Ea, 40
Eagle, 164
Eagle B., 242
Eagle I, 195–96
Ecopesca IV, 55
Egli, Dane, 239
Eliason, Alan, 177
Ellis, James, 14
El Paso Intelligence Center: described, 93;
  expansion of, 207
El Toro, 159
Encounter Bay, 246–48
English, Glenn, 94, 107, 126, 132–33

Ercius, Walter R., 24, 25
Erwin, James C., 272
Escanaba, USCGC, 237
Escobar, Pablo, 103, 126, 282
Esso Bonaire III, 261, 263
Everglades City: legacy of, 268–69; location of, 51; pacification of, 211–12; as smuggling center, 106–7
Everglades National Park, as offload zone, 25
Exon Valdez, 283

Fairchild, Larry, 272
Falcon. *See* Aircraft
Farallon, USCGC, 168
Farnol, J. E., 21
Farragut, USS, 96
Fast and Easy, 184
Fatuk, 161–62, 164, 224, 225
Federal Drug Identification Number, 181
Federal Drug Seizure System, 181
Federal Rules of Criminal Procedure: #11, 172, 210; #35, 172, 209, 213, 248
Federal Witness Protection Program, 268
Feldkamp, Robert, 39
Fidelity, USS, 96
Fishery Conservation and Management Act, 83
Fishery enforcement patrols, 21, 52, 102
FL3254FR, 259
FL9362EM, 254, 255, 256–57, 259
FL9980EY, 260
Fleming, Mike, 154
FLIR (forward looking infrared radar), 217, 220, 256, 259
Floaters, described, 88
Flopper-stoppers, 19
Florida: close to drug sources, 10–11, 80; Gold Coast, 22, 52; off-loading in Keys, 17; offload procedures, 50–51; record seizures in, 26; seizures decreased, 230; statewide grand jury of, 31–32, 41
Florida Department of Law Enforcement, 24, 106
Florida Marine Patrol, 46, 47, 57, 81, 83
Flynn, Theresa, 232
Fokker. *See* Aircraft
Foley, Kevin, 44
Foreman, Percy, 25
Forwell, Michael, 248
Fourwinds, 102

Frazier, Douglas, 232
French Connection, 2
French Customs, 8
Fuel drums, as indicators of suspicion, 11
Fuller, Craig, 110
Furr, Walter, 190

Gallatin, USCGC, 52–54, 133–34, 158–59, 227
Galves-Diaz, Alfonso, 140
Gap, definition of, 20
Gehring, Howard, 109–10, 204
Gemini, USS, 215
General Accounting Office reports: amounts of drugs seized, 172; comments on National Drug Policy Board, 232–33; interdiction case follow-ups, 93; NNBIS audit of, 181; primary seizing agencies, 165
Georgia Bureau of Investigation, 36
Gilma I, 14–16
Gina IV, 36
Gladstone, 67, 68
Golden Lamb, 13
Golden Triangle, 2
Gollan, Antoni, 4–5
Gonzalez-Uribe, Miguel, 254, 258, 261
Gorman, Paul, 231
Goodwin, David, 47
Gould, Charles, 36
Goza Now, 153–54
Grace Caroline, 238–39, 239
Gracey, James S., 133
Graham, Bob, 176
Grass. *See* Marijuana
Gray, Dave, 160–61
Green, Ben, 22
Green, D. E., 14
Grimurkamban. See *Trio Senior*
Grindstaff, Clark, 154
Guajira Peninsula, 57, 76, 130
Guardship, British Navy, 22
Guillot Lara, Jaime, 106
Guinee, Paul, 235
Gunsmoke, 46–47

Halycon, 278
Hamilton, USCGC, 137
Handoga, Ted, 221
Hart, Terry, 109
Hashish, definition of, 88
Hawkeye. *See* Aircraft

Hawkins, Mary Ellen, 211–12
Heim, George, 275–76
Helen L II, 56–57, 58
Henrickson, David, 13–14
Henry Morgan II, 120
Herbicides: glyphosate, 133; 2,4-D and
    paraquat, 51, 61
Hercules. *See* Aircraft
Hercules, USS, 215, 224, 225
Heroin: Colombian, 147; Mexican black-
    tar, 2; Middle Eastern, 1, 2
Hewitt, Gaynor M., 134
Hidden compartments. *See* Concealed
    compartments
Hood, Douglas, 46
Horizonte, 262
Hostages, in Florida Keys, 126–27
Hovering Vessel Act, 36, 57, 114
How, A. B., 16–17
Howell, Jim, 109
Hughey, Dennis, 235
Humpers, 77
Hysell, Ken, 280
Hyuandai #23, 145

Immigrants: Chinese, 1, 160; Cuban, 3
Infrared sensors, 113
Ingersol, USS, 278
Ingersoll, John, 4
Intelligence (drug): all source center
    proposed, 174; essential elements
    of information, 204; human, 213;
    special, 181, 245, 278
Inter-American Commission for Drug
    Control, 174
Intrepid Venture, 244–46, *245*
IRT (infrared radiation thermometer), 20
Isla de Aruba, 55
Islander, 89
Island Express, 159–60

Jackowski, Mark, 261
Jacobsen, Stanley, 163–64
Jamaica Defense Force Coast Guard, 21
James Island, 56
Jane K, 195
J. J. Lorick, 264, 265
Joint Marine Interdiction Command
    Center, 202
John L. Hall, USS, 214
Johnson, Lyndon B., 4
Jones, Duane, 237

Jose Gregorio 70
Jubilee, 71
Juliana I, 52
Kaki, 38
Kane, R. E., 258, 259
Kang, Soo-Jin, 157–58
Karen Danica, 65
Karia, 184
Keating, Francis A. II, 177
Keating, Richard, 56
Kidd, USS, 116
Kilcoyne, Paul, 232
Kime, J. W., 283
Kingpin smugglers, 50, 60, 112
Knight, Michael J., 24
Kobakoff, Rich, 204
Korn, Barry W., 24
Kovachevich, Elizabeth, 268
Krentzman, Ben, 40
Kristen Jane, 66
Krumm, Lee, 132
Kuomintang Army, 2

Labrador. See *Night Train*
Lacouture, John E., 174–75
Lady Bridgid, 262
Lady Christina, 215
Lady Virgo, 191–92
Lamb, Steven G., 24
LAMPS. *See* Aircraft
Lanasa II, 156
Lara Bonilla, Rodrigo, 125
Larson, Jack, 210, 232
Larzelere, A. R., 14–16
LaToto, 215
Latuso, Tony, 45, 47
Laura Lee, 158
La Violencia, 9
Lawn, John, 176, 177
Layton, Ron, 177
Lead agencies, 201, 203, 233
Leahy, William P., 272
Lehder, Carlos, 60, 103, 150, 201, 232
Leland, W. T., 284
Line Island Trader, 196
Lion Heart, 119
Lipan, USCGC, 118, *119,* 137, 139–40
Lloyd B. Gore, 247, 249–50
Lober, Jerry, 153–54
Local User Terminal, 124
Lockwood, John, 178, 208
Lookout list, definition of, 65

LORAN (long-range navigation): in
Caribbean, 19; positions determined
by, used as evidence, 218; smuggler
incompetence with, 261; smuggler use
of, 255–56, 257
Lucky Star, 278
Lucy, 38
Luz Maria, 237, 255
Luz Marina. See *Luz Maria*

McAdams, Sandy, 46
McAdams, Sheila, 46
McCloy, USS, 193, *194,* 215
McCoy, Mike, 254, 255
McCoy, William S., 30
McCutcheon, John, 44
McKenney, Mark, 160–61
McLellan, Art, 210
McNamara, R. T., 126
McRich, 82–83
Maher, Tom, 217–18
Malargo I, 192
Mallow, USCGC, 242–43
Manatee County Sheriff's Department, 219
Mandatory minimum sentences, 172, 210,
227, 261, 283
Manitou, USCGC, 185, 255, 256, 260,
264
Marania, 55
Maria B, 278
Mariel boatlift, 58, 64, 68, 72, 90
Marielitos, 68
Marijuana: Acapulco Gold, 3, 5; Belizian,
129, 265; Boggs Act of 1951, 3;
Colombian, 9 *passim;* Colombian
Gold, 9, 31; cultivation of, 9; delivered
to Europe, 145; domestic production
of, 64, 198, 270; fall harvest of, 193;
famine, 5; flood of 1978, 61; ganja, 21;
increased use of, in 1994, 283;
Jamaican, 9, 21, 103; largest maritime
seizure of, 37; largest Pacific seizure of,
248; Mexican, 2, 3, 103, 128–29, 146,
165–66; unique packaging of, 260;
prices of, 198, 207, 270, 279; profile
transports of, 32, 44, 218; sailboat
smugglers of, 21–22; shortage of, in
1979, 64; shortage of, in 1990, 279;
smuggled through Cuba, 34–35, 240;
smuggled through Mexico, 207–8;
Southeast Asian, 227, 241, 262; Tax
Act of 1937, 3; tetrahydrocannabinol,

186; tonnage attrition of, 278; use of,
in 1967 and 1968, 4
Maritime Defense Zones, 206
Maritime smuggling: aspects of early, 3–4,
10, 27; changing methods and routes,
112; decline of, 284; early California
boats used in, 28; early limiting factors
in, 2; early phases of, 25; early voyages
involving, 18–20; expenses of, 79–80;
along Florida east coast, 28; along Flor-
ida gulf coast, 22, 27; patterns of, 41;
pro-fits in, 79; risks in, by 1988, 238;
security measures for, 51, 74–75, 78–79,
113–14, 265–66; specialized efforts in, 72
Martha. See *Sea Crust*
Maslanka, James G., 24
Master Mike, 162–63
Masters, Thomas O., 3
Matagorda, USCGC, 255, 256, 257–58
Matthews, David, 211–12
Matthews, Frank, 26
Maui, USCGC, 255, 256, 257, 258–59, 264
Mauro Hoyes, Carlos, 231
Meader, Bruce, 154
Medellin Cartel, 60, 89, 103, 125, 231, 282
Media: criticism of anti-narcotics efforts
by, 125–26, 127–28, 132, 133; decline
in drug interest by, 201; defeatist atti-
tude of, 150, 282; distraction of, 278;
drug war focus of, 277, 282; failure of,
to note passing of marijuana fleet, 231,
232, 270; influences on public opinion,
124; positive press, 147, 173
Meese, Edwin III, 173, 177, 228, 231, 235
Meinster, Robert, 39
Melpo Jr., 262
Mercedes, 214
Mercy Wiggins, 8, 24, 39
Merlin, 163
Mermelstein, Max, 89, 103–4
Mexican Bypass, 226
Mexican Navy, 191, 226, 264, 266
Miami Beach Shore Patrol, 152
Miami Citizens Against Crime, 90, 92
Miami/Dade Police Department, 154
Midget, USCGC, 67
Minski, Michael, 81–83
Miss Beverly Ann, 262–63
Miss Cecile, 96
Miss Connie, 55
Miss Debbie, 118
Missing boat cases, 47

Mississippi, USS, 97, *97*
Miss Jill II, 82–83
Mister Sidney, 58
Mizer, Lynn, 38
Moby Dick (cabin cruiser), 16
Moby Dick (freighter), 99
Moctezuma, 57
Modoc, USCGC, 55
Mohawk. *See* Aircraft
Mont Baron, 96
Morales, Ricardo, 60
Morgenthau, USCGC, 243
Moritz, Susan I., 66
Morris, Stan, 276
Motherships: cocaine, 241, 264; crews of, 77; hashish, 278; loading of, 76; marijuana, 30, 41, 265; name changes of, 75; operations of, 31, 58, 68, 71, 98–100, 254; Pacific, 76
Mr. Lucky, 13–14
Mrs. White, 139–41, 182
Mules (low-level smugglers), 112, 177, 280
Mulik, Linda, 213
Mullen, Francis, 92–93, 111
Mulvihill, Thomas, 240
Murad, Sam, 261
Murphy, Daniel J., 93, 109, 110, 111, 121
Murphy, John M., 40–41
Murtagh, Michael, 84
My Girls, 216

Nana II, 39
Naples, Donald, 206
Narcotics, supply and demand of, 2, 3, 129
Narcotics and Dangerous Drugs Information System, 112
Narwal, 114–15, 118
National, 39
National Data Buoy Program, 124
National drug control strategy, 275
National Drug Enforcement Policy Board, 173, 177, 201, 275
National Drug Intelligence Center, 271
National Drug Interdiction Operations Oversight Group, 111
National Drug Policy Board, 202, 205, 232–33, 234, 275; Interdiction Committee of, 233
National Foreign Intelligence Community: as regional advisers, 204; counter-narcotics mission of, 94, 271
National Guard, 175; of Georgia, 186

National Household Survey on Drug Abuse, 270
National Institute on Drug Abuse, 270
National and International Drug Law Enforcement Strategy, 201
National Marine Fisheries Service, 53, 80, 81, 126, 164
National Narcotics Border Interdiction System: audit of, 181; concerns about, 273; decline of, 233–34; described, 108–12; disestablishment of, 251; eulogy of, 275; internal audit by, 204; last day of, 272–73; regional evaluations of, 204; threat assessments/operation orders by, 205
National Narcotics Intelligence Consumers Committee, 60, 103, 165
National Narcotics Leadership Act, 276
National Oceanic and Atmospheric Administration, 46–47, 124
National Park Service, 184
National Security Decision Directives, 175–76, 277
National Student Association, 4
Naval Institute, 206
Naval War College: drug interdiction games at, 168; drug policy game at, 275–76
Navesink, 182–83
Nella, 222–23
Nelson, Alan, 177
Nerma, 264, 265
New Triton, 242
Nightstalker. *See* Aircraft, Nomad
Night Train, 44–45, 48
Nimitz, USS, 96–97
Nina I, 278
Nistanova, 118
Nite Hawk Two, 139
Nixon, Richard M., 5, 26
Nomad. *See* Aircraft
Noonan, Michael, 232
Noriega, Manuel, 231, 261, 264, 277
Northwind, USCGC, 130, *131,* 132
Nunez, Pete, 235
Nutri I, 38

Ocean Lady, 156
Ocean Queen, 142
Ochoa, Jorge, 89, 103
Ochoa Sanches, Arnoldo, 35, 241, 269
Ocracoke, USCGC, 215
Odessa, 36

Odin, 15
Offensive operations, 121, 124, 129, 152, 167
Office of National Drug Control Policy: absorbed NNBIS, 110; Border Interdiction Committee of, 274; established, 250; targeted for cuts, 283
Offload organizations, 61, 79, 200, 270, 278
Oil rig service and supply vessels, 40, 134–36, 137
Olarte Morales, Boris, 190
Olaug, 66
Olson, James Lee, 8
Onalay, 59
O'Neal, Harold, 24
Operations: Alliance, 177; Backribs, 130; Bahamas and Turks and Caicos, 106, 155, 175; Blue Lightning, 151–52, 175, 202, 275; Checkmate, 178; Chemcon, 124; Cuban Reunification, 58; Everglades, 107; Grouper, 87; Hat Trick, 129–32, 147, 175, 202; Hat Trick II, 132, 151–52, 158; Hat Trick III, 177–78, 274, 275; Intercept, 5; Peacemaker, 211, 226, 232, 255, 261; Spoke Outrider, 130; Spoke Tailgate, 130; Stopgap, 57; Wagon Wheel, 130, 147
Opium: Far Eastern, 2; Pacific coast smuggling of, 1; production of, 2
Oppenheimer, Andres, 269
Orca, 102
Organization of American States, 174, 231
Organized Crime Drug Enforcement Task Forces, 95
Orion. *See* Aircraft
Orion, state patrol boat, 81–83, *81*
Ouellet, USS, 243

Pacific Equatorial Route, 242
Pacific Great Circle Route, 196–97, 230
Pacific Star, 145–46, *147*
Panamco II, 196
Parks, Michael, 11–12
Patricia, 71
Perez, Andrew, 254
Perry, Dennis, 232
Persistence, 71
Petrel, USCGC, 263
Phillips, Mark, 39
Pickup boats: described, 79; name changes of, 75

Picon, Jorge, 16
Pindling, Lyndon, 106
Pirate's Lady, 45–47
Platform transmitter terminal, 124
Platshorn, Robert, 39
Platte, USS, 261
Point Barnes, USCGC, 15, 137
Point Barrow, USCGC, 8
Point Countess, USCGC, 195–96, 268
Point Francis, USCGC, 66, 69
Point Franklin, USCGC, 66
Point Jackson, USCGC, 161
Point Spencer, USCGC, 70
Point Steel, USCGC, 216
Point Swift, USCGC, 56, 160, 219, 221, 237
Point Thatcher, USCGC, 55, 255, 256, 258
Polaris (Gulf), 70
Polaris (Pacific), 89
Pompero, 25
Popeye. *See* Wooten, Willard
Poseydon, 245
Posse Comitatus Act: amended, 89, 93–94; legal test of, 98; mentioned, 57, 64, 89–90
Post-seizure procedures, 143, 182, 221–22, 271–72
Pot. *See* Marijuana
Pot Revolution, 3
Potomac, 71–72
President Monroe, 145
Primeau, Tom, 247
Profiteer, 184–85
Prohibition, 3, 17

Querube II, 115–16
Quester, 65

Rama Cay, 137
Ramsden, Donald, 159
Ramsland, 143–44
Ranger, 116
Rauch, Diana Robinson, 244, 246
Ravelo-Renedo, Fernando, 34–35, 105
Reagan, Ronald: addressed nation on drugs, 173; awarded PUC to *Dauntless,* 101; contributions to anti-narcotics efforts, 124; created SFTF, 92; emphasis on drug war, 205; established OCDETFs, 95; issued Executive Order 12590, 202; NSDD by, 175; signed legislation establishing ONDCP, 251

Recently departed master syndrome, 33
Recife, 97–98
Red Baron, 39
Red Beech, USCGC, 88
Reno, Janet, 283
Revolutionary Armed Forces of
    Colombia, 125
RG-8A. *See* Aircraft
Ricardo, 100
Rinkevich, Charles F., 92
Rinsi-Cadena, Nino, 44–45
Rio de Janeiro Conference, 174
Rio Panuco, 96
Robinson, Calvin, 244, 246
Robinson, Frank, 244
Robinson, John, 244
Robinson, William, 244
Rodney, Roosevelt, 241–43
Rodriguez Cruz, Rene, 105
Rogers, Don, 173
Rogers, T. J., 248
Roon Diep, 71
Roosevelt, Franklin D., 72
Rosangle, 139
Rose Marie, 10, 193
Route 26: described, 156; drug seizures
    on, 156, 215–16, 226, 237, 255
Royal Canadian Mounted Police, 67, 71,
    221, 249, 250
Royal Navy, 263
Ruby R, 244
Ruiz, Reinaldo, 240
Rum War, 17, 30
Running Bear, 56
Rush, USCGC, 278
Russo, Jeffrey F., 158
Ryan, John, 224

Sabrina, 237
Safe Boating Act, 41
Sagebrush, USCGC, 48, 116
Saint Nicholas, 118
Saja, 162, 164, 224, 225
Samarkanda, 67
Sandinistas, 152
Sandy Creek massacre, 46–47
San Nicholas, 137, 138
Santamaria Cuadrado, Aldo, 105–6
Santo Domingo Express, 241
Satellites: environmental, 124; rumors of
    tracking by, 64; surveillance by, 57–58
Savoie, Ken, 263

Schmoke, Kurt, 236
Schowengerdt, Nick, 109
Scott Bader, 59
Scuttling, of Pacific drug boats, 146
Sea Chariot, 280–81, *281*
Sea Crust, 53–54
Seagull. *See* Aircraft
Sea Hawk, USCGC, 136–37, 185
Sea Point, 264
Sea Wanderer, 193
Secure radio system, need for, 224
Seidler, Gerald, and Mary Beth, 3
Seized vessels, geographical distribution
    of, 146
Sellers, Jim, 153
Semmes, USS, 215, 224–25
Seneca, USCGC, 278
Shaffer, Gregory, 216
Shanti, 100
Shapiro, Herbert, 134
Shearwater, USCGC, 142, 263
Sherman, USCGC, 37
Shinkashu Maru, 145
Shkor, John, 110
Shrimpers: drug smuggling by, 17–18;
    Mexican, 191; multi-ton loads on, 27
Shuck, Patrick L., 97
Siboney, 39
Siler, Owen W., 41
Silvano, 71
Silverware, 39
Sims, George, 46
Singer, Robert, 242–44
Sitkinak, USCGC, 263
Slater, Charles D., 45, 47
Smuggler air reconnaissance, 78
Smuggler operation, code-named Denver,
    246, 248
Smuggling ventures: middleman, 75–76;
    principal, 75
Snowflake. See *Break Sea*
Snyder, William, 243
Sonner, Brian, 211–12
Soto-Rivera, Armando, 190
South C. Express, 187–90, *189*
South Florida Task Force: described,
    92–93; detractors of, 92–93; successes
    of, 94
Southern Belle, 59
Southern Governors Conference, 94–95
Soviet brigade in Cuba, 64, 90
Spivey, Larry, 36

Square grouper, 17
Stansel, Raymond Grady, Jr., 31–32
Starship, 38
Statement of no objection, explained, 33
Steadfast, USCGC, 65, 85–86, 157–58
Stealth boats, 238, 281
Steele, John D., 30–31, 36
Steinberg, Donald, 38, 52
Steinhatchee Seven, 24, 25, 47
Steinhorst, Walter, 47
Strongosky, David, 24
Struggle, 37–38
Sullivan, Pat, 14
Sunbird, 185–86
Sunburst, 102
Sunfish, 88
Sununu, John, 273
Surprise, 100
Suspicionless boardings, 120–21

Tagged targets, 111
Tamaroa, USCGC, 71
Tambs, Lewis, 133
Tampa, USCGC, 235
Taney, USCGC, 164
Teal, 40
Terrorist attacks, Colombia, 133, 152
Terry II, 162
Terry and Joe, 71
Terry's Dream, 59
Thomas E, 69
Thompson, D. C., 95–96
Thorsen, Howard B., 178, 200
Tice, R. Dean, 175
Tiki, 89
Tiki X, 100, 101
Tomoka, 30
Torrijos, Moises, 36
Torrijos, Omar, 36
Tortugas shrimp grounds, 17
Trainor, J. C., 271
Trampolining, 177, 280
Tranquilandia raid, 124–25, 132
Treasury Enforcement Communications
    System, 112
Trebach, Arnold S., 282
Trio Senior, 100
Triton Express, 217–18, *217*
Tsalickis, Michael, 238
Tuell, Les, 268
Turtola, 254–61, *259*, 262, 263, 273,
    278, 279

Tusker, 59
Two meter radios, as smuggling indica-
    tors, 74
Tysfjord, 70

Uithol, J. C., 44–45
Unimak, USCGC, 195
United Kingdom Agreement, 87, 114,
    139, 140
U.S. Air Force, Sector Operations Control
    Centers, 206
U.S. Army, helicopters for OPBAT, 106
U.S. Border Patrol, 177
U.S. Coast Guard: armed boarding par-
    ties, 17; Atlantic Area Command, 52;
    Auxiliary, 215; entry into drug war, 17;
    Famous-class cutters, 215; first drug
    seizure by, 11–13; Flag Plot, 33;
    Hamilton-class cutters, 1; Intelligence
    Coordination Center, 271; Inter-
    national Maritime Law Enforcement
    Teams, 284; Island-class patrol boats,
    168; Law Enforcement Detachments
    (defined), 114; Pacific Area Command,
    143, 272; Patrol Boat Squadron One,
    255, 256; Rescue Coordination Center,
    136; Seventh District, 83; surface-effect
    cutters, 95, 284; Tactical Law
    Enforcement Teams (defined), 90, 96
U.S. Customs: air fleet, 180–81; Bureau
    of, 28; Contraband Enforcement
    Teams of, 192, 226; decommissioning
    of boats, 184; designated service, 28;
    fast boats of, 180; Patrol, 26, 34
U.S. Marine Corps, 284
U.S. Navy: drug-hunting configuration,
    169; first assisted in drug seizure,
    96; first drug seizure from ship of,
    97; patrol hydrofoils (Gray Terrors)
    of, 169, 215, 284, *285*; role of, in
    providing ships, 90; summary of
    seizures, 169
U.S. v. Cruz-Valdez, 141
U.S. v. Vidal-Hungria, 141, 182, 190
U.S. v. Villamonte-Marquez, 120
Ute, USCGC, 115–16

V&S, 142
Valborg, 38
Valdez, Juan, 240
Valkyure, 71–72
Valley Forge, USS, 281

Vashon, USCGC, 262
Venture, 262
Venture Three, 242
Vera, 138
Vesco, Robert, 60
Victory at sea, 278, 285
Vienna Drug Control Conference, 228
Vietnam: anti-war movement, 4; commitment of American troops in, 4
Vigorous, USCGC, 59, 70, 186
Von Raab, William, 126, 132–33, 176, 177

W&V, 118
Wagnor, Pete, 38
Wammer Jammer, 118
Warren, Roy, 11
Weatherly, David, 232
Weaver, Bill, 273
Webster, William H., 271
Weed, Ted, 13
Wharton study, 206–7
Wha Yang. See Saja

White, Dick, 271
White, Mark, 176
White Sumac, USCGC, 237
Wood, Janet, 32
Wooten, Willard, 39, 210–11, 216, 222–23, 232

Xiphias, 114

Yamandai, 226
Yarborough, Larry, 84
Yoko Maru No. 77, 162, 224–25
Yost, Paul, 278
Young, Elvin, 213
Young, Richard, 205–6
Youth rebellion, 3
Yvette, 96

Zadareky, Joe, 109
Zedon Sea, 265, 270, 281
Zero-tolerance: policy, 235–36; seizures under, 230
Zoila, 117

ABOUT THE AUTHOR

Charles Fuss's government career spanned thirty-six years, from Naval Training Station San Diego to the Executive Office of the President. His service in the U.S. Navy and the Marine Corps Reserve included two combat tours off Korea in the USS *Bataan* (CVL-29). In 1959, having earned a Master's degree in biology from the University of Southwestern Louisiana, Mr. Fuss joined the old Bureau of Commerical Fisheries as a seagoing researcher. Eleven years later he became a National Marine Fisheries Service enforcement agent in the then-new National Oceanic and Atmospheric Administration and, eventually, special-agent-in-charge of the southeast region.

In 1983 Senior Agent Fuss was detailed to the Office of the Vice President, National Narcotics Border Interdiction System, as his agency's representative. Fisheries expertise was needed because one-third of the drug-smuggling boats came from the fishing fleets. Mr. Fuss developed vessel post-seizure and crew debriefing procedures that received national recognition. He was selected to prepare the maritime scenarios for the 1988 Drug Interdiction Games at the Naval War College and participated as leader of the Red Force Maritime Team.

In the spring of 1989 Mr. Fuss was redetailed to the newly established Office of National Drug Control Policy (ONDCP) in the Executive Office of the President. His proposal for a national cooperating-defendant debriefing program was included in the first National Drug Control Strategy issued by President George Bush in September of that year. Mr. Fuss received a letter of commendation from the president, was selected for a special achievement award by the Federal Investigators Association, and was awarded the Commerce Department's Silver Medal. He remained at ONDCP as a maritime-smuggling expert until his retirement in 1990.

Mr. Fuss is the author of forty-two articles and a fishing vessel identification guide. He lives in St. Pete Beach, Florida, with his wife, Carol.

The **Naval Institute Press** is the book-publishing arm of the U.S. Naval Institute, a private, nonprofit, membership society for sea service professionals and others who share an interest in naval and maritime affairs. Established in 1873 at the U.S. Naval Academy in Annapolis, Maryland, where its offices remain today, the Naval Institute has members worldwide.

Members of the Naval Institute support the education programs of the society and receive the influential monthly magazine *Proceedings* and discounts on fine nautical prints and on ship and aircraft photos. They also have access to the transcripts of the Institute's Oral History Program and get discounted admission to any of the Institute-sponsored seminars offered around the country. Discounts are also available to the colorful bimonthly magazine *Naval History*.

The Naval Institute's book-publishing program, begun in 1898 with basic guides to naval practices, has broadened its scope in recent years to include books of more general interest. Now the Naval Institute Press publishes about 100 titles each year, ranging from how-to books on boating and navigation to battle histories, biographies, ship and aircraft guides, and novels. Institute members receive discounts of 20 to 50 percent on the Press's nearly 600 books in print.

Full-time students are eligible for special half-price membership rates. Life memberships are also available.

For a free catalog describing Naval Institute Press books currently available, and for further information about joining the U.S. Naval Institute, please write to:

Membership Department
U.S. Naval Institute
118 Maryland Avenue
Annapolis, MD 21402-5035
Telephone: (800) 233-8764
Fax: (410) 269-7940
Web address: www.usni.org